CHINA:

ECONOMIC, POLITICAL AND SOCIAL ISSUES

CHINA:

ECONOMIC, POLITICAL AND SOCIAL ISSUES

JACK M. PHILLIPS
AND
LOGAN J. MOORE
EDITORS

Nova Science Publishers, Inc.
New York

For permission to use material from this book please contact us:
Telephone 631-231-7269; Fax 631-231-8175
Web Site: http://www.novapublishers.com

LIBRARY OF CONGRESS CATALOGING-IN-PUBLICATION DATA

China : economics, political and social issues / Jack M. Phillips and Logan J. Moore (editors).
p. cm.
ISBN 978-1-60456-727-4 (hardcover)
1. China--Economic conditions--2000- 2. China--Social conditions--2000- 3. China--Politics and government--2002- I. Phillips, Jack M. II. Moore, Logan J.
HC427.95.C4374 2008
330.951--dc22 2008018225

Published by Nova Science Publishers, Inc. ✢ New York

CONTENTS

PREFACE

China's economic, political and societal issues have become major points of interest to countries all over the globe. This new book presents in-depth analyses of issues such as foreign policy, political reform, and overall economic developments.

Chapter 1 - The Asia-Pacific Economic Cooperation (APEC) has been universally acknowledged as the major regional economic cooperation organization for the liberalization and facilitation of trade and investment (TILF) in the Asia-Pacific region. However, APEC's role as leader in the Asia-Pacific region is being challenged. In 2004, an emerging China entered into a landmark agreement with ASEAN, which is the 2004 ASEAN-China accord that portends to establish the world's largest free trade area by the year 2010. As a result, the fate of APEC largely became intertwined with the fate of China.

APEC was formed in 1989, and evolved from a regional economic consultative body, into an organization explicitly addressing political concerns in the region. APEC is the by-product of evolving international political economy concerns, from the post-Cold War, post-East Asian financial crisis, to post-9/11 and global threats of mega-terrorism. APEC has suffered a crisis in lack of credibility since the East Asian financial crisis; many perceive that APEC failed to adequately respond to the crisis. However, APEC's credibility has been more harmed by a perceived inability to accomplish the Bogor goals. In 1994, APEC member economies signed the Bogor Declaration, and developed economies pledged to eliminate trade and investment barriers by 2010, while developing economies pledged to eliminate trade and investment barriers by 2020. Some critiques link accomplishing the Bogor goals to APEC's survival and relevancy in the new millennium.

A critique of APEC based solely on the Bogor goals results in a denial of other equally important relevancies, serving as harbingers for survivability and continuing relevancy. In the new millennium, APEC's survival and continuing relevancy will lie in its historical commitment to TILF. However, historical relevancies must also allow for adjustments reflecting new international political economy concerns, such as, global threats of mega-terrorism, the 2004 ASEAN-China accord, termination of the WTO Multi-Fibre Agreement (MFA) of 1974, and what is being dubbed "JACIK," a prospective free trade super mega zone, comprising ASEAN, China, Japan, India and the Republic of Korea. Moreover, survival for APEC in the new millennium means encompassing an explicit economic agenda, in conjunction with an explicit international relations (political) agenda. APEC will survive in the new millennium by incorporating the latter relevancies, which reflect both historical relevancies, and evolving relevancies from changing and dynamic international political economy environments.

Chapter 2 –This chapter outlines the trade barriers in China. The U.S. goods trade deficit with China was $232.5 billion in 2006, an increase of $31 billion from $201.5 billion in 2005. U.S. goods exports in 2006 were $55.2 billion, up 31.7 percent from the previous year. Corresponding U.S. imports from China were $287.8 billion, up 18.2 percent. China is currently the 4th largest export market for U.S. goods.

U.S. exports of private commercial services (i.e., excluding military and government) to China were $9.1 billion in 2005 (latest data available), and U.S. imports were $6.5 billion. Sales of services in China by majority U.S.-owned affiliates were $5.1 billion in 2004 (latest data available), while sales of services in the United States by majority China-owned firms were not available in 2004 ($321 million in 2002 is latest data available).

Chapter 3 - Asia presents one of the most vibrant economic environments in the world. China and India have emerged as the leaders in the Asian region due to their rapid growth and market size. Consequently, equity markets in both China and India have significantly developed following liberalization in the early 1990s. The rapid growth of these economies coupled with the development of their financial markets has attracted significant portfolio investment from U.S. investors. For example, U.S. equity portfolio flows have increased from 0.63 billion to 7.14 billion in China and from 0.5 to 11 billion in India between 1994 and 2005.

This research examines the dynamic nature of the relationship between U.S. portfolio equity flows and equity returns in China and India. To understand the linkages between equity flows, market returns, and other variables we dissect our empirical findings as follows: first, the authors examine the correlations between stock market returns and portfolio flows; second, they decompose flows into expected and unexpected components to analyze how returns are influenced by different flow components; and third, they explore the dynamic relationships among flows, returns, and related variables. The authors' findings show that flows are 'pulled' into China and India by returns greater than U.S. market returns. Additionally, they find that the Indian equity index is influenced by U.S. investment activity and dividend yields, whereas the Chinese equity index is statistically unaffected by foreign investor behavior and fundamental determinates of value. This supports the ideas espoused in the popular press that the Chinese government still plays a major role in determining equity prices. A unique finding of this research is that the variance of the flow sequence in both China and India is better explained by shock to fundamentals vs. shocks to returns. This indicates that large American investors are making portfolio allocation decisions not simply on the basis of simple 'return chasing', but are at least partially informed about the markets of China and India. The authors anticipate that the strong relationship between equity flows and fundamentals should strengthen in the future as information asymmetries decline and U.S. investors continue to develop more sophisticated methods of assessing underlying value in these markets.

Chapter 4 - Oriental cultures differ from white, Christian cultures in the structure by which the family is organized and the way children are brought up. The formal representation of the Oedipus complex in Confucian Chinese society shows a distinct difference from that of white, Christian, Western societies. The classic oedipal situation as described by Freud seldom, if ever, exists in pre-modern Chinese literary works, but variant forms do appear even in classical Chinese literature. In this chapter, the author attempts to explore to what extent the Oedipus complex as the "fate of all of us" is true of other cultures. The author inquires, however, not by conducting a case study of social data collected in a non-Western culture, but by analyzing textual data contained in a literary masterpiece in an approach adopted by Freud when he formulated his initial idea of the Oedipus complex. The literary text is China's greatest classical novel, the *Hongloumeng*, authored by Cao Xueqin, which has two complete English translations: *A Dream of Red Mansions* and *The Story of the Stone*. This masterpiece offers an encyclopedic representation of traditional Chinese family life and narrates deeply hidden oedipal themes. Although their formal structure is very different from the triadic structure of the classical Freudian concept, it still falls within what Ernest Jones calls "the nuclear family complex." The author's case study will be conducted in relation to various debates on the Oedipus complex in the West.

Chapter 5 - The purpose of this chapter is to present a framework for understanding Chinese business culture and negotiating style. The author has had opportunities to discuss this topic with a large number of foreign executives. Many of them said they loved to negotiate and work with the Chinese. They perceived Chinese businesspeople as sincere business “gentlemen” who worked at a high level of mutual trust and respect. However, many others gave a diametrically different picture; they hated to negotiate with the Chinese and they were fed up with the tricky Chinese style of negotiating. In their eyes, the Chinese are “immoral” businesspeople who can “cheat”, “lie”, or just do whatever is necessary to knock you off balance at the negotiation table.

The author was struck by this contradictory image and was very much a part of this Chinese phenomenon some years ago when negotiating (as a Chinese negotiator) with foreign businesspeople: the Chinese negotiator is a both sincere and deceptive negotiator. This chapter aims to decode the paradox of Chinese negotiating style. The author starts by discussing the philosophical foundation of Chinese culture. Next, he presents will present a model of Chinese business culture. The chapter will conclude with managerial implications about how to do business effectively in China. A case study of Chinese negotiation behavior will be presented in the Appendix.

Chapter 6 - The modern concept of child abuse as a public health concern originates from Western societies. The various forms of child maltreatment have been extensively studied in the past 40 years. However, studies of child abuse among Chinese communities are extremely limited. The purpose of this study is to examine the clinical characteristics of child physical abuse seen in a regional hospital that provides acute and ambulatory care to one-sixth of the childhood population in Hong Kong. Children admitted into the hospital from January 1998 to June 2004 for management of suspected physical abuse were included. They were examined by one of the designated paediatricians, Medical Coordinators on Child Abuse, and were managed according to a hospital protocol and a set of inter-professional procedures. The management included medical and health evaluation, injury documentation, nursing observations, and a social enquiry into the family background and functioning, and the child's academic and behavioural problems at school. Seven hundred and twenty children had been evaluated for suspected physical abuse during the study period. An increasing annual incidence was seen and the number of cases had been rising by an average of 20% per year. Boys (392, 54%) outnumbered girls (328, 46%). The mean and median ages were both 8.8 years. A sharp rise in the number of cases was seen after the age of 6 years, the time when children started their primary school education. The male predominance was also evident only during the pre-primary and primary education ages. The highest number of cases was seen during May and June each year, the time when most students were preparing for their year-end examination. 568 (79%) cases were eventually substantiated as child abuse. The more severe injuries included intracranial bleeding (n=7), fractures (n=17), poisoning (n=16), burns (n=12), and soft tissue lacerations (n=41). Two children died, one from shaken baby syndrome and the other from carbon monoxide poisoning. Family dysfunction, including dependency on social security (48%), parental conflicts (30%) and single-parenthood (29%), was prevalent. Genuine behavioural problems (14%) and problems in studying (12%) of the child concerned were less frequently seen. Hence, the pattern of physical abuse and vulnerabilities in families revealed in this study are comparable to those of the Western culture. The bias in the age and gender of the battered children may reflect the traditional and higher expectation on the male offspring to excel academically, and the culturally fostered practice of corporal punishment under such circumstances.

Chapter 7 - With two questionnaires named Money Ethics Scale (MES) and Propensity to Engage in Unethical Behavior Scale (PEUBS), which are designed by the authors, this study investigates randomly 204 managerial staffs and 395 university students, to analyze their money profiles, and the relation between money profiles and unethical activity. The results show that Achieving Money Worshiper and Careless Money Admirer have more possibility to involve unethical activity than Apathetic Money Handler and Money Repeller when they are faced with work stress, but Apathetic Money Handler and Money Repeller have more possibility to involve unethical activity than Achieving Money Worshiper when they are faced with unethical organizational context; university students have more possibility to involve unethical activity than managerial staffs when they are faced with work stress, conformity and organizational context.

Chapter 8 - Contrary to the expectations of many outside observers at the beginning of the 1990's the political system of the People's Republic of China (PRC) experienced remarkably little transformation during the last decade of the twentieth century. The Chinese Communist Party (CCP) weathered the aftermath of the bloody repression of the Tiananmen democracy movement of 1989 as well as the demise of other Communist Party dictatorships in Russia and Eastern Europe. Neither the transition of authority from the late Deng Xiaoping to Jiang Zemin nor the passing of the helm from the latter to Hu Jintao at the Sixteenth Party Congress convened in Beijing in November 2002 have ushered in large-scale elite in-fighting or a systemic succession crisis disabling the functioning of the political system. Against this backdrop of stability, it has been the more subtle changes to that system on which most authors have pinned their hopes for a political transformation. These include *inter alia* the building of the rule of law, a more independent role for people's congresses at different levels of the political hierarchy, changing state-society relations and new intellectual trends. However, one of the aspects receiving most attention in recent years has been ongoing political reform in the Chinese countryside. The very dearth of other eye-catching reforms in the political realm has made the adoption of direct elections at the basic-level of a Leninist Party-state seems even more spectacular. These elections pertain to villagers' committees (VCs), the executive body at the rural grassroots-level which was instituted with the demise of collective farming and the people's commune system in the early 1980s. Only after a special law was passed in 1987 did these elections begin to resemble democratic procedures and during the 1990s the spread of these was still quite uneven. Yet, problems of implementation notwithstanding these elections have served as an impetus to pioneer elections for other positions of the Party and state apparatuses. All of these reforms, to be dealt with in more detail below, have raised the eyebrows of Western China-watchers.

While it appears easy to explain the attention paid to grassroots political reforms in rural China, the extent of these changes and their impacts remain hard to gauge given the huge area and diverse nature of the Chinese countryside. In fact, Jonathan Unger aptly called rural politics in China "kaleidoscopic" because of the wide variations existing between different localities. Nevertheless, it is probably not too early to raise questions pertaining to the nature of these political transformations. Specifically, this article addresses the question which driving forces behind them can be identified. The author argues that political change at the grassroots-level in rural China has neither been a story of top-down reform, nor of bottom-up initiative, but rather a mixture of both and that during the process new actors which he terms bureaucratic entrepreneurs, policy advocates and policy entrepreneurs came to play significant roles. First, it will be necessary to sketch the economic transformations in rural China during the reform era to elaborate different reform patterns. The author then turns to the political reforms taking place in this new context and attempt to identify which pattern best serves to explain these. In doing so, he focuses on political reforms defined as a restructuring of formal political institutions. Accompanying changes in political attitudes and the political culture of rural China are addressed only where they are perceived as either driving forces or results of these institutional reforms.

Chapter 9 - This chapter provides an overview of the Muslim separatist movement in China's northwestern Xinjiang Uighur Autonomous Region, China's attempts to stifle activities, which it considers terrorism, and implications for U.S. policy. Some analysts suggest that the U.S.-led campaign against terrorism may make it difficult to pressure the Chinese government on human rights and religious freedoms, particularly as they relate to Uighur Muslims in Xinjiang.

China also has reportedly stepped up its suppression of Uighur Muslims following the attacks in the United States on September 11, 2001. A policy question for the United States is how to balance the anti-terrorist campaign with traditional concerns over human rights in China's western region, and how to react should Beijing use the threat of terrorism to abrogate rights of autonomy in Xinjiang as provided for in China's constitution.

Chapter 10 - The technology market was built upon under the circumstance of the large-scale reform on the system of economy as well as science and technology. The core of the reform was to improve the integration among Science and Technology with economic and social development, accelerate the application and dissemination of the S&T achievements as well as give full play to S&T as the primary productive force.

In accordance with reforming on the whole system of science and technology, China also reformed the technology transfer system. The orientation was to discard the drawbacks of the former application and dissemination system on S&T system, to establish a market-guided technology transfer system and enhance the motivation and energy of technology development and transfer.

In: China: Economic, Political and Social Issues
Editors: J. M. Phillips and L. J. Moore
ISBN: 978-60456-727-4

Chapter 1

THE NEW MILLENNIUM: APEC AND EMERGING CHINA

*M. Ulric Killion**
Visiting Professor in International Law,
Shanghai International Studies University, P.R.C.

ABSTRACT

The Asia-Pacific Economic Cooperation (APEC) has been universally acknowledged as the major regional economic cooperation organization for the liberalization and facilitation of trade and investment (TILF) in the Asia-Pacific region. However, APEC's role as leader in the Asia-Pacific region is being challenged. In 2004, an emerging China entered into a landmark agreement with ASEAN, which is the 2004 ASEAN-China accord that portends to establish the world's largest free trade area by the year 2010. As a result, the fate of APEC largely became intertwined with the fate of China.

APEC was formed in 1989, and evolved from a regional economic consultative body, into an organization explicitly addressing political concerns in the region. APEC is the by-product of evolving international political economy concerns, from the post-Cold War, post-East Asian financial crisis, to post-9/11 and global threats of mega-terrorism. APEC has suffered a crisis in lack of credibility since the East Asian financial crisis; many perceive that APEC failed to adequately respond to the crisis. However, APEC's credibility has been more harmed by a perceived inability to accomplish the Bogor goals. In 1994, APEC member economies signed the Bogor Declaration, and developed economies pledged to eliminate trade and investment barriers by 2010, while developing economies pledged to eliminate trade and investment barriers by 2020. Some critiques link accomplishing the Bogor goals to APEC's survival and relevancy in the new millennium.

A critique of APEC based solely on the Bogor goals results in a denial of other equally important relevancies, serving as harbingers for survivability and continuing relevancy. In the new millennium, APEC's survival and continuing relevancy will lie in its historical

* E-mail address: mulrickillion@netscape.net. All observations and analysis are the author's own and by no means reflect the views of Shanghai International Studies University or its affiliates.

commitment to TILF. However, historical relevancies must also allow for adjustments reflecting new international political economy concerns, such as, global threats of mega-terrorism, the 2004 ASEAN-China accord, termination of the WTO Multi-Fibre Agreement (MFA) of 1974, and what is being dubbed "JACIK," a prospective free trade super mega zone, comprising ASEAN, China, Japan, India and the Republic of Korea. Moreover, survival for APEC in the new millennium means encompassing an explicit economic agenda, in conjunction with an explicit international relations (political) agenda. APEC will survive in the new millennium by incorporating the latter relevancies, which reflect both historical relevancies, and evolving relevancies from changing and dynamic international political economy environments.

INTRODUCTION

The importance of Asian Pacific Economic Cooperation (APEC) lies in the numbers, in particular, economic data. At the time of the 2004 APEC-Chile summit, APEC comprised twenty-one member economies, spans four continents, represents more than one-third of the world's population (2.6 billion), constitutes over fifty percent of world gross national product (GNP) (US $19,254 billion), and represents more than forty-one percent of global trade.[1]

Nonetheless, APEC has been described as "four adjectives in search of a noun."[2] This statement reflects the understandings and misunderstandings of APEC as an international intergovernmental organization (IGO) and the role of APEC in the global economy, especially in terms of the new millennium. In addition, this statement reflects problems experienced by APEC since its 1989 birth as an international economic cooperation organization, especially defining itself, setting goals, and accomplishing goals such as the Bogor goals. In 1994, APEC member economies signed the Bogor Declaration, which is dubbed the Bogor goals, and developed economies pledged to eliminate trade and investment barriers by 2010, while developing economies pledged to eliminate trade and investment barriers by 2020.[3] The history of APEC lends understanding to how it grew from a simple economic consultative forum into a more complex anomaly in terms of IGOs, its role in promoting multilateral trade as opposed to regionalism, and the prospect of APEC as a major player in the new millennium, which some critiques link to accomplishing the seemingly all-important Bogor goals.

Moreover, given the growing maturity of the People's Republic of China (China) in economics, diplomacy and politics, the fate of APEC may well be contingent on the direction and vision of a maturing Chinese polity. The economic data also reflects the growing importance of China. In 2004, China's export and import figures were estimated at US $325,642 million in exports and US $295,303 million in imports. Notwithstanding growing

---

1 *See* APEC OUTCOMES AND OUTLOOKS 2003/2004, Asian-Pacific Economic Cooperation Publication 2004, at 4, [hereinafter 2004 APEC Outcomes].

2 *See* Walden Bello, *APEC: The Unauthorized History*, 18th May 1998, http://www.hk.super.net/~daga/walden01.htm, "To borrow the classic definition of the forum by former Australian Foreign Minister Gareth Evans, APEC is still "four adjectives in search of a noun."

3 APEC ECONOMIC LEADERS' DECLARATION OF COMMON RESOLVE
Bogor, Indonesia, 15 November 1994, Asia-Pacific Economic Cooperation, Member Economies, at http://www.apec.org/apec/.

U.S. – China trade deficit,[4] the leader remains the United States with US $693,103 million in exports and US $1,161,366 million in imports. The estimates in exports and imports for APEC economies demonstrate that China only lags between the economies of the U.S. and Japan, whose trade was estimated at US $417,165 million in exports and US $337,957 million in imports.[5] In 2004, China continued to experience robust economic growth,[6] and most important, in terms of foreign diplomacy, pushed its relations with the Association of Southeast Asian Nations (ASEAN) into a new stage.[7]

An emerging China combining its growing economic strength with the economic potential of ASEAN, challenges APEC's leadership in the Asian region. The ASEAN region has a population of about 500 million, a combined gross domestic product of US $737 billion, and a total trade volume of US $720 billion.[8] On 29 November 2004, China joined ASEAN in signing an agreement that established regional cooperation between them; they paved the way for establishing the world's largest free trade zone, or free trade area (FTA).[9] Whether perceived as good or bad, the fate of APEC became largely intertwined with the fate of China.

APEC is generally regarded as the major forum for facilitating economic growth, cooperation, trade and investment in the Asia-Pacific region,[10] or trade and investment liberalization and facilitation (TILF). APEC from its original inception and membership of twelve economies has expanded to a membership of twenty-one economies.[11] An APEC

---

4 *See* Robert E. Scott, *Soaring Imports of Oil and Chinese Goods Drive Trade Deficits to New Record, Trade Picture*, (Econ. Pol'y Inst.), Aug. 13, 2004 (The deficit rose from $22.7 billion in 1993 to $124 billion in 2003.).

5 2004 APEC Outcomes, *supra* note 1, at 18, *citing Current Price GDP, Current GDP per Capita, Exports and Imports*, The APEC Region Trade and Investment 2003.

6 *See* Fu Jing, *Rosy Forecast of Economic Growth*, CHINA DAILY, Nov. 6, 2003, at 2003 WL 57560665; *see also* Lena Lee, *Foreign Investors, Retail Sales Set the Pace in China,* THE ASIAN WALL STREET JOURNAL, Mar. 26, 2004, at A2, at 2004 WL 56592469; *see also China set 7% growth target for 2004,* NEWS GUANGDONG, Dec. 3, 2003, http://www.newsgd.com/business/prospective/200312030031.htm.

7 *See* Editor's Note, *China more mature in Diplomacy*, CHINA DAILY, December 16, 2004; *see also* Association of Southeast Asian Nations, Overview, http://www.aseansec.org/64.htm, "ASEAN was established on 8 August 1967 in Bangkok by the five original Member Countries, namely, Indonesia, Malaysia, Philippines, Singapore, and Thailand. Brunei Darussalam joined on 8 January 1984, Vietnam on 28 July 1995, Laos and Myanmar on 23 July 1997, and Cambodia on 30 April 1999." *Id.*

8 Association of Southeast Asian Nations, Overview, http://www.aseansec.org/64.htm. [hereinafter ASEAN].

9 See Deal forms free-trade megazone, China, ASEAN sign landmark accord, SHANGHAI DAILY, 30 November 2004; see also T.N. Srinivasan, Preferential Trade Agreements with Special Reference to Asia, (Paper presented at the Asian Economic Outlook Workshop, Manila, November 2001), Yale University, January 2002, http://www.econ.yale.edu/~srinivas/PrefTradeAgreements.pdf.
Preferential Trade Agreements (PTAs) are agreements among a set of countries involving preferential treatment of bilateral trade between any two parties to the agreement relative to their trade with the rest of the world. Preferences, however, need not extend to all trade between the two, and the coverage could depend on the type of PTAs. Customs unions and the so-called free trade areas are common forms of PTAs. Members of most PTAs belong to a well-defined geographical area, such as for example, the European Union (EU), North American Free Trade Area (NAFTA) and Association of Southeast Asian Nations (ASEAN). For this reason regional PTAs are called Regional Trade Agreements (RTAs). The most common form of RTAs are the euphemistically named Free Trade Areas (FTAs), with few Customs Unions (CU) which require the partners to maintain a common external trade policy, in addition to free trade with each other.

10 Takeshi Isayama, Commissioner of JPO, Keynote Speech: *APEC Region Intellectual Property Right Protections beyond the Year 2000*, February 22, 1999.

11 2004 APEC Outcomes, *supra* note 1, "The word 'economies' is used to describe APEC members because the APEC cooperative process is predominantly concerned with trade and economic issues, with members engaging one another as economic entities." *Id.*, at 2.

annual cycle begins and ends with the annual joint ministerial meeting of foreign affairs and trade ministers. Since 1993, there was also added to the annual cycle an annual APEC economic leaders' meeting.[12] APEC is the only IGO in the world operating on the basis of non-binding commitments, open dialogue and equal respect for the views of all participants, or member economies. In comparison with other IGOs, unlike the World Trade Organization (WTO),[13] or other international instruments and treaty bodies, APEC has no international treaty obligations required of its member economies; perhaps it is not even a formal agreement.[14] Decisions made within APEC are reached by consensus. As a result, commitments are undertaken only on a voluntary basis.[15] APEC's management style is characteristically consensus building and a step-by-step approach.[16] As for the four adjectives in search of a noun, an examination of the history of APEC should lend to both the search for and greater understanding of the manifest noun, which describes APEC in the new millennium.

HISTORY OF APEC

A true historicism of the birth of APEC directly relates to the post-Cold War era. Contrary to the prognostications of Samuel Huntington and his clash of cultures thesis,[17] a post-Cold War era may best be described as one of growing global economic tensions, rather than cultural or ideological tensions.[18] These global economic tensions evolved from fear that at the close of the Cold War (1945-1991), the United States would not be able to resolve its trade disputes with Europe and Japan. In the advent of the U.S. retreating into economic isolationism because of these unresolved disputes, there was fear of the formation of three major tracing blocs based on the dollar, yen and deutschmark, respectively, the U.S., Japan and Germany.[19] The creation of the North American Free Trade Agreement (NAFTA) only heightened these fears.[20] This pre-history of APEC prompted the initiatives of Robert Hawke and others, which eventually led to the formation of APEC. The post-Cold War era has been

---

12 *See* Heather Gibb, *Gender Front and Center An APEC Primer*, Chapter 2, in *How APEC Works*, (The North-South Institute 1999), http://www.nsi-ins.ca/ensi/publications/apec/.

13 Marrakesh Agreement Establishing the World Trade Organization [hereinafter WTO Agreement], The Legal Texts: The Results of the Uruguay Round of Multilateral Trade Negotiations, 1867 U.N.T.S. 154, 33 I.L.M. 1144 (1994).

14 Aziz Choudry, *APEC and Free Trade*, Seminar to Development Studies, Massey University, Palmerston North, Aotearoa/New Zealand, 2 May 1997.

15 About APEC – Asian-Pacific Economic Cooperation, http://www.apecsec.org.sg/apec/about_apec.html.

16 Takeshi Isayama, *supra* note 10.

17 *See* Samuel P. Huntington, The Clash of Civilizations and the Remaking of World Order 19 (1996).

18 *See* Tim Harcourt, APEC'S LABOR AGENDA: NEGOTIATING THE FUTURE, at 4-5, Foreword by R. J. L. Hawke, A.C., (2000).

19 *See* Paul Bowles, *APEC: Progress Based on the Wrong Model?*, Canadian Business Economics 48, 57, Fall 1997 (Discussing different definitions for regional blocs.).

20 *See* Lincoln Wright, *APEC--Australia's Pragmatic Asia Policy?*, Japan Policy Research Institute, JPRI Working Paper No. 8: April 1995, http://www.jpri.org/publications/workingpapers/wp8.html, "The initial rationale in Canberra for enmeshing itself with Asia was the fear of being excluded from a regional trade agreement, such as a Yen bloc, as well as from the European Community and a Dollar bloc in the Americas. The creation of NAFTA added to Australia's fear;" *see also generally* North American Free Trade Association, NAFTA Secretariat, Legal text of NAFTA, http://www.nafta-sec-alena.org/DefaultSite/index_e.aspx?CategoryId=42.

described as the advent of acceleration in economic regionalization, which was accompanied by a corresponding increase in transnational political interactions that were also associated with regional*ism*.[21] Asia-Pacific regionalism was necessarily defined in terms of the contours of the post-Cold War international political economy.

The international political economy of the East Asian financial crisis (1997-98) equally influenced Asia-Pacific regionalism. In the 1970s and 1980s, Japan, South Korea, Taiwan, Hong Kong, and Singapore, followed by Thailand, Malaysia and Indonesia, were being hailed as miracles of capitalist development. In terms of Western taxonomies, dominant interpretations of the making of the East Asian Miracle were linked to the rise and spread of neo-liberalism or economic liberalism, while many commentators used the dynamic new Asian capitalism to support the case for *laissez-faire* economic policies. The post-Cold War period and the miracle economies of Northeast and Southeast Asia were perceived as a challenge to the West. However, the East Asian financial crisis (1997-98) did eventually precipitate changes in the contours of the post-Cold War international political economy.[22]

A third admixture to the forces of international political economy, or macroeconomic forces, were the terrorist attacks on September 11, 2001, or what has been dubbed 9/11, other incidents of mega-terrorism, and the resulting economics of terrorism that ensued. Subsequent to 9/11, a 2002 Organisation for Economic Co-operation and Development (OECD) report on the economics of terrorism found that heightened terrorist threats do have some long-lasting, if diffuse, macroeconomic repercussions.[23] Indeed, the international political economy of the post-9/11 world and new geo-political realities, in conjunction with a general global economic slowdown, posed a challenge to all economies, both Asian and non-Asian economies.[24] The international political economy of the post-Cold War period, the East Asian financial crisis, the events of 9/11, other incidents of mega-terrorism, and resulting economics of terrorism affected the growth of Asian regionalism. APEC in the 1980s and early 1990s seemed the perfect venue for both benefiting from and facilitating a post-Cold War preoccupation with economic development and integration, and managing relations among

---

21 *See* Mark T. Berger & Mark Beeson, *APEC, ASEAN+3, and American Power: The History and Limits of the New Regionalism in the Asia-Pacific*, at 1, 2003, University of Queensland, Australia, http://eprint.uq.edu.au/archive/00000732/; *see also* Mark Beeson, *Re-thinking Regionalism: Europe and East Asia in Comparative Historical Perspective*, at 3, (This paper was presented at the Oceanic Conference on International Studies, Canberra July 14-16, 2004), Consequently, much recent scholarship about regional processes makes a basic distinction between regional*ism* and regional*ization*. In this formulation, regionalism refers to the political process in which states drive cooperative initiatives. Regionalization, by contrast, refers to processes of economic integration which, while they may be influenced by state policies, are essentially the uncoordinated consequence of private sector activities.

22 *See* Mark T. Berger, *Bringing History Back In: The Making and Unmaking of the East Asian Miracle*, Politik und Gesellschaft Online, International Politics and Society 3/1999, at http://www.fes.de/ipg /ipg3_99/artberger.html.

23 *See* ORG. FOR ECON. CO-OPERATION AND DEV. (OECD), Overview of the OECD: What is it? History? Who Does What? Structure of the Organization?, at http://www.oecd.org/document/18/0,2340,en_2649_ 201185_2068050_1_1_1_1,00.html (OECD's role has been "to build strong economies in its member countries, improve efficiency, hone market systems, expand free trade and contribute to development in industrialised as well as developing countries."); *see also* Patrick Lenain et al., *The Economic Consequences of Terrorism* (Org. for Econ. Co-operation and Dev., Econ. Dept, Working Paper No. 334, 2002), at http://appli1.oecd.org/olis/2002doc.nsf/linkto/ecowkp (2002)20/$FILE/ JT00129726.PDF.

24 *See* Yeo Lay Hwee, *Culture and Civilizations Dialogue*, Lecture Tour of Asia-Europe Foundation (ASEF) on Countering Unilateralism, Preserving Diversity: Dimensions of Asia-Europe Cooperation, December 2-4, 2003, http://www.iias.nl/asem/index.html?http://www.iias.nl/asem/asem2003/ASEMConference_CulturesCivi lizationsDec2003.html.

the miracle economies of East Asia (Northeast Asia and Southeast Asia). However, changing international political economy environments such as a post-East Asian financial crisis and post-9/11 gravely affected the credibility of APEC.[25]

In addition, one should understand just what is, or includes, the region known as the Asia-Pacific. The region does not include South Asia (India, Pakistan, Afghanistan, Bangladesh and Sri Lanka), and Southwest Asia (the Arab Peninsula, Iraq and Iran). More specifically, the Asia-Pacific region comprises East Asia and Southeast Asia, two socio-geographical subsets (along with Oceania, North America and South America) all constituting the pacific basin. It is a region that is larger than Europe. Some consider it as characterized by geographical, historical, cultural and political diversity, while still maintaining a high degree of mutual interaction among its nation-states. The Asia-Pacific is also a region consisting of some Asia nation-states that are grounded in strong tradition, if not ontological bases in tradition, such as China, Japan, Korea and some Southeast Asia nation-states.[26]

Southeast Asian countries emerged from colonialism in the 1950s and 1960s. These countries faced problems of poverty, overpopulation, high birth rates, undeveloped economies and the weight of tradition. For instance, the Malaysian economy was mostly dependent on rubber (40 percent of GDP in the 1950s), with about half of its workforce engaged in the agricultural sector. In the 1980s, these economies underwent restructuring, mostly by shifting from an emphasis on agriculture to industrial development and export-based growth. In addition, many of these economies began to benefit from the transfer of technology such as Japan, Korea and Taiwan. It is a pattern of technology transfer broadly ranging from manufacturing to electronics.[27]

In the 1980s, China became a significant economic partner of most of these ASEAN nation-states. In the mid-1980s, ASEAN nation-states sought to expand exports in the wake of falling commodity prices and growing protectionist sentiment in developed countries. Consequently, expanding economic relations with China ensued. In addition, Japan, under the umbrella of the Fukuda Doctrine (1972), improved its relations with Southeast Asia by forging a special relationship with ASEAN as an organization, which included bilateral relations with ASEAN members.[28]

In comparison to APEC, ASEAN, which was formed in 1967,[29] originally comprised Indonesia, Malaysia, the Philippines, Singapore, and Thailand, and was formed more for political rather than economic reasons. Later joining ASEAN were Brunei in 1984, Vietnam

---

25 *See* Mark Beeson, *Multilateralism: American Power and East Asian Regionalism*, at 1, Working Paper Series, No 64, City University of Hong Kong, May 2004, http://www.cityu.edu.hk/searc/WP.html (This paper looks at multilateral processes in the Asia-Pacific region and the impact of American foreign policy on them.).

26 *See* Tan Tai Yong, *The Post-War History of East and Southeast Asia*, Asia-Europe Environment Forum, ASEF University, 2000, http://www.asef.org/asef-uni/3_infohub/infohub_m_library.html.

27 *Id.*

28 *See* Jiro Okamoto, *Japan's View on "East Asian Economic Zone,"* (Institute of Development Economy, Jetro, October 8, 2001), http://www.npf.org.tw/English/Publication/TE/TE-R-090-026.htm, "The "Fukuda Doctrine" declared, among other things, that Japan would never become a military power again, it would pursue mutual confidence building with ASEAN members, and it would assist their economic development as an equal partner;" *see also* Tadahiro Yoshida, *East Asian Regionalism and Japan*, IDE APEC Study Center, Working Paper Series 03/04 – No. 9, March 2004, APEC Study Center Institute of Developing Economies, Jetro, at http://www.ide.go.jp/English/Publish/Apec/pdf/apec15_wp9.pdf, "The Fukuda Doctrine was epoch-making because it signaled Japan's official recognition of the ASEAN nations as friendly partners in Asia. The Fukuda Doctrine was a sign of the growing importance of Asia to Japan."

29 ASEAN, *supra* note 8.

in 1995, and Laos and Myanmar in 1998. Before 1992, ASEAN was mostly concerned with political issues affecting the region. A watershed event in the history of ASEAN was the 1992 summit, when the vision of establishing an ASEAN Free Trade Area (AFTA) was adopted. Consequently, ASEAN shifted from an emphasis on politics to economic cooperation.[30]

In 1989, APEC presented an alternative to ASEAN nations. However, the idea of APEC had to be first borne, and then affected into a regional economic cooperation organization. There are several historical accounts offered in explanation for the beginnings of APEC. Some of these historical accounts are distinctive, while others offer histories that overlap other historical accounts.

In the late 1980s and 1990s, there was a growing inclination towards Pacific regionalism. Regional cooperation in Western developed economies provided ample example and incentive. For instance, there was the deepening European integration or the EC-92 that led to a fear of a fortress Europe, and the U.S. decision to form a preferential trade agreement (PTA) with Canada.[31] In 1980, the Pacific Economic Cooperation Conference (PECC) was formed.[32] PECC was a government-supported private body, and a novel initiative striving for creation of a new regional economic framework. However, ASEAN showed little enthusiasm for its agenda. ASEAN perceived the larger institution alternative as potentially threatening to its integrity and solidarity.

During an earlier 1986 meeting of the PECC, a standing committee created the Trade Policy Forum (TPF) for purpose of regularly reviewing macroeconomic conditions, other conditions in the Asia-Pacific region, monitoring GATT trade round negotiations, and exploring trade policy issues deemed important to the region. Subsequent to APEC being established in 1989, the TPF contributed to APEC's Committee on Trade and Investment (CTI), various sub-fora and expert groups. In 1989, when APEC was established, PECC became the only non-government observer of APEC. The TPF both formally and informally subsequently contributed to the CTI,[33] and other forums, such as, the WTO, Asian Development Bank (ADB)[34] and United Nations Conference on Trade and Development (UNCTAD).[35]

---

30 *See* Jose L. Tongzon, *The Challenge of Regional Economic Integration: The Vietnamese Perspective*, The Developing Economies, XXXVII-2 (June 1999), 137-61, 137 n.1, *see also* Kernial Singh Sandhu, et al., THE ASEAN READER, Singapore: Institute of Southeast Asian Studies (1992).

31 See Maurice Schiff, Small Is Beautiful: Preferential Trade Agreements and the Impact of Country Size, Market Share, Efficiency, and Trade Policy, World Bank, Working Paper 1688, October 1966, http://www.worldbank.org/html/dec/Publications/Workpapers/wps1668-abstract.html.

32 Pacific Economic Cooperation Council (PECC), http://www.pecc.org/, "PECC is a unique tripartite partnership of senior individuals from business and industry, government, academic and other intellectual circles."

33 TPF WWW Homepage, http://www.pacific.net.id/content/TPF/public.htm, "Trade Policy Forum is one of the key policy groups of the Pacific Economic Cooperation Council, an organization of business, government and academic."

34 Asian Development Bank (ADB), http://www.adb.org/, "ADB is a multilateral development finance institution dedicated to reducing poverty in Asia and the Pacific."

35 United Nations Conference on Trade and Development (UNCTAD), UNCTAD XI Home, http://www.unctadxi.org/templates/Startpage____4.aspx, "The Member States of UNCTAD gathered in São Paulo, agreed on a Declaration that they called "The Spirit of São Paulo". The decisions adopted at UNCTAD XI, in addition to the Bangkok Plan of Action, form a solid basis to build upon and are essential instruments in the Member State's continued commitment to support UNCTAD in fulfilling its mandate as the focal point within the United Nations for the integrated treatment of trade and development, on the road to its twelfth session in 2008."

There were other pre-1989 attempts at Asian regionalism. In the late 1960s, although not effected, the concept of a Pacific free trade area (PAFTA) was advanced. In 1966, there was a first meeting of the Southwest Asian Ministerial Conference for Economic Development. In 1968, the Pacific Basin Economic Council was established.[36] In the 1970s, there was also advanced, but not affected, a concept of an Organization for Pacific Trade and Development (OPTD), which many hail as an Asian-Pacific version or clone of the Organization for Economic Cooperation and Development (OECD).[37]

There is also a more Asian-specific viewpoint to the history of APEC that contains slight variations from the Hawke-originating theme, which attributes the original idea of APEC to former Prime Minister Robert Hawke of Australia. The issue of an Asian regional trading bloc was of great concern to Asian leaders. In particular, the controversial Malaysian Prime Minister Mahathir Mohamad proposed the formation of an East Asian economic group in response to perceived threats from North America, Europe and Australia. Fearing marginalization, Mahathir invited several East Asian countries to Canberra, Australia to discuss a new regional group. This initial proposal did not include the U.S. and Canada. It was at the insistence of Japan that these North American countries be included, to avoid harming the existing trans-Pacific trading relationship.[38] Moreover, even Hawke's initial proposal did not envision the participation of the U.S. and Canada. Rather, his initial vision focused on the importance of regional cooperation among Australia, New Zealand, South Korea, Japan and the six members of ASEAN.[39] Historically, what became the ASEAN Plus Three group comprises the nations that Mahathir earlier proposed for an East Asian Economic Caucus (EAEC). Practically speaking, the idea of an EAEC evolved into the ASEAN Plus Three group.[40]

Most recognize the origin of ASEAN as dating back to 1989, as a part initiative of Robert (Bob) Hawke, then Prime Minister of Australia (1983-1991), and Australia; part Japan;[41] and others. However, Hawke more than any other source is credited with the initial idea of an economic gathering of nation-states. The stimulus for this meeting was Hawke's January

---

36 Japan Ministry of Foreign Affairs, APEC Information, History of Asia-Pacific Cooperation, http://www.mofa.go.jp/policy/economy/apec/1995/info/history.html.

37 *See* David MacDuff & Yuen Pau Woo, *APEC as a Pacific OECD Revisited,* (Paper was prepared for the APEC International Assessment Network (APIAN) and presented to the APEC Study Centres International Consortium Meeting, Merida, Mexico, May 23-24, 2002; *see also* Merit E. Janow, *APEC: An Assessment,* (Discussion Paper Series, APEC Study Center, Columbia University, January 1997), at 7-9.

38 Bowles, *supra* note 19, at 57-58.

39 Janow, *Id.,* at 8, at footnote 17, "Press reports indicate that Japan's Prime Minister Takeshita wrote Prime Minister Hawke in March supporting the Seoul plan. In April, Hawke sent a senior Australian diplomat, Dick Woolcott on a series of talks throughout Asia on the proposed grouping and its draft agenda." (Internal citations omitted).

40 *See* Edward J. Lincoln, *Taking APEC Seriously,* Policy Brief No. 92, Brookings Institute, December 2001, at 4.

41 Takeshi Isayama, *supra* note 10, During the 1980s, North America and Europe had initiated steps toward regional integration. The question of Asian integration resulted in Japan's Ministry of International Trade and Industry (MITI), which was earlier call the Trade Agency and the Ministry of Commerce and Industry, fearing that the development of regional blocs in North American and Europe would leave the Asia-Pacific region behind others. The MITI established a research group for purpose of debating the future of the Asia-Pacific region, subsequently concluded that an organization such as APEC was needed. This finding paralleled a similar debate that occurred in Australia at about the same time; *see also* Japan Ministry of Economy, Trade and Industry (METI), http://www.meti.go.jp/english/.

1989 call for more effective cooperation among Asia-Pacific economies.[42] An APEC declaration from the 1989 meeting contains a special acknowledgement to the people and government of Australia. Conversely, APEC ascribes as its beginning that, "APEC was established in response to the growing interdependence among Asia-Pacific economies and to the need to advance Asia-Pacific economic dynamism and sense of community."[43] Nonetheless, the origin of the APEC forum is mostly attributed to an earlier initiative of Robert Hawke, who as a member of the Australian Labor Party, and a former trade union leader, believed in government by consensus.[44] As early as 1983, Hawke envisioned the future of Australia as being intertwined with the Asia-Pacific region.[45]

In 1989, Australia proposed the formation of an intergovernmental forum called APEC. Thereafter, the first APEC meeting of foreign and trade ministers from twelve Asia-Pacific economies was convened in Canberra, Australia. The initial member economies were Australia, Brunei Darussalam, Canada, Indonesia, Japan, the Republic of Korea, Malaysia, New Zealand, the Republic of the Philippines, Singapore, Thailand and the United States. In, 1989, there were six ASEAN members of APEC, being Brunei, Indonesia, Malaysia, Philippines, Singapore, and Thailand. As a result, the original nation-states included ASEAN members, Australia, Canada, Japan, Korea, New Zealand and the U.S. In later years, APEC expanded its members to include Chile, China, Chinese Taipei, Hong Kong, Mexico, Papua New Guinea, Peru, Russia, and Viet Nam.[46]

In order to understand the Bogor goals and how it affects APEC in the new millennium, an APEC history of its annual meetings and minister meetings, including leaders' meetings, should be considered in reference to three historical periods. These periods are the pre-Bogor goals period, Bogor goals period, and post-Bogor goals period. One source described the earlier history of APEC in terms of the historical categorizations of birth and childhood (1989-1991), adolescence (1992-1994), and proliferation and accelerated development (1995-present).[47] However, the present for this source constituted the 1997 APEC summit, and this source could not have reasonably anticipated the directional growth of APEC, especially the growth and evolution manifest in the 2004 APEC-Chile summit. Categorizations built around the Bogor goals are more appropriate, because as previously mentioned some critiques link

---

42 Chairman's Summary Statement, Asia-Pacific Economic Cooperation, Ministerial Meeting, Canberra, 6-7 November 1989.

43 Canada Foreign Affairs, Canada-APEC, A Brief History of APEC, http://www.dfait-maeci.gc.ca/canada-apec/history-en.asp.

44 National Museum of Australia Home, Prime Ministers of Australia – Hawke, http://www.nma.gov.au /primeministers/12.htm.

45 *See Moves Towards Asianisation: Australia's "Asian Future", and the "Labor" Side of Politics*, The Asianisation of Australia: volume 1, section 8 (Last updated October 2000), *citing* Halliwell, Malcolm, *Fighting over Asia*, (Letter), The Australian, 31 October 1994, p. 8. "In 1994, former Labor prime minister Bob Hawke continued on with his previous pronouncements when he proclaimed that 'I said in my first days as prime minister that Australia's future depended upon becoming more enmeshed with Asia;'" *see also Moves Towards Asianisation: Australia's "Asian Future", and the "Labor" Side of Politics*, The Asianisation of Australia: volume 1, section 8 (Last updated October 2000), *citing* The Sunday Mail, 23 June 1985; cited in: Dique, Dr. J.C.A., *Immigration - A Policy of Perfidy*, Veritas, Bullsbrook, Western Australia, c1985, p. 61.

46 Asia-Pacific Economic Cooperation, Member Economies, http://www.apec.org/apec/member_economies.html.

47 The leaders of Asian Pacific Economic Cooperation (APEC), APEC FAQ, International Economics, Chinese University of Hong Kong (2000), http://intl.econ.cuhk.edu.hk/topic/index.php?did=16#ref, *citing* Lu Jianren, *Asian Pacific Economic Cooperation and China* (1997) (Discussing relationship between APEC and China). [hereinafter APEC FAQ].

APEC's survivability and continuing relevancy to the success or failure in accomplishing the Bogor goals.

A more official history, rather than pre-history, of APEC ranges from the first minister meeting at Canberra, Australia in 1989 to the minister meeting and leaders' meeting convened at Santiago, Chile in 2004. Understanding the history of APEC meetings should lend understanding to the importance of the 1994 Bogor goals and issues of survivability and relevancy of APEC in the new millennium.

Pre-Bogor Goals Period (1989-1993)

The pre-Bogor goals period comprises the ministerial meetings at Canberra, Australia (1989), Singapore (1990), Seoul, Republic of Korea (1991), Bangkok, Thailand (1992) and Blake, Island, in Seattle, Washington (1993). In addition, this period encompasses the first leaders' meeting convened at Blake Island (1993).

First APEC Ministerial Meeting (Canberra, Australia 1989)

The first APEC Ministerial Meeting is held 6-7 November 1989 at Canberra, Australia.[48] This economic consultation addressed issues of strengthening the multilateral trading system and enhancing the potential for success of the then pending Uruguay trade round, assessing both prospects and obstacles to increasing trade and investment flows in the region, and identifying practical common economic interests. The agenda was relatively simple and reflected APEC's early organizational structure. The Chairman's Summary Statement, at paragraph 17 (Carrying Forward Regional Economic Cooperation), expressed the consensus of member economies that at this stage in the development of APEC it was too early to decide upon a particular organizational structure for a ministerial-level forum and the necessary support needed for this sort of mechanism. Rather, paragraph 21 (Carrying Forward Regional Economic Cooperation), despite preferences of some participants, evidences a consensus that a proper support mechanism will be the by-product of both reflection and evolution of APEC's cooperation process.

APEC defined itself in terms of a consensus-based organization, rather than rules-based organization. The Chairman's Summary Statement, at paragraph 16 (General Principles of Asia-Pacific Economic Cooperation), outlines broad areas that the member economies have in common. Paragraph 16 stresses cooperation, non-informal consultation, and most importantly, consensus. Electing to be a consensus-based organization was possible because of lack of more formally structured organization and APEC's earlier emphasis on cooperation, non-formal consultation, and recognition and respect for all participants, including both differing socio-economic systems and levels of development.

In addition, the issue of China participating in these economic consultations was expressly addressed. Paragraph 24 (Carrying Forward Regional Economic Cooperation) acknowledges the importance of China and the respective economies of Hong Kong and Taiwan to the future prosperity of the region. There was a consensus that it is desirable to

[48] Chairman's Summary Statement, First APEC Ministerial Meeting, Canberra, Australia, 6-7 November 1989.

further consider the involvement of these three economies in the process of Asia-Pacific Economic Cooperation. While the desirability of China's participation was obvious, it was still problematic. Obtaining the participation in economic consultations of China, more so than either Taiwan or Hong Kong, was imperative to Asia-Pacific regionalism. A problem for APEC was that participation of China posed political problems, and not economic problems, in terms of the participation of the three economies at the same time.

Political problems surrounding the participation of China were also linked to China's bid for resumption of membership in GATT 1947. In 1989, China, unlike other APEC member economies, was not a member of GATT.[49] Nonetheless, and despite its non-GATT-member status, China in the 1980s had already emerged as a major player in the global economy. At the close of the infamous Cultural Revolution (1966-76), China's trade grew dramatically faster than world trade. China's foreign trade rose from about $20 billion in the 1970s to about $475 billion in 2000, or, comparatively, from 0.6 percent of world trade (1977) to 3.7 percent of world trade (2000).[50]

The problem confronting APEC was how to get the three economies of China, Hong Kong and Taiwan to participate at the same time. In 1947, the Republic of China (ROC) was one of the original members of GATT 1947. However, in 1949, the People's Republic of China (China) was established on the mainland and Republic of China (ROC) moved to Taiwan. In 1950, the Republic of China (ROC) resigned from GATT, and the People's Republic of China (China) denounced GATT for ideological reasons. In 1986, the People's Republic of China applied to renew, or resume membership in GATT.[51] A working party was convened to consider China's request of resumption of its original membership.[52] In 1988, a Chinese delegation indicated that China originally assumed contracting party status by accepting the protocol of provisional acceptance, dated 30 October 1947.[53]

A problem for APEC is the China (P.R.C.) – Chinese Taipei debate. More particularly Chinese Taipei includes the separate customs territory of Taiwan, Penghu, Kinmen and Mastu.[54] Previously, in 1965, Taiwan was granted observer status at sessions of the GATT 1947. Observer status was subsequent removed in 1971 following a decision by the United Nations Assembly (UN) that recognized the People's Republic of China as the legitimate government of China. In September 1992, GATT's Council of Representatives did establish a separate working party that examined request for accession of Chinese Taipei. During consultations of the working party, eventually, all contracting parties acknowledged China's viewpoint that Chinese Taipei, as separate customs territory, should not accede to GATT 1947 before China. Issues of China's accession, or resumption, also involved the territories of

---

49 General Agreement on Tariffs and Trade, Oct. 30, 1947, 61 Stat. A-11, T.I.A.S. 1700, 55 U.N.T.S. 194 [hereinafter GATT].

50 *See* Nicholas R. Lardy, INTEGRATING CHINA INTO THE GLOBAL ECONOMY, 4, 178 M. 25, Brookings Institution Press (2002) 4, 178 n.25.

51 See Penelope B. Prime, *China joins the WTO: how, why, and what now? The overall, long-term, effects should be positive, but don't expect too much, too soon,* (Statistical Data Included), Business Economics (April 2002), at Table 1, China and Taiwan Join the WTO: Major Milestones, http://www.findarticles.com/ cf_dls/m1094/ 2_37/86851408/p8/article.jhtml?term=.

52 *See* Wang Yi, (ed.), GATT & WTO – LAW AND RULES FOR WORLD TRADE, Publishing House of Law Beijing (1998), 168-74.

53 *Id.*, at 168-74.

54 WTO News: 2001 Press Releases, WTO Successfully Concludes Negotiations on China's Entry, Press/243 17 September 2001, Notes to Editors, http://www.wto.org/english/news_e/pres01_e/pr243_e.htm.

Hong Kong, then a British Crown Colony, which China resumed sovereignty over on 1 July 1997, and Macao, then a Portuguese colony, which China resumed sovereignty over on 20 December 1999.[55]

Second APEC Ministerial Meeting (Singapore 1990)

The Joint Statement of the Ministerial Meeting shows that present at this meeting, as observers were the ASEAN Secretariat, the PECC and the South Pacific Forum (SPF).[56] The initial tone of the meetings was delivered by then Prime Minister Lee Kuan Yew in a keynote address. An excerpt from his address follows.

> All countries present today have grown faster because of the GATT-IMF multilateral free trade regime. It is in all our interests to keep open the system of free and fair trade. Indeed APEC countries should set themselves up as examples of good GATT abiding citizens of the world and oppose the formation of trading blocs. In that way we will contribute to world economic growth.

At paragraph 4 of the Joint Statement, ministers while recognizing the need for strong regional economic performance, noted that without economic performance neither democratic institutions, nor social justice can flourish and be promoted. Economic growth was therefore seen as a contingent for promoting security in the Asia-Pacific region. The 1990 agenda fairly conformed to and reflected the first agenda of 1989. The agenda, set forth at paragraph 5 of the Joint Statement, included a broad range of topics such as world and regional economic developments/regional economic outlook, global trade liberalization through the GATT Uruguay trade round, and APEC work projects and future participation. Ministers, at paragraph 12 of the Joint Statement, recognized the opening of the Central and East European economies to the world, and perceived this as possibly leading to an increase flow of goods, technology, capital and investment in the region, and possibly new export markets. However, at paragraph 14, there is some reservation, in that ministers hoped that creation of a single European market would lead to the emergence of a more outward-looking economy, rather than a more restrictive trade bloc.

At the 1989 Canberra meeting, there was a consensus that in order for APEC to eventually lead to tangible benefits, there was a need to progress beyond mere agreement on general principles. For this purpose, ministers reached a consensus on more substantive work projects. At paragraph 20 of the Joint Statement, they identified broad areas of cooperation, which included economic studies, trade liberalization, investment, technology transfer and human resource development, and sectoral cooperation. It was also during this meeting that APEC formed seven working groups, addressing trade and investment data, trade promotion, investment and technology transfer, human resource development, regional energy cooperation, marine resource conservation, and telecommunications. Ministers, at paragraph 27 of the Joint Statement, further reaffirmed their earlier commitment at the 1989 Canberra

---

55 *Id.*

56 Joint Statement, Second APEC Ministerial Meeting, Singapore, 29-31 July 1990.
It was also during the 1990 meeting that APEC formed seven working groups, addressing trade and investment data, trade promotion, investment and technology, transfer, human resource development, regional energy cooperation, marine resource conservation, telecommunications.

meeting to seek the participation of the three economies, China, Taiwan and Hong Kong, in future consultative meetings of APEC.

Finally, at paragraph 17 of the Joint Statement, there is consensus continuing from the 1989 meeting that the primary objective of APEC was to ensure a successful conclusion of the GATT Uruguay trade round. Pursuant to this purpose, at paragraph 18, the ministers issued the Singapore APEC Declaration on the Uruguay Round, which is contained at Annex B of the Joint Statement. The Singapore Declaration essentially directed that consultations concerning the trade round between APEC representatives should be intensified.

Third Ministerial Meeting (Seoul, South Korea 1991)

The Joint Statement of Ministers reflects several important changes in the goals, agenda, especially future participation of APEC. The most obvious change is the participation of the three economies, China, Taiwan and Hong Kong, all at the same time. This was a significant accomplish for APEC. Paragraph 3 also recognized a keynote speech by H.E. Roh Tae Woo, President of the Republic of Korea from 1988 to 1993.[57] Former President Woo emphasised that APEC, "whose fifteen economies are producing one half of the global output, has reached a stage where an institutional base should be established in order to represent the common economic interests of the region and to promote intraregional trade and economic cooperation."

There are two important aspects of APEC addressed in Woo's keynote speech. Following the enlarged participation of the three economies, especially that of China, it is reasonable to assume that this enlarged participation resulted in both increase to fifteen member economies and a regional body producing one-half of global output. His speech also addressed a problem remnant of the first meeting concerning the organizational structure of APEC. A consensus-based body, rather then rules-based body, reliant on cooperation and non-form consultations was now encouraged to establish a more formal organizational structure. It is perhaps in light of this concern that ministers, at paragraph 23 of the Joint Statement recognised the need to consider possibility of establishing a mechanism on a permanent basis that would provide support and coordination for APEC activities at various levels such as financing APEC activities, apportionment of expenses, and other organisational matters.

The agenda remained in conformity with agendas from previous years. Except for consolidation of APEC's principles and objectives, at paragraph 6 of the Joint Statement, the general goals correspond with that of earlier meetings. The general announced goals are consolidation of APEC's principles and objectives, regional economic trends and issues, Uruguay trade round and regional trade liberalization, APEC work program, and future steps for APEC. In the Seoul Declaration, at paragraph 4, Mode of Operation, APEC reaffirmed cooperation based on consensus building.

The agenda was also expanded. In terms of the APEC work program, ministers increased the work projects by addition of projects in the areas of fishers, transportation and tourism. As a result, the work projects were increased from the ten established at the 1990 Singapore meeting to fifteen work projects. In addition, during this meeting that the idea of open

57 Country Briefings: South Korea, Political forces, Economist (Economist.com), Mar 26th 2004, at http://www.economist.com/countries/SouthKorea/PrinterFriendly.cfm?Story_ID=2536193.

regionalism, as a core concept of APEC, begins to take shape. Open regionalism is generally defined as a concerted and unilateral trade liberalization that is along the lines of the most-favoured-nations (MFN) status.[58] Because one of the four Seoul Declaration goals reads, "to reduce barriers to trade in goods and services and investment among participants in a manner consistent with GATT principles." The Seoul Declaration represented the clearest statement to-date of the goals of APEC. The other three Seoul Declaration goals are: "to enhance the positive gains resulting from increasing economic inter dependence...; to develop and strengthen the open multilateral trading system...; to reduce barriers to trade in goods and services and investment among participants in a manner consistent with GATT principles."[59]

Fourth Ministerial Meeting (Bangkok, Thailand 1992)

During this ministerial meeting, the goals and objectives of APEC remain substantial the same as in earlier years, with only a few noticeable changes. One noticeable change was a move toward greater institutionalization. In terms of future steps of APEC, at paragraph 23 of the Joint Statement, ministers expressed appreciation to senior officials for conducting, pursuant to Joint Statement from Seoul (1992), a study based on the Thai Secretariat Working Paper, being Future Steps of APEC. Recognizing that APEC had evolved to a stage where institutionalization could possibly strengthen APEC and enhance efficiency in promoting regional cooperation, ministers agreed, per recommendations of senior officials, that it was time to set up an APEC Secretariat, as an effective support mechanism. It was agreed to establish an APEC fund for financing APEC activities. Ministers endorsed both the Consolidated Report on the Future Steps for APEC and the Bangkok Declaration on APEC Institutional Arrangements, which is contained in Appendix 3 of the Joint Statement.

The most significant change pursuant to greater institutionalization was the establishment of a permanent Secretariat. It was agreed that the seat of APEC Secretariat would be in Singapore. The members agreed to make annual contributions to the APEC fund on proportional basis for covering administrative and operations costs. However, members still remained committed to a consensus-based organization, especially at paragraph 27 of the Joint Statement, by reaffirming APEC is an open and evolving process, and recalling the criteria for participation earlier set forth in the Seoul APEC Declaration, "[T]hat decisions regarding participation be made on the basis of a consensus of all existing participants, and that participation in APEC be open, in principle, to those economies in the Asia-Pacific region."

In terms of future participation, at paragraph 29 of the Joint Statement, members agreed to examine the case of Mexico's membership in APEC and report these findings to the next ministerial meeting (United States 1993). The impetus for considering Mexico as a new member was the growing integration of a North American economy and growing economic links between the North American economy and the Asia-Pacific region.

---

58 Berger, *supra* note 22, at 24, note 38, *citing* Peter Drysdale, David Vines and Brett House, EUROPE AND EAST ASIA: A SHARED GLOBAL AGENDA? in Peter Drysdale and David Vines, eds., EUROPE, EAST ASIA AND APEC: A SHARED GLOBAL AGENDA?, (Cambridge: Cambridge University Press, 1998), 6-9.

59 Janow, *supra* note 37, at 10 n.31.

During this meeting, an Eminent Persons Group (EPG) was also established, comprising individuals from each member economy. Initially, the concept of EPG was to develop a vision in the Asia-Pacific for year 2000, identify problematic constraints, and report to the next ministerial.[60]

Fifth Ministerial Meeting (Seattle, Washington 1993)

Many contend that the dynamics of APEC as a ministerial-level organization made an abrupt change after President Clinton's 1993 invitation to leaders to attend a meeting at Blake Island, which is attributed as commencing the annual APEC leaders' meetings. The fifth ministerial meeting was convened with the first leaders' meeting, with leaders calling for continuing reductions in trade and investments barriers.[61]

This meeting constitutes the first ministerial meeting of a more institutionalized APEC. Pursuant to greater institutionalization, an APEC Secretariat is now in attendance. In terms of future participation, at paragraph 37 of the Joint Summary, APEC welcomed the admission of two new economies, Mexico and Papua New Guinea. It was also decided to admit Chile at the next ministerial meeting in 1994. As for other possible participation, APEC deferred consideration of other possible new memberships pending senior officials study on APEC's membership policies. The latter also reflected APEC growing institutionalisation. As a result of growing institutionalisation, the agenda is also expanded, reflecting a more structured organization. The items on the agenda listed at paragraph 5 of the Joint Statement are generally the Report of the EPG, economic trends and issues, trade and investment issues, the APEC work program, participation issues, and organizational issues.

The Report of the EPG bears mention.[62] At this time, C. Fred Bergsten chairs the EGP. This EPG report emphasized a need for APEC to accelerate and expand cooperation in order to respond to three pending threats to the continued vitality of the region, being the erosion of the multilateral global trading system, evolution of inward looking regionalism, and the risk of fragmentation within the Asia-Pacific region. The EPG recommended that APEC undertake initiatives in four key areas, which were regional and global trade liberalization, trade facilitation programs, technical cooperation, and further institutionalising APEC. In response, the ministers agreed to develop a more long term vision for open trade in the APEC region, and further proposed a program of initiatives to implement their vision.

At paragraph 10 of the Joint Statement, ministers instructed senior officials to implement the EGP recommendations by developing pragmatic programs for trade liberalization and facilitation, technical cooperation, and most importantly, the structural development of APEC and its decision-making process. Senior officials were further requested to prepare a strategy and program that would advance regional and global open trade, and identify mechanisms for achieving that goal. Ministers, at paragraph 11, also requested the EPG to present specific proposals on achieving long-terms goals. Ministers, as in earlier years, at paragraph 17,

---

60 Janow, *supra* note 37, at 11 n. 36.

61 White House, Office of the Press Secretary, Highlight of the APEC Leaders' Meetings, November 11, 2000, http://clinton4.nara.gov/WH/new/html/Mon_Nov_13_094715_2000.html.

62 Janow, *supra* note 37, at 12 n.37, Report of the Eminent Persons Group, A Vision for APEC: Towards an Asia Pacific Economic Community, at 8 APEC Doc. No. 93-EP-01 (Oct. 1993).

reaffirmed that trade and investment liberalization was the cornerstone of APEC. "Strengthening the multilateral trading system, expanding regional and global trade and improving investment rules and procedures in a GATT-consistent manner are, therefore, central APEC objectives. The Uruguay Round must conclude by December 15."

Notwithstanding the namesake of first annual economic leaders meeting, this meeting also established committees on trade and investment, budget and administration, and shows that the EGP was established for a two-year period.

Bogor Goals Period (1994)

This is the year of the Bogor, Indonesia ministry, which resulted in the Bogor goals, being the Bogor Declaration, or the APEC Economic Leaders' Declaration of Common Resolve.[63] The Bogor Declaration or Declaration of Common Resolve reflected a consensus earlier reached at Blake Island. The Bogor Declaration, at paragraph 2, expressed this declaration as a pledge or vision statement of member economies. This vision statement reads as follows.

> 1. [T]o find cooperative solutions to the challenges of our rapidly changing regional and global economy: to support an expanding world economy and an open multilateral trading system; to continue to reduce barriers to trade and investment to enable goods, services and capital to flow freely among our economies; to ensure that our people share the benefits of economic growth, improve education and training, link our economies through advances in telecommunications and transportation, and use our resources sustainably.

It is a vision statement, at paragraph 3, based on recognition of a growing interdependence of an economically diverse region, comprising developed, industrializing and developing economies. APEC's approach is intended to be coherent and comprehensive, and embracing the pillars of sustainable growth, equitable development and national stability. The statement contained in paragraph 6 of the Bogor Declaration, however, is the most important consequence of the Bogor ministry. In anticipation of the new millennium, or twenty-first century, at paragraph 6, ministers agree to adopt a long-term goal of free and open trade and investment in the region. A goal that will be accomplished by further reductions in barriers to trade and investment, and promoting free flows of goods, services and capital, or what they referred to as being in a GATT-consistent manner. Pursuant to this announced goal, ministers also committed to accomplish this goal by a specific date. In particular, ministers agreed to the following.

> [T]o complete the achievement of our goal of free and open trade and investment in the Asia-Pacific no later than the year 2020. The pace of implementation will take into account differing levels of economic development among APEC economies, with the industrialized economies achieving the goal of free and open trade and investment no later than the year 2010 and developing economies no later than the year 2020.

---

63 APEC Economic Leaders' Declaration of Common Resolve, Bogor, Indonesia, 15 November 1994.

In pursuance of this goal by a certain date, they emphasized the creation of an outward-looking, rather than inward-looking, trade bloc. A possible drawback to their commitment may be found at paragraph 9, which, while recognizing that APEC economies are ready to implement a cooperative arrangement, still allowed those that are not ready to participate to join at a later date. However, the Bogor Declaration did not specify which member economies fit in the year 2010 category and the year 2020 category. As a result, there has been debate concerning which economies fit in these categories such as the case of China, and even debate concerning whether the Bogor Declaration did bind all member economies such as the case of Malaysia.[64]

Another important development stemming from the Bogor Declaration is a renewed interested in creating a dispute settlement service. Its proposed creation was justified as resolving trade and other economic disputes and their recurrences, which hamper the implementation of agreed cooperation arrangements. Ministers agreed, at paragraph 9, to explore possibility of a voluntary consultative dispute mediation service, which would supposedly supplement the WTO dispute settlement mechanism.

However, in fairness to APEC, especially in terms of setting the Bogor-date-specific-goals, they recognized, at paragraph 10, that this was an ambitious goal. "Our goal entails a multiple year effort. We will start our concerted liberalization process form the very date of this statement." A firm implementation plan had yet to be developed for the accomplishment of this ambitious and seemingly larger than life goal. Ministers and senior officials were directed to immediately begin preparing detailed implementation proposals. The history of APEC reveals that there were several attempts and several plans implemented for the purposes of accomplishing the Bogor goals within the specified periods. To-date, all of the implementation strategies have failed. Nonetheless, a focal point of this meeting was also the elemental concern of how best to advance APEC's ambitious Bogor goals.[65]

Ministers and senior officials were also requested to consider the recommendations contained in the second reports prepared by the EPG and the Pacific Business Forum. The second EPG report is significant because it attempted to explain the concept of open regionalism, mostly in response to notions of the concept of APEC being a regional initiative. Instead, APEC should be outward looking, rather than inward looking, by ensuring that whatever opportunities are available in the APEC context are equally available to both non-member Asiatic nations and the global economy.[66] Another important aspect of this meeting is the establishment of the economic committee and policy-level group on small and medium-sized enterprises.

Finally, during the economic leaders' meeting, Jiang Zemin, then China President, in a keynote speech stressed that trade liberalization should be based on the principle of non-discrimination, and that it should accommodate the diversity of the Asian-Pacific region. He

---

64 Janow, *supra* note 37, at 17 n. 57.
Malaysia's Prime Minister initially asserted that he did not consider the timetable binding, since the proposal was delivered to the leaders without proper vetting at the level of senior officials. He later introduced the caveat that it was unclear where Malaysia would fit by 2020. Some trade analysts have questioned whether it is fully appropriate to include all of China in the 2020 timetable. They note that some parts of China, such as Guangzhou and Shanghai, will be industrial areas in 2010.

65 White House, *supra* note 61.

66 Janow, *supra* note 37, at 15.

urged APEC members to proceed in a gradual, orderly and phased manner,[67] perhaps reminiscent of China's "gradualist" approach to economic development.

Post-Bogor Goals Period (1995-Present)

During this period, APEC enlarged the areas of economic and technical cooperation. The milestones of this period are the 1995 Osaka Action Agenda, requiring economic and technical cooperation among APEC members; and the 1996 Manila Action Plan (MAPA 1996) that included a collective action plan and individual action plans from its eighteen members.[68] The post-Bogor goals period include the ministerial meetings and leaders' meetings at Osaka, Japan (1995); Subic, Philippines (1996); Vancouver, Canada (1997) Kuala Lumpur, Malaysia (1998); Auckland, New Zealand (1999); Brunei Darussalam (2000); Shanghai, China (2001); Los Cabos, Mexico (2002); and Bangkok, Thailand (2003), and Santiago, Chile (2004).

1995 APEC - Osaka, Japan Summit

On 16-19 November 1995, the seventh APEC ministerial and the third leader's meeting were hosted in Osaka, Japan. Ministers adopted the Osaka Action Agenda,[69] a blueprint for implementing APEC's commitment to free and open trade and investment, business facilitation and economic and technical cooperation.[70] A significant aspect of this meeting was the creation of individual and collective action plans. At paragraph 5 of the Joint Statement, the ministers recognized that, in response to the decisions made by the economic leaders at the Bogor, Indonesia ministry (1994), APEC activities this year focused on the formulation of the Action Agenda to achieve the Bogor Declaration goals. For this reason, the most significant aspect of this meeting was the Osaka Action Agenda. It was the first strategy implemented by APEC for purpose of accomplishing the Bogor goals.[71]

This new focus required intensive and wide-ranging deliberations in all APEC fora.[72] The ministers also agreed to establish the APEC Business Advisory Council (ABAC) in 1996. This need was deemed based on a recognized need for continued cooperation and active involvement of the business and private sectors in APEC activities. In addition, the EPG recommended a fifty percent rule, in that members should reduce by fifty percent or half the transition period for implementing trade liberalization and rule-making reforms that they had committed to in the Uruguay trade round.[73]

---

67 APEC 2001 in China, Role of China in APEC, http://www.china.org.cn/e-apec/china-aspec/2.htm (Discussing China's Participation in APEC's Important Activities and APEC activities sponsored by and held in China.) [hereinafter Role of China].

68 APEC FAQ, *supra* note 47.

69 APEC Economic Leaders' Declaration for Action, Osaka, Japan, 19 November 1995.

70 White House, *supra* note 61.

71 *See* C. Fred Bergsten, (speech), *Back to the Future: APEC Looks at Subregional Trade Agreements to Achieve Free Trade Goal*, Institute for International Economics, October 31, 2000, Washington, DC (Institute for International Economics), http://www.iie.com/publications/papers/bergsten1000.htm.

72 APEC, Joint Statement, Seventh Ministerial Meeting, Osaka, Japan, Nov 16-17, 1995.

73 APEC Eminent Persons Group, Implementing the APEC Vision, (1995), http://www.apecsec.org.

Finally, Jiang, then China President, stressed that the importance of revitalizing developing countries to the prosperity of both the Asian-Pacific region and the world should be recognized from a historical viewpoint. Jiang suggested that APEC should evolve into an economic organization with distinctive characteristics of the Asia-Pacific region.[74] As in the previous year, Jiang's speech arguably contains political rhetorical cultural relativism reflecting Chinese notions of Asian values.

1996 APEC – Philippines, Manila Summit

The President of the Republic of the Philippines, H.E. Fidel V. Ramos, opened the meeting by stating that this year's APEC chair, the Philippines, has set three leadership tasks for itself, carrying out the Manila Action Plan for APEC 1996 (MAPA 1996), strengthening economic and technical cooperation, and further engaging the private sector in the APEC process. Ramos stressed that APEC has moved from the commitment-making phase of setting a vision, goals and agenda to an action phase of carrying out individual initiatives and collective initiatives.[75]

Ministers adopted the Manila Action Plan (MAPA '96) for APEC, which included individual and collective action plans for purposes of achieving the Bogor goals. An important aspect of this meeting was the endorsement of improved individual action plans (IAPs). The first strategy manifest in the Osaka (1995) action agenda was being followed by detail in Manila (1998) with implementation of the IAPs.[76] In addition, the ministers endorsed the Information Technology Agreement, which led to the conclusion of the agreement in the WTO. Ministers further agreed that APEC's economic and technical cooperation activities should focus on six priority areas for cooperation, which were identified as human resources, efficient capital markets, economic infrastructure, technologies of the future, sustainable development, and small and medium-sized enterprises.

Jiang Zemin noted that APEC economic and technical cooperation differs from traditional development. The reciprocity for cooperation is equality, mutual benefit and "complementarity." For Jiang, an APEC-approach encompassed recognition of diversity, flexibility, a "gradualist" approach and openness, mutual respect, equality, mutual benefit, consensus and "voluntarity," and combination of individual and collective action.[77]

1997 APEC – Vancouver, Canada Summit

The ministers agreed that the East Asian financial crisis (1997-1998) reinforced the importance of APEC laying the foundation for realizing their longer-term growth potential, which was expressed as still being exceptionally strong.[78] The most important event of this meeting is adoption of the Early Voluntary Sectoral Liberalization (EVSL) initiative. Ministers endorsed the EVSL initiative, which sought to cut tariffs in key economic sectors.

---

[74] Role of China, *supra* note 67.

[75] Joint Statement, Eighth APEC Ministerial Meeting, Manila, Philippines, 22-23 November 1996.

[76] Bergsten, *supra* note 71.

[77] Role of China, *supra* note 67.

[78] Joint Statement, Ninth Ministerial Meeting, Vancouver, Canada, Nov 21-22, 1997.

Nine priority sectors were identified for immediate action, being chemicals, fish products, forestry products, energy goods and services, environmental goods and services, gems and jewelry, medical equipment, the Telecommunications Mutual Recognition Agreement and toys. Ministers further endorsed a framework of public-private partnerships in infrastructure development that aimed at making more resources available for infrastructure investment in the Asia-Pacific region.[79]

During this meeting, Jiang Zemin emphasized that the APEC approach responds to the reality of the Asia-Pacific region, in that it is conducive to achieving a balance of rights, interests and needs of various member economies, while better enabling member economies to give full play to respective capabilities for common development. Moreover, members should decline financial policies in light of their specific conditions. In terms of trade and investment liberalization, Jiang stressed that APEC members should realize the Bogor goals based on the principles of self-determination, voluntarism and flexibility, and by adopting a pragmatic approach to the Bogor timetable. The point stressed was that APEC members should be allowed adjustments in speed and means, in accordance with individualistic nation-specific characteristics resulting in what was deemed an active and steady way.[80]

The most important event of this meeting was the EVSL initiative. APEC now perceived that the Osaka Action Agenda (1995) was experiencing difficulty toward achieving the Bogor goals. As a result, APEC employed a second strategy of sectoral liberalization, the EVSL initiative. Its initial start is a success that is attributable to the first sectoral liberalization in the Information Technology Agreement (1996), which was ratified by the Europeans and others. Facing a perceived failure with the IAPs, despite MAPA '96, APEC considered sectoral liberalization as a more probable means of achieving the Bogor goals.[81]

1998 APEC – Kuala Lumpur, Malaysia Summit

The ministers expressed concern that the East Asian financial crisis (1997-1998) with its associated contagion effects has had serious socio-economic implications for growth, employment and poverty levels in member economies.[82] The ministers requested senior officials to intensify APEC efforts in addressing the social impact of the crisis. Ministers also endorsed the submission of improved individual action plans (IAPs). In addition, joining the ranks of APEC are three new members, which were Peru, Russia and Vietnam.

Ministers also agreed to place the tariff-cutting elements of the priority sectors of the EVSL initiative into the WTO, intending to obtain an early WTO agreement on these sectors by the time of the 1999 Seattle WTO ministerial. In addition, leaders re-committed to help the Asia-Pacific region emerge from the East Asian financial crisis and return to economic growth. The strategy for doing so was a call for economic reforms and stronger international financial architecture.[83]

---

79 White House, Office of the Press Secretary, Highlight of the APEC Leaders' Meetings, November 11, 2000, http://clinton4.nara.gov/WH/new/html/Mon_Nov_13_094715_2000.html [hereinafter White House].

80 Role of China, *supra* note 67.

81 Bergsten, *supra* note 71.

82 Joint Statement, Tenth APEC Ministerial Meeting, Kuala Lumpur, Malaysia, 14-15 November 1998.

83 White House, *supra* note 79.

1999 APEC – Auckland, Australia Summit

The Joint Statement shows that the APEC agenda was broadened to reflect three themes of APEC 99. The themes are expanding business opportunities in the region, strengthening the functioning of markets, and, most importantly, broadening support for APEC.[84] Broadening support for APEC is undoubtedly based upon, as set forth at paragraph 46 of the Joint Statement, building greater understanding of APEC's goals.

The ministers were attempting to maintain the momentum for economic reform as many regional economies emerged from the East Asian financial crisis. Ministers also approved an agenda designed to foster a new dynamic for the region, strengthen and open markets, reform regulatory regimes, enhance competition, and create greater opportunities for businesses. In addition, there were the goals of launching a new round of WTO trade negotiations and ensuring preparations for possible Y2K problems.[85] Finally, in 1999 and beyond potential new members include Russia, India, Sri Lanka, Pakistan, Ecuador, Mongolia, Panama, and Colombia.

This meeting also evidences a third strategy toward accomplishing the Bogor goals, implying the earlier strategies, such as, Osaka Action Agenda (1995), IAPs (MAPA 1996), and the EVSL initiative (1997), are deemed to be failing. It is a strategy built around a greater dependence that is within a broader liberalization through the launch of a new round of trade talks, which focused on the trade talks in Seattle (WTO 1999).[86] As for China's participation, Jiang stressed that APEC can only maintain its vitality and make achievements, by keeping its nature as an economic form, maintaining the APEC approach, and attaching importance to economic and technical cooperation.[87]

2000 APEC – Brunei Darussalam Summit

It was hoped that the APEC leaders' meeting in Bandar Seri Begawan, Brunei Darussalam on November 15-16, 2000, would build on the progress of the seven previous leaders' meetings. In 1994, the ministers had reached a landmark agreement to achieve the goal of free and open trade and investment in the region no later than 2010 for industrialized economies and 2020 for developing economies, the Bogor goals. In 1993, APEC leaders envisioned an Asia-Pacific that harnessed the energy of its diverse economies, strengthened cooperation and promoted prosperity. To that end, ministers called for continued reduction of trade and investment barriers to allow goods, services, capital and investment to flow freely among APEC economies. [88]

In 2000, C. Fred Bergsten, former EGP chairperson, observed that the origins of APEC, in conjunction with the work of the EPG, provided a perspective on where APEC then stood and what needed to be accomplished in the up-coming ministerial meetings.[89] Bergsten perceived APEC to have been functioning on a two-track system. One track was captured in

[84] Joint Statement, Eleventh APEC Ministerial Meeting, Auckland, New Zealand, 9-10 September 1999.

[85] White House, *supra* note 79.

[86] Bergsten, *supra* note 71.

[87] Role of China, *supra* note 67.

[88] White House, *supra* note 79.

[89] Bergsten, *supra* note 71.

the Seattle (1993) and Bogor (1994) ministerial meetings. The emphasis of the first track is best described by former President Clinton, host of the Seattle summit, in exclaiming, "We want to put together a community of Asia-Pacific economies." The other track characterized the 1994 Bogor goals of achieving free and open trade in the Asia-Pacific region by 2010 or 2020. While the 1993 Seattle summit may have been praiseworthy, the 1994 Bogor summit was more spectacular for having set a free-trade goal. The Osaka Summit showed the way to accomplish the Bogor goals, while the 1996 Subic summit is hailed for the Information Technology Agreement.

As for accomplishing the Bogor goals, Bergsten had doubts, perceiving APEC as experiencing an eroding process over the years. The Bogor goals have been extremely difficult to implement. By the year 2000, APEC had attempted three different strategies for achieving the Bogor goals, all of which failed. Bergsten proposed a fourth strategy for APEC. It was a strategy of developing on a *de facto* basis, what economists refer to as revealed preferences. He perceived this strategy in terms of an evolution in regionalism. It is an evolutionary process suggesting the evolution of a large number of subregional trade and financial arrangements. This proposed strategy required that member economies work in smaller groups, and set their own respective timetables with selected partners. In 2000, there was a small occurrence of such agreements at various stages: some agreed upon, some were being negotiated, some were being studied, and others were being considered. Free trade areas represented part of global movement toward subregional and plurilateral trade agreements, for example, the arrangements of Singapore-New Zealand, Japan-Singapore, Japan-Korea, Japan-Mexico, and Korea-Chile.[90]

APEC leaders earlier foresaw this problem during the 1994 Bogor, Indonesia ministry, when setting a goal of free trade by 2010. Later in the Bogor Declaration, leaders raised the issue of the creation of sub regional arrangements. It was an issue of the compatibility of sub regional arrangement with APEC goals and strategies.

2001 APEC – Shanghai, China Summit

The year of 2001 is a challenging year for APEC because of two primary reasons. APEC had to contend with both a near global economic shutdown and the events of September 11, 2001. It is the first APEC meeting following the 9/11 attacks. This also presented the issue of whether APEC as an economic forum was capability of confronting this crisis. In Shanghai, APEC leader maintained a commitment to a traditional economic mission, while also taking a strong stance against the threat of global terrorism. As a result, a counter terrorism program evolved, with initiatives also launched that focused on both advancing APEC's Bogor goals and development of an e-APEC strategy, which was also in response to fear of an economic shutdown.[91]

APEC's 2001 theme was, "Meeting New Challenges in the New Century: Achieving Common Prosperity through Participation and Cooperation." There had been an economic slowdown in the U.S., Japan and Europe, which the ministers perceived as dampening

---

90 *Id.*

91 California Chamber of Commerce Home Page, What's Happening in APEC?, Business Briefing, Vol. 12– February 2002, http://www.calchamber.com/documents/apec_happening.htm [hereinafter What's Happening in APEC?].

prospects of a global and regional economy. Recent 9/11 terrorists attack in the U.S., posed risk to industries and consumer confidence. Nonetheless, ministers agreed to strengthen cooperation in confronting short-term problems, while emphasizing the importance of achieving the Bogor goals within the agreed period.[92]

Ministers also urged that China's accession be finalized at the forthcoming WTO ministerial conference. Ministers reiterated strong support for approval of accession to the WTO by Chinese Taipei at that conference and the advancement of WTO accession by the Russian Federation and Viet Nam. In addition, ministers supported the participation of all acceding economies in the new round of WTO negotiations.

The issue of confronting the threat of global terrorism is of critical importance because APEC had historically, at least explicitly, confined itself to economic issues. APEC, now, when confronting threat of global terrorism, explicitly addressed political issues. As a result, the significance of this first post-9/11 meeting is APEC, as a gathering of world leaders after the attacks, committed to both coordinating a response to terrorism and trying to minimize the economic effects of terrorism. The threat of terrorism had become a global concern, in that it now manifests a risk both to security of nations and economic prosperity, for Asian and non-Asian nations alike.[93]

Finally, in the Shanghai Declaration, leaders endorsed the pathfinder approach for attaining the Bogor goals of free and open trade and investment. "Leaders reaffirm that those economies ready to initiate and implement a cooperative arrangement may proceed to do so, consistent with the Bogor Declaration.... Use of 'pathfinder initiatives' based on a group of members piloting the implementation of the initiatives, will invigorate progress towards the Bogor Goals." A problem of pathfinder approach was the subsequent interpretation of its concept by members. A narrow interpretation would still require a full consensus of members, despite some members desiring to delay implementation. Contrarily, it could be interpreted as being consistent with the spirit of the Shanghai Accord and the principle of voluntarism. The essence of pathfinder approach is that it allowed members to join when they were ready. For instance, the non-binding investment principles can be implemented, in part or in full, in accordance with an agreed timetable that reflects a coalition of the willing. The principles on trade facilitation could also have been readily transformed into an APEC action agenda.[94]

2002 APEC – Los Cabos, Mexico Summit

The 2002 theme for APEC is "Expanding the Benefits of Cooperation for Economic Growth and Development, Implementing the Vision." The keynote speech of Luis Ernesto Derbrez highlighted growth policies for trade and investment, building human capital and micro enterprises, the participation of women and young people, and improving the functioning of APEC.

---

92 Joint Statement, Thirteenth APEC Ministerial Meeting, Shanghai, People's Republic of China, 17-18 October 20001.

93 What's Happening in APEC?, *supra* note 91.

94 APEC International Assessment Network (APIAN), Remaking APEC as an Institution, The Third APIAN Policy Report, August 2002, at 9, [hereinafter APIAN Assessment].

APEC continued with the theme of TILF. One source, however, argued that APEC should also address the controversial "Singapore issues," which the WTO would not address until 2003.[95] In the following year, the fifth ministerial conference of the WTO in Cancun, 10-14 September 2003, ended without a consensus.[96] In 2003, then WTO Chairperson Luis Ernesto Derbez attributed lack of consensus partly to members remaining entrenched on the "Singapore issues,"[97] which are issues of trade and investment, trade and competition policy, trade facilitation, and transparency of government procurement.[98] It was also suggested that growing regionalism is a major concern, because the WTO rules, Article XXIV of GATT 1947, did not provide an adequate standard ensuring that they are non-discriminatory. The importance of RTAs being consistent with the WTO was a major concern.

In regards to the new and evolving political agenda of APEC, one source observed that the 2001 APEC meeting would probably be recorded in history as the occasion on which Bush, Jiang and Putin realigned the globe. In some viewpoints, especially Bush, the credibility of APEC is becoming dependent on an agenda for counter terrorism. Some, perhaps not so critical of tying APEC's credibility to an agenda for counter terrorism, found that these deliverables were no more than a repackaging of what APEC was already doing in finance and transportation.[99]

This meeting is also heavily influenced by the events of 9/11. The history of APEC lets us know that APEC was formed as an economic consultative group, which allowed leaders of Asian-Pacific economies to get together and discuss trade and the global economy. A distinguishing feature of the Los Cabos meeting was the dominance of security issues. Bush had a priority of issues concerning Saddam Hussein and Iraq. The problem of impending war in Iraq, in conjunction with the meeting being led by Mexico, naturally lent to President Bush's priorities. Because Mexico was one of the rotating seats on the United Nations Security Council, and Bush wanted Mexico's backing on a resolution, or ultimatum, concerning Saddam and Iraq.[100] While APEC had positively expanded to become a useful venue for discussing security and diplomatic issues, the negative consequences were an economic agenda that had largely disappeared, resulting in formal statements that were seemingly vague and lacking in content.[101]

---

95 *See* C. Rammanohar Reddy, *Decision time on Singapore issues at WTO*, THE HINDU, Online Edition of India's National Newspaper, July 28, 2003, http://www.hinduonnet.com/thehindu/2003/07/28/stories/2003072803001200.htm.

96 WTO News, Summary of 14 September 2003, Day 4: Conference ends without consensus, http://www.wto.org/english/thewto_e/minis_e/min03_14sept_e.htm.

97 *Id.*

98 WTO news: 2002 news items, 16 January 2002, International Conference on Financing for Development, Statement by Mr. Ouedraogo, WTO Deputy Director-General to the final Preparatory Committee, 14-25 January 2002, New York, USA, http://www.wto.org/english/news_e/news02_e/ ouedraogo_stat_fin%26 dev_conf_e.htm.

99 Asia Pacific Foundation of Canada, APEC Study Centre in Canada, Report on International Symposium on Perspectives for APEC: 2002 and Beyond December 3 and 4, Mexico City, http://www.asiapacific.ca/about/ apec/apec2002.pdf.

100 Bush Meets With Asian Leaders at APEC Summit, CNN Transcript, Aired October 26, 2002, http://edition.cnn.com/TRANSCRIPTS/0210/26/cst.11.html

101 Edward Lincoln, *supra* note 40, at 1.

2003 APEC – Bangkok, Thailand Summit

As one source noted, "APEC 2003 was not a disaster for the U.S. but neither was it a crowning success."[102] In the past thirty years, Indonesia had led ASEAN and Southeast Asia. In 1997, during the East Asian Financial Crisis and stepping down of President Suharto, leadership had passed to Singapore. Because of Singapore Prime Minister Goh Chok Tong and Malaysian Prime Minster Mahthir Mohammed stepping down, Thailand and Thaksin arose as the new leadership.[103]

During 2003, China made state visits to Thailand and Australia. The problem of terrorism seemed not to be a primary concern for China, in that China did not talk much about the problem of terrorism. Rather, China more so talked about the future, China's role in the future, China's intent to become a major player in the region, the need for free trade, and China's intention to increase investment and prosperity for the region via increased trade. Comparatively, the U.S., represented by President Bush appeared more so focused on the past and issues of security and war on terrorism, including war on Iraq.[104] Finally, a Counter Terrorism Task Force and other initiatives related to the problem of growing terrorism were established, eventually producing the APEC Counter Terrorism Action Plan.[105]

2004 APEC – Santiago, Chile Summit

The theme for this year is "One Community, One Future." In 2004, the goal of APEC remains the advancement of free trade. However, in retrospective, when one examines the history of APEC from its 1989 inception to its present body in 2004, one notices discernible, albeit subtle, differences in organization structure, policies, and goals. The leaders' meeting in the Chilean capital of Santiago on 21-22 November 2004 is an organization different in appearance and substance. The most important new ingredient of the APEC agenda is explicit concerns of a political nature, rather than the former APEC promotion of aid and trade in the Asia-Pacific region.

As a reminder of the 2003 summit, U.S. President Bush continued his diplomatic agenda concerning the fight against terrorism. In terms of politics, most problematic for an American populace is that economics, and not politics, dominate the agenda. Conversely, in terms of economics, this meeting is dominated by moves for bilateral free trade agreements.

Initially, APEC, as a forum of only twelve members that met at ministerial-levels, emphasized helping poorer member economies promote economic growth through technical assistance and trade. APEC has grown to now include Japan, the U.S., China, Australia, Southeast Asia and Latin American countries. APEC continues to operate by consensus approach and without legally binding text such as an international treaty. It had experienced some degree of institutionalization, but remained a loose institutional structure by virtue of

---

102 Christopher W. Runckel, APEC 2003 and The U.S. Role in Asia, Runckel & Associates, 2003, http://www.business-in-asia.com/apec2003.html.

103 Report on International Symposium on Perspectives for APEC: 2002 and Beyond, December 3 and 4, Mexico City, http://www.business-in-asia.com/apec2003.html.

104 Business-In-Asia.Com, APEC 2003 and The U.S. Role in Asia, http://www.business-in-asia.com/apec2003.html.

105 2004 APEC Outcomes, *supra* note 1.

consensus approach and continuing voluntarism. It is for this reason, membership in APEC is loosely defined. Membership is a simple criterion of geography, belonging to the Asia-Pacific region. Russia's membership exemplifies the looseness of this criterion for membership.

On the positive side, due to President Clinton's 1993 proposal at Seattle, APEC's economic consultative forum evolved into an annual meeting of top-level presidents and prime ministers. Clinton's 1993 proposal is significant because it represented APEC transition from economic only forum to both economic and, at least implicitly, political forum. What was hailed as an apolitical forum did implicitly commence an evolution to wider agenda embracing economic and political regional concerns. There has always been an implicit and hidden political agenda of APEC. At its inception, it is announced that the nomenclature of economies in reference to members should enjoy a freedom apart from typical political concerns. The reference of economic leaders' meeting, as opposed to, simply, a meeting of Asia-Pacific nations, was arguably done so in pursuance of political objectives.

In Bogor, Indonesia (1994), APEC set a goal for trade and investment liberalization to be accomplished by 2010 for industrialized members and 2020 for developing members. The Bogor goals were to be accomplished by action guidelines adopted at the Osaka ministry (1995). As continuing proof of a commitment to consensus approach and voluntarism, the Bogor goals and pledges of implementation were not to be coerced, and in the absence of a more formally structured enforcement mechanism, implementation was depended on no more than peer pressure.

Initially, APEC pursued a liberalization agenda that supplemented and accelerated the WTO goal of multilateral trade negotiations. However, due to complications and speed in pursuing liberalization within the WTO structure, there evolved a growing preference for FTAs on a bilateral basis. The Chile summit evidenced this growing international trend and saw many opportunities for members to search for new bilateral trade agreements.

Before the WTO and pending Uruguay round trade talks, the prevailing fear of Asian nations was trade blocs dominated by the U.S., Japan and Germany. History now reveals a new growing fear born of a new international political economy concern. In 2004, the new and prevailing fear is being left behind in the region-wide moves for FTAs, with China seen as taking the initiative. Moreover, the scope of these FTAs are directed to agreements to make the flow of investment and manpower resources easier, and not just simply trade liberalization. These agreements are called Economic Partnership Agreements (EPA), which seek to strengthen bilateral economic relations.

The APEC-Chile summit leaves us with the question of the future role of APEC. Because the summit's showing of diplomacy leaves one with no doubt of the growing importance of politics to APEC's agenda. During this summit, the latter is evidenced by Japan's Prime Minister Junichiro Koizumi's attempt to break a diplomatic stalemate between China and Japan, while reaffirming a Japan-U.S. alliance. This presents critical concerns of what happened to the original economic only agenda of APEC for free-world trade, and prospects of APEC playing a leading role in promoting free trade in the new millennium.[106]

---

[106] Advancing Free Trade Remains Key Goal of the APEC, Foreign Press Center/Japan, November 24, 2004, http://www.fpcj.jp/e/shiryo/jb/0453.html.

APEC: CREDIBILITY AND REGIONALISM

APEC has been criticized as being an undemocratic and non-transparent structure, and examining economic issues to the exclusion of social issues. Separating economic issues from social issues denies reality. Consequently, some social issues that manage to make it on the agenda, such as sustainable human development, are seriously truncated.[107] However, there are many criticisms of APEC, ranging from a failure to respond to the East Asian financial crisis (1997-98), to failing to adequately meet challenge of growing regionalism.

APEC failures are partly attributable to the East Asian financial crisis.[108] This crisis brought into question whether the Asian development model after all lacked substance, especially in merely relying on foreign capital. There is also the question of whether in the beginning too much had been expected of Asian industrialization. Debates also ensued concerning how to deal with the Asian financial crisis and whether the International Monetary Fund's (IMF) prescription was correct.[109] There was also the question concerning the problem of an influx of international short-term capital. During this period, the U.S., Europe and Japan were criticized for doing too little, too late. The East Asian financial crisis left the Asia-Pacific region feeling the blunt of uncertainty, especially about the future. The East Asian financial crisis has been described as Asian economies forgetting to steadfastly pursue an industrialization pattern reflective of Asian reality.[110] Asian economies depended on international short-term capital via financial liberalization for combating capital shortages. If Asian economies had developed their soft infrastructures such as human resources, and hard infrastructures such as road, factories and transportation, and then pursued a more orthodox industrial development path of cultivating industries, this problem would have never intensified to the degree that it did.

The severity of the financial crisis varied from economy to economy, as did the IMF's prescription and proposed solutions to the problems of economic globalization that ensued. One source described the theories of origin of the Asian financial crisis as either a failure in Asian capitalism or Western capitalism. A problem of these theories is that both treat Asia as a block, failing to take cognizance of differing economies, cultures, religions and polities. Treating Asia as a block also ignores the fact that Asian economies were hit at different times, in different ways, with some not even being directly hit.[111] Proposing liberalization and facilitating trade without consideration of the particularities of the various economies, and without confirmation of time needed to weather such crisis, or where the greater problems lie, inevitably created the problem of restructuring economies in a vacuum.

APEC is also criticized for losing sight of its original goals. In an increasingly borderless world, industrial development seeks markets generating maximum benefits for investors, that

---

107 Canada and APEC: Perspectives from Civil Society, First Draft, April 22, 1997, Prepared by the Policy Working Group, Canadian Organizing Network for the 1997 People's Summit on APEC.

108 Takeshi Isayama, *supra* note 10.

109 The International Monetary Fund (IMF), http://www.imf.org/, "The IMF is an organization of 184 countries, working to foster global monetary cooperation, secure financial stability, facilitate international trade, promote high employment and sustainable economic growth, and reduce poverty."

110 Takeshi Isayama, *supra* note 10.

111 *See* Susan Glazebrook, *The Role of the Law in the Asian Financial Crisis*, The paper is based on the Presidential address given by Dr. Glazebrook at the Plenary session of the Inter-Pacific Bar Association Ninth Annual Conference, Bangkok, Thailand, May 1, 1999, http://www.ipba.org/membersonly/papers/documents/glazebrook.pdf.

is, a global market where industries choose and reject economies. Economic alignments are necessary, because a single economy in the global economy cannot maintain international competitiveness and growth in all sectors of an economy. There are comparative and absolute advantages in trade, and every economy tends to enjoy a comparative advantage and even comparative disadvantage.[112] Outward-looking directions are necessary, because an economy cannot close its borders indefinitely in today's global economy. An economy must search for means to form economic links with other economies, or suffer the consequences of autarky. For these reasons, some argue that APEC should return to its origins, and redirect its attention to this new environment.

APEC became the leading forum for political and economic collaboration in the Asia-Pacific region. APEC, by its member economies, was granted a broad agenda for promoting trade and economic cooperation. Pursuant to this broad agenda, APEC members signed the 1994 Bogor Declaration. However, the accomplishment of the Bogor goals would experience a serious setback because of the East Asian financial crisis. Many expected that APEC would find solutions to the financial crisis. A problem for APEC is that it was generally perceived as indecisive and ineffective in meeting this challenge. As recession and economic slowdown took its toll on economies in the region, the prestige of APEC suffered. The political economy of the financial crisis found Asian economies looking to other forms of economic cooperation, if not regionalism. A perception of APEC failing to adequately respond to the financial crisis negatively affected its credibility.[113]

A new thinking about Asian regionalism begins to evolve, which is at least partly attributable to the failure of APEC to deal with the financial crisis. The idea of a new East Asian regionalism was embraced by many Asian economies. There was a commonly held view in Asia, especially Korea and the ASEAN countries, that they had been let down by the West, in particular, the United States and Japan, during the crisis. This view was based on a belief that the West, or the G-7 nations, now G-8, made the financial crisis worst by pulling

---

112 *See* Richard N. Block, et al., *Economic Perspectives on International Labor Standards*, 11 MSU-DCL J. INT'L L. 417, 419 (2002):

Traditionally, economist have referenced the "factor cost model" when discussing international trade. Specifically, the theory suggests that countries should specialize in the production of goods in which they can produce at least cost. . . . [T]heorists take into account a country's productive factor endowments, including land, capital, labor and climate. In applying the factor cost model, economists compare the costs of production of each product both within and between countries. When a jurisdiction has the capability to produce a particular product at least cost compared to other jurisdictions, it is said to have an "absolute advantage." Meanwhile, that country is said to have a "comparative advantage" in a certain product if it can produce that output cheaper relative to other products within its boundaries.

113 *See* Shalendra D. Sharma, *Beyond ASEAN and APEC: Towards a New Asia-Pacific Economic Regionalism*, Vol. 14, No. 3 East Asian Review, 37-48 (Autumn 2002)

from their region funds from their banking and financing institutions.[114] For this reason, they felt that more assistance should have come from the West. [115]

This feeling of abandonment by the West was intensified in two respects. The G-7 nations either refused to assist, as in the case with the U.S. and Japan concerning Thailand, or when assisting, as through the IMF, imposed seemingly excessive and stringent demands. Despite the merits of these contentions, there was a consensus among Asian economies that they should reduce their dependence on the G-7 nations and multilateral financial institutions such as the IMF and World Bank.[116]

The aftermath of a growing proclivity toward East Asian regionalism is a resulting credibility problem for APEC. It is a credibility problem only attenuated by its failure at the 1997 Vancouver ministerial meeting to support Japan's proposal for an Asian Monetary Fund (AMF), and further, its endorsement of central role of the IMF in resolving the crisis.[117] This event on the part of APEC alienated many Asian economies. However, the growing idea of East Asian regionalism is claimed not to be an explicit rejection of multilateralism, or global economic integration, rather a claimed consensus of Asian economies regarding mostly regional autonomy, especially in economic matters. Asian economies claimed that a more regionally focused institution could better design more appropriate conditionality than the IMF.[118] This was perceived to be mostly due to closer geographical proximity of Asian economies.[119]

During this period of growing global regionalism, APEC seems caught in the midst of the regionalism versus multilateralism debate. There has yet to be resolved the debate contrasting

---

114 University of Toronto G8 Information Center: What is the G8?, http://www.g7.utoronto.ca/what_is_g8.html, The six countries at the first summit, held at Rambouillet, France in November 1975, were France, the United States, Britain, Germany, Japan and Italy. They were joined by Canada at the San Juan Summit of 1976 in Puerto Rico, and by the European Community at the London Summit of 1977. From then on, membership in the G7 was fixed, although 15 developing countries' leaders met with the G7 leaders on the eve of the 1989 Paris Summit, and the USSR and then Russia participated in a post-summit dialogue with the G7 since 1991. Starting with the 1994 Naples Summit, the G7 met with Russia at each summit (referred to as the P8 or Political 8). The Denver Summit of the Eight was a milestone, marking full Russian participation in all but financial and certain economic discussions; and the 1998 Birmingham Summit saw full Russian participation, giving birth to the G8 (although the G7 continued to function along side the formal summits).

115 Sharma, *supra* note 113.

116 The International Bank for Reconstruction and Development (IBRD) or (World Bank) or (The World Bank Group), http://www.worldbank.org/ (Explaining that The World Bank consists of five institutions: International Bank for Reconstruction and Development; International Development Association; International Finance Corporation; Multilateral Investment Guarantees Agency; International Centre for Settlement of Investment Disputes. In the World Bank Group, there are also the regional development banks, such as the Inter-American Development Bank).

117 Edward Lincoln, *supra* note 40, at 5,
A key motive behind the Chiang Mai Initiative on currency swaps has been to insulate Asian nations from the behavior of Western "speculators" and the policy demands of the IMF. This is a scaled back approach from the AMF proposed by the Japanese government in 1997, but the motive remains the same. In fact, talk of an AMF has not disappeared, though the concept is now carefully couched in terms of making it a clear subsidiary or supplement to the IMF— disbursing funds to troubled Asian countries only with IMF approval. Still, there is an underlying desire to gain more independence from IMF or Western demands.

118 Articles of Agreement of the International Monetary Fund, Art. V, sec. 3(a),
"The Fund shall adopt policies on the use of its general resources, including policies on stand-by or similar arrangements, and may adopt special policies for special balance of payments problems, that will assist members to solve their balance of payments problems in a manner consistent with the provisions of this Agreement and that will establish adequate safeguards for the temporary use of the general resources of the Fund."

119 Sharma, *supra* note 113.

regionalism to multilateralism in trade.[120] Some criticisms focus on APEC as a regional trading agreement. These critiques perceive liberalization as the cause of social and economic problems, rather than as a solution. In this respect, APEC by adopting a neo-liberal agenda had adopted an incorrect model. There are criticisms that simply center on APEC's adoption of economic liberalization or neo-liberalism. This is mostly an issue of state sovereignty that results from models of regionalism embracing both developed and developing economies. Some development theorists, in challenging liberalization as the best option, argue that the retention of state control over strategic economic instruments and sectors provides more options for development. There are simply critiques such as liberal economists that encourage a multilateral approach, rather regional approach, to trade liberalization. Regionalism for these critiques is a second best choice to multilateralism.[121]

There are also criticisms that speak to APEC's vagueness and generalities. APEC is perceived by some as saying much the same every year since its 1989 formation, and suffering a failure in its primary goal of TILF and the Bogor goals. The 2004 APEC-Chile summit has been described as an APEC weekend resulting in with a 9,000-word, 24-page commitment to continue being vague, and as, "a voluntary come-along-to-the-party-if-you-wish organisation."[122] The 2005 APEC-Busan, South Korea summit hardly differed and reflected the same routine, especially formal statements that continue to be seemingly vague and lacking in content.

A growth in FTAs may also have challenged APEC's goal of TILF. While the world witnesses a struggling WTO Doha Development Agenda, there are increasing numbers of FTAs or PTAs.[123] Between 1990-1994, the number of FTAs substantially jumped, in that twenty-nine new FTAs were reported to the WTO. From 1995-1999, the number of FTAs grew by an additional sixty-four agreements with twenty-eight of these FTAs being transition economies. After 2000, South-South agreements accounted for a larger percentage of the new

---

120 Bowles, *supra* note 19.

121 Id., citing A. Singh, Openness and the Market Friendly Approach to Development: Learning the Right lessons from Development Experience, World Development, Vol. 22, No. 12 (December 1994).

122 *See Red tape chokes Apec, Focus*, November 24, 2004, THE STANDARD, Sing Tao Newspaper Group and Global China Group, http://www.thestandard.com.hk/stdn/std/Focus/FK22Dh02.html.

123 *See* Andrew L. Stoler, *Preferential Trade Agreements and the Role and Goals of the World Trade Organization*, Institute for International Business, Economics & Law, The University of Adelaide, Conference on Free Trade Agreements in the Asia-Pacific Region: Implications for Australia, 4-6 July 2004, Perth, Australia, at 2 n. 3.

In the time since the launch of the Doha Round, Australia – long seen as one of the most ardent backers of the GATT-WTO – has negotiated and agreed PTAs with Singapore, Thailand and the United States. Canberra has embarked on a feasibility study of a PTA with China and has been invited by ASEAN members to consider joining New Zealand in a PTA with the regional grouping. And Australia's pace of PTA activity, while impressive, pales in comparison with that of the United States. As of this writing, Washington is simultaneously negotiating PTA's with the Andean Group, SADC, Bahrain and Thailand and there are signs that a negotiation might be possible with Malaysia. Pending before the Congress are recently negotiated PTAs with Australia, the Central American Common Market, the Dominican Republic and Morocco. And the United States has not given up in its now-stalled effort to negotiate a PTA encompassing nearly all of the countries of the Western Hemisphere. Japan and Mexico have concluded a PTA, as have Korea and Chile. Singapore and Panama are exploring a deal. The European Union is in active negotiations on a PTA with Mercosur.

Id., at 2.

FTAs reported to the WTO. In a three-year period (2000-2002), there was a fifty-five percent growth in the number of new FTAs.[124]

The growing proliferation of FTAs pose a threat to the WTO goal of free trade, in that political considerations for entering FTAs may be overriding economic considerations offered via the avenue of the WTO. The world has witnessed a growth in both FTAs motivated solely by political considerations, and FTAs motivated by a combination of economic and political considerations. If motivations for FTAs are grounded in political considerations, then the WTO may lose its appeal as a feasible alternative.[125] The problem of FTAs motivated by solely political considerations, or even in part by political considerations, is that they can in terms of economics have a negative effect, both nationally and globally. FTAs have a potential to result in trade diversion, which is welfare reducing.[126] Politically motivated FTAs may potentially undermine the WTO and multilateral trade,[127] if not APEC's primary goal of TILF.

Most problematic for the non-Asian economies with the advent of growing interests in regionalism and a perceived weak APEC, Asian nations began to actively pursue regional dialogues to the exclusion of non-Asian economies. In light of a perceived weak and ineffective APEC, Asian nations started turning to ASEAN, or ASEAN Plus Three, and FTAs between Asian nations,[128] such as, the 2004 ASEAN-China accord. The consequence of a growth in Asian FTAs or PTAs, especially the new potential of Asian regionalism proposed by ASEAN at the 10th ASEAN summit in Vientiane, Laos, may pose a threat to multilateral trade, the WTO and APEC. The ASEAN summit struck an accord between China and ASEAN that could result in the world's largest FTA.

2004 ASEAN – CHINA ACCORD

Since 1991, China has been an active participant in APEC.[129] The participation of China during the present reign of China President Hu Jintao reflects the earlier posturing of former

---

124 WTO: Regional Trade Agreements: Facts and Figures, http://www.wto.org/english/tratop_e/region_e/regfac_e.htm; *see also* Stoler, *Id.*, at 2-3, *citing* World Trade Report 2003, Table IB.9, page 47 (World Trade Organization, Geneva, 2003).

125 *Id.*, at 6. "For example, political considerations drove the negotiations of the U.S.-Israel, U.S.-Jordan or U.S. Morocco PTAs. In addition, the Mercosur agreement linking Brazil, Argentina, Uruguay and Paraguay was also an agreement motivated by political considerations."

126 *Id.*, at 7.

There is a potentially dark side to the economic justification for a PTA. If there is a concern one hears expressed frequently by economists in respect of PTA's it is that they are likely to produce some degree of trade diversion. Trade diversion is welfare reducing, but that does not mean that it cannot be saleable on a sectoral basis. It is not impossible that a government might pursue a PTA as a way to realize economic rents from trade in sectors where its companies might not be competitive internationally. In classic trade diversion scenarios, the most efficient suppliers are shut out of the market when less efficient overseas producers (in the PTA partner) are granted preferential access through discriminatory tariff reductions. Clearly, a PTA grounded in an exclusionary motivation will be neither welfare enhancing nor complementary to the WTO multilateral process as participants in such a PTA will have little interest in seeing progress at the multilateral level.

127 *Id.*, at 11.

128 Edward Lincoln, *supra* note 40, at 1.

129 Role of China, *supra* note 67 (For instance, For instance, President Hu, at the 2003 Bangkok summit made a three-point proposal expressly language similar to Jiang; i.e. " . . . voluntarism and consensus, should be upheld;" " . . . reform and innovation by willingly adapting itself to changing circumstances.").

President Jiang Zemin. Hu Jintao, not unlike Jiang Zemin, continues to present a positive image of China's active participation in APEC.[130]

A vision and understanding of China's active participation in APEC becomes blurred, if not suspect, however, when one considers China's relation with ASEAN, especially in the year 2004. As previously mentioned, on 29 November 2004, at the 10th ASEAN summit in Vientiane, Laos, China and ASEAN signed a landmark agreement to cut tariffs, resulting in a substantial step towards creating the world's largest FTA by 2010.[131] The most prominent of the series of agreements and mechanisms produced by the summit are the Agreement on Trade in Goods of the Framework Agreement on Comprehensive Economic Cooperation between ASEAN and China, and the Agreement on Dispute Settlement Mechanism.[132] An important aspect of this accord is that it requires the two regions to begin building a massive tariff-free market over the next five years in an area comprising nearly two billion people.[133]

The establishment of this FTA will boost the development of this region, which already has about 1.7 billion consumers, about US $1.8 trillion in GDP, and US $1.2 trillion in trade volume. Statistics from the China Ministry of Commerce (MOFCOM) shows that since 1990, ASEAN has been China's fifth largest trade partner for eleven consecutive years. Trade volume in the first ten months of 2004 hit US $84.61 billion, which is up by 35.2 percent over the same period in 2003.[134] The accord between China and ASEAN is expected to build on two-way trade that is expected to surpass US $100 billion in 2004.[135] Notwithstanding a trade deficit with ASEAN, China anticipates that trade will balance out with growth in the region, and as noted by one Chinese source, the agreements are expected to create a win-win situation for economic and trade relations.[136]

---

130 Hu outlines China's ideas on improving APEC process, Embassy of the People's Republic of China in Australia, November 24, 2003, http://www.chinaembassy.org.au/eng/xw/t45610.htm; *see also* Advancing Win-Win Cooperation for Sustainable Development, Speech by President Hu Jintao of China at the APEC CEO Summit, November 19, 2004, http://www.apec2004.cl/imc/economy.asp?id=12.

131 *See* Sun Shangwu, *ASEAN deal hailed as milestone for regional co-operation*, CHINA DAILY, November 30, 2004.

132 *See* Sun Shangwu, *ASEAN links push free trade,* CHINA DAILY, November 29, 2004.

133 10th ASEAN Summit Vientiane, Laos 2004, ASEAN Overview, Paragraphs 10-11, ASEAN Free Trade Area, http://www.10thaseansummit.gov.la/asean_view.htm, [hereinafter 10th ASEAN Summit 2004].
10th paragraph In realising the ASEAN Free Trade Area (AFTA), 98.62% of the products in the CEPT Inclusion List (IL) of ASEAN-6 have been brought down to the 0-5% tariff range. As of September 2004, products in the IL, which continue to have tariffs of above 5% are those that have been transferred from the Sensitive Lists (SL) and General Exception Lists (GE) in 2003. Tariffs on 60.89% of the products in the IL of ASEAN-6 have been eliminated. The average tariff for ASEAN-6 under the CEPT Scheme is now down to 1.91% from 12.76% in 1993. For the new ASEAN Member Countries (Cambodia, Laos, Myanmar and Viet Nam), 79.13% of the products traded in the region have been moved into the IL and tariffs on 69.88% of these items have already been brought down within the 0-5% band.
11th paragraph Regional financial cooperation has also strengthened. The bilateral swap arrangements network under the Chiang Mai Initiative now comprises 16 agreements with a combined size of US$36.5 billion. The Finance Ministers of ASEAN are also working on a series of promotional activities to attract more funds from developed capital markets outside Southeast Asia to move into ASEAN to strengthen the regional financial markets.

134 Sun Shangwu, *ASEAN links push free trade, supra* note 132.

135 Deal forms free-trade megazone, China, ASEAN sign landmark accord, supra note 9.

136 *See* Sun Shangwu, *ASEAN links push free trade, supra* note 132, "Zhai Kun, a researcher on Southeast Asian affairs with the China Institute of Contemporary International Relations." . . . "The agreements have paved the way for building up a China-ASEAN FTA, and are expected to create a win-win situation for economic and trade relations, said Zhai; *see also* 10th ASEAN Summit Vientiane, Laos 2004, ASEAN Overview, supra note 133, at Paragraphs 7-9.

Moreover, the significance of 2004 ASEAN-China accord is enhanced by China's increasingly growing global trade volume. In 2005, MOFCOM reported that in 2004 China registered a 34.7 percent surge in foreign trade, with US $1.15 trillion being exchanged. As a result, China became the world's third largest trading power, only lagging behind the U.S. and Germany. Conversely, Chinese sources fearing that some analysts will use these figures for promoting trade protectionism, are insisting that China is not a large trading power or strong trading power. In defense of a large trade volume, and yearly surplus that amounted to US $32 billion, which is up by 25.5 percent year-on-year, Chinese sources are arguing that China's trade accounts for just 5.5 percent of global trade volume, its per capital trade value is only US $850 compared to world average of US $2,400, and that in the first quarter of 2004 it registered a trade deficit of US $8.4 billion.[137] Admittedly, becoming the world's third largest trader by volume may not necessarily be commensurate with being a strong trading power. However, it is difficult to deny that the economic data, especially potential gross trade volume, enhances the potential and threat of the 2004 ASEAN-China accord.

As for implementing the 2004 ASEAN-China accord, ASEAN plans to accomplish this task by strengthening economic relations and expanding trade through the establishment of FTAs and Closer Economic Partnerships (CEPs).[138] A Vientiane Action Programme, adopted by the 10th ASEAN summit, calls for the ten-member group to develop strategies for attracting the investment required to sustain economic growth.[139] In the past decades, economic growth was largely driven by FDI and exports. Exports have stabilized and show signs of expanding. However, since the East Asian financial crisis (1997-98), ASEAN had experienced a sustained decline in FDI.[140] Therefore, the action program calls for a strategy that will strengthen links and promote agreements with major trade partners such as China, Japan, South Korea, the U.S., Australia, New Zealand, the EU, and emerging India.[141]

ASEAN members also signed an agreement that will move them closer to formation of a EU-style single market. They also linked the pact for reduction of tariffs to Bogor-type target dates. ASEAN economic ministers called for tariffs to be abolished by 2007 for the more developed members such as Brunei, Malaysia, Indonesia, the Philippines, Singapore and

---

7th paragraph ASEAN's trade performance grew significantly in 2003. Total ASEAN exports grew by 12.12% from US$ 383.85 billion in 2002 to US$ 430.39 billion in 2003. Total ASEAN imports grew by 9.51% or from US$ 328.11 billion in 2002 to US$ 359.32 billion in 2003.

8th paragraph Intra-ASEAN exports grew higher than the total ASEAN exports. The overall growth was 15.4% or in value term it grew from US$ 86.39 billion in 2002 to US$ 99.7 billion in 2003. Intra-ASEAN imports experienced modest growth in 2003, from US$ 72.23 billion in 2002 to US$ 74.49 billion in 2003.

9th paragraph The United States, Japan, the European Union, China and the Republic of Korea (ROK) remained ASEAN's largest trading partners. The share of ASEAN's total trade with these countries in overall ASEAN trade in 2003 were 14.1%, 13.7%, 11.5%, 7.0% and 4.1%, respectively.

137 *See* Zhang Jin, *Nation now No. 3 global trader*, CHINA DAILY, January 12, 2005; *see also* Zhi Ming, *Large trade volume itself not a reason for being content*, CHINA DAILY, January 13, 2005.

138 Sun Shangwu, ASEAN deal hailed as milestone for regional co-operation, supra note 131.

139 Association of Southeast Asian Nations, Vientiane Action Programme, http://www.aseansec.org/VAP-10th%20ASEAN%20Summit.pdf.

140 10th ASEAN Summit *supra* note 133.
Despite the unfavourable external outlook and against the backdrop of slowdown in global foreign direct investment (FDI) flows, FDI flows to ASEAN increased by 48%, up from $ 13.7 billion in 2002 to $20.2 billion in 2003, resulting in ASEAN being one of the highest FDI growth regions. The overall improved ASEAN investment environment and strong regional economic growth and integration have increased the attractiveness of ASEAN to foreign investors. The increase in FDI flows in 2003 was the highest since 2000.

141 Sun Shangwu, ASEAN deal hailed as milestone for regional co-operation, supra note 131.

Thailand. The other four members, being Cambodia, Myanmar, Laos and Viet Nam will have to abolish tariffs in sectors including autos, textiles and electronics by 2010.[142] In addition, the Agreement on Dispute Settlement Mechanism sets up a three-person panel of independent experts to resolve trade dispute between ASEAN and China.[143]

China and ASEAN present genuine probability of accomplishing what APEC failed to accomplish, more particularly, accomplishing Bogor-type target goals within an earlier period than APEC. China and ASEAN appear to be moving forward in the new millennium, while APEC seems stalled by an inability to accomplish the all-important Bogor goals. Earlier failures in the Osaka Action Agenda, the IAPs, the EVSL initiative, a strategy of greater dependence within a broader global liberalization through launch of the new rounds of trade talks at the WTO, and being seemingly outraced by the ASEAN-China Accord in attempting to form the world's largest FTA, may serve as a harbinger for demise of APEC as the major IGO for TILF in the Asia-Pacific region.[144] However, in the new millennium, factors contributing to the continued relevancy and survivability of APEC may warrant new definitions and meanings. The critical issue of the role that APEC will play in the new millennium, especially after the ASEAN-China accord, may well warrant the balancing of both economic and political considerations, in gauging APEC's relevancy and survivability.

THE NEW MILLENNIUM: APEC AND CHINA

China appears to be an active participant in the economic consultative forums of APEC. However, a second glance reveals China more in pursuance of a political agenda rather than economic consultations. Moreover, the issue of a political rather than economic agenda engenders problems for APEC, especially in terms of preserving its relevancy in the new millennium.

APEC experienced an evolution, albeit limited in scope, to encompass both an explicit economic and explicit political agenda. Many attribute APEC's evolution to an explicit political agenda to the 2001 APEC – Shanghai summit. Moreover, the political economy of post-9/11 further heightened the need for an explicit political agenda at both the 2001 APEC – Shanghai summit and 2002 APEC – Mexico summit. As previously mentioned, one suspects that APEC since its 1989 inception has always had a hidden or implicit political agenda. The first evidence of a political agenda was clearly shown at the first ministers meeting, when ministers discussed both the need and means to bring abroad the three economies of China, Taiwan and Hong Kong. Political problems require political solutions. As a result, the solution to the problem implied a political, rather than economic, solution.

In 1989, APEC was presented to the world with both implicit politics and explicit economics as stock of its agenda. The prevailing international political economy, politics intertwined with economics, makes this true. As earlier mentioned, one criticism of APEC is the examination of economic issues to the exclusion of other societal or social issues.[145]

---

142 *See ASEAN Summit stresses integrated region*, CHINA DAILY, November 30, 2004.

143 Sun Shangwu, ASEAN links push free trade, supra note 132; Deal forms free-trade megazone, China, ASEAN sign landmark accord, supra note 9.

144 Takeshi Isayama, *supra* note 10.

145 Canada and APEC: Perspectives from Civil Society, First Draft, April 22, 1997, Prepared by the Policy Working Group, Canadian Organizing Network for the 1997 People's Summit on APEC.

Suggesting that solely an economic consultative forum can resolve economic development issues, is an attempt to redress economic issues in a void not only divorced from reality, but, more particularly, political reality. It is the problem of economic modeling and attendant general assumption that economic actors taken individually or *en masse* are rational decision makers. For Alfred Marshall (1842-1924), the father of neoclassicism, a definition of economics had to encompass the terms of political economy and economics.[146] As a result, the term of political economy implied that economics and politics were interrelated, implying value statements and normative judgments. As previously noted, generally, regionali*zation* refers to economic integration process mostly driven by private sector activities, while, conversely, regional*ism* refers to the political process that is driven by state cooperative initiatives.[147]

APEC was commenced during periods of evolving, if not enlarging, international political economy concerns. APEC is a by-product of the international political economy concerns of the Cold War, post-Cold War, East Asian Financial crisis, 9/11 and the economics of terrorism that ensued. However, international political economy concerns are not static, they are dynamic and evolve with changing world trends such as the growth of FTAs or PTAs. A Western world should not be dismayed at both the present posture of APEC and China's geo-political posturing, because the new concept of Asian regionalism was, in part, borrowed from Western models of FTAs such as the EU and NAFTA.[148]

China will eventually demonstrate to a multilateral-inclined, free trade world the difference between traditional and West-centric trade methodologies and the praxis of PTAs with Chinese characteristics. A problem for APEC and the global economy may be a lack of understanding of China's dual participation in APEC and ASEAN. It is a question of the economic, political, or combination of both motivations that influence China in its respective relations with APEC and ASEAN.

Whether perceived as a good or bad consequence, when China began to assume role of world player, the fate of APEC became increasingly intertwined with the economic and political development of China. In the international arena, China in a bid for world player extended growing economic powers into forming a corresponding center, if not region, of international political power. While Western economists and politicians debated the merits and likelihood of success and failure in East Asian regionalism, in terms of ASEAN, and APEC's Bogor goals, China in the interim continued to both engage ASEAN and pursue regional FTAs or PTAs. To the dismay of the Western world and especially Western regional theorists,[149] Asian regionalism now seems a likely probability, despite thematic discourses in doubt such as the following. "There is no Asian regionalism based strictly on regional identity

---

146 *See* Harry Landreth, HISTORY OF ECONOMIC THEORY SCOPE, METHOD, AND CONTENT, Houghton Mifflin Company Boston, 1976, at 285.

147 Berger, *supra* note 22.

148 *See* Tianshu Liu, *Implication of Trade Creation and Trade Diversion Effect on Trade between RTAs and China and Australia*, Proceedings of the 16th Annual Conference of the Association for Chinese Economics Studies, Australia (ACESA) Brisbane, QLD, 19 - 20 July 2004, (PhD Thesis), at 2, "After fifteen years of the long awaited WTO membership . . it is merely the beginning of China's free trade goal considering that other countries around the world, like European Union (EU), the United States and Canada, have been pursuing economic and trade cooperation within a particular region."

149 *See* Walden Bello, *Viewpoint: Is ASEAN irrelevant?*, PHILIPPINE DAILY INQUIRER (Dec 17, 2004), http://www.bilaterals.org/article.php3?id_article=1060 (Filipino academic and writer Walden Bello discussing problems of ASEAN regionalism.).

or ideology, except perhaps for the original ASEAN 6. Even that may have diluted as ASEAN 10, comprising six relatively more developed and rich states and four poorer transition economies, was forged by politics and security."[150] Thus, China is demonstrating to a doubting Western world and its West-centric taxonomies of regionalism, the difference between West-centric regional trade taxonomies and the praxis of regionalism with Chinese characteristics. Moreover, because of an increasing connectedness between China and ASEAN, rather than APEC, the fate of APEC became largely intertwined with China's fate.

The combined regional force of China and ASEAN presents a problem for APEC, because the recent ASEAN summit held in Vientiane, Laos on 28-29 November 2004, may have broken new ground in Asian regionalism and community building. Albeit other agreements are effected, this meeting most importantly resulted in the landmark 2004 ASEAN-China accord. In particular, the 2004 ASEAN-China accord also laid the groundwork for the introduction of a new possible rival for APEC. The future of Asian regionalism, which garnered some support at the 10th ASEAN summit, may well be what is being dubbed "JACIK," comprising Japan, ASEAN, China, India and the Republic of Korea.[151] As a result, APEC, which had been universally acknowledged as the major IGO for TILF in the Asia-Pacific region,[152] has been relegated to minimum importance. The ASEAN-China accord created the prospect for a free trade mega zone, while a prospective "JACIK" FTA, turned the prospect of a free trade mega zone, more accurately, into the prospect of a free trade super mega zone.

The latter presents critical issues of the significance and role of APEC in the new millennium. One witnesses China actively participating in both APEC and ASEAN, and suspects that China's supposed active participation in APEC is more politically motivated, rather than motivated by economic concerns. The verbiage contained in the speeches of former China President Jiang Zemin and later China President Hu Jintao during earlier APEC summits, when measured against actions undertaken, especially in geopolitical posturing in the Asian region, reflected China's grave doubts about APEC providing an effective mechanism for promoting the political and, especially, economic interests of China. There is a seeming commonality in the postures of Asian leaders, such as Jiang, Hu and former Malaysian Prime Minister Mahathir Mohamad. Because these leaders spoke, and continue to speak, the language of political rhetorical cultural relativism, reflecting a model of East Asian regionalism that views cultural differences as the cause of Asia's path to economic success.[153] Perhaps it is a East Asia-centric fear of Western institutions and models for development that are reminiscent of the international politically economy concerns of the Cold War, post-Cold

150 *See* Linda Low, *East Asian Regionalism: Would that Help Globalisation, Growth and (In) Equality?,* Paper for Globalisation, Growth and (In) Equality, 5th Centre for the Study of Globalisation and Regionalisation Annual Conference, coorganised by University of Warwick, CSGR and Economic &V Social Research Council, University if Warwick, 15-17 March 2002, http://ww.warwick.ac.uk/fac/soc/GSGR/PLow.pdf, *citing* William D. Coleman, and Geoffrey Undershill, (eds.), Regionalism and Global Integration: Europe, Asia and the America*s*, London and New York: Routledge (1998), at 11; Donald Barry and Ronald C. Keith, (eds.), Regionalism, Multilateralism, and the Politics of Global Trade, Vancouver: University of British Columbia Press (1999), 10-13.

151 *See* Eric Teo Chu Cheow, *Bigger Steps towards Asian Integration, China Daily*, November 21, 2004.

152 Takeshi Isayama, *supra* note 10.

153 *See* Katharina Pistor & Philip A. Wellons, (eds.), The Role of Law and Legal Institutions in Asian Economic Development 1960-1995, New York, Oxford University Press (1998), 34-35 (Culture theory, such as Asian values, can be associated with the theories of Baron de Montesquieu.).

War, the East Asian financial crisis, and the seemingly rigorous conditionalities of the IMF and World Bank. Moreover, developing countries more often than not perceive that their development agendas are bypassed in the WTO for rules benefiting the rich and powerful, the developed countries. It is a recurrent theme in international law and politics, especially concerning the WTO and other Bretton Woods institutions.[154] In addition, because of the potentiality in the particular development of the East Asian region, rather than more generally described Asian-Pacific region, the Bogor goals became increasingly irrelevant. The issue of accomplishing the Bogor goals pales in comparison to the magnitude of what may now transpire in the new millennium, being a potential ASEAN-China FTA and "JACIK" FTA.

The significance of APEC seems tied to a past period. In the 1990s, it was APEC threatening the relevancy of ASEAN by creating a trans-Pacific free trade area. Nonetheless, the growth of West-centric regionalism in the EU, then NAFTA, may have precipitated the demise of APEC as leader in the Asia-Pacific region. One could argue that regionalism prognosticated APEC's demise, because of the growing trend of regionalism and APEC's seeming incapability to respond to this growing trend. If APEC had shown a capability to accomplish the Bogor goals, or even perhaps better responded to the East Asian financial crisis, then its credibility may have been spared. For now, it is perhaps rightly characterized as a loosely institutionalized, consensus-based organization that appears ineffective and inefficient. APEC's agenda turned from implicit politics and explicit economics, to explicit politics and implicit economics, which ran contrary to the changing goals and emphasis on economic cooperation adopted by ASEAN in 1992, when planning to establish an AFTA. From 1989 to 2004, one witnessed the apolitical concerns of APEC evolve to the implicit political concerns, then manifest as the explicit political concerns. In light of this historical evolution, APEC seems to do well in political posturing, especially in its recent leaders' meetings. Conversely, in light of failings in pursuance of the Bogor goals, it seems not to do well as the supposed major forum and IGO for TILF in the Asia-Pacific region.[155]

It is perhaps in terms of international relations (politics) such as promoting regional security and continuing the fight against mega-terrorism, rather than economic cooperation, that APEC will somehow manage to survive and discover new relevancies in the new millennium. Moreover, in the new millennium, the latter political agenda would represent an important role for APEC in the Asia-Pacific, which would lend to substantive relevancy. Admittedly, some that might argue that the refocusing of APEC goals towards political concerns and security measures might further weaken its efficacy as an IGO or regional economic cooperation organization. A problem for APEC is a weakened credibility dating back to the East Asian financial crisis, and most recently, a doubtful ability to accomplish the Bogor goals.

Nonetheless, and most important, APEC remains relevant to China. First, although China is a member of other East Asia sub regional groups, before China acceded to the WTO in 2001, the only international economic organization that China was a member of was APEC. Second, China stands to benefit from APEC's continuing role in promoting trade negotiation rounds in the WTO, especially the Doha Development Agenda. In terms of multilateralism,

---

154 *See* Fatoumata Jawara & Aileen Kaw, BEHIND THE SCENES AT THE WTO: THE REAL WORLD OF INTERNATIONAL TRADE NEGOTIATIONS, (Zed Books, 2003) (Discussing WTO trade negotiations and dominance by the EU and US, and lack of full participation by poor countries.).

155 Takeshi Isayama, *supra* note 10.

the promotion of free trade and investment, or TILF, benefits China. Third, APEC, as seen in the 2004 APEC-Chile summit and earlier summits, presents China with an international stage for self-promotion of political and diplomatic interests. APEC summits have allowed China to interchange and interact with major world powers such as the United States, EU, Mercosur (South American Common Market, Mercado Comun del Cono Sur or Southern Cone Common Market)[156] and others. Fourth, although in China the ASEAN Regional Forum (ARF) became the most important official channel for multilateral security dialogue, APEC is still important to China in terms of security in the Asia-Pacific region.[157] In terms of political considerations, many deem China ambitious to dominate the Asian region.[158] One Chinese source described China's maturing diplomacy in 2004 as "omni-directional foreign policy."[159] Notwithstanding a relevancy more couched in political considerations, than economic considerations, APEC remains relevant to China in the new millennium.

In addition, in terms of possible roles that APEC may play in the new millennium, APEC's survival being intertwined with China's economic and political development presents a potential dilemma. The proposed ASEAN-China FTA implies an exclusionary model of regionalism that is primarily based on political considerations, and may pose a threat to TILF, the WTO, multilateral trade, and the APEC.

The latter model of regionalism presents an FTA motivated by exclusionary motivations, which is probably more trade diverting than trade creating. In terms of trade liberalization, trade diversion is the welfare change caused by consumer and producers substituting higher cost imports from an exporting economy for lower cost imports from third economies.[160] Trade creation is the welfare improvement that arises because high-cost domestic production in one economy is replaced by lower-cost production in another economy. Thus, trade creation allows aligned economies to better exploit their comparative advantage. In terms of more liberalized trade, both economies supposedly further specialize their production, hence, serving the markets of aligned economies with products at lower prices. In terms of FTAs, trade creation improves resource allocation and welfare. Whether overall a net static welfare gain in an economy will be the result of aligned economies, is contingent on whether trade creation outweighs trade diversion or vice versa.[161]

---

156 The official site of the Mercosur Secretariat, http://www.mercosur.org.uy/. The EU's Relation with Mercosur – Overview, http://europa.eu.int/comm/external_relations/mercosur/intro/, "Mercosur was created by Argentina, Brazil, Paraguay and Uruguay in March 1991 with the signing of the Treaty of Asuncion. It originally was set up with the ambitious goal of creating a common market/customs union between the participating countries."

157 China's National Defense 2004, White Papers of the Government, China Information Office of the State Council, http://www.china.org.cn/e-white/.

158 *See Potential Chinese dominance of North Korea*, CHINA REFORM MONITOR No. 572, Editor: Al Santoli, American Foreign Policy Council, Washington, DC, December 21, 2004, http://www.afpc.org, (This source notes that China is ambitious to dominate Asia and discussion examples involving North Korea and Taiwan.); *see also* Chen Zhou and Deng Hongzhou, *Paper maps military future*, CHINA DAILY, December 28, 2004. "But the old security problems in the region have not been fundamentally removed while new insecure elements are emerging. The United States is realigning and beefing up its military presence in the region and strengthening military alliances."

159 *See* Hu Xuan, *Maturing diplomacy in 2004*, CHINA DAILY, (January 1-2, 2005).

160 *See generally* Jacob Viner, THE CUSTOMS UNION ISSUE, New York: Carnegie Endowment for International Peace (1950) (In 1950, Viner introduced the concepts of trade creation and trade diversion.).

161 See Viner, Id; see also Stefan Szepesi, Coercion or engagement?, Economics and institutions in ACP-EU trade negotiations, ECDPM Discussion Paper No. 56, June 2004, at 8.

Assuming net trade creation, and not diversion, custom unions or regional trade arrangements such as NAFTA should enjoy greater economic efficiency, and further benefits stemming from increased trade and investment.[162] Even the former U.S. Trade Representative, Robert Zoellick, advocated PTAs as triggering "competitive liberalization," and as an alternate route to free trade with economies competing to open markets to each other. A fear of exclusion serves as impetus of non-members to either join the group or accept broader agreements.[163] However, the factor of political motivation engenders a tacit assumption of trade diversion. FTAs or PTAs grounded in exclusionary motivations such as political motivations are neither welfare enhancing, nor complementary to the WTO and multilateralism.[164] Thus, models of regionalism motivated by political considerations threaten multilateral trade and, most important, create trade distortion and are welfare reducing.[165]

Most problematic in terms of the 2004 ASEAN-China accord portending the world's largest FTA is that typical trade areas comprising subsets of nations are not necessarily welfare enhancing for all participating nations.[166] The harm from discrimination in trade affects exports to a PTA market and terms of trade, such as, decreased export prices required to maintain competitiveness in a preferential market.[167] A PTA and its discriminatory nature especially have potential to adversely affect the poorest economies. Due to trade diversion, especially stemming mostly from non-participants in the global economy, the global economy will be adversely affected by impending trade distortion.[168]

---

162 *See* Viner, *Id*; *see also* James E. Meade, THE THEORY OF CUSTOMS UNION (1955); *see also* Kym Anderson, *The Challenge of Reducing Subsidies and Trade Barriers*, University of Adelaide, World Bank and CEPR, World Bank Policy Research Working Paper 3415, September 2004, at 4, *citing* Jagdish N. Bhagwati, THE GENERALIZED THEORY OF DISTORTIONS AND WELFARE, in TRADE, BALANCE OF PAYMENTS AND GROWTH, edited by J.N. Bhagwati et al, Amsterdam: North-Holland (1971), In terms of the general theory of the welfare effect of trade distortion, "The standard comparative static analysis of national gains from international trade emphasizes the economic benefits from production specialization and exchange so as to exploit comparative advantage in situations where a nation's costs of production and/or preferences differ from those in the rest of the world."

163 Soamiely Andriamananjara, *On the Relationship between Preferential Trade Agreements and the Multilateral Trading System*, U.S. International Trade Commission, Remarks prepared for the PECC Trade Forum Meetings at the Institute for International Economics, Washington, DC., April 22, 2003, at 3.
"The term "competitive liberalization" has been widely used in APEC dialogue, and was first coined by Bergsten in 1996 in C. Fred Bergsten, *Competitive Liberalization and Global Free Trade: A Vision for the Early 21st Century*, Working Paper 96-15, Institute for International Economics. He argues for instance that the United States initiated the Kennedy Round in the 1960s and the Tokyo Round in the 1970s to counter the discrimination inherent in the creation and expansion of the European Community."
Id., at 3 n. 4.

164 Stoler, *supra* note 123, at 7.

165 Edward Lincoln, *supra* note 40, at 6. Conversely, "Despite trade diversion concerns, the United States has clearly moved in the direction of free trade areas itself, creating the North American Free Trade Area with Canada and Mexico, and now discussing a broader Free Trade Area of the Americas."

166 Edward Lincoln, *Id.*, at 6, Conversely, "Despite trade diversion concerns, the United States has clearly moved in the direction of free trade areas itself, creating the North American Free Trade Area with Canada and Mexico, and now discussing a broader Free Trade Area of the Americas."

167 Soamiely, *supra* note 163, On the Relationship between Preferential Trade Agreements and the Multilateral Trading System, U.S. International Trade Commission, Remarks prepared for the PECC Trade Forum Meetings at the Institute for International Economics, Washington, DC., April 22, 2003, at 2.

168 *Id.*, at 8, *citing* R. Pomfret, THE ECONOMICS OF REGIONAL TRADING ARRANGEMENTS, London: Oxford University Press (1997); M. Schiff and L.A. Winters, REGIONAL INTEGRATION AND DEVELOPMENT, London and New York: Oxford University Press for the World Bank (2003).

Notwithstanding an exception to general theory of the welfare effect of trade distortion,[169] an ASEAN-China FTA constituting the world's largest FTA may pose a serious threat to the global economy.[170] Admittedly, free trade might not be best policy for lesser-developed countries or economies (LDCs) that are facing what economists refer to as a market distortion.[171] Nonetheless, FTAs such as even NAFTA, and the European experiment that was clearly driven by both politics and economics,[172] "inevitably politicize trade more than multilateral trade agreements do."[173] However, China and ASEAN members are developing countries, as opposed to LDCs, thus voiding any arguable exceptions to the general theory prognosticating a welfare reducing effect. The advent of politically motivated ASEAN-China FTA as the world's largest FTA more probable, than not, will produce trade distortion in the global economy.[174] Assuming *arguendo* trade distortion, the world's largest FTA could produce immeasurable and exponentially growing welfare reducing effects.

The latter presents an issue of the WTO rules governing FTAs, at Article XXIV of GATT 1947,[175] which implicitly tolerates trade diversion. Conversely, an important feature of multilateralism is supposed to be the absence of discrimination among trading partners, because multilateral trade is welfare enhancing.[176] An assumed characteristic of international trade agreements, such as NAFTA and EU, is that by their nature as international agreements, they assumedly frustrate protectionism. Whether these international agreements are in fact welfare enhancing is perhaps another issue, because this conclusion does not necessarily apply in reality to liberalization between selective groups of nations. [177]

As early as APEC's third ministerial meeting (Seoul 1991), the idea of open regionalism as a core concept of APEC begins to take form. As reflected in APEC's Seoul Declaration

---

169 Anderson, *supra* note 162, at 2.

The reluctance to reduce trade distortions is almost never because such policy reform involves government treasury outlays. On the contrary, except in the case of a handful of low-income countries still heavily dependent on trade taxes for government revenue, such reform may well benefit the treasury (by raising income and/or consumption tax revenues more than trade tax revenues fall, not to mention any payments foregone because of cuts to subsidy programs).

170 *Id.*, at 2 n. 1, "Not all subsidies are welfare-reducing, and in some cases a subsidy-cum-tax will be optimal to overcome a gap between private and social costs that cannot be bridged à la Coase (1960);" *see also* Rajiv Sethi & Peter Skott, *Uneven Development and the Dynamics of Distortion*, Department of Economics, Working Papers 1997-23, University of Aarhus, http://ideas.repec.org/p/aah/aarhec/1997-23.html (Discussing trade distortion and instances where distorted industrial policies of LCDs may be welfare enhancing).

171 *See* Jagdish Bhagwati, FREE TRADE TODAY 26-27 Princeton University Press, 2002, "We also realized, as no one had pointedly done earlier, that if a suitable policy was addressed to offset that distortion, then we could get back to endorsing free trade."

172 *See* J. F. Francois and M. Rombout, *Preferential Trade Arrangements, Induced Investment, and National Income in a Heckscher-Ohlin-Ramsey Model*, TI 2000-061/2, Tinbergen Institute Discussion Paper, June 2000, at 2, http:// www.tinbergen.nl/discussionpapers/00061.pdf.

173 Bhagwati, *Id,* at 110.

174 Liu, *supra* note 148, at 3-4.

Generally speaking, a country will benefit from importing commodities that are once highly protected in domestic market with a lower-cost member, while suffer a loss when diverts her imports from a low-cost third country to a high-cost member country because of tariff deduction within the regional free trade area. The former is known as the trade creation effect in comparison with the trade diversion effect defined by the latter. As a member country and the whole world will decrease their welfare when trade diversion effect occurs, many studies have been done to observe if it is worth to form or participate in a RTA.

175 GATT, Part III, Article XXIV: Territorial Application - Frontier Traffic- Customs Unions and Free-trade Areas, 5, http://www.wto.org/english/docs_e/legal_e/gatt47_02_e.htm.

176 The European Union's Trade Policies and their Economic Effects, OECD 2000, at 8.

177 Szepesi, *supra* note 161, at 8.

goals (1991), it would be open regionalism, rather than closed or exclusionary regionalism, generally definable as a concerted and unilateral trade liberalization that is along the lines of the most-favored-nations (MFN) status. For this reason and others, Article XXIV has been referred to as the GATT loophole for FTAs. This clause exempts FTAs and customs unions from the obligation in Article I to accord MFN treatment.[178] This loophole is justified for two historical reasons: First, for encouraging membership in GATT, political reality meant accommodating a long history of custom unions that predated GATT, and second, exceptions were permitted under specific or controlled conditions, intending to avoid ad hoc and partial discrimination practiced during the interwar period.[179] In addition, the WTO Memorandum of Understanding on Article XXIV fails to clear up existing ambiguities and contradictions.[180] As a result, Article XXIV remains a continuing source of debate concerning FTAs. A problem only exasperated by fact that only one working party has ever determined that a FTA or regional trade agreement (RTA) satisfied Article XXIV, while, conversely, no FTAs or RTAs have been found to be incompatible with GATT. A GATT Study Group concerning Article XXIV reads, "They have set a dangerous precedent for further special deals, fragmentation of the trading system, and damage to the trade interests of non-participants... GATT rules on customs unions and free trade areas should be examined, redefined so as to avoid ambiguity, and more strictly applied."[181]

An additional problem for global trade is that the 2004 ASEAN-China accord came at a time that the WTO agreement on textiles and clothing would conclude, being January 1, 2005, ending the Multi-Fibre Agreement (MFA) of 1974.[182] The MFA was widely acknowledged as trade distorting with distortions having paradoxical effects. The MFA protected developed economy markets, in that it limited clothing imports from developing economies by quotas. At the Uruguay round in 1994, it was agreed that the MFA would be dismantled in phases, ending on January 1, 2005, when developed economies would remove all quota allocations. Developing and less-developed economies agreed, perceiving the removal would benefit them. However, termination of the MFA is producing mixed results.

The effect of removing this trade barrier will mostly accrue to China first, India second. China and India can produce clothing at lower cost than any other developing economies because of labor-intensive industries. As a result, nine developing and lesser-developed economies, being Bangladesh, the Dominican Republic, Fiji, Madagascar, Mauritius, Sri Lanka, Uganda, Jamaica and Nepal, on September 2004, requested the WTO's Council for Trade in Goods to conduct country-specific analyses for measuring the effect of the MFA's termination. They are seeking assistance for large scale restructuring to prevent impending disastrous economic and social consequences that will befall their countries. These nations, not unlike the rest of the world, have had difficulty competing with China. In their particular situation, China clothing imports raised from 11 million units in 1995 to 213 million units in

---

178 GATT 1947, Art. I, (Outlining most favored-nation treatment).

179 Srinivasan, *supra* note 9, at 2-3.

180 WTO: Understanding on the Interpretation of Article XXIV of the General Agreement on Tariffs and Trade 1994, http://www.wto.org/english/tratop_e/region_e/regatt_e.htm.

181 *See* Kerry A. Chase, *Multilateralism Compromised: The Origins of GATT Article XXIV*, Tufts University (2004), *citing* WTO: REGIONALISM AND THE GLOBAL TRADING SYSTEM (Geneva: WTO, 1995), 69-70, n. 8.

182 GATT, Multi-fibre Agreement, which was in force from 1974 to 1994; *see* WTO Legal Texts: The Uruguay Round agreements, http://www.wto.org/english/docs_e/legal_e/ursum_e.htm#cAgreement.

2003. Estimates indicated that at the termination of the MFA, job losses would be between 27 million and 31 million worldwide.[183] A prospective ASEAN-China FTA, in conjunction with termination of the MFA, further enhances the anticipated welfare reducing effect.

In 2005, both the European Union and the United States entered into Memorandum of Understanding with China regarding the pending global trade crisis of Chinese textile and apparel products. In 2009, the latter Memorandums of Understanding and the WTO safeguards will have ended. The pending global trade crisis in textiles and apparel will present itself as still unresolved in 2009, if not sooner. The Memorandums of Understanding offer at best short-term solutions to a still pending crisis. The latter will eventually present the issue of the need for buffers sanctioning trade distortions such as non-tariff barriers (NTBs) or measures, pursuant to the greater interests of the global economy. It is perhaps a matter of choosing the lesser of two evils, that is, seemingly prospective immeasurable trade distortions from a proposed ASEAN-China FTA versus seemingly more quantitative and measurable trade distortions implicitly tolerated by the WTO rules.

It must be borne in mind that ten years subsequent to the Uruguay Round of multilateral trade negotiations, many subsidies and trade distortions remain. In terms of the implicitly tolerated trade distortions, there is Article XX(b) of the GATT, which does allow an importing country to impose measures necessary to protect human, animal or plant life or health.[184] In addition, the WTO Agreement on Technical Barriers to Trade governs the imposition of technical requirements on products by an importing country.[185] They include trade taxes-cum-subsidies, protection measures such as anti-dumping, regulatory standards and domestic production subsidies. In addition, insufficient or excessive taxation or quantitative regulations also lead to inefficiencies and can be trade distorting.[186] Most important, FTAs or PTAs that are primarily motivated by exclusionary motivations, especially non-economic motivations, which are implicitly tolerated by the WTO rules,[187] produce trade and investment diversion rather than creation. In terms of the WTO rules, the same holds true for FTAs, and proposed buffers such as NTBs to offset trade distortion, both produce implicitly tolerated trade distortion. However, most discerning is that the purported world's largest FTA, the ASEAN-China FTA, taken in conjunction with termination of the MFA, could produce immeasurable and exponentially growing welfare reducing effects.

Notwithstanding employing NTBs as a buffer, which are possibly the only alternatives available following a failed Istanbul Declaration,[188] in the event a proposed ASEAN-China

---

183 *See Textiles Trade Reform: Unstitched By China, WTO*, EFU, (October 22, 2004), http://www.efu.com.cn/eng/onllinesales/promotion/allround/2004-10-22/6605.htm.

184 See Joel P. Trachtman, Decisions of the Appellate Body of the World Trade Organization European Communities-Measures Affecting Asbestos and Asbestos-Containing Products, EJIL-Current Developments, 5 April 2001, http://www.ejil.org/journal/curdevs/sr13.html#TopOfPage (Discussing Article XX(b)).

185 *See* Willy Lin, (speech), *Implications of the end of the WTO Agreement on Textiles and Clothing*, Pacific Economic Cooperation Council's 15th General Meeting held September 1, 2003 in Brunei, http://www.tdctrade.com/shippers/vol26_5/vol26_5_chairman_03.htm.

186 Anderson, *supra* note 162, at 2.

187 GATT, Part III, Article XXIV: Territorial Application - Frontier Traffic- Customs Unions and Free-trade Areas, 5, http://www.wto.org/english/docs_e/legal_e/gatt47_02_e.htm; *see also* John H. Jackson, THE JURISPRUDENCE OF GATT & WTO - INSIGHTS ON TREATY LAW AND ECONOMIC RELATIONS, Higher Education Press, 2002, at 101-102.

188 *See* Seventy-two textile and apparel groups from thirty-six countries made the Istanbul Declaration to the WTO, requesting the WTO extend the MFA quota free deadline from December 31, 2004 to December 31, 2007, but it failed, *Istanbul has no Future, Press Release, Fair Trade Association*, Brussels, June 14, 2004,

FTA is motivated in part or in entirety by exclusionary motivations, then APEC could conceivably serve as a possible "non-NTB-type" buffer to trade distortions that may ensue. Regardless of likelihood of accomplishing the Bogor goals, there are many reasons to believe APEC can, and will, play an important role in buffering anticipated trade distortions. Because, as observed by one assessment of APEC's continuing and substantive relevancies, "[S]trategically, APEC helps stabilize relations among its diverse membership by providing a unique forum for regular discussions among leaders, ministers, technical experts and corporate executives."[189] No other international economic cooperation organization or other IGO is better suited for this task.

> APEC helps to keep the United States engaged in the region, assists the accommodation of China, and facilitates exchange between the wealthier and poorer nations of the region and between East Asia and nations of North and South America. And while it is difficult to measure its precise contributions, APEC has added its weight to those reformers throughout the Asia Pacific that advocate for more open markets and effective government and, especially in recent years, for more focus on human capacity building and on a more equitable sharing of the fruits of globalization.[190]

The latter presents an additional substantive relevancy of APEC that benefits global trade and all economies participating in global trade. APEC has always been relevant in promoting free trade and new rounds of trade negotiations with the WTO, a relevancy that continues into the new millennium. The latter relevancy is also enhanced by the promotion of regional security and continuing the fight against mega-terrorism. Despite difficulties in implementing the Bogor goals, the original commitment of APEC to TILF continues and bears relevancy in the new millennium. In addition, the latter relevancy of promoting free world trade benefits developed and developing economies, because free trade benefits all participating countries.[191] In this respect and others, APEC remains relevant to all participating economies in global trade, and most important, remains relevant in the new millennium. APEC is not expendable as an international economic cooperation organization.

Admittedly, the 2004 ASEAN-China accord may not establish a trade region that is welfare reducing. It may create a trade region manifesting a net static welfare gain, that is,

---

http://www.fta-eu.org/en/new/pmpdf.php?site=fta&pm_id=79; *see also* Brussels Communiqué by the Istanbul Declaration Partners in the Global Alliance for Fair Trade in Textiles and Clothing Brussels, June 17, 2004, http://www.deik.org.tr/genel/ 2004625141610brusselscommunique-june2004.pdf, The Istanbul Declaration is a call to their individual governments to undertake the following actions:

1. Request an emergency meeting of the WTO in order to analyze and identify WTO solutions to the pending crisis associated with the expiration of textile and clothing quotas on January 1, 2005. These could include an extension of the current system, the development of a new system or the use of other WTO mechanisms.
2. Implement automatic and seamless transitional safeguard mechanisms in order to prevent massive disruptive surges of trade from a few countries. The damage associated with the removal of a limited number of quotas in 2002 under the third stage of the phase – out must not be repeated. For example, during that removal, almost all the benefits went to a single supplier, which significantly cut prices.
3. Demand expedited and effective remedies to all types of unfair trading practices employed by certain major supplying countries, including currency manipulation, state sponsored subsidies and state provided non – performing loans, among others.

189 APIAN Assessment, *supra* note 94, at 3, Preface.

190 *Id.*

191 *See* Peter Malanczuk, AKEHURST'S MODERN INTRODUCTION TO INTERNATIONAL LAW 231 (Routledge 7th ed. 1997).

trade and investment creation, and not diversion. A welfare-enhancing ASEAN-China FTA is based on the existence of three key assumptions. First, most ASEAN economies did in fact make the transition from an emphasis on agriculture to industrial development and export-based growth.[192] Second, ASEAN nations have addressed a post-East Asian financial crisis of declining FDI.[193] Third, an ASEAN-China FTA is primarily motivated by economic concerns or economic cooperation, rather than political concerns. However, it is suggested that most ASEAN economies fail in one or more of these respects, especially transition from food, agriculture and forestry,[194] to industrial development and export-based growth. ASEAN is still a relatively weak economic body,[195] with intra-ASEAN exports in 2001 accounting for only twenty percent of ASEAN's total exports, an export figure reflecting the same proportions from the 1970s.[196] Although ASEAN nations have witnessed an increase in FDI, ASEAN nations are still addressing a post-East Asian financial crisis of declining FDI.

In addition, China in anticipation of the termination of the MFA on January 1, 2005, imposed tariffs commencing on January 1, 2005, on six categories of textile exports. On January 1, 2005, many countries removed textile-trading quotas as scheduled, including the U.S., E.U. and Canada. The export tariff was imposed by China's MOFCOM for purpose of addressing concerns of trade partners. On May 20, 2005, China again imposed export duties on another 74 ten-digit tariff lines.[197] In terms of an impending ASEAN-China FTA, the

192 Tan Tai Yong, *supra* note 26.

193 10th ASEAN Summit 2004, supra note 133.

194 *See* Ching-Cheng Chang and Shih-Hsun Hsu, *A Partial Equilibrium Analysis on the Effects of Trade Liberalization in APEC Food Sector*, APEC Study Centre Consortium-1999 Conference, Auckland, New Zealand, May 31-June 2, 1999, http://www2.auckland.ac.nz/apec/papers/Chang.html, "[M]ost of the ASEAN countries possess comparative advantages in exporting rice, vegetable oils, and sugar;" *see also* Joint Press Statement, The Twenty Sixth Meeting of the ASEAN Ministers on Agriculture and Forestry (26th AMAF), Myanmar, Oct. 7, 2004, http://www.aseansec.org/16432.htm; *see also* Deputy PM highlights co-operation among Asian countries at Boao forum, (Deputy Prime Minister Vu Khoan of Vietnam), Nov. 4, 2003, http://www.nhandan.org.vn/english/20031104/bai-news2.html,

> Yet, Asian countries are at different levels of development. Many are still backward agriculture-based economies, thus being in a disadvantageous position in international competition. The service sector, financial and banking systems, science and technology, including information technology, which all are crucial for development in today's world, are still very weak in Asian economies, except for a few.

195 Edgardo S. Santiago, Chapter 4 Economic Development, in ASEAN State of the Environment Report 2000, 24-37, (2000 UNEP RRC.AP), http://www.rrcap.unep.org/sub-region/aseansoe/, "Most AMC economies, although developing rapidly, continue to depend heavily on agriculture and other food-based industries, which are relatively high polluters." *Id.*, at 25; "[A]griculture was the dominant sector for the economies of Cambodia, the Lao PDR and Myanmar, contributing over 50% of GDP in 1997. For other AMCs, agriculture was a much lower percentage of GDP than industry or services." *Id.*, at 27; "Agriculture absorbs over half of ASEAN's employment." *Id.*, at 28.

196 *See* Bello, *supra* note 149, China's motivation, says Chinese economist Angang Hu is in two parts. One, integrate China into global economy as "center of the world's manufacturing industry." Two, while opening up ASEAN markets to manufactured products, attract investments from ASEAN into China's western region;. *see also* Teofilo C. Daquila, *Asean's Economic Performance Reviewing the Past, Looking to the future,* 6(2) HARV. ASIA Q. 10 (2002), http://www.fas.harvard.edu/~asiactr/haq/200203/daquila.pdf, "[I]n 1999-2000, the region showed some signs of economic recovery but was interrupted by poor export performance and low FDI inflows. The September 11 incident further worsened conditions in the region, by causing economic slowdowns in ASEAN's major trading and investment partners—the US, Japan and the European Union."

197 *See* Dai Yan, *Textile tariff details unveiled*, CHINA DAILY, December 28, 2004; *see also* Dai Yan, *Textile export curbs to remain*, CHINA DAILY, January 5, 2005; *see also* Ministry of Commerce of the People's Republic of China, *Commerce Minister Bo Xilai Attending Press Conference Hosted by the State Council Information Office*, ASIA REPORT, June 1, 2005, http://english.mofcom.gov.cn/aarticle/counselorsreport/asiareport/ 200506/20050600106396.html.

MOFCOM's tariff impositions may or may not exhibit genuine multilateralism on the part of China, and may or may not sufficiently address fears of the global economy.

A problem of regionalism is that it may well constitute the movement of polities in terms of politics, rather than economies in terms of globalization.[198] Assuming *arguendo* the latter is true, then regionalism is compromised in its capacity as a supposed complement to a multilateral trade approach. Conversely, it may be that nations have acted politically, in pursuance of national and regional interests, rather, as a dual approach to development, seeking to both liberalize and define the terms of their liberalization. Nonetheless, and regardless of whether China is pursuing unilateral trade practices, or pursuing a dual approach to development, APEC will continue to be relevant in the new millennium, because of its historical commitment to TILF, and continuing promotion of regional security and the fight against mega-terrorism.

APEC's relevancy and survivability somehow became contingent on accomplishing the all-important Bogor goals. A problem of the Bogor-goals contingency is that it ignores other relevancies, past, present, and perhaps future relevancies of APEC as an international economic cooperation organization, especially its historical commitment to TILF. APEC was essentially meant to be a loosely institutionalized, consensus-governed body serving as an economic consultative forum for Asia-Pacific nations. APEC is the by-product of prevailing international political economy concerns of the 1980s and 1990s, the Cold War and post-Cold War eras. APEC has undergone growth and evolution, mostly due to changing international political economy environments, ranging from the post-Cold War, post-East Asian financial crisis (1997-98), to the events of 9/11 and the economics of terrorism that ensued. APEC experienced a transition from a seemingly apolitical agenda to a combined political and economic agenda. In the new millennium, the role of APEC must necessarily be understood and defined in terms of changing, dynamic and prevailing international political economy environments, and count as examples the East Asian financial crisis, the proliferation of regional trade agreements such as the impending ASEAN-China FTA, termination of the WTO Multi-Fibre Agreement (MFA) of 1974, and global threats of mega-terrorism. Perhaps more so for this reason than any other, it is unrealistic to expect that APEC can return to its humbler beginnings, that is, a simple economic consultative forum, rather than what it became, an international forum addressing both economic and political concerns in the Asia-Pacific region. Most will agree that APEC enjoys some tacit relevancies and remains relevant in the new millennium, albeit for different reasons, including an emerging China. However, APEC's organizational structure and goals, which were relevant in the 1980s and 1990s, may be insufficient and inadequate for the new millennium challenges.[199] Despite tacit relevancies, for purposes of survival and continuing relevancy in the new millennium, APEC will have to develop more creative and realistic goals, and perhaps commit to reforms and organizational restructuring, in light of China, ASEAN, and especially the prospects of a future "JACIK" FTA.

---

[198] Bowles, *supra* note 19.

[199] APIAN Assessment, *supra* note 94, Executive Summary, at 1.

CONCLUSION

APEC remains relevant in the new millennium. As for the Bogor goals, they should never been given the prominence attributed by many. APEC members when adopting these seemingly bigger than life goals well knew the road ahead in terms of implementing them. Critiques judged APEC harshly for failings, one seemingly after another, in implementing the Bogor goals, all the while ignoring other relevancies of APEC. A failure to accomplish the Bogor goals will not, and should not, result in the demise of APEC because of the same reasons. In the new millennium, the survival and continuing relevancy of APEC will lie in its historical commitment to trade and investment liberalization and facilitation (TILF), while allowing adjustments reflecting new international political economy concerns, such as, global threats of mega-terrorism, the 2004 ASEAN-China accord, termination of the WTO Multi-Fibre Agreement (MFA) of 1974, new WTO trade negotiation rounds, and what is being dubbed "JACIK." Moreover, survival for APEC in the new millennium means encompassing an explicit economic agenda, in conjunction with an explicit international relations (political) agenda.

In: China: Economic, Political and Social Issues
Editors: J. M. Phillips and L. J. Moore
ISBN: 978-60456-727-4

Chapter 2

TRADE BARRIERS IN CHINA*

Office of the United States Representative

TRADE SUMMARY

The U.S. goods trade deficit with China was $232.5 billion in 2006, an increase of $31 billion from $201.5 billion in 2005. U.S. goods exports in 2006 were $55.2 billion, up 31.7 percent from the previous year. Corresponding U.S. imports from China were $287.8 billion, up 18.2 percent. China is currently the 4th largest export market for U.S. goods.

U.S. exports of private commercial services (i.e., excluding military and government) to China were $9.1 billion in 2005 (latest data available), and U.S. imports were $6.5 billion. Sales of services in China by majority U.S.-owned affiliates were $5.1 billion in 2004 (latest data available), while sales of services in the United States by majority China-owned firms were not available in 2004 ($321 million in 2002 is latest data available).

The stock of U.S. foreign direct investment (FDI) in China in 2005 was $16.9 billion (latest data available), up from $15.0 billion in 2004. U.S. FDI in China is concentrated largely in the manufacturing, wholesale trade, mining and non-bank holding companies sectors.

When China acceded to the World Trade Organization (WTO) on December 11, 2001, it committed to implement over time a set of sweeping reforms that required it to lower trade barriers in virtually every sector of the economy, provide national treatment and improved market access to goods and services imported from the United States and other WTO Members, and protect intellectual property rights (IPR). Five years later, the deadlines for almost all of China's commitments have passed, and China's transition period as a new WTO Member is now essentially over.

China has taken significant and often impressive steps to reform its economy since acceding to the WTO. During this period, China has repealed, revised or enacted more than one thousand laws, regulations and other measures in an effort to bring its trading system into basic compliance with WTO standards. China has also taken steps to implement numerous

* Excerpted from the Office of the United States Representative report "Foreign Trade Barriers."

specific commitments pursuant to schedules set forth in its WTO accession agreement. Each year, China has made annual reductions in its tariff rates, eliminated non-tariff barriers, expanded market access for foreign services providers and improved transparency. All of these steps were designed to deepen China's integration into the international trading system, as well as to facilitate and strengthen economic reforms that China had begun 20 years earlier.

Nevertheless, despite significant progress in many areas, China's record in implementing WTO commitments is decidedly mixed. China continues to pursue problematic industrial policies that rely on trade-distorting measures such as local content requirements, import and export restrictions, discriminatory regulations and prohibited subsidies, all of which raise serious WTO concerns. China's shortcomings in enforcing laws in areas where detailed WTO disciplines apply, such as intellectual property rights, have also created serious problems for the United States and its other trading partners.

Many of the United States' most difficult trade issues with China can be traced to excessive Chinese government intervention in the market through policy directives and the actions of individual officials. This government intervention, evident in many areas of China's economy, is a reflection of China's historic yet unfinished transition from a centrally planned economy to a free-market economy governed by rule of law. To some extent, these difficulties were anticipated. During the fifteen years of negotiations leading up to China's WTO accession, the United States and other WTO Members were aware of the state's large role in China's economy and carefully negotiated conditions for China's WTO accession that would, when implemented, lead to significantly reduced levels of government intervention in the market, and a corresponding reduction in trade distortions and market access barriers.

While China did make noteworthy progress as a result of economic reforms adopted before and in the first few years after its accession to the WTO, recently we have seen an upsurge in industrial planning measures as tools of economic development by China's central government authorities. China appears to want to expand the government's role in directing the economy and in developing internationally competitive Chinese enterprises, while also restricting the role of international companies in certain sectors.

Recognizing these challenges, USTR announced, in a "top-to-bottom" review of U.S.-China trade relations issued in February 2006, that it would adopt a dual-track approach to resolving its WTO concerns. The United States would continue to seek cooperative and pragmatic resolutions through bilateral dialogue with China, including the Joint Commission on Commerce and Trade (JCCT), as well as *ad hoc* bilateral meetings and a variety of sector-specific dialogues. However, when bilateral dialogue fails to succeed in addressing U.S. concerns, the United States will not hesitate to exercise its WTO rights through the initiation of dispute settlement against China, as it would with any other mature WTO trading partner.

The United States achieved some important successes through bilateral dialogue in 2006, including at a JCCT meeting in April. At that meeting, China made several commitments related to IPR protection and enforcement. It also committed to eliminate duplicative testing and certification requirements applicable to imported medical devices, to make adjustments to its registered capital requirements for telecommunications service providers and to finalize a protocol allowing the resumption of trade in U.S. beef and beef products. China also reaffirmed past commitments to technology neutrality for 3G telecommunications standards and to ensuring that foreign express couriers would not be impacted negatively by new rules in the postal area. In addition, China committed to commence, by no later than December 31, 2007, formal negotiations to join the WTO's Government Procurement Agreement. Since the

JCCT meeting in April 2006, the United States has been working with China to make sure that it implements all of these commitments.

However, to date, other issues have evaded bilateral resolution, despite extensive dialogue. Issues like WTO-prohibited subsidies, IPR enforcement and certain market access concerns have resisted resolution. Although the United States has been making earnest efforts to resolve these concerns through bilateral discussions, it is prepared to pursue other options if the bilateral approach is not fruitful, as it recently did when it initiated a WTO dispute settlement case challenging apparent WTO-prohibited subsidies.

In several areas, Chinese policies and practices continued to cause particular concern for the United States and U.S. industry in 2006, particularly in light of China's WTO commitments, as is detailed below and in the 2006 USTR Report to Congress on China's WTO Compliance. First, the lack of effective IPR enforcement remains a major challenge, as counterfeiting and piracy in China remain at unacceptably high levels and cause serious economic harm to U.S. businesses in virtually every sector of the economy. Second, China has continued to resort to industrial policies that limit market access for non-Chineseorigin goods and foreign service providers, and that provide substantial government resources to support Chinese industries and increase exports. Third, capricious practices by Chinese customs and quarantine officials can delay or halt shipments of agricultural products into China, while sanitary and phytosanitary standards with questionable scientific bases and a generally opaque regulatory regime frequently bedevil traders in agricultural commodities. Fourth, Chinese regulatory authorities continue to frustrate efforts of

U.S. providers of banking, insurance, motor vehicle financing, direct selling, telecommunications, construction and engineering, legal and other services to achieve their full market potential in China through the use of an opaque regulatory process, overly burdensome licensing and operating requirements, and other means. They have also imposed new restrictions on foreign providers of financial information services and have so far failed to open up the China market to foreign credit card companies. Fifth, transparency remains a concern, as many of China's regulatory regimes continued to suffer from systemic opacity, frustrating efforts of foreign – and domestic – businesses to achieve the potential benefits of China's WTO accession.

Overall, while China has a more open and competitive economy than 25 years ago, and China's WTO accession has led to the removal of many trade barriers, there are still barriers to trade that have yet to be dismantled. The central government continues to implement industrial policies that protect a number of noncompetitive or emerging sectors of the economy from foreign competition. In many sectors, import barriers, opaque and inconsistently applied legal provisions and limitations on foreign direct investment often combine to make it difficult for foreign firms to operate in China. In addition, some ministries, agencies and government-sponsored trade associations have renewed efforts to erect new technical barriers to trade. Meanwhile, many provincial governments at times have strongly resisted reforms that would eliminate sheltered markets for local enterprises or reduce jobs and revenues in their jurisdictions, although they have also supported market access for other foreign investors that do not pose a threat to local vested interests.

To meet its obligations as a responsible stakeholder in the world trading system, China will need to institutionalize market-oriented reforms and eliminate mechanisms that allow government officials to intervene in the Chinese economy in a manner that is inconsistent with market principles. China also needs to take additional steps to make its trade regime more predictable and transparent. Despite its remarkable transformation over the past quarter century, China continues to suffer from its command economy legacy, and Chinese government policymaking often operates in a way that prevents U.S. businesses from achieving their full potential in the China market. Through the new high-level Strategic Economic Dialogue launched in December 2006 and ongoing bilateral dialogues like the JCCT, the United States is pushing China to accelerate its transformation into a more market-based economy.

IMPORT BARRIERS

Prior to its WTO accession in December 2001, China restricted imports through high tariffs and taxes, quotas and other non-tariff measures, and restrictions on trading rights. Beginning in 2002, its first year in the WTO, China significantly reduced tariff rates on many products, decreased the number of goods subject to import quotas, expanded trading rights for Chinese enterprises and increased the transparency of its licensing procedures. Subsequently, China has continued to make progress by implementing tariff reductions on schedule, phasing out import quotas and expanding trading rights for foreign enterprises and individuals. Nevertheless, some serious problems remain, such as China's tariff treatment of imported automotive parts and China's refusal to grant trading rights for certain industries.

Trading Rights

Prior to its WTO accession, China restricted the types and numbers of entities with the right to trade. Only those domestic and foreign firms with trading rights could import goods into, or export goods out of, China. Restrictions on the type and number of firms with trading rights contributed to systemic inefficiencies in China's trading rights system and created substantial incentives to engage in smuggling and other corrupt practices.

In 1995, liberalization of China's trading rights system began to proceed gradually. The pace accelerated in 1999 when the Ministry of Foreign Trade and Economic Cooperation (MOFTEC), the predecessor to China's existing Ministry of Commerce (MOFCOM), announced new guidelines allowing a wide variety of Chinese firms with annual export volumes valued in excess of $10 million to register for trading rights. In August 2001, China extended this regulation to allow foreign-invested firms to export their finished products. Import rights for foreign-invested firms were still restricted to the importation of inputs, equipment and other materials directly related to their manufacturing or processing operations. Firms and individuals without trading rights, including foreign-invested firms with a manufacturing presence in China seeking to import products made outside of China, were required to use a local agent.

In its WTO accession agreement, China committed to substantial liberalization in the area of trading rights. Specifically, China committed to eliminate its system of examination and approval of trading rights and to make full trading rights automatically available to all Chinese enterprises, Chinese-foreign joint ventures, wholly foreign-owned enterprises and foreign individuals, including sole proprietorships, within three years of its accession, or by December 11, 2004, which was the same deadline for China to eliminate most restrictions in the area of distribution services. China further committed to expand the availability of trading rights pursuant to an agreed schedule during the first three years of its WTO membership.

Although China did not fully adhere to the agreed phase-in schedule in some instances, it put in place a registration system implementing the required liberalization of trading rights, both for Chinese enterprises and for Chinese-foreign joint ventures, wholly foreign-owned enterprises and foreign individuals, including sole proprietorships. This liberalization is reflected in China's revised Foreign Trade Law, issued in April 2004. It provides for trading rights to be automatically available through a registration process for all domestic and foreign entities and individuals, effective July 1, 2004, almost six months ahead of the scheduled full liberalization required by China's accession agreement. In June 2004, MOFCOM issued implementing rules establishing the procedures for registering as a foreign trade operator. U.S. companies have reported few problems with the new trading rights registration process.

In December 2004, as required by its WTO accession agreement, China also ended its practice of granting import rights or export rights for certain products, including steel, natural rubber, wools, acrylic and plywood, only to designated enterprises. Any domestic or foreign enterprise or individual can now trade in these products.

Consistent with the terms of China's WTO accession agreement, the importation of some goods, such as petroleum and sugar, is still reserved for state-trading enterprises. In addition, for goods still subject to tariff-rate quotas such as grains, cotton, vegetable oils and fertilizers, China reserves a portion of the in-quota imports for state-trading enterprises, while it committed to make the remaining portion (ranging from 10 percent to 90 percent, depending on the commodity) available for importation through non-state traders. In some cases, the percentage available to non-state traders increases annually for a fixed number of years.

Meanwhile, however, China has not yet given foreign entities trading rights for the importation of books, newspapers, periodicals, electronic publications and audio and video products. Under the terms of China's accession agreement, China's trading rights commitments appear to apply fully to these products, as they are not among the products for which China reserved the right to engage in state trading. As a result, trading rights for these products should have been automatically available to all Chinese enterprises, Chinese-foreign joint ventures, wholly foreign-owned enterprises and foreign individuals as of December 11, 2004. Nevertheless, China continues to wholly reserve the right to import books, newspapers, periodicals, electronic publications and audio and video products to state trading enterprises.

Import Substitution Policies

Throughout the 1990s, China gradually reduced formal import substitution policies. When it acceded to the WTO, China agreed to eliminate all subsidies prohibited under Article 3 of the WTO Agreement on Subsidies and Countervailing Measures (Subsidies Agreement), including all forms of subsidies contingent on the use of domestic over imported goods. In its WTO accession agreement, China also committed that it would not condition import or investment approvals on whether there are competing domestic suppliers or impose other performance requirements. In anticipation of this commitment, China enacted legal changes in 2000 and 2001 to eliminate local content requirements for foreign investments. Under the prevailing rules, however, investors are still "encouraged" to follow some of the formerly mandated practices. Instances in which the Chinese government has reportedly pursued import substitution or similar policies are described below.

Corporate Tax Deductions to Foreign-Invested Firms

Measures issued by the Ministry of Finance and the State Administration for Taxation (SAT) make income tax and value-added tax (VAT) refunds available to foreign-invested firms in connection with their purchases of domestically manufactured equipment. These refunds are not available in connection with purchases of imported equipment or equipment assembled in China from imported parts. A similar measure makes an income tax refund available in connection with domestic firms' purchases of domestically manufactured equipment for technology upgrading.

Automotive Parts

Before China's WTO accession, China's automobile industrial policy offered significant advantages for foreign-invested factories using high levels of local content. In 2001, in anticipation of China's new obligations as a WTO Member, the State Economic and Trade Commission (SETC) issued Bulletin No.13, which provided that the preferential policy for automobile localization rates would be cancelled upon China's WTO accession. However, U.S. automobile manufacturers reported that some local government officials continued to require local content and cited the old automobile industrial policy's standards. China also committed to issue a revised automotive industrial policy within two years of its WTO accession, or by December 11, 2003, but missed this deadline. In May 2004, China issued a new automobile industrial policy. It included provisions discouraging the importation of automotive parts and encouraging the use of domestic technology. It also required new automobile and automobile engine plants to include substantial investment in research and development facilities, even though China expressly committed in its WTO accession agreement not to condition investment rights or approvals on the conduct of research and development in China.

In 2005, China began to issue measures implementing the new automobile industrial policy. One measure that generated strong criticism from the United States, the EU, Japan and Canada was the *Measures on the Importation of Parts for Entire Automobiles*, which was issued by the National Development and Reform Commission (NDRC) in February 2005 and became effective in April 2005. These rules impose charges that unfairly discriminate against imported automotive parts and discourage automobile manufacturers in China from using imported automotive parts in the assembly of vehicles. Specifically, the rules require all vehicle manufacturers in China that use imported parts to register with China's Customs Administration and provide specific information about each vehicle they assemble, including a list of the imported and domestic parts to be used, and the value and supplier of each part. If the number or value of imported parts in an assembled vehicle exceeds specified thresholds, the regulations assess each of the imported parts a charge equal to the tariff on complete automobiles (typically 25 percent) rather than the tariff applicable to automotive parts (typically 10 percent). These rules appear to be inconsistent with several WTO provisions, including Article III of GATT 1994 and Article 2 of the Agreement on Trade-Related Investment Measures, as well as the commitment in China's accession agreement to eliminate all local content requirements relating to importation. In March and April 2006, the United States, the EU and Canada initiated dispute settlement against China by filing formal WTO consultations requests. Joint consultations were held in May 2006. However, these consultations did not lead to an agreed resolution. In September 2006, the United States, the EU and Canada filed requests for the establishment of a panel to hear the dispute. A panel was established at the October 2006 meeting of the WTO's Dispute Settlement Body.

Steel

China issued a new Steel and Iron Industry Development Policy in July 2005. Although many aspects of this new policy have not yet been implemented, it still includes a host of objectives and guidelines that raise serious concerns. For example, this policy requires that foreign enterprises seeking to invest in Chinese iron and steel enterprises possess proprietary technology or intellectual property in the processing of steel. Given that foreign investors are not allowed to have a controlling share in steel and iron enterprises in China, this requirement would seem to constitute a *de facto* technology transfer requirement, calling into question China's implementation of its WTO accession agreement commitment not to condition investment rights or approvals on the transfer of technology. This policy also appears to discriminate against foreign equipment and technology imports. Like other measures, this policy encourages the use of local content by calling for a variety of government financial support for steel and iron projects utilizing newly developed domestic equipment. Even more troubling, however, it calls for the use of domestically-produced steel-manufacturing equipment and domestic technologies whenever domestic suppliers exist, calling into question China's implementation of its WTO accession agreement commitment not to condition the right of investment or importation on whether competing domestic suppliers exist.

Semiconductors

China's 10th Five-Year Plan calls for an increase in Chinese semiconductor output from $2 billion in 2000 to $24 billion in 2010. In pursuit of this policy, China has attempted to encourage the development of China's domestic integrated circuit (IC) industry through, among other things, discriminatory VAT policies. In particular, through a series of measures, China has provided for the rebate of a substantial portion of the 17 percent VAT paid by domestic manufacturers on their locally-produced ICs. China, meanwhile, charged the full 17 percent VAT on imported ICs, unless they were designed in China. After bilateral meetings on this issue failed to yield a change in China's policy, in March 2004, the United States filed the first WTO case against China. In the ensuing consultations, China signaled its willingness to discuss a possible resolution. In July 2004, the United States and China reached a settlement in which China agreed to immediately cease certifying new Chinese IC manufacturers or products as eligible for the VAT rebate and to issue the necessary regulations to eliminate the VAT rebate entirely by November 1, 2004, with an effective date no later than April 1, 2005. China also agreed to repeal the relevant implementing rules that had made VAT rebates available for ICs designed in China but manufactured abroad by September 1, 2004, with an effective date no later than October 1, 2004. China followed through on each of these agreed steps in a timely manner, and the two sides notified the WTO in October 2005 that their dispute had been satisfactorily resolved. Nevertheless, the United States continues to monitor closely new financial support that China is making available to its domestic producers for consistency with the WTO Subsidies Agreement's disciplines.

Fertilizer

In 2001, China began exempting all phosphate fertilizers except diammonium phosphate (DAP) from the VAT. DAP, a product that the United States exports to China, competes with other phosphate fertilizers produced in China, particularly monoammonium phosphate. Both the United States Government and U.S. producers have complained that China has employed its VAT policies to benefit domestic fertilizer production.

Telecommunications Equipment

There have been continuing reports of the Ministry of Information Industry (MII) and China Telecom adopting policies to discourage the use of imported components or equipment. For example, MII has reportedly still not rescinded an internal circular issued in 1998 instructing telecommunications companies to buy components and equipment from domestic sources.

Tariffs and other Import Charges

Under the terms of its WTO accession, China committed to substantial annual reductions in its tariff rates, with most of them taking place within five years of China's WTO accession. The largest reductions took place in 2002, immediately after China acceded to the WTO, when the overall average tariff rate fell from over 15 percent to 12 percent.

China's post-WTO accession tariff rates are "bound," meaning that China cannot raise them above the bound rates without "compensating" WTO trading partners (i.e.: re-balancing tariff concessions or, in accordance with WTO rules, being subject to withdrawal of substantially equivalent concessions by other WTO Members). "Bound" rates give importers a more predictable environment. China may also apply tariff rates significantly lower than the WTO-required rate, as in the case of goods that the government has identified as necessary to the development of a key industry. For example, China's Customs Administration has occasionally announced lower applied tariff rates for items that benefit key economic sectors, in particular for the automotive, steel and chemical industries.

U.S. exports continued to benefit from China's participation in the Information Technology Agreement (ITA), which requires the elimination of tariffs on computers, semiconductors and other information technology products. China began reducing and eliminating these tariffs in 2002 and continued to do so in the ensuing years, achieving the elimination of all ITA tariffs on January 1, 2005, as the tariffs dropped to zero from a pre-WTO accession average of 13.3 percent. U.S. exports of ITA goods continued to perform well in 2006, as they totaled $9.2 billion, an increase of 52 percent over the 2005 figure.

China completed its timely implementation of another significant tariff initiative, the WTO's Chemical Tariff Harmonization Agreement, in 2005. The United States exported $6.5 billion in chemicals to China in 2006, up from $5.6 billion in 2005, an increase of 16.7 percent.

However, China still maintains high duties on some products that compete with sensitive domestic industries. For example, the tariff on large motorcycles will only fall from 60 percent to 45 percent. Likewise, most video, digital video and audio recorders and players still face duties of approximately 30 percent. Raisins face duties of 35 percent.

U.S. exports of some bulk agricultural commodities have increased dramatically in recent years, and continue to perform strongly, especially soybeans and cotton. Exports of soybeans rose to more than $2.5 billion in 2006, a 12 percent increase over the previous year. Cotton exports rose 47 percent in the same period to nearly $2.1 billion, a new record. Exports of forest products such as lumber also continued to perform strongly, increasing by 16 percent over 2005, to reach $547 million in 2006. Fish and seafood exports rose 25 percent to $440 million in 2006. Meanwhile, exports of consumer-oriented agricultural products increased by 34 percent to $731 million in 2006.

Overall, China's tariff changes have increased market access for U.S. exporters in a range of industries, as China continued the process of reducing tariffs on goods of greatest importance to U.S. industry from a base average of 25 percent (in 1997) to 7 percent over a period of five years, starting on January 1, 2002. It made similar reductions throughout the agricultural sector. These tariff changes contributed to another significant increase in overall U.S. exports, which rose approximately 33 percent from January through December 2006, when compared to the same time period in 2005.

Tariff Classification

Chinese customs officers have wide discretion in classifying a particular import. While foreign businesses might at times have benefited from their ability to negotiate tariff classification into tariff categories with lower import duty rates, lack of uniformity makes it difficult to anticipate border charges.

Customs Valuation

In January 2002, shortly after acceding to the WTO, China's Customs Administration issued the Measures for Examining and Determining Customs Valuation of Imported Goods. These regulations addressed the inconsistencies that had existed between China's customs valuation methodologies and the WTO Agreement on Customs Valuation. The Customs Administration subsequently issued the Rules on the Determination of Customs Value of Royalties and License Fees Related to Imported Goods, effective July 2003. These rules were intended to clarify provisions of the January 2002 regulations that addressed the valuation of royalties and license fees. In addition, by December 11, 2003, China had issued a measure on interest charges and a measure requiring duties on software to be assessed on the basis of the value of the underlying carrier medium, meaning, for example, the CD-ROM or floppy disk itself, rather than the imputed value of the content, which includes, for example, the data recorded on a CD-ROM or floppy disk.

More than three years later, China has still not uniformly implemented these various measures. U.S. exporters continue to report that they are encountering valuation problems at many ports. According to U.S. exporters, even though the 2002 regulations and 2003 implementing rules provide that imported goods normally should be valued on the basis of their transaction price, meaning the price the importer actually paid, many Chinese customs officials are still improperly using "reference pricing," which usually results in a higher dutiable value. For example, imports of wood products are often subjected to reference pricing. In addition, some of China's customs officials are reportedly not applying the provisions in the 2002 regulations and 2003 implementing rules as they relate to software royalties and license fees. Following their pre-WTO accession practice, these officials are still automatically adding royalties and license fees to the dutiable value (for example, when an imported personal computer includes pre-installed software), even though China's 2003 implementing rules expressly direct them to add those fees only if they are import-related and a condition of sale for the goods being valued.

U.S. exporters have also continued to express concerns about the Customs Administration's handling of imports of digital media that contain instructions for the subsequent production of multiple copies of products such as DVDs. The Customs Administration has been inappropriately assessing duties based on the estimated value of the yet-to-be-produced copies.

More generally, U.S. exporters continue to be concerned about inefficient and inconsistent customs clearance procedures in China. These procedures vary from port to port, massive delays are not uncommon, and the fees charged appear to be excessive and are rising rapidly, giving rise to concerns about China's compliance with its obligations under Article VIII of GATT 1994.

Rules of Origin

In September 2004, nearly three years after China acceded to the WTO, the State Council finally issued the regulations intended to bring China's rules of origin into conformity with WTO rules for import and export purposes. These regulations took effect on January 1, 2005. Importers have not reported problems stemming from inappropriate application of rules of origin.

Border Trade

China's border trade policy continues to generate MFN and other concerns. China provides preferential import duty and VAT treatment to certain products, often from Russia, apparently even when those products are not confined to frontier traffic as envisioned by Article XXIV of GATT 1994. China addressed some of these concerns in 2003 when it eliminated preferential treatment for boric acid and 19 other products. Nonetheless, it appears that large operators are still able to take advantage of border trade policies to import bulk shipments across China's land borders into its interior at preferential rates. In addition, U.S. industry reports that China continues to use border trade policies to provide preferential treatment for Russian timber imports, to the detriment of U.S. timber exporters.

Antidumping, Countervailing Duty and Safeguard Measures

Since acceding to the WTO, China has emerged as a significant user of antidumping measures, with a total of 91 antidumping measures in place affecting imports from 21 countries, and 17 antidumping investigations in progress, by the end of 2006. China continued to actively apply its antidumping law in 2006, initiating several new investigations, although none of them involved U.S. products. Chemical products remain the most frequent target of Chinese antidumping actions.

Most of the rules and regulations used by MOFCOM to conduct its antidumping investigations were issued as provisional measures by MOFCOM's predecessor agencies – MOFTEC and SETC – shortly after China acceded to the WTO. While these measures generally represent good-faith efforts to implement the relevant WTO commitments and to improve China's pre-WTO accession measures, they also contain vague language, have gaps in areas of practice and allow inordinate discretion. Meanwhile, China's handling of antidumping investigations and reviews continues to raise concerns in key areas such as transparency and procedural fairness. Concerns with transparency, including access to information, are especially acute with regard to the injury portion of investigations.

To date, China has not initiated a countervailing duty investigation. China's only safeguard measure was removed at the end of 2003 after being in place for less than two years.

The Supreme People's Court has issued a judicial interpretation covering the review of antidumping and other trade remedy decisions. To date, however, judicial review of these types of decisions remains untested.

In one antidumping investigation involving imports of kraft linerboard from the United States, following an affirmative final determination and the imposition of antidumping duties in September 2005, the affected U.S. exporters filed for administrative reconsideration with MOFCOM. The exporters raised concerns with various aspects of the final determination, particularly the injury finding. In January 2006, immediately after the United States notified China that it intended to commence dispute settlement at the WTO, MOFCOM issued a decision repealing the antidumping order.

Non-Tariff Barriers

China's WTO accession agreement obligated China to address many of the non-tariff barriers it had historically used to restrict trade. For example, China is obligated to phase out its import quota system, apply international norms to its testing and standards administration, remove local content requirements, and make its licensing and registration regimes transparent. At the national level, China made progress following its WTO accession in reforming its testing system, revising regulations requiring local content and improving overall regulatory transparency, including in the licensing area. Despite this progress, however, as China's trade liberalization efforts moved forward, some non-tariff barriers remained in place and others were added.

Five years after China's WTO accession, many U.S. industries complain that they face significant non-tariff barriers to trade, which are discussed in more detail in various sections below. These barriers include, for example, regulations that set high thresholds for entry into service sectors such as banking, insurance and telecommunications, selective and unwarranted inspection requirements for agricultural imports and the use of questionable sanitary and phytosanitary measures to control import volumes. Many U.S. industries have also complained about China's manipulation of technical regulations and standards to favor domestic industries.

Import Quotas

In the past, China often did not announce import quota amounts or the process for allocating import quotas. China set import quotas through negotiations between central and local government officials at the end of each year. Import quotas on most products were eliminated or are scheduled for phase-out under the terms of China's WTO accession. China's accession agreement required China to eliminate existing import quotas for the top U.S. priority products upon accession and to phase out remaining import quotas on industrial goods, such as air conditioners, sound and video recording machines, color TVs, cameras, watches, crane lorries and chassis, and motorcycles, by January 1, 2005. While China's post-WTO accession import quota system was beset with problems, China did fully adhere to the agreed schedule for the elimination of all of its import quotas, the last of which China eliminated on January 1, 2005.

Tariff-Rate Quotas

In 1996, China claimed to have introduced a tariff-rate quota (TRQ) system for imports of wheat, corn, rice, soy oil, cotton, barley and vegetable oils. The quota amounts were not publicly announced, application and allocation procedures were not transparent, and importation occurred through state trading enterprises. China later introduced a TRQ system for fertilizer imports. Under these TRQ systems, China places quantitative restrictions on the amount of these commodities that can enter at a low "in-quota" tariff rate; any imports over that quantity are charged a prohibitively high duty.

As part of its WTO accession commitments, China was to establish large and increasing TRQs for imports of wheat, corn, rice, cotton, wool, sugar, rapeseed oil, palm oil, soybean oil and fertilizer, with most in-quota duties ranging from 1 percent to 9 percent. Each year, a portion of each TRQ is to be reserved for importation through non-state trading entities. China's accession agreement sets forth specific rules for administration of the TRQs, including increased transparency and reallocation of unused quotas to end-users that have an interest in importing. China phased out the vegetable oil TRQs in 2006, but currently maintains a TRQ regime on six agricultural products including wheat, cotton, corn, rice, wool and sugar, as well as three chemical fertilizers including di-ammonium phosphate.

For the first two years after China's WTO accession, China's implementation of its TRQ systems generated numerous complaints from foreign suppliers, with the most serious problems being lack of transparency, sub-divisions of the TRQ, small allocation sizes and burdensome licensing procedures. Repeated engagement by U.S. officials led to regulatory and operational changes by NDRC for shipments beginning January 1, 2004. Key changes included the elimination of separate allocations for general trade and processing trade, the elimination of certain unnecessary licensing requirements, and the creation of a new mechanism for identifying allocation recipients. In 2004, improvements in NDRC's TRQ administration became evident, although transparency continued to be problematic for some of the commodities subject to TRQs.

While NDRC was implementing the systemic changes in 2004, exports of some bulk agricultural commodities from the United States showed substantial increases, largely due to market conditions. In particular, despite some continuing problems with NDRC's handling of the cotton TRQs, U.S. cotton exports totaled a record $1.4 billion in both 2004 and 2005, followed by a new record of $2.1 billion in 2006. In addition, U.S. wheat exports totaled $495 million in 2004, as the TRQ allocations for wheat did not appear to act as a limiting factor, but declined significantly to $78 million in 2005 and then to $23 million in 2006. The drop in U.S. wheat exports was due to higher production and lower prices in China, which reduced China's overall import demand.

Meanwhile, the administration of China's TRQ system for fertilizer, handled by SETC and subsequently MOFCOM, has suffered from systemic problems since China's WTO accession. By 2006, this system was still operating with insufficient transparency, and administrative guidance still seemed to be affecting how the allocated quota was used. U.S. fertilizer exports to China have declined throughout the post-WTO accession period, due in part to continuing problems with MOFCOM's administration of the fertilizer TRQ system and in part to increasing subsidization, and resulting overcapacity, of China's domestic fertilizer industry. U.S. fertilizer exports to China decreased from $676 million in 2002 to $355 million in 2005. In 2006, U.S. fertilizer exports to China declined sharply again, totaling $232 million for the year.

In October 2006, perhaps in an attempt by the central authorities to rein in provincial and local efforts to build further unneeded capacity, the Tariff Policy Commission of the State Council announced a temporary reduction of the in-quota tariff rate for fertilizer from 4 percent to 1 percent, effective November 2006. It is too early to tell what effect this change may have on U.S. fertilizer exports to China. However, U.S. and other foreign fertilizer producers were anticipating increased exports after December 11, 2006, when China was scheduled to begin allowing foreign enterprises to engage in the wholesale and retail distribution of fertilizer within China.

Import Licenses

In the early 1990s, China began to reduce substantially the number of products subject to import licensing requirements. With its WTO accession in December 2001, China committed to the fair and nondiscriminatory application of licensing procedures. Among other things, China also committed upon its WTO accession to limit the information that a trader must provide in order to receive a license, in order to ensure that licenses are not unnecessarily burdensome, and to increase transparency and predictability in the licensing process.

MOFTEC issued new regulations and implementing rules to facilitate licensing procedures shortly after China's accession to the WTO. However, license applicants initially reported that they had to provide sensitive business details unnecessary for simple import monitoring. In some sectors, importers also reported that MOFTEC was using a "one-license-per-shipment" system rather than providing licenses to firms for multiple shipments. MOFTEC began to allow more than one shipment per license in late 2002 following U.S. interventions, without modifying the measure authorizing the "one-license-per-shipment" system. In December 2004, MOFCOM issued revised licensing procedures for imported goods. Among other changes, import licenses no longer have quantitative restrictions, provisions related to designated trading were removed, and provisions allowing more than one license per shipment and an "under or over provision" for overloaded or short shipments were added.

China is the world's largest importer of iron ore, accounting for over 40 percent of global iron ore imports (based on 2006 data). Increasing global steel production, led by Chinese growth, has contributed to significant price increases over the past several years. In May

2005, after Chinese steel producers negotiated contracts with major foreign iron ore suppliers, the Chinese government began imposing new import licensing procedures for iron ore without prior WTO notification. Even though the WTO's Import Licensing Agreement calls for import licensing procedures that do not have a restrictive effect on trade, China reportedly restricted licenses to 48 traders and 70 steel producers and has not made public a list of the qualified enterprises or the qualifying criteria used. While the Chinese government maintained that it did not impose any qualifying criteria, it did acknowledge that two organizations affiliated with the Chinese government -- the China Steel Industry Association and the Commercial Chamber for Metals, Minerals and Chemicals Importers and Exporters -- had been discussing a set of rules regarding qualifying criteria such as production capacity and trade performance. In 2006, the United States continued to engage China and monitor developments, as this situation could set a troubling precedent for the handling of imports of other raw materials.

China's inspection and quarantine agency, the State Administration of Quality Supervision, Inspection and Quarantine (AQSIQ), has also imposed inspection-related requirements that have led to restrictions on imports of many U.S. agricultural goods. In particular, two AQSIQ measures issued in 2002 require importers to obtain a Quarantine Inspection Permit (QIP) prior to signing purchase contracts for nearly all traded agricultural commodities. QIPs are one of the most important trade policy issues affecting the United States and China's other agricultural trading partners.

AQSIQ sometimes slows down or even suspends issuance of QIPs at its discretion, without notifying traders in advance or explaining its reasons, resulting in significant commercial uncertainty. Because of the commercial necessity to contract for commodity shipments when prices are low, combined with the inherent delays in having QIPs issued, many cargoes of products such as soybeans, meat and poultry arrive in Chinese ports without QIPs, creating delays in discharge and resulting in demurrage bills for Chinese purchasers. In addition, traders report that shipment are often closely scrutinized and are at risk for disapproval if they are considered too large in quantity.

Some improvements were made to the QIP system in 2004 following repeated U.S. engagement, both bilaterally and at the WTO. In June 2004, AQSIQ issued Decree 73, the Items on Handling the Review and Approval for Entry Animal and Plant Quarantine, which extended the period of validity for QIPs from three months to six months. AQSIQ also began issuing QIPs more frequently within the established time lines. Nevertheless, a great deal of uncertainty remains even with the extended period of validity, because a QIP still locks purchasers into a very narrow period to purchase, transport and discharge cargoes or containers before the QIP's expiration, and because AQSIQ continues to administer the QIP system in a seemingly arbitrary manner.

In 2006, the QIP system saw little improvement, and traders continued to be concerned that the rules and regulations of the QIP system remain available as an administrative tool to limit the quantity of imports. However, traders remain hesitant to press AQSIQ for change because they would risk reprisals. Many of them would at least like AQSIQ to eliminate the quantity requirements that it unofficially places on QIPs. These quantity requirements have been used often by AQSIQ during peak harvest periods to limit the flow of commodity imports. Eliminating this requirement would help to ensure that QIPs do not interfere with the market.

Internal Policies

Taxation

Income Taxes

In April 2001, the National People's Congress passed long-awaited changes to the tax collection law, designed to standardize and increase the transparency of China's tax procedures. The State Council issued detailed regulations for the implementation of this law in September 2002. As part of a broader campaign to "rectify market order" and eliminate inter-provincial barriers to domestic commerce, the Chinese central government also implemented measures to prevent local governments from applying tax treatment that discriminated in favor of locally owned firms.

In order to narrow the widening urban-rural income gap, the Central Committee of the Communist Party of China and the State Council issued Document No. 1 of 2004, which instructed the governments at all levels to reduce the agricultural tax rate of 8.4 percent by 1 percent in 2004, along with the removal of all taxes on special farm produce except for tobacco. Document No. 1 also calls for further reductions in the agricultural tax rate until it is totally eliminated within five years. Where fiscally feasible, local governments were also called upon to reduce or eliminate agricultural taxes more quickly. Agricultural taxes were abolished nationwide effective January 2006.

Foreign investors, including those who have used investment as an entry point to the Chinese domestic market, have benefited from investment incentives such as tax holidays and grace periods, which allow them to reduce substantially their tax burden. Domestic enterprises have long resented rebates and other tax benefits enjoyed by foreign-invested firms, and these benefits may be gradually phased out. According to the tax laws and regulations currently in place, domestic and foreign-invested companies in China are subject to an income tax rate of 33 percent, but because of various tax waivers and incentives most domestic enterprises pay 24 percent and most foreign businesses pay 15 percent.

In December 2006, the Standing Committee of China's National People's Congress conducted its first deliberations over a draft law that proposes to unify corporate income tax rates for domestic and foreign companies in China. The draft law reportedly calls for a universal tax rate of 25 percent, with a 5-year grace period for foreign businesses. The draft law also reportedly includes the following preferential policies: (1) a 20 percent tax rate for small-sized businesses that are marginally profitable; (2) a 15 percent tax rate for government-supported key high technology enterprises; (3) preferential policies to venture capital and investments in environment protection, resource and water conservation and work safety; (4) extension of current preferential tax policies for investment in agriculture, forestry, husbandry, fishery and infrastructure (such as airports, railways and irrigation works); and (5) alternative preferential policies replacing the current preferential policy of awarding direct tax holidays to businesses created for laid off workers and disabled as well as businesses performing resource recycling. Because the draft law has not been circulated publicly, it is not clear whether, or on what timetable, existing preferential export-related policies benefiting foreign-invested enterprises (discussed below in the section on Export Subsidies) would be withdrawn. If the draft law comes into effect, the impact on foreign-invested firms whose businesses have benefited from lower taxes could be significant. Chinese companies, in general, will have a reduced tax burden, making them more competitive with these foreign-invested firms. At the same time, investment in the production of goods with higher technological content and in infrastructure could well rise as a result of the contemplated preferential policies.

Value-Added Taxes

Application of China's single most important revenue source – the VAT, which ranges between 13 percent and 17 percent, depending on the product – continues to be uneven. Importers from a wide range of sectors report that, because taxes on imported goods are reliably collected at the border, they are sometimes subject to application of a VAT that their domestic competitors often fail to pay. As discussed above in the section on Import Substitution Policies, the United States was successful in obtaining China's agreement to remove discriminatory VAT policies favoring domestically-produced semiconductors. In addition, China's selective exemption of certain fertilizer products from the VAT has operated to the disadvantage of imports from the United States.

Meanwhile, China maintains a measure that provides VAT refunds for foreign-invested enterprises when they purchase domestically made equipment, as discussed above in the section on Import Substitution Policies. These refunds are not available for purchases of imported equipment or equipment assembled in China from imported parts. In addition, another measure makes VAT exemptions available to foreign-invested enterprises with regard to imported equipment used to produce their products, provided that they export 100 percent of their production, as discussed below in the section on Export Subsidies.

China retains an active VAT rebate program for exports, although rebate payments are often delayed. In 2003, China announced the reduction of VAT rebates for exports by 3 percentage points, partly in response to foreign complaints about an under-valued renminbi (RMB). Although State Administration of Taxation officials reportedly plan to eliminate rebates eventually in order to increase tax revenues, China has continued this practice in order to spur domestic economic growth. In December 2004, for example, the Ministry of Finance and the State Administration of Taxation issued a circular announcing an increase in the VAT rebate rate from 13 percent to 17 percent for the export of certain information technology products, including integrated circuits, independent components, mobile telecommunication equipment and terminals, computers and periphery equipment, and numerically controlled machine tools. In 2005, China adjusted the ratio of the share of the export VAT refund burden between the central and local governments, from 75-25 to 92.5-7.5. China also halted refunds for some products in high demand domestically in order to discourage their export. For example, China eliminated a 13 percent VAT rebate for exports of steel billets and ingots, although it maintained VAT rebates of 8 percent to 13 percent for more processed steel products. In September 2006, China sought to discourage exports by eliminating VAT rebates for exports of coal, non-ferrous metal and waste and scrap, silicon and certain primary wood products, among other products, and by lowering existing VAT rebates for a variety of steel, non-ferrous metal, textiles and ceramics products.

Meanwhile, China continues to consider fundamental reform of its VAT regime and, in particular, the transformation from a production-based regime to one that is consumption-based. China has pursued a pilot program in the Northeast, but it is unclear when this reform might be extended nationwide.

Consumption Taxes

China's 1993 consumption tax system continues to raise concerns among U.S. exporters. Because China uses a substantially different tax base to compute consumption taxes for domestic and imported products, the tax burden imposed on imported consumer goods ranging from alcoholic beverages to cosmetics to automobiles is higher than for competing domestic products.

STANDARDS, TESTING, LABELING AND CERTIFICATION

In its WTO accession agreement, China committed to ensure that its regulatory authorities apply the same standards, technical regulations and conformity assessment procedures to both imported and domestic goods and use the same fees, processing periods and complaint procedures for both imported and domestic goods. China also committed that, in order to eliminate unnecessary barriers to trade, it would not maintain multiple or duplicative conformity assessment procedures and would not impose requirements exclusively on imported products. China further committed to ensure that its standards developers, regulatory authorities and conformity assessment bodies operated with transparency and allowed reasonable opportunities for public comment on proposed standards, technical regulations and conformity assessment procedures.

In anticipation of these commitments, China devoted significant energy to reforming its standards and testing and certification regimes prior to its WTO entry. In April 2001, China merged its domestic standards and conformity assessment agency and entry-exit inspection and quarantine agency into one new organization, AQSIQ. Chinese officials explained that this merger was designed to eliminate discriminatory treatment of imports, including requirements for multiple testing simply because a product was imported rather than domestically-produced. China also formed two quasi-independent agencies administratively under AQSIQ: (1) the Certification and Accreditation Administration of China (CNCA), which is charged with the task of unifying, implementing and administering the country's conformity assessment regime; and (2) the Standardization Administration of China (SAC), which is responsible for setting mandatory national standards, unifying China's administration of product standards and aligning its standards and technical regulations with international practices and China's commitments under the WTO Agreement on Technical Barriers to Trade (TBT Agreement).

In January 2002, China began the task of bringing its standards regime more in line with international practice with AQSIQ's issuance of rules designed to facilitate China's adoption of international standards. China subsequently embarked on the task of reviewing all of its existing 21,000 technical regulations to determine their continuing relevance and consistency with international standards. In November 2005, China reported that as of October 2005 it had nullified 1,416 national standards as a result of this review. China has since continued its review of existing standards ands technical regulations, but has not provided an update on its progress.

Nevertheless, in a number of sectors, including automobiles, automotive parts, telecommunications equipment, Internet protocols, wireless local area networks (see the "WAPI" section below), radio frequency identification technology, audio and video coding, food products and consumer products such as cosmetics, concern has grown as China has pursued the development of unique technical requirements, despite the existence of well-established international standards. These China-specific standards, which sometimes appear to lack a sound technical or scientific basis, could create significant barriers to entry into China's markets because of the high cost of compliance for foreign companies.

The lack of transparency in China's standards development process also troubles many foreign companies. The vast majority of Chinese standards-setting bodies are not fully open to foreign participation, in some cases refusing membership to foreign firms and in other cases refusing to allow companies with majority foreign ownership to vote. In some cases, foreign firms are allowed non-voting observer status, but are required to pay membership fees far in excess of those paid by the domestic voting members. Nevertheless, in 2005, some U.S. companies and industry groups concluded that China had begun to make progress in reforming its standardization system by strengthening its links with standards-setters in other countries and by moving its standards regime into closer conformity with international practice.

China's designated notification authority, MOFCOM, has been notifying proposed technical regulations and conformity assessment procedures to WTO Members, as required by the WTO Agreement on Technical Barriers to Trade. Almost all of these notified measures, however, have emanated from AQSIQ or SAC, and few of the trade-related technical regulations drafted by other agencies have been notified. Lack of meaningful comment periods also remains an issue. In many cases, an agency provides insufficient time for the submission of comments, and allots little time for the agency's consideration of those comments, before it finalizes a measure.

Despite China's commitment to apply the same standards and fees to domestic and imported products upon its accession to the WTO, many U.S. industries have complained about China's manipulation of technical regulations and standards to favor domestic industries. In fact, SAC issued a strategy report in September 2004 promoting China's development of standards and technical regulations as a means of protecting domestic industry as tariff rates fall. At the sub-national level, importers have expressed concern that local officials do not understand China's WTO commitments and apply arbitrary technical regulations and standards to protect local industries. These problems are compounded by the fact that coordination between AQSIQ and its affiliated bodies, CNCA and SAC, is lacking, as is coordination between these bodies and China Customs and other ministries and agencies, at both the central and local government levels, on issues related to technical regulations.

China's China Compulsory Certification (CCC) mark system took full effect in August 2003, following a transition period that lasted for fifteen months. The CCC mark replaced the prior "Great Wall" and "CCIB" marks and is now required for more than 130 product categories, such as electrical machinery, information technology equipment, household appliances and their components. In 2006, as in prior years, U.S. companies continued to complain that the regulations lack clarity regarding the products that require a CCC mark. They also have reported that China is applying the CCC mark requirements inconsistently and that many domestic products required by CNCA's regulations to have the CCC mark are still being sold without it. U.S. companies in some sectors also complained that certification remains a difficult, time-consuming and costly process. The process involves on-site inspection of manufacturing facilities outside of China, the cost of which is borne by producers. In addition, small- and medium-sized

U.S. companies without a presence in China find it particularly burdensome to apply for CCC mark exemptions, such as for replacement and re-export, because China requires the applications to be done in person in the Beijing offices of CNCA. China also continues to require the CCC mark for products that would no longer seem to warrant mandatory certification, such as low-risk products and components.

To date, CNCA has accredited well over one hundred Chinese enterprises accreditation to test and certify for purposes of the CCC mark. Despite China's commitment that qualifying minority foreign-owned (upon China's accession to the WTO) and majority foreign-owned (two years later) joint venture conformity assessment bodies would be eligible for accreditation and would be accorded national treatment, China so far has not accredited any foreign-invested conformity assessment bodies. As a result, exporters to China are often required to submit their products to Chinese laboratories for duplicative tests that have already been performed abroad, resulting in greater expense and a longer time to market.

The concerns of U.S. exporters about the CCC mark are heightened by the increasing product scope of the CCC mark certification system. Beginning in 2004, several new categories of products have been added to the list of products requiring the CCC mark, including the addition of six categories of toy products, beginning on June 1, 2007. Additionally, the "China RoHS" scheme discussed below will utilize the CCC mark certification process for certain products to ensure compliance.

In other conformity assessment contexts, some importers report discriminatory treatment and uneven enforcement of technical regulations and standards. For example, foreign companies' products can only be tested in certain designated laboratories. Limited testing and certification capacity means that evaluations sometimes take much longer than international best practice would suggest is appropriate. As testing and certification capacity expands to meet this demand, U.S. companies with multi-country operations worry that inexperienced laboratories might make negative determinations that would have global consequences for the company.

Meanwhile, redundant testing requirements continue to trouble U.S. companies, particularly in cosmetics, new chemicals, pharmaceuticals, medical equipment, cellular telephones and other telecommunications products, consumer electronic products and automobiles. For example, China often requires telecommunications and information technology equipment to be tested and certified to the same electromagnetic compatibility requirements by both MII and CNCA. In December 2004, SAC created technical committees to develop standards for testing environmental equipment, products developed through biotechnology, and new plant and animal varieties, suggesting that foreign companies may soon see additional requirements in these industries as well.

U.S. companies also cite problems with a lack of transparency in the certification process, lack of coordination among standards bodies, burdensome requirements and long processing times for licenses. Some companies have also expressed concern that their intellectual property will be released to competitors when they submit samples of high technology products for mandatory testing. Technical committees that evaluate products for licensing and certification are generally drawn from a pool of government, academic and industrial experts that companies fear may be too closely associated with their competitors. In some cases, laboratories responsible for testing imported products are affiliated with domestic competitors, making the possibility of intellectual property theft more likely.

WAPI

A particularly significant example of China's development of unique technical requirements, despite the existence of well-established international standards, arose in May 2003, when China issued two standards for encryption over Wireless Local Area Networks (WLANs), applicable to domestic and imported equipment containing WLAN (sometimes referred to as Wi-Fi) technologies. Conformance to these standards was scheduled to become mandatory in June 2004. The standards incorporated the WLAN Authentication and Privacy Infrastructure (WAPI) encryption algorithm for secure communications. This component of the standards differed significantly from internationally recognized standards. China sought to enforce the use of WAPI by mandating a particular algorithm (rather than mandating the need for encryption, and leaving the choice of the algorithm to the market) and providing the necessary algorithm only to a limited number of Chinese companies. U.S. and other foreign manufacturers would have been compelled to work with and through these companies, some of which were competitors, and provide them with their proprietary technical product specifications. Following high-level bilateral engagement, China agreed in April 2004 to postpone indefinitely implementation of WAPI and to work within international standards bodies on future development of wireless standards. This commitment led China to submit WAPI for consideration in the International Organization for Standardization (ISO) and International Electrotechnical Commission's (IEC) Joint Technical Committee 1 (ISO/IEC JTC1). In 2006, following balloting of ISO/IEC JTC1 members, the proposed WAPI amendment did not get enough votes to be accepted as an international standard.

In December 2005, the Ministry of Finance (MOF), MII and NDRC jointly issued the Opinions for Implementing Government Procurements of Wireless Local Areas Network. This measure seems to require all government agencies, quasi-government bodies and government-affiliated organizations, when procuring WLAN and related products using fiscal funds, to give priority to WAPI-compliant products. This measure took effect in February 2006. The United States has been monitoring developments in this area, but so far the trade effects of this policy appear to be limited.

Chemical Registration

In September 2003, China's State Environmental Protection Administration (SEPA) issued a regulation requiring manufacturers and importers of new chemicals to apply to SEPA's Chemical Registration Center (CRC) for approval and to provide extensive test data to substantiate the physical properties, consumer safety and environmental impact of the new chemical. U.S. industry's primary concerns are that CRC has not been able to make decisions on the approval of new chemicals in a timely manner and that the governing rules and testing requirements are not transparent and accessible. SEPA's CRC acknowledges receipt of more than 40 completed applications for new chemicals since October 2003. According to the most recent information available from U.S. industry, only a small number of new chemical applications have been approved.

U.S. industry notes that a number of applications have been pending well beyond the 120-day timeline set forth in the regulation. U.S. industry also complains of shifting requirements and implementation changes, such as recently expanded eco-toxicity testing requirements, which mandate that certain ecotoxicity testing, particularly fish eco-toxicity and bio-degradation studies, be carried out in one of six SEPA-accredited laboratories in China. These accredited laboratories have all been established since mid-2004 in response to the

September 2003 regulation, and U.S. industry fears that if inexperience leads one of these new laboratories to declare a product unsafe, it could affect sales globally. China's lack of a low-volume exemption, meaning an exemption where trade in a given chemical falls below an annual volume threshold, also appears to hinder the importation of U.S. chemicals, particularly for high-value specialty chemicals sold in small quantities.

Toxic Chemicals

In December 2005, SEPA and the General Administration on Customs issued the Circular on the Highly Restricted Import/Export Toxic Chemicals List five days before it entered into force. In response to U.S. complaints that the notice period was too short, SEPA provided a transition period until June 2006 during which the regulation was apparently not enforced against shipments of chemicals imported from the United States. China subsequently notified the measure to the WTO TBT Committee in June 2006, with no opportunity for comment and no transition period. In addition to these problems, U.S. industry has expressed concerns about excessive fees required to register chemical products, as well as a lack of clarity on the scope of coverage of the measure.

Hazardous Substances

MII and six other Chinese agencies jointly issued the Administrative Measures on the Control of Pollution Caused by Electronic Information Products (China RoHS) in February 2006, with a March 2007 effective date. China did not notify China RoHS to the WTO TBT Committee until May 2006. China had notified an earlier measure setting out the broad framework for China RoHS, the Administrative Measure on Electronic Information Pollution Control, in September 2005, but it provided little detail on how China RoHS would operate.

The objective of China RoHS is to restrict the use of lead, mercury, cadmium, hexavalent chromium, poly-brominated bi-phenyls (PBB) and poly-brominated di-phenyl ethers (PBDE) in certain electrical information products. China RoHS has two main components. One component involves labeling and marking requirements for a long list of electrical information equipment products, which goes into effect in March 2007. The other component involves a planned requirement for in-country testing and certification using China's CCC mark system; however, the effective date for this requirement, and the products to which it will be applicable, remain unclear.

China RoHS is similar to a pre-existing European Union measure (EU RoHS Directive). However, China RoHS differs from the EU RoHS Directive in several ways, including through a different scope of products, unique requirements for labeling and marking across a wide range of electrical information equipment products and a requirement for CCC mark registration to test and certify the absence of the restricted substances in an as yet undetermined catalogue of products.

The China RoHS scheme has created substantial concern for U.S. and other foreign companies in several ways. These companies have expressed concerns about the justification for, and the burdensome nature of, China's labeling and marking requirements for a long list of products. The EU RoHS regulations do not require labeling. Additionally, the issue of how China's labeling and marking requirements will be applied to products containing many electrical information product components has not been adequately addressed by Chinese regulators, nor have the mandated labeling and marking requirements been notified to the WTO TBT Committee for review and comment.

Companies have also expressed concern about China's plans to require an in-country testing and certification process using the CCC mark system for the as yet to be determined catalogue of products that will be banned if they contain the hazardous substances identified above. No other country regulating hazardous substances in electrical information products requires in-country, government-administered testing for compliance, according to U.S. industry. For example, the EU requires companies to self-declare their conformity with the EU RoHS Directive.

Scrap Recycling

Scrap exports from the United States to China exceeded $4 billion in 2006, making scrap one of the United States' largest exports to China by value. In late 2003, China's AQSIQ issued a notice requiring overseas scrap material exporters to register with AQSIQ. The stated purpose of the new requirement was to better monitor the entry of scrap shipments into China reportedly due to high occurrences of receiving dangerous waste and illegal material in past shipments from overseas. It was not until May 2004 that AQSIQ issued the implementing rules. These rules established registration procedures, including an application deadline of July 2004, and set substantive requirements. In response to U.S. and other WTO Members' concerns that the application period was too short, AQSIQ extended the application deadline to August 2004, allowed companies who submitted incomplete applications to supplement required documents and extended the new requirement's effective date from November 2004 to January 2005.

In 2004, AQSIQ made public on its website the names of overseas exporters approved to ship scrap to China in two postings, the first in mid-October and the second at the end of December, only days before the new registration would take effect. In total, about 85 percent of worldwide applicants were granted approval, including hundreds of U.S. exporters. AQSIQ indicated that it would notify applicants that were not approved and that these exporters would be able to apply again six months after receiving notice of their rejection.

In July 2005, AQSIQ posted Bulletin No. 103/2005 on its website, announcing the resumption of the review and approval of registration applications for scrap imports. According to the bulletin, as of August 2005, scrap suppliers must wait three years to reapply for registration if they are denied eligibility. A December 2005 AQSIQ notice reported that an additional 260 company registrations had been approved, including 55 U.S. companies.

Since Bulletin No. 103/2005 was published, U.S. scrap exporters continue to experience problems related to inconsistent and unexplained rejections of licenses, confusing requirements imposed with little or no notice, and rejections of shipments at the point of entry. Problems are also being encountered within the United States as a result of pre-inspection requirements imposed by the Chinese authorities and conducted by Chinese-authorized inspectors at the shipment origin point.

Scrap Waste

In December 2004, China's President Hu Jintao signed Presidential Order No. 31, publishing the amended Law for the Prevention of Solid Scrap Waste Pollution, which went into effect in April 2005. According to this law, firms manufacturing, selling and importing items listed in the mandatory reclamation catalogue must recycle these items, and it is illegal to import scrap waste as component materials that cannot be rendered safe. Depending on the particular item, items that can be safely used as component materials are subject to either restricted import procedures or automatic licensing procedures. SEPA is charged with coordinating with MOFCOM, NDRC, China Customs and AQSIQ to design, adjust and publish the catalogues of imported solid scrap waste subject to the restricted or automatic licensing regimes. SEPA and MOFCOM, meanwhile, are responsible for reviewing and issuing licenses for the items subject to restricted import procedures.

Medical Devices

China still requires outdated type-testing (batch testing) for medical devices. Quality systems audits, a common practice in other major markets, address product safety and efficacy in a more rigorous manner than type-testing. As a result, requiring firms that have undergone internationally recognized quality systems audits to also be type-tested is redundant and does not provide any additional safety benefits, while it adds unnecessary costs and delays in getting needed medical device products to Chinese patients. Certain electro-medical devices also face redundant testing by two different agencies, the State Food and Drug Administration (SFDA) and AQSIQ, which administers the "CCC" mark for electrical safety. Both agencies perform virtually identical product tests and factory inspections prior to registration, but they do not recognize the results of one another's tests and inspections. The U.S. medical devices industry reports that this redundancy adds significant time and costs to bringing a new technology to market in China without providing any additional safety benefits.

At the April 2006 JCCT meeting, China committed to eliminate the testing and certification redundancies in the medical devices sector. However, AQSIQ/SFDA Notice No. 70, issued in April 2006, intended by China to fulfill the JCCT commitment, only eliminated a single redundancy. It only eliminated redundant testing and redundant testing fees, while failing to address separate and redundant AQSIQ and SFDA application fees, certification processes and inspection teams for inspecting the manufacturing facilities of medical device makers in the United States and other countries.

A similar concern exists for imported pacemakers, which are inspected by AQSIQ after clearing customs. This review adds unnecessary delay and costs to the distribution of these pacemakers, without providing any additional safety benefits, as pacemakers are scanned and re-calibrated by the hospital before implantation into patients.

Sanitary and Phytosanitary (SPS) Measures

In 2006, China's general lack of transparency remained a problem. China either failed to notify or belatedly notified to the WTO numerous SPS measures, resulting in measures that were adopted without the benefit of comments from other interested WTO Members. In addition, in some cases, the adopted measures were overly burdensome, appeared to lack a scientific foundation, or raised significant national treatment concerns. U.S. engagement with China at the WTO and bilaterally, including through the provision of technical assistance, has helped to ensure China's compliance with certain WTO transparency obligations. At the same time, however, various U.S. agricultural exports continued to be subjected to unnotified entry, inspection and labeling requirements or faced unwarranted import bans. The most problematic of China's SPS measures are described below.

Bovine Spongiform Encephalopathy (BSE)-Related Bans on Beef and Low-Risk Bovine Products

In December 2003, China and other countries imposed a ban on U.S. cattle, beef and processed beef products in response to a case of BSE found in a dairy cow which had been imported from Canada into the United States. Since that time, the United States has repeatedly provided China with extensive technical information on all aspects of its BSE-related surveillance and mitigation measures, internationally recognized by the World Organization for Animal Health (OIE) as effective and appropriate, for both food safety and animal health.

After three years, China still has not provided any scientific justification for continuing to maintain its ban, nor has it identified any of the administrative and regulatory steps necessary to lift the ban. Although China finally sent a technical team to the United States in October 2005, this visit did not advance a resolution of the impasse. At the April 2006 JCCT meeting, China agreed to conditionally reopen the Chinese market to U.S. beef, subject to the negotiation and finalization of an import protocol by technical experts on an expedited basis. Jointly negotiated protocols, and accompanying export certificates, are normal measures necessary for the export of any livestock products from the United States to China or other trading partners. At the end of June 2006, after three inconclusive rounds of negotiations, China's food safety regulators unilaterally announced a limited market opening, restricted to the entry of U.S. boneless beef from animals 30 months of age or less. One month later, they followed up that announcement with an announcement of 22 onerous entry conditions, many of which were unrelated to BSE. These unilateral announcements had no practical effect, because, as with any trading partners seeking to engage in livestock trade, the United States and China would have had to agree on language for actual export safety certificates before the trade could resume. Since then, the United States has pressed China to reconsider its position and to negotiate an appropriate protocol in light of China's WTO SPS Agreement obligations and relevant OIE guidelines.

At the same time that it banned U.S. cattle, beef and processed beef products, China also banned low-risk or "safe to trade" bovine products (i.e.: bovine semen and embryos, protein-free tallow and non-ruminant feeds and fats) even though they are deemed tradable based on OIE guidelines regardless of a country's BSE status. After numerous bilateral meetings and technical discussions in 2004, including a visit to U.S. bovine facilities by Chinese food safety officials, China announced a lifting of its BSE-related ban for low-risk bovine products in late September 2004. However, China conditioned the lifting of the ban on the negotiation of protocol agreements setting technical and certification parameters for incoming low-risk bovine products. In November 2004, U.S. and Chinese officials finalized and signed protocols that would enable the resumption of exports of U.S.-origin bovine semen and embryos, contingent on facility certification by China's regulatory authorities, as well as a resumption of exports of U.S.-origin non-ruminant feeds and fats. In July 2005, China finally announced the resumption of trade in bovine semen and embryos, following certifications for 52 U.S. facilities made earlier in the year. However, trade in U.S.-origin non-ruminant feeds and fats did not resume, as China's regulatory authorities insisted on a series of onerous, detailed and unnecessary information requirements that are not consistent with OIE guidelines and contrast sharply with U.S. requirements. As a result of further negotiations in December 2005, export certificates were finalized, and trade resumed in early 2006. Meanwhile, trade in protein-free tallow had not resumed by the end of 2006, as U.S. and Chinese officials had not reached agreement on provisions of a protocol.

Avian Influenza (AI)

In February 2004, China imposed a nationwide ban on U.S. poultry in response to cases of low-pathogenic AI found in Delaware. Throughout 2004, the United States provided technical information to China on the U.S. AI situation, and in August 2004 a high-level Chinese delegation conducted a review of the status of AI eradication efforts in the United States. In December 2004, China lifted its nationwide ban on U.S. poultry, leaving in place a ban only for the states of Connecticut and Rhode Island. In early 2005, following the announcement of low-pathogenic AI found in the state of New York, China did not impose a nationwide ban. Instead, demonstrating progress in following OIE guidelines, China imposed a ban limited to poultry from the state of New York.

In 2006, China imposed an import ban on poultry and poultry products originating from the state of Pennsylvania, based on incidents of low-pathogenic AI. China also suspended the importation of heat-treated and cooked poultry and poultry products at the same time, even though the OIE's AI chapter makes clear that products that have been heat-treated in a manner to inactivate the virus should not be subject to an AI-related import ban. Despite China's progress in imposing limited bans, as opposed to nationwide bans, in response to cases of AI, China's actions are problematic because any ban in response to cases of low-pathogen AI is inconsistent with international standards. The United States is attempting to work with China's regulators to address these issues.

Wheat

The 1999 U.S.-China Agricultural Cooperation Agreement established an agreed level of TCK fungus tolerance in U.S. wheat, and China no longer routinely blocks U.S. wheat exports from the Pacific Northwest on the basis of the TCK fungus. Nevertheless, China has imposed a maximum residue level (MRL) for selenium that is more stringent than the international standard and threatens U.S. wheat exports to China. In addition, China has imposed an MRL for vomitoxin in wheat in the absence of any international standard or scientific justification. Although these measures are problematic, U.S. exports of wheat to China appear to be unaffected by them. A drop in U.S. wheat exports in 2006 was attributable to other factors.

Zero Tolerance for Pathogens

Since 2002, China has applied SPS-related requirements on imported raw meat and poultry that do not appear to be consistent with Codex Alimentarius (Codex) guidelines or current scientific testing practices. One requirement establishes a zero tolerance limit for the presence of Salmonella bacteria. A similar zero tolerance standard exists for E. Coli and Listeria pathogens. Meanwhile, the complete elimination of these enteropathogenic bacteria is generally considered unachievable without first subjecting raw meat and poultry to a process of irradiation. Moreover, China apparently does not apply this same standard to domestic raw poultry and meat, raising national treatment concerns.

In late 2005 and early 2006, 14 U.S. pork and poultry plants were de-listed by China for alleged violations of zero tolerance standards for pathogens or detection of certain chemical residues. Despite positive results from USDA Food Safety and Inspection Service investigations of the plants, the majority of the plants were not re-listed as approved to ship products to China until April 2006, following extensive engagement between U.S. and Chinese regulatory officials because of differences between Codex guidelines and China's SPS related requirements on imported raw meat and poultry. Two U.S. plants remain de-listed while U.S. regulatory officials continue to press Chinese regulatory officials to re-list the plants or to provide scientific justification.

Meanwhile, China continues to maintain maximum residue levels (MRLs) for certain heavy metals, veterinary drugs and other residues that are inconsistent with Codex and other international standards. China also enforces a zero tolerance standard for some residues, even where Codex has adopted guidelines that many of China's major trading partners have adopted. U.S. regulatory officials have encouraged their Chinese counterparts to adopt MRLs that are scientifically based, safe and minimally trade disrupting.

Distilled Spirits

Until August 2006, China maintained a mandatory standard on distilled spirits that set maximum limits on naturally occurring substances, known as superior alcohols or fusel oils, which result from the production process. However, the Joint UN FAO/WHO Expert Committee on Food Additives, like U.S. regulators of alcohol, has recognized that superior alcohols are safe for human consumption. In August 2006, after several years of bilateral engagement and interventions by the United States at WTO TBT Committee meetings, China notified a proposed revision of its distilled spirits standard and indicated that it was accepting public comment. According to China's notification, the proposed revision would eliminate the requirement for tolerance levels of superior alcohols, or fusel oil. If adopted, it would bring China's standard in line with international norms.

Food Additive Standards

Another problematic area involves China's overly restrictive food additive standards. China continues to block many U.S. processed food products from entering the Chinese market by banning certain food additives that are widely used in other countries and have been approved by the World Health Organization. The most recent example is China's proposed *Hygienic Standard for Uses of Food Additives*, notified to the WTO in July 2005 so that WTO Members could comment on it. This proposed technical regulation is 237 pages long and covers dozens of residues and additives for nearly 1,000 commodities. In some cases, it employs domestic nomenclature rather than internationally recognized technical terms, making it difficult to assess the impact that it would have on specific products. The United States recently submitted detailed comments on the proposed technical regulation and asked China to delay its adoption until a thorough review could take place.

Biotechnology Regulations

In January 2002, the Ministry of Agriculture (MOA) issued new rules implementing June 2001 regulations on agricultural biotechnology safety, testing and labeling. The product most affected by these rules was soybeans, while corn and other commodities were also potentially affected. However, the rules did not provide adequate time for completion of required safety assessments before their effective date of March 20, 2002. In response to U.S. interventions,

China issued interim rules, which allowed trade to continue while authorities carried out safety assessments of biotechnology products. These interim rules were extended twice and were set to expire in April 2004. In December 2003 talks, MOA officials promised that approval of Round-up Ready soybeans would be completed at least 60 days before expiration of the interim rules in order to prevent any trade disruption. China followed through on this promise and approved Round-up Ready soybeans, along with two cotton events and two corn events, in February 2004. Two months later, China issued final safety certificates for four additional corn events and seven canola events. China issued a formal safety certificate for another corn event later in 2004, leaving only one corn event still awaiting final approval. During the July 2005 JCCT meeting, MOA issued the final safety certificate for the remaining corn event. All of the approvals made in 2004 and 2005 were for three-year renewable safety certificates. In January 2007, MOA renewed safety certificates for all of the events that had originally been approved three years earlier.

Other U.S. concerns with China's biotechnology regulations remain. Areas of concern include limited timelines for submission of products, lack of clarity on assessment requirements for stacked (multiple trait) products and, at times, duplicative and unprecedented testing requirements.

Food Labeling

The U.S. processed food industry has registered concerns with a number of standards and labeling requirements on its exports to China. The meat industry in particular is concerned that labeling regulations issued in late 2002 contain several requirements that go beyond those of any other country. It asserts that these requirements are unnecessary and costly.

Chinese agricultural importers and importers of processed foods are also concerned about measures requiring labels for products containing material developed through the use of biotechnology, such as soybeans and corn. The June 2001 biotechnology regulations issued by MOA require labeling of bulk commodities, but implementation has been limited and sporadic. Future implementation of these measures remains uncertain.

The distilled spirits industry is concerned that China will require its products to comply with all existing food labeling requirements. The industry believes that some of these requirements are inappropriate. For example, China requires distilled spirits product labels to include a bottling date. According to accepted international practice relating to wines and spirits, however, the date of manufacture (production or bottling date) is not required. Because many spirits products consist of a blend of spirits that are aged for varying periods, a single "date of manufacture" is often not possible to specify, would not represent the actual age of the product and would confuse consumers regarding the actual age of the product. China also requires the labels of distilled spirits products to include a list of ingredients, even though the original ingredients (e.g., corn, wheat, rye and barley) are completely transformed and are no longer present after distillation. Furthermore, China maintains typeface specifications and translation requirements that are inconsistent with international standards.

Export Regulation

Export Licenses and Quotas

Over the last several years, China has progressively reduced the number of products requiring some type of export license. In 2005, China continued this trend, as it freed up three additional categories of products from this requirement (man-made jade, satin and some kinds of silk). As of the end of 2006, China continued to maintain export licensing requirements for 46 categories of products (totaling 312 items at the 8-digit tariff level), including important industrial raw materials like coke, fluorspar and rare earth oxides, as well as certain grains, cotton, livestock, certain metals, lethal chemicals and food products. In addition, China occasionally imposes new export licensing requirements on strategically sensitive commodities.

For some products, such as coke (a key steel input) and fluorspar (a key ingredient in a wide range of downstream products made with fluorocarbons), the export licensing system raises serious concerns under WTO rules that generally prohibit export restrictions. Export licenses for these two products are accompanied by export quotas and at times have required the payment of high export license fees beyond the administrative costs of administering an export license system.

In 2004, China's export restrictions on coke began to have a significant, adverse effect on U.S. integrated steel producers and their customers, as China's increasingly restrictive export restrictions pushed the export price of Chinese coke to the vicinity of $500 per metric ton (MT), more than three times the price in 2003. After a series of meetings in which the United States urged China to eliminate the practice of using export restrictions, not just for coke but also for other products, China raised the 2004 quota allotment for coke to 12.3 million MT, and it indicated that it would eventually raise the quota to the 2003 level of 14.3 million MT. Shortly thereafter, MOFCOM also issued an urgent notice reiterating that the sale of export licenses was illegal. In the ensuing months, with the increased supply of Chinese coke and the crackdown on the sale of export licenses, the export prices for Chinese coke declined significantly.

U.S. industry was also able to obtain a substantially larger quantity of Chinese coke in 2004 than it had in 2003.

In May 2005, consistent with earlier indications from China, an NDRC official stated publicly that China would eliminate the coke export quota system as of January 1, 2006. A MOFCOM official also noted that while WTO rules allow Member countries to impose quotas on exports under certain circumstances, the rules simultaneously require restrictions on domestic consumption, which had not been done to date. In November 2005, when MOFCOM announced the 2006 export quota levels for agricultural, industrial and textile products, coke was absent from the list. MOFCOM later indicated that coke would still be subject to an export quota, except the export quota would now be administered by the NDRC, not MOFCOM. The reason given for the switch in coke export quota administration is that NDRC is responsible for dealing with industrial products that have significant influence on the national economy. In early December 2005, the NDRC released a list of 2006 coal export quotas, but did not include coke. In late December 2005, the NDRC finally issued the coke export quota, set at 14 million MT for 2006.

In 2006, even though the export price for Chinese coke remained relatively low compared to the $500 per MT price of 2004, the export quota kept world coke prices artificially high in 2006, and a significant differential existed between China's domestic coke prices and world coke prices. However, the Chinese government continued its efforts to direct market outcomes by maintaining the export quota on coke for 2007. In addition, in October 2006, China took the additional step of imposing a 5 percent duty on exports of coke.

In October 2006, China announced new export duties on certain steel inputs and semi-processed steel products. Applied in combination with differential VAT rebate policies, these export duties act to restrict exports of raw materials and semi-processed inputs (including coke) while promoting the production and export of more processed steel products.

China has imposed quotas and high license fees on exports of fluorspar since before its accession to the WTO, apparently with the objective of supporting China's downstream producers of the numerous products derived from fluorspar, such as non-ozone depleting hydrofluorocarbon refrigerants and foam blowing agents. While their foreign competitors pay higher world market prices for fluorspar, China's downstream producers benefit from the artificially low domestic prices for fluorspar and are able to export their products around the world at prices well below those of their foreign competitors. China has refused to modify its practices in this area, despite repeated U.S. requests. In fact, China has increased the protection afforded to its downstream producers by lowering the export quota on fluorspar each year and, in October 2006, by imposing a 10 percent duty on exports of fluorspar.

In December 2004, China announced plans to impose export duties on certain categories of textile and apparel products in an apparent effort to manage the export growth of textile and apparel products in response to concerns raised by its trading partners as the January 1, 2005 deadline for removal of global textile quotas drew near. In February 2005, MOFCOM issued rules imposing automatic licensing requirements for textile exports to the United States, the European Union and Hong Kong. Subsequently, China suspended the licensing requirements only to restore similar measures in June 2005 and July 2005 after the United States imposed safeguards on certain categories of textile imports from China. China claimed the measures were needed to avoid uncertainty among Chinese textile exporting firms, to encourage exports of high value-added items and to avoid rent seeking in license distributions. Under the June 2005 measures, MOFCOM, China Customs and AQSIQ jointly issued and made adjustments to a catalogue of subject items, listed by tariff codes, destination countries and regions, implementing periods and total licensed export quantities of subject items. Included in the catalogue were textile products subject to foreign safeguard actions or those subject to temporary quantitative regulation in accordance with bilateral agreements. In November 2005, USTR and MOFCOM signed a memorandum of understanding (MOU), under which China agreed to limit export growth rates in 34 categories of textiles, representing approximately 40 percent of bilateral trade in textiles, through 2008. The United States in turn agreed to dismiss all pending China-specific textile safeguard investigations and agreed to exercise restraint in invoking safeguards for categories of textiles falling outside the MOU. The United States and China also established an Electronic Visa Information System Arrangement to monitor trade in the affected products.

China requires export licenses on products that are the subject of antidumping duties in a foreign market. As was initially the case in 2005 for textile exports subject to safeguard limitations in the United States, the central government has often delegated responsibility for issuing these licenses to quasi-governmental industry associations formed to take the place of the ministries that governed production during the earlier central planning era. Foreign investors report that the industry associations are using the power to issue export licenses to force companies to participate in association-supported activities. For example, the steel producers' industry association will not issue an export license to any company that does not contribute to its antidumping defense funds.

Export Subsidies

China officially abolished subsidies in the form of direct budgetary outlays for exports of industrial goods on January 1, 1991. In its WTO accession agreement, China committed to eliminate all subsidies prohibited under Article 3 of the WTO Agreement on Subsidies and Countervailing Measures, including all forms of export subsidies on industrial and agricultural goods, upon its accession to the WTO in December 2001.

A general lack of transparency makes it difficult to identify and quantify possible export subsidies provided by the Chinese government. China's subsidy programs are often the result of internal administrative measures and are not publicized. Sometimes they take the form of income tax reductions or exemptions. They can also take a variety of other forms, including mechanisms such as credit allocations, low-interest loans, debt forgiveness and reduction of freight charges. U.S. industry has alleged that subsidization is a key reason that Chinese exports are undercutting prices in the United States and gaining market share. Of particular concern are China's practices in the steel, petrochemical, high technology, forestry and paper products, textiles, hardwood plywood, machinery and copper and other non-ferrous metals industries.

In April 2006, China finally submitted its long-overdue subsidies notification to the WTO's Subsidies Committee. Although the notification is lengthy, with over 70 subsidy programs reported, it is also notably incomplete, as it failed to notify any subsidies provided by China's state-owned banks or by provincial and local government authorities. In addition, while China notified several subsidies that appear to be prohibited under WTO rules, it did so without making any commitment to withdraw them, and it failed to notify other subsidies that appear to be prohibited.

Through the remainder of 2006, the United States pressed China to withdraw the subsidies that appear to be prohibited, which include both export subsidies and import substitution subsidies and benefit a wide range of industries in China, principally through income tax and VAT exemptions and reductions. However, China was unwilling to commit to the immediate withdrawal of these subsidies. Accordingly, the United States initiated a challenge to these subsidies under the WTO's dispute settlement procedures in early 2007.

Shortly after China acceded to the WTO, U.S. corn exporters began to complain that China was subsidizing its corn exports. In 2002 and 2003, it appeared that significant quantities of corn had been exported from China, including corn from Chinese government stocks, at prices that may have been 15 percent to 20 percent below domestic prices in China. As a result, U.S. corn exporters were losing market share for corn in their traditional Asian markets, such as South Korea and Malaysia, while China was exporting record amounts of corn. In 2004, however, trade analysts began to conclude that, because of several economic factors, including changes in the relationship between domestic prices and world prices, China was trending toward becoming a net importer of corn. One result appears to be that

China's exports are largely made on a commercial basis, although concern remains regarding the operation of China's VAT rebate system for corn.

INTELLECTUAL PROPERTY RIGHTS (IPR) PROTECTION

With its acceptance of the TRIPS Agreement, China took on obligations to adhere to generally accepted international norms to protect and enforce the intellectual property rights held by U.S. and other foreign companies and individuals in China. Specifically, the TRIPS Agreement sets minimum standards of protection for copyrights and neighboring rights, trademarks, geographical indications, industrial designs, patents, integrated circuit layout designs and undisclosed information. Minimum standards are also established by the TRIPS Agreement for IPR enforcement procedures and remedies. The TRIPS Agreement additionally requires that, with very limited exceptions, WTO Members provide national and most favored nation (MFN) treatment to the nationals of other WTO Members with regard to the protection and enforcement of intellectual property rights.

Since its accession to the WTO, China has overhauled its legal regime and put in place a comprehensive set of laws and regulations aimed at protecting the intellectual property rights of domestic and foreign entities in China. At the same time, some key improvements in China's legal framework are still needed, and China has continued to demonstrate little success in actually enforcing its laws and regulations in the face of the challenges created by widespread counterfeiting, piracy and other forms of infringement. Indeed, USTR's April 2006 report under the Special 301 provisions of U.S. trade law cited inadequate IPR enforcement as one of China's greatest shortcomings as a trading partner. As a result, in 2006, the United States' bilateral engagement with China continued to focus on obtaining improvements to multiple aspects of China's system of IPR protection and enforcement so that significant reductions in IPR infringement in China could be realized and sustained over time.

Several factors contribute to China's poor IPR enforcement record. One major factor is China's chronic underutilization of deterrent criminal remedies. For example, legal measures in China that establish high thresholds for criminal investigation, prosecution and conviction preclude criminal remedies in many instances of commercial-scale counterfeiting and piracy, creating a "safe harbor" for infringers and raising concerns among the United States and some of its major trading partners relating to China's obligations under Article 61 of the TRIPS Agreement. With criminal remedies circumscribed, China's enforcement authorities rely instead on toothless administrative enforcement, which primarily results in small fines, administrative injunctions and other minor inconveniences for infringers. Meanwhile, procedures in civil actions are frequently cumbersome, and civil damages are generally low.

Another exacerbating factor – which also raises WTO concerns – is China's continued maintenance of import restrictions and restrictions on wholesale and retail distribution that reduce and delay market access for certain types of legitimate foreign products, such as movies, video games and books. These restrictions inadvertently help to ensure that infringing products continue to dominate those sectors within China.

China's leaders began to demonstrate a willingness to address U.S. concerns in October 2003, when a new IPR Leading Group was formed, signaling a more focused and sustained effort by China to tackle the IPR enforcement problem. Many officials in China, led by

President Hu Jintao, Premier Wen Jiabao and Vice Premier Wu Yi, continued to give voice to China's commitment to protecting intellectual property rights in 2006 and worked hard to make it a reality, as they attempted to improve not only public awareness but also training and coordination among the numerous Chinese government entities involved in IPR enforcement while simultaneously fighting local protectionism and corruption. Sustained involvement by China's leaders is critical if China is to deliver on the IPR commitments that it made at the April 2004, July 2005 and April 2006 JCCT meetings, including China's core commitment to significantly reduce IPR infringement levels across the country.

Building on earlier engagement with China, the United States conducted an out-of-cycle review under the Special 301 provisions of U.S. trade law in 2004 and 2005. This review involved a systematic evaluation of China's entire IPR enforcement regime and concluded in April 2005 with the Administration's elevation of China to the Special 301 "Priority Watch" list and the creation of a comprehensive strategy for addressing China's ineffective IPR enforcement regime, which included the possible use of WTO mechanisms, as appropriate.

Pursuing this new strategy at the July 2005 JCCT meeting, the United States sought and obtained China's agreement to take a series of specific actions designed to: (1) increase criminal prosecutions of IPR violators; (2) improve border enforcement and reduce exports of infringing goods; (3) counter piracy of movies, audio visual products and software; (4) address Internet-related piracy; and (5) assist small- and medium-sized U.S. companies experiencing China-related IPR problems, among other things. To date, China has taken steps to fulfill many of these commitments. It adopted amended rules governing the transfer of administrative and customs cases to criminal authorities, and it took some steps to pursue administrative actions against end-user software piracy. China posted an IPR Ombudsman to its Embassy in Washington, who has facilitated contacts between U.S. Government officials and their counterparts in Beijing, and has been a source of information for U.S. businesses, including small- and medium-sized companies. China has also sought to expand enforcement cooperation.

In October 2005, the United States submitted a request to China under Article 63.3 of the TRIPS Agreement, as did both Japan and Switzerland, seeking more transparency on IPR infringement levels and enforcement activities in China, with the objective of obtaining a better basis for assessing the effectiveness of China's efforts to improve IPR enforcement since China's accession to the WTO.

However, despite the United States' extensive efforts to follow up on its Article 63.3 request bilaterally, China has since provided only limited information in response, hampering the United States' ability to evaluate whether China is taking all necessary steps to address the rampant IPR infringement found throughout China.

In 2006, the United States again used the JCCT process, including the IPR Working Group created at the April 2004 JCCT meeting, to secure new IPR commitments and, in a few instances, specific actions to implement past commitments. During the run-up to the April 2006 JCCT meeting, China took enforcement actions against plants that produce pirated optical discs, and it also issued new rules that require computers to be pre-installed with licensed operating system software. At the meeting itself, China further committed to ensure the legalization of software used in Chinese enterprises and to take up issues of government and enterprise software asset management in the JCCT IPR Working Group. China also agreed to work on cooperation to combat infringing goods displayed at trade fairs in China and to intensify efforts to eliminate infringing products at major consumer markets in China, such as the Silk Street Market in Beijing. The two sides further agreed that they would increase cooperation between their respective law enforcement authorities and customs authorities and that the United States would provide China with additional technical assistance to aid China in fully implementing the WIPO Internet treaties (i.e.: the WIPO Copyright Treaty and the WIPO Performance and Phonograms Treaty). In addition, China reaffirmed its prior commitments to continue efforts to ensure the use of legalized software at all levels of government and to adopt procedures to ensure that enterprises use legal software, beginning with state-owned enterprises and other large enterprises.

To date, China has made some progress in implementing its April 2006 JCCT commitments, but it has been slower than in the past. One bright spot appears to be China's implementation of the new rules requiring computers to be pre-installed with licensed operating system software, as U.S. industry has been pleased with the initial results of that effort.

Legal Framework

In most respects, China's framework of laws, regulations and implementing rules remains largely satisfactory. However, reforms are needed in a few key areas, including certain aspects of the Criminal Law and rapidly emerging fields, such as Internet copyright protection. In particular, right holders have pointed to a number of continuing deficiencies in China's criminal measures. For example, it appears that China would need to eliminate thresholds for criminal prosecution that provide a legal "safe harbor" for many commercial infringers if it is to bring its legal framework into compliance with its TRIPS Agreement obligations. In addition, while China introduced new regulations in 2006 that represent a positive step toward meeting the requirements of the WIPO Internet treaties, more work is needed at both the national level and the provincial level to meet the challenges of Internet piracy and fully implement the WIPO Internet treaties.

At the time of its accession to the WTO, China was in the process of modifying the full range of IPR laws, regulations and implementing rules, including those relating to patents, trademarks and copyrights. China had completed amendments to its Patent Law, Trademark Law and Copyright Law, along with regulations for the Patent Law. Within several months of its accession, China issued regulations for the Trademark Law and the Copyright Law, followed by implementing rules. China also issued regulations and implementing rules covering specific subject areas, such as integrated circuits, computer software and pharmaceuticals. U.S. experts carefully reviewed these measures after their issuance and, together with other WTO Members, participated in a comprehensive review of them before the WTO's TRIPS Council in 2002.

Since 2003, China has periodically issued new IPR laws, regulations and other measures. The U.S. Government has reviewed these measures through bilateral discussions and subsequent TRIPS Council reviews. Encouragingly, China has also become more willing to circulate proposed measures for public comment and to discuss proposed measures with interested trading partners and stakeholders.

In 2006, China announced a new Action Plan for revising its legal regime in order to better protect intellectual property rights. Among other things, this Action Plan sets out China's intentions for revising the Patent Law, the Trademark Law and related measures, and

China subsequently did release new versions of both the Patent Law and the Trademark Law for public comment. Since then, the United States has been assessing the potential ramifications of the contemplated revisions for U.S. right holders. The U.S. Government and U.S. industry groups have also submitted written comments, along with invitations to continue dialogue on these important pieces of legislation.

China has also been working on other proposed legal measures that could have significant implications for the intellectual property rights of foreign right holders. In particular, China is drafting an Anti-Monopoly Law and has considered rules relating to the treatment of IPR by standards-setting organizations. The United States is carefully monitoring both of these efforts and has raised concerns with particular aspects of these proposals, both in bilateral meetings and at the WTO.

The United States, meanwhile, has repeatedly urged China to pursue additional legislative and regulatory changes, using both bilateral meetings and the annual transitional reviews before the WTO's TRIPS Council. The focus of U.S. efforts is to persuade China to improve its legal regime in certain critical areas, such as criminal IPR enforcement and legislative and regulatory reform, especially with regard to China's high criminal thresholds and other obstacles to effective enforcement. Other obstacles in the area of criminal enforcement include, for example, the lack of criminal liability for certain acts of copyright infringement, the profit motive requirement in copyright cases, the requirement of identical trademarks in counterfeiting cases and the absence of minimum, proportionate sentences and clear standards for initiation of police investigations in cases where there is a reasonable suspicion of criminal activity. At the same time, the United States has also been pressing China for a variety of changes to its administrative and civil enforcement regimes, such as the restoration of minimum (and deterrent) fines in administrative trademark enforcement cases, increased referral of administrative enforcement actions for criminal prosecution, elimination of the need for legalization and consularization of foreign evidence, implementation of a discovery process with compulsory measures for evidence protection, provision of meaningful injunctive relief and enforcement of judicial orders. While some of these issues do not raise specific WTO concerns, all of them will continue to detract from China's enforcement efforts until addressed.

In its 2006 Action Plan, China did not embrace reform of the Criminal Law, although it did undertake to "improve" its December 2004 judicial interpretation on the handling of criminal IPR cases. Improvement of that measure could include, for example, clarification of some issues related to China's problematic thresholds, but Chinese government officials have given no indication that this process will lead to the reduction or elimination of these thresholds – a key concern for U.S. right holders, particularly in light of China's obligations under Article 61 of the TRIPS Agreement. In the United States' view, China's high thresholds for criminal prosecution help to explain why criminal remedies are so underutilized in China, as these thresholds create a substantial "safe harbor" for commercial-scale infringers. The United States is determined to resolve this problem and, in November 2006, informed China that it would be filing a formal request for WTO consultations on this issue and certain other IPR enforcement issues. However, China asked the United States to delay that filing so that further bilateral discussions could take place. With the support of U.S. industry, the United States agreed to hold further bilateral discussions, with the objective of seeking a resolution in the near term.

The United States has also sought improvements in China's copyright protection in the context of electronic information networks since the April 2004 JCCT meeting. China took an important step at the time of that meeting when the National Copyright Administration (NCA) issued the Measures for Administrative Protection of Copyright on the Internet. That measure requires Internet service providers to take remedial actions to delete content that infringes on copyrights upon receipt of a complaint from the right holder, or face administrative penalties ranging from confiscation of illegal gains to fines of up to RMB100,000 ($12,500).

During the run-up to the July 2005 JCCT meeting, the United States also urged China to accede to the WIPO Internet treaties and to fully harmonize its regulations and implementing rules with them. Compliance with these treaties is not required under WTO rules, but they still reflect important international norms for providing copyright protection over the Internet. These treaties have been ratified by many developed and developing countries since they entered into force in 2002. In the case of China, this type of copyright protection is especially important in light of its rapidly increasing number of Internet users, many of whom have broadband access. At the July 2005 JCCT meeting, the United States obtained China's commitment to submit the legislative package necessary for China's accession to the WIPO Internet treaties to the National People's Congress by June 2006. Although China's fulfillment of this commitment has been delayed for technical reasons relating to coordination with Hong Kong and Macau, the Standing Committee of the National People's Congress issued a notice in late December 2006 indicating that China had decided to accede to the WIPO Internet treaties. Even before that decision, China had moved forward with the harmonization of some of its regulations and implementing rules in 2005 and 2006. In May 2006, for example, the State Council adopted an important Internet-related measure, the Regulations on the Protection of Copyright Over Information Networks, which went into effect in July 2006. Overall, this measure represents a welcome step, demonstrating China's determination to improve protection of the Internet-based right of communication to the public while China continues its preparations for accession to the WIPO Internet treaties. This measure is not comprehensive, however. A number of gaps remain to be filled for China to meet the challenges of Internet piracy and fully implement the WIPO Internet treaties.

With respect to software piracy, China issued new rules during the run-up to the 2006 JCCT meeting that require computers to be pre-installed with licensed operating system software and government agencies to purchase only computers satisfying this requirement. Combined with ongoing implementation of previous JCCT commitments on software piracy, it is hoped that these rules will contribute to significant further reductions in industry losses due to software piracy, which were estimated to have declined from $1.48 billion in 2004 to $1.27 billion in 2005. Achieving sustained reductions in end-user software piracy will require more enforcement by China's authorities, followed by high profile publicity of fines and other remedies imposed.

In the customs area, the United States was encouraged in 2006 by the Customs Administration's increased efforts to provide effective enforcement against counterfeit and pirated goods destined for export. Nevertheless, the United States remains concerned about the rapid growth in infringing products originating from China (discussed in the Enforcement section below). The United States also remains concerned about various aspects of the Regulations on the Customs Protection of Intellectual Property Rights, issued by the State Council in December 2003, and the Customs Administration's May 2004 implementing rules.

Disposal of confiscated goods, for example, remains a problem under the implementing rules. Among other things, the implementing rules appear to mandate auction following removal of infringing features, rather than destruction of infringing goods not purchased by the right holder or used for public welfare. Allowing goods to re-enter the channels of commerce under these circumstances raises questions of consistency with provisions of the TRIPS Agreement and, in some cases, safety concerns. The United States raised these issues with China bilaterally and at the WTO in 2006, but so far China has not indicated that it will be addressing them.

The United States also remains concerned about a variety of weaknesses in China's legal framework that do not effectively deter, and may even encourage, certain types of infringing activity, such as the abusive registration of trademarks, the "squatting" of foreign company names and designs, the theft of trade secrets, the registration of other companies' trademarks as design patents and vice versa, the use of falsified or misleading license documents or company documentation to create the appearance of legitimacy in counterfeiting operations, and false indications of geographic origin of products. In 2006, the United States continued to discuss these and other problems with China and seek solutions for them.

In the pharmaceuticals sector, the United States continues to have a range of concerns. The United States has urged China to provide greater protection against unfair commercial use of undisclosed test and other data submitted by foreign pharmaceuticals companies seeking marketing approval for their products. The United States has also encouraged China to undertake a more robust system of patent linkage and to consider the adoption of a system of patent term restoration. In addition, built-in delays in China's marketing approval system for pharmaceuticals continue to create incentives for counterfeiting, as does China's inadequate regulatory oversight for the production of active pharmaceutical ingredients by domestic chemical manufacturers. In 2006, as in prior years, the United States sought to address all of these issues as part of its broader effort to work with China to improve China's regulatory regime for the pharmaceuticals sector.

Enforcement

The TRIPS Agreement requires China to ensure that enforcement procedures are available so as to permit effective action against any act of infringement of intellectual property rights covered by the TRIPS Agreement, including expeditious remedies to prevent infringement and remedies that constitute a deterrent to further infringement. Although the central government displayed strong leadership in modifying the full range of China's IPR laws and regulations in an effort to bring them into line with China's WTO commitments, effective IPR enforcement has not been achieved, and IPR infringement remains a serious problem throughout China. IPR enforcement is hampered by a lack of coordination among Chinese government ministries and agencies, a lack of training, the allocation of resources, a lack of transparency in the enforcement process and its outcomes, and local protectionism and corruption.

Despite repeated anti-piracy campaigns in China, an increasing number of civil IPR cases in Chinese courts and other efforts, overall piracy and counterfeiting levels in China remained unacceptably high in 2006. IPR infringement continued to affect products, brands and technologies from a wide range of industries, including films, music and sound recordings, publishing, business and entertainment software, pharmaceuticals, chemicals, information technology, apparel, athletic footwear, textile fabrics and floor coverings, consumer goods, food and beverages, electrical equipment, automotive parts and industrial products, among many others.

U.S. industry in 2006 continued to estimate that levels of piracy in China across all lines of copyright business range between 85 percent and 93 percent, indicating little or no improvement over 2005. Trade in pirated optical discs continues to thrive, supplied by both licensed and unlicensed factories and by smugglers. Small retail shops continue to be the major commercial outlets for pirated movies and music (and a wide variety of counterfeit goods), and roaming vendors offering cheap pirated discs continue to be visible in major cities across China. Piracy of books and journals and end-user piracy of business software also remain key concerns. In addition, Internet piracy is increasing, as is piracy over enclosed networks such as universities.

Although China made a commitment at the July 2005 JCCT meeting to take aggressive action against movie piracy, including enhanced enforcement for titles not yet authorized for distribution, right holders have monitored China's efforts and report little meaningful improvement in piracy of pre-release titles in several major cities. However, NCA began to undertake campaigns to combat Internet piracy in 2006. In addition, with the assistance of the Ministry of Education, NCA took initial steps to address textbook piracy on university campuses in late 2006. The continuation of these efforts, along with follow-up monitoring and consistent publicity, are needed to create lasting improvements.

China's widespread counterfeiting not only harms the business interests of foreign right holders, but also includes many products that pose a direct threat to the health and safety of consumers in the United States, China and elsewhere, such as pharmaceuticals, food and beverages, batteries, automotive parts, industrial equipment and toys, among many other products. At the same time, the harm from counterfeiting is not limited to right holders and consumers. China estimated its own annual tax losses due to counterfeiting at more than $3.2 billion in 2002, and this figure could only have grown in the ensuing years.

The United States places the highest priority on addressing the IPR protection and enforcement problems in China, and since 2004 it has devoted significant additional staff and resources, both in Washington and in Beijing, to address these problems. A domestic Chinese business constituency is also increasingly active in promoting IPR protection and enforcement. In fact, Chinese right holders own the vast majority of design patents, utility models, trademarks and plant varieties in China and have become the principal filers of invention patents. In addition, the vast majority of China's IPR enforcement efforts are undertaken at the behest of Chinese right holders seeking to protect their interests. Nevertheless, it is clear that there will continue to be a need for sustained efforts from the United States and other WTO Members and their industries, along with the devotion of considerable resources and political will to IPR protection and enforcement by the Chinese government, if significant improvements are to be achieved.

As in prior years, the United States worked with central and local government officials in China in 2006 in a determined and sustained effort to improve China's IPR enforcement, with a particular emphasis on the need for dramatically increased utilization of criminal remedies. A variety of U.S. agencies held regular bilateral discussions with their Chinese counterparts and have conducted numerous technical assistance programs for central and local government officials on TRIPS Agreement rules, enforcement methods, patent and trademark practices and procedures, transparency and rule of law issues. In addition, in 2006, the United States organized another annual roundtable meeting in China designed to bring together U.S. and Chinese government and industry officials. The United States also continued to use the IPR Working Group created at the April 2004 JCCT meeting and the JCCT process itself to press China for needed changes.

The United States' efforts have also benefited from cooperation with other WTO Members in seeking improvements in China's IPR enforcement, both in China and at the WTO during meetings of the TRIPS Council. For example, the United States, Japan and Switzerland made coordinated requests under Article

63.3 of the TRIPS Agreement in October 2005 in order to obtain more information about IPR infringement levels and enforcement activities in China and provide a better basis for assessing the effectiveness of China's efforts to improve IPR enforcement since China's accession to the WTO. In addition, the United States and the EC have increased coordination and information sharing on a range of China IPR issues over the last year. China's membership in the Asia Pacific Economic Cooperation Forum (APEC) also brings increased importance to APEC's work to develop regional IPR best practices.

The United States has also continued to pursue a comprehensive initiative to combat the enormous global trade in counterfeit and pirated goods, including exports of infringing goods from China to the United States and the rest of the world. That initiative, the Strategy Targeting Organized Piracy (STOP!), was announced in October 2004 and is a U.S. Government wide effort to stop fakes at the U.S. border, to empower U.S. businesses to secure and enforce their intellectual property rights in overseas markets, to expose international counterfeiters and pirates, to keep global supply chains free of infringing goods, to dismantle criminal enterprises that steal U.S. intellectual property and to reach out to like-minded U.S. trading partners in order to build an international coalition to stop counterfeiting and piracy worldwide.

China's share of infringing goods seized at the U.S. border increased from 69 percent in Fiscal Year 2005 to 81 percent in Fiscal Year 2006, with the value of infringing goods from China totaling more than $125 million. The continuing growth in both the absolute value and China's relative share of infringing goods seized at the border is a major challenge that calls for serious actions by the Chinese government.

China is making genuine efforts to improve IPR enforcement. U.S. industry has confirmed that some of China's special campaigns, such as the continuing "Mountain Eagle" campaign against trademark infringement crimes, have in fact resulted in increased arrests and seizures of infringing materials, although the disposition of seized goods and the outcomes of criminal cases remain largely obscured by a lack of transparency. The 2006 Action Plan announced that China will launch more of these "special crackdown efforts" with respect to various IPR infringement problems. The United States has urged China to use its implementation of the 2006 Action Plan as an opportunity to tackle emerging enforcement challenges, particularly the sale of pirated and counterfeit goods on the Internet. In addition, the United States has suggested that China use this opportunity to examine the potential benefits of specialized national IPR courts and prosecutors, providing faster trademark examination procedures and ensuring that the resources available to local administrative, police and judicial authorities charged with protecting and enforcing intellectual property rights are adequate to the task.

Nevertheless, despite its many positive efforts to improve IPR enforcement, China pursues other policies that continue to impede effective enforcement. China refuses to make needed changes to its legal framework that would facilitate the utilization of criminal remedies. These changes should be an important objective for China, given the lack of deterrence clearly evident in China's current enforcement regime, which relies too heavily on administrative enforcement. But, China continues to maintain counter-productive measures such as its high thresholds for criminal prosecution, which continue to constrain China's enforcement authorities while creating a "safe harbor" for substantial commercial-scale infringement. At the same time, China maintains market access barriers, such as import restrictions and restrictions on wholesale and retail distribution, which discourage and delay the introduction of a number of legitimate foreign products into China's market. These barriers create additional incentives for infringement of products like movies, video games and books and inevitably lead consumers to the black market, again compounding the severe problems already faced by China's enforcement authorities.

SERVICES BARRIERS

Until China's entry into the WTO, China's service sectors were among the most heavily regulated and protected sectors of the national economy. Foreign service providers were largely restricted to operations under the terms of selective "experimental" licenses. However, both as a matter of policy and as a result of its WTO commitments, China decided to significantly liberalize foreign investment in its service sectors. At present, the market for services, underdeveloped due to historical attitudes and policies, has significant growth potential in both the short and long term.

China's WTO commitments are designed to provide meaningful access for U.S. service providers. In its accession agreement, China committed to the substantial opening of a broad range of service sectors through the elimination of many existing limitations on market access at all levels of government, particularly in sectors of importance to the United States, such as banking, insurance, distribution, telecommunications and professional services. These commitments are far-reaching, particularly when compared to the services commitments of many other WTO Members.

China also made certain "horizontal" commitments, which apply to all sectors listed in its Services Schedule. The two most important of these cross-cutting commitments involve acquired rights and the licensing process. Under the acquired rights commitment, China agreed that the conditions of ownership, operation and scope of activities for a foreign company, as set out in the respective contractual or shareholder agreement or in a license establishing or authorizing the operation or supply of services by an existing foreign service supplier, will not be made more restrictive than they were on the date of China's accession to the WTO. In other words, if a foreign company had pre-WTO accession rights that went beyond the commitments made by China in its Services Schedule that company could continue to operate with those rights.

In the licensing area, prior to China's WTO accession, foreign companies in many sectors did not have an unqualified right to apply for a license to operate in China. They could only apply for a license if they first received an invitation from the relevant Chinese regulatory authorities, and even then the decision-making process lacked transparency and was subject to inordinate delay and discretion. In its accession agreement, China committed to licensing procedures that were streamlined, transparent and more predictable.

At present, many challenges remain in securing the benefits of China's services commitments. While China continued to keep pace nominally with the openings required by its WTO accession agreement, it also continued to maintain or erect terms of entry in some sectors that were so high or cumbersome as to prevent or discourage foreign suppliers from gaining market access. For example, excessive and often discriminatory capital requirements continued to restrict market entry for foreign suppliers in many sectors, such as insurance, banking, motor vehicle financing, securities, asset management, telecommunications, construction and freight forwarding, among others. In addition, in sectors such as insurance, banking and legal services, branching and related restrictions have been put into effect that raise concerns. In other sectors, such as construction services, problematic measures appear to be taking away previously acquired market access rights.

Meanwhile, the Administrative Licensing Law, which took effect in July 2004, has increased transparency in the licensing process, while reducing procedural obstacles and strengthening the legal environment for domestic and foreign enterprises. As a result, the licensing process in many sectors continued to proceed in a workman-like fashion in 2006, although concerns about unfair discrimination remained, particularly in the banking and insurance sectors. In addition, in some sectors, such as direct selling and telecommunications, the licensing process was characterized by inordinate delays.

Insurance Services

In its WTO accession agreement, China agreed to phase in expanded ownership rights for foreign companies, for the most part during the first three years of China's WTO membership. Upon China's accession to the WTO, foreign life insurers were to be permitted to hold 50 percent equity share in a joint venture; within two years of accession, foreign property, casualty and other non-life insurers were to be permitted to establish as a branch, joint venture or a wholly foreign-owned subsidiary; and, within three years of accession, or by December 11, 2004, foreign insurers handling large scale commercial risks, marine, aviation and transport insurance, and reinsurance were to be permitted 51 percent foreign equity share in a joint venture (with the right to establish as a wholly foreign-owned subsidiary within two more years). China further agreed that all foreign insurers would be permitted to expand the scope of their activities to include group, health and pension lines of insurance by December 11, 2004. In addition, China agreed to eliminate geographic restrictions on all types of insurance operations by December 11, 2004.

With regard to branching, China scheduled a WTO commitment to allow non-life firms to establish as a branch in China upon accession and to permit internal branching in accordance with the lifting of China's geographic restrictions. China further agreed that foreign insurers already established in China that were seeking authorization to establish branches or sub-branches would not have to satisfy the requirements applicable to foreign insurers seeking a license to enter China's market.

Shortly after China acceded to the WTO, the China Insurance Regulatory Commission (CIRC) issued several new insurance regulations, including ones directed at the regulation of foreign insurance companies. These regulations implemented many of China's commitments, but they also created problems in three critical areas – capitalization requirements, transparency and branching. In particular, China's capitalization requirements were significantly more exacting than those of other major economies, and they limited the ability of foreign insurers to make necessary joint venture arrangements. The regulations also continued to permit considerable bureaucratic discretion and to offer limited predictability to foreign insurers seeking to operate in China's market.

In May 2004, CIRC issued implementing rules, the Detailed Rules on the Regulations for the Administration of Foreign-Invested Insurance Companies. These rules lowered capital requirements for national licenses from RMB500 million ($62.5 million) to RMB200 million ($25 million) and for branch offices from RMB50 million ($6.25 million) to RMB20 million ($2.5 million). These changes have been welcomed by some U.S. insurers, but others still consider them to be too high. The rules also streamlined licensing application procedures and shortened approval times, although some procedures remain unclear. Meanwhile, the rules did not adequately address branching rights, as many aspects of this issue remain vague. The rules also did not address another issue that U.S. and other foreign insurers had begun to complain about – in practice, it appeared that Chinese insurers were being granted new branch approvals on a concurrent basis (more than one branch approval at a time), while foreign insurers had only received approvals on a consecutive basis (one branch approval at a time). In addition, while the rules provide some guidance regarding foreign insurers wishing to apply for approval to convert from a branch to a subsidiary, CIRC has continued to have difficulty adhering to its own regulatory requirement that it act on applications within 60 days, as long delays are routine.

By December 2004, in accordance with its WTO commitments, China had lifted all of its geographic restrictions on foreign insurers. China also took steps in 2005 to permit foreign insurers to offer health and group insurance as well as pension/corporate annuities and increased the 50 percent ceiling on foreign ownership of joint venture insurance brokerages to 51 percent. In 2006, with all geographic restrictions having been removed and most business scope restrictions lifted, the operations of foreign insurers in China continued to grow. Currently, 47 foreign insurers, including a large number of U.S. insurers, operate in China. Foreign insurers had nearly a 7 percent share of the national market (according to data through 2005), and they continued to capture encouraging market shares in major municipalities such as Beijing (20 percent), Shanghai (17 percent), Shenzhen (10 percent) and Guangzhou (9 percent).

Banking Services

In its WTO accession agreement, China committed to a five-year phase-in for banking services by foreign banks. Specifically, China agreed that, immediately upon its accession, it would allow U.S. and other foreign banks to conduct foreign currency business without any market access or national treatment limitations and conduct domestic currency business with foreign-invested enterprises and foreign individuals, subject to certain geographic restrictions. The ability of U.S. and other foreign banks to conduct domestic currency business with Chinese enterprises and individuals was to be phased in. Within two years after accession, foreign banks were also to be able to conduct domestic currency business with Chinese enterprises, subject to certain geographic restrictions, which were to be lifted gradually over the following three years. Within five years after accession, foreign banks were to be able to conduct domestic currency business with Chinese individuals, and all geographic restrictions were to be lifted. Foreign banks were also to be permitted to provide financial leasing services at the same time that Chinese banks were permitted to do so.

Shortly after China's accession to the WTO, the People's Bank of China (PBOC) issued regulations governing foreign-funded banks, along with implementing rules, which became effective February 1, 2002. The PBOC also issued several other related measures. Although these measures kept pace with the WTO commitments that China made, it became clear that the PBOC had decided to exercise extreme caution in opening up the banking sector. In particular, it imposed working capital requirements and other prudential rules that far exceeded international norms, both for the foreign banks' headquarters and branches, which made it more difficult for foreign banks to establish and expand their market presence in China. Many of these requirements, moreover, did not apply equally to foreign and domestic banks. For example, a foreign bank branch licensed to conduct business in all currencies for both corporate and individual clients had to satisfy an operating capital requirement of RMB500 million ($62.5 million), while a domestic bank branch with the same business scope needed only RMB300 million ($37.5 million) in operating capital. In addition, the PBOC allowed foreign-funded banks to open only one branch every 12 months.

In early 2004, following extensive engagement by the United States and other WTO Members, the PBOC reduced working capital requirements for various categories of foreign banks. With the issuance of the Implementing Rules for the Administrative Regulations on Foreign-Invested Financial Institutions later that year, the China Banking Regulatory Commission (CBRC) also removed the restriction that had limited foreign-funded banks to opening only one new branch every 12 months. Meanwhile, China kept up with its commitments regarding the lifting of geographic restrictions on foreign banks conducting domestic currency business with foreign enterprises and individuals and Chinese enterprises.

One area still raising concerns involves the establishment of Chinese-foreign joint banks. In the Services Schedule accompanying its WTO accession agreement, China agreed that qualified foreign financial institutions would be permitted to establish Chinese-foreign joint banks immediately after China acceded, and it did not schedule any limitation on the percentage of foreign ownership in these banks. To date, however, China has limited the sale of equity stakes in existing state-owned banks to a single foreign investor to 20 percent, while the total equity share of all foreign investors is limited to 25 percent.

By September 2006, despite high capital requirements and other impediments, 191 foreign banks, including a number of U.S. banks, reportedly had branches or representative offices in China, although only major banks have been large enough to satisfy the application requirements. In addition, the business that foreign banks were most eager to pursue in China – domestic currency business – had expanded tremendously, although China's regulatory authorities continued to shield domestic banks from foreign competition in some areas, such as by limiting product innovation by foreign banks. According to the PBOC and CBRC, the domestic currency business of U.S. and other foreign banks grew rapidly in the first two years after China's WTO accession, even though the banks' clients were then limited to foreign-invested enterprises and foreign individuals. Following the PBOC's December 2003 announcement that foreign banks would be permitted to conduct domestic currency business with Chinese enterprises subject to geographic restrictions allowed by China's WTO commitments, the growth in U.S. and other foreign banks' domestic currency business accelerated. By September 2006, the total assets of foreign banks in China reportedly had reached $105 billion, representing approximately 2 percent of total banking assets in China. In some coastal cities, the amount was higher. For example, in Shanghai, foreign banks' assets reportedly represented 12.4 percent of total banking assets in October 2005.

Notably, the five-year phase-in period for banking services by foreign banks was scheduled to end on December 11, 2006. By that time, China had committed to remove remaining geographic limitations and to allow foreign banks to conduct domestic currency business with Chinese individuals. Full implementation of these commitments should allow U.S. and other foreign banks to benefit tremendously from new business opportunities, and China should realize important benefits from having greater access to world-class banking services. In November 2006, however, the State Council issued the Regulations for the Administration of Foreign-Funded Banks. While the United States continues to work closely with

U.S. banks to assess these regulations, which are intended to implement China's December 11, 2006 commitments, these regulations have generated some immediate concerns. For example, the regulations mandate that only foreign-funded banks that have had a representative office in China for two years and that have total assets exceeding $10 billion can apply to incorporate in China. After incorporating, moreover, these banks only become eligible to offer full domestic currency services to Chinese individuals if they can demonstrate that they have operated in China for three years and have had two consecutive years of profits. The regulations also restrict the scope of activities that can be conducted by foreign banks seeking to operate in China through branches instead of through subsidiaries. In particular, the regulations restrict the domestic currency business of foreign bank branches. While foreign bank branches can continue to take deposits from, and make loans to, Chinese enterprises in domestic currency, they can only take domestic currency deposits of RMB1 million ($125,000) or more from Chinese individuals and cannot make any domestic currency loans to Chinese individuals. Foreign bank branches also cannot issue domestic currency credit cards to Chinese enterprises or Chinese individuals.

Securities Services

Pursuant to the terms of China's WTO accession agreement, foreign securities firms were to receive the right to form joint ventures for fund management upon China's accession to the WTO in December 2001, while joint ventures for securities underwriting were to be permitted within three years after accession.

The China Securities Regulatory Commission (CSRC) issued regulations on the establishment of joint venture fund management companies and securities underwriting by Chinese-foreign joint ventures shortly after China's WTO accession. China's decision to limit foreign partners to a minority stake of these joint ventures (49 percent for fund management and 33 percent for securities trading), however, continues to limit their appeal to leading foreign firms and only a handful of joint ventures have been formed. In addition, China continues to limit the security underwriting joint ventures to underwriting A-shares and to underwriting and trading government and corporate debt, B-shares and H-shares. In December 2005, CSRC instituted a moratorium on foreign investment in the securities sector, claiming the need to clean up domestic securities companies and further develop the sector.

The Chinese stock market performed well in 2006, and some observers were predicting that CSRC may lift the moratorium in the second half of 2007.

Since December 2002, China has allowed Qualified Foreign Institutional Investors (QFIIs) to trade in A-shares via special accounts opened at designated custodian banks. In 2006, prior stringent criteria were loosened considerably, allowing more foreign institutions to qualify as QFIIs. However, other requirements limit the extent to which QFIIs can trade in A-shares. In addition, by the end of 2006, CSRC had distributed over $9 billion of the $10 billion overall QFII quota, but had not indicated when it will increase the quota.

Financial Information Services

In its WTO accession agreement, China committed that, for the services included in its Services Schedule, the relevant regulatory authorities would be separate from and not accountable to, any service suppliers they regulated, with two specified exceptions. One of the services included in China's Services Schedule – and not listed as an exception – is the "provision and transfer of financial information, and financial data processing and related software by suppliers of other financial services."

Nevertheless, concerns have been raised that China has still not established an independent regulator in the financial information services sector. Xinhua, the Chinese state news agency, is both a major market competitor of, and the regulator of, foreign financial information service providers in China.

In September 2006, a major problem developed when Xinhua issued the Administrative Measures on News and Information Release by Foreign News Agencies within China. These rules abolished the Measures for Administering the Release of Economic Information in China by Foreign News Agencies and Their Information Subsidiaries, which had been issued in 1996. Among other things, under one aspect of the 2006 rules, which has not yet been implemented, Xinhua would preclude foreign providers of financial information services from contracting directly with, or providing financial information services directly to, domestic Chinese clients. Instead, foreign financial information service providers would have to operate through a Xinhua-designated agent, and the one agent designated to date is a Xinhua affiliate. These new restrictions do not apply to domestic financial information service providers and, in addition, contrast with the rights previously enjoyed by foreign information service providers since the issuance of the 1996 rules, well before China's accession to the WTO in December 2001.

In response to complaints from the United States and the European Union, China's Premier publicly promised in September 2006 that the new rules would not change how foreign financial information service providers did business in China. Shortly thereafter, Xinhua told foreign financial information service providers that the new rules would not be applied to them until after an implementing measure was issued, although Xinhua subsequently began to pressure foreign financial information service providers to comply with the new restrictions.

Credit Cards

In the Services Schedule accompanying its Protocol of Accession, China committed to remove market access limitations and provide national treatment for foreign suppliers providing "payment and money transmission services, including credit, charge, and debit cards," with this commitment becoming effective with regard to the RMB business of retail clients no later than December 11, 2006. China also extended this commitment to cover the provision and transfer of financial information, financial data processing and advisory, intermediation and other financial services auxiliary to payments and money transmission services.

Under its existing rules, China restricts access to its market by foreign credit card companies. The rules only permit a bank in China to issue a credit card with a foreign logo on it if the card is co-branded with the logo of China Union Pay (CUP), an entity created by the PBOC and owned by participating Chinese banks. In addition, all RMB transactions must be processed through CUP's network, while the network of the foreign credit card company is used only to process foreign currency transactions.

In the second half of 2006, a number of troubling proposals were attributed to CUP and apparently supported by the PBOC. The common theme of these proposals was that CUP would be designated as a monopoly provider of payment and money transmission services for Chinese consumers for RMB processing and that no other providers would be able to enter this market. To date, China has taken no steps to implement its commitment to open up its market to foreign credit card companies. China reportedly is in the process of drafting regulations in this area, but no drafts have been made publicly available.

Wholesaling Services and Commission Agents' Services

In its WTO accession agreement, China committed to provide national treatment and eliminate market access restrictions for foreign enterprises seeking to provide wholesaling and commission agents' services and related services, such as repair and maintenance services, through a local presence within three years of China's accession (or by December 11, 2004), subject to limited product exceptions. In the interim, China agreed to progressively liberalize its treatment of these services pursuant to a set schedule. The phase-in of these services was supposed to start with minority foreign-owned joint ventures by December 11, 2002, followed by majority foreign-owned joint ventures by December 11, 2003.

Shortly after acceding to the WTO, China fell behind in its implementation of the required progressive liberalization, as foreign enterprises continued to face a variety of restrictions. It was not until mid-2004, following high-level U.S. engagement that China began to take steps to liberalize. At that time, MOFCOM issued regulations providing national treatment and eliminating market access restrictions on joint ventures providing wholesaling services and commission agents' services. These regulations also established a timetable for extending this liberalization to wholly foreign-owned enterprises on December 11, 2004.

While these regulations were welcome, MOFCOM was very slow to implement them, and it still has not implemented them fully. Initially, MOFCOM did not issue any guidance regarding how its approval system would operate, and the application process remained opaque. In most instances, the application process turned into a protracted negotiation, as the central and local approving authorities were still in the process of determining the appropriate procedures and documentation requirements. When approvals were issued, moreover, the central and local approving authorities imposed a variety of restrictions, such as limits on the scope of products that could be distributed and limits on the specific services that could be supplied. Registered capital requirements have also varied.

In addition, through the first six months of 2005, the Chinese authorities rarely issued approvals for existing enterprises seeking to expand their business scope to include wholesale distribution, in part because the Chinese authorities were sorting out historical tax treatment and Free Trade Zone (FTZ) issues. The Chinese authorities did issue some approvals for the establishment of new wholesale distribution enterprises, but this route did not make business sense for many enterprises already established in China.

By June 2005, the Chinese authorities had begun to make progress in resolving many of the problems that had plagued the application and approval process, including how it would handle the tax and FTZ issues that had stalled many enterprises' applications. In July 2005, MOFCOM and the General Administration of Customs (Customs Administration) issued the Circular on Issues Concerning the Trade Administration of Bonded Zones and Bonded Logistics Parks, which clarified the handling of applications from enterprises located in FTZs. At the July 2005 JCCT meeting, China also committed to improve the transparency of the application and approval process. Consistent with this commitment, in September 2005, MOFCOM issued the Application and Approval Guidelines for Foreign Investments, which clarify many aspects of the application and approval process. Some improvements subsequently took place in the application and approval process, but it was not until MOFCOM issued the Notice on Entrusting National Economic and Technological Development Zones with the Authority to Approve Foreign-Funded Distribution Firms and International Forwarding Agents in February 2006 that the problems with the application and approval process largely disappeared. With the issuance of that measure, MOFCOM devolved the right to grant distribution licenses from the central authorities to provincial-level authorities, making the application and approval process more efficient and less time-consuming, although some technical challenges remain with regard to, for example, manufacturing enterprises seeking to expand the scope of their business to include distribution activities.

These developments have enabled U.S. companies to improve the efficiency of their China supply chain management, and as a result many of them are restructuring their legal entities to integrate their China operations into their global business more fully and efficiently. At the same time, U.S. companies in some industries continue to have concerns with regard to product and services restrictions that China has yet to remove.

U.S. industry remains seriously concerned about continuing restrictions on the rights of foreign enterprises to engage in wholesale (and retail) distribution of books, newspapers, periodicals, electronic publications and audio and video products. Some measures, such as the April 2004 distribution services regulations, purport to allow foreign enterprises to engage in wholesale (and retail) distribution of these products. However, a host of other measures appear to impose market access or national treatment limitations, such as the State Council's April 2005 Several Opinions on Canvassing Foreign Investment into the Cultural Sector; NDRC's November 2004 Catalogue for the Guidance of Foreign Investment Industries; the Provisions on the Administration of the Publication Market, issued by the General

Administration of Press and Publication (GAPP) in June 2004; the Rule on Management of Foreign-Invested Book, Magazine and Newspaper Distribution Enterprises, issued by GAPP and MOFTEC in March 2003; and the Administrative Regulations on Electronic Publications, issued by GAPP in December 1997. Under these measures, for some of the products at issue, distribution is limited to Chinese state-owned enterprises. For others, only Chinese-foreign joint ventures with minority foreign ownership are permitted to engage in distribution or foreign enterprises face restrictive requirements not imposed on domestic enterprises.

China began to implement several measures governing the distribution of automobiles by foreign enterprises in 2005, including the Implementing Rules for the Administration of Brand-Specific Automobile Dealerships, jointly issued by MOFCOM, the NDRC and the State Administration for Industry and Commerce (SAIC) in February 2005. The NDRC followed up with the Rules for Auto External Marks in November 2005, and MOFCOM issued the Implementing Rules for the Evaluation of Eligibility of Auto General Distributors and Brand-specific Dealers in January 2006. While U.S. industry has generally welcomed these measures, they do contain some restrictions on foreign enterprises that may not be applied to domestic enterprises.

China delayed the implementation of its wholesale distribution services commitments with regard to pharmaceuticals, despite the fact that the exception for pharmaceuticals contained in China's accession agreement expired as of December 11, 2004. Although the April 2004 distribution services regulations indicated that separate regulations would be issued for the pharmaceuticals sector, China did not issue any further regulations and continued to require foreign pharmaceutical companies to sell their finished products through Chinese wholesalers (after hiring Chinese importers to bring their finished products into the country) through the remainder of 2004 and the first half of 2005. In the second half of 2005, China began allowing the acceptance of applications from foreign pharmaceutical companies for wholesale distribution licenses under the April 2004 distribution services regulations and the State Food and Drug Administration's Rules on the Management of Drug Business Licenses. Since then, U.S. and other foreign pharmaceutical companies have been able to obtain wholesale distribution licenses. However, it appears that some provincial-level authorities have not yet begun issuing these licenses because of uncertainty generated by the provision in the April 2004 distribution services regulations indicating that MOFCOM would issue separate regulations covering pharmaceuticals. At the same time, despite overall progress in this area, many other restrictions affecting the pharmaceuticals sector make it difficult for foreign pharmaceutical companies to realize the full benefits of China's wholesale distribution commitments. The United States continues to engage the Chinese regulatory authorities in these areas as part of an effort to promote comprehensive reform of China's healthcare system and to reduce unnecessary trade barriers.

U.S. industry remains concerned about the uncertainty created by the provision in the April 2004 distribution services regulations that allows the local approving authorities to withhold wholesale (and retail) distribution license approvals when, as is the case in most cities, urban commercial network plans have not yet been formulated. This provision could operate as a *de facto* restriction on the operations of foreign wholesalers (and retailers).

In early December 2006, China issued the Measures for the Administration of the Market for Crude Oil and the Measures for the Administration of the Market for Refined Oil Products. These measures are intended to implement China's significant market-opening WTO commitments, scheduled for December 11, 2006, to permit foreign enterprises to engage in wholesale distribution of crude oil and processed oil (e.g., gasoline), in China. China's full implementation of these commitments would allow U.S. industry to begin to take advantage of China's earlier, partial opening of the retail distribution sector to foreign enterprises. However, these regulations impose high thresholds and other potential impediments on foreign enterprises seeking to enter the wholesale distribution sector, such as requirements relating to levels of storage capacity, pipelines, rail lines, docks and supply contracts. These requirements appear designed to maintain the monopolies enjoyed by state-owned China National Petroleum Corporation and China Petrochemical Corporation.

Retailing Services

In 1999, the Chinese government broadened the scope for foreign investment in the retail sector. New regulations encouraged the entry of large international retailers (such as hypermarkets and warehouse-style stores) into China. China's subsequent WTO commitments were designed to further expand the ability of foreign retailers to enter the market through a much wider range of modalities. China committed to allow 100 percent foreign ownership of smaller retail operations, some large retail operations, gas stations and even car dealerships within three years to five years of China's December 2001 WTO accession, although certain types of large retail operations could still face ownership limitations.

As in the area of wholesaling and commission agents' services, China fell behind in its implementation of the required progressive liberalization of retailing services shortly after acceding to the WTO, as foreign enterprises continued to face a variety of restrictions. China only began to take steps to liberalize in mid2004, when MOFCOM issued regulations providing national treatment and eliminating market access restrictions on joint ventures supplying retailing services. These regulations also established a timetable for extending this liberalization to wholly foreign-owned enterprises on December 11, 2004.

Many of the same problems that plagued the application and approval process for wholesaling and commission agents' services also arose in the area of retailing services. The changes that took place in the application and approval process in 2005 helped to improve the situation, but it was MOFCOM's issuance of the Notice on Entrusting National Economic and Technological Development Zones with the Authority to Approve Foreign-Funded Distribution Firms and International Forwarding Agents in February 2006 that made the problems with the application and approval process largely disappear.

U.S. industry continues to have concerns with regard to the provision in the April 2004 distribution services regulations allowing the approving authorities to withhold retail distribution license approvals when, as is the case in many cities, urban commercial network plans have not yet been formulated. It appears that China may be applying this provision in a discriminatory manner. In April 2006, MOFCOM issued a notice explaining that foreign-invested enterprises would not be granted approvals for projects in cities that had not yet finalized their urban commercial network plans, while it appears that domestic enterprises continue to receive approvals for their projects.

Meanwhile, it appears that China may not be fully implementing its commitment to allow foreign enterprises to sell gasoline at the retail level. Although China's retail services commitments initially did not apply to processed oil, as it was one of the excepted goods under China's Services Schedule, that exception expired on December 11, 2004, and by that time China committed to permit wholly foreign-owned enterprises to operate gas stations. However, according to some recent reports, China is now claiming that gas stations fall under the chain store provision in its Services Schedule, which applies to "those chain stores which sell products of different types and brands from multiple suppliers with more than 30 outlets" and permits only joint ventures with minority foreign ownership.

Franchising Services

As part of its services commitments, China committed to permit the cross-border supply of franchising services immediately upon its accession to the WTO. It also committed to permit foreign enterprises to provide franchising services in China, without any market access or national treatment limitations, by December 11, 2004. In December 2004, MOFCOM issued new rules governing the supply of franchising services in China, the Measures for the Administration of Commercial Franchises, which became effective in February 2005. These rules raised a number of concerns. Of particular concern is a requirement that a franchiser own and operate at least two units in China for one year before being eligible to offer franchises in China. The business models of many U.S. franchising companies, including some large hotel chains, are adversely affected by this requirement because they do not own and operate units, instead relying exclusively on franchisees to distribute goods and services. The rules also impose high capital requirements and require broad and vague information disclosure by franchisers, with uncertain liability if these disclosure requirements are not met. Following U.S. Government and U.S. industry requests that China address these issues by revising the December 2005 franchising rules, China reported in November 2006 that revised franchising rules had been submitted to the State Council for review and would be issued in due course.

Sales Away from a Fixed Location

In 1998, China banned all direct selling activities (or sales away from a fixed location) after some foreign and domestic firms used direct selling techniques to operate fraudulent pyramid schemes and other less-than-legitimate operations disguised as direct selling to bilk participants. No U.S. firms were implicated in these schemes. Meanwhile, some large U.S. and other foreign direct selling firms were allowed to continue operating in China after altering their business models. In its WTO accession agreement, China committed to the resumption of direct selling activities by December 2004.

In August and September 2005, nine months overdue, the Chinese authorities issued the measures designed to implement China's direct selling commitments – the Measures for the Administration of Direct Selling and the Regulations on the Administration of Anti-Pyramid Sales Scams. These measures became effective on December 1, 2005, and contained several problematic provisions. For example, one provision outlaws practices allowed in every country in which the U.S. industry operates – reportedly 170 countries in all – by refusing to allow direct selling enterprises to pay compensation based on team sales, where upstream personnel are compensated based on downstream sales. In addition, there is a cap limiting the amount of compensation based on sales revenue to 30 percent, which inhibits direct selling companies from employing compensation as a tool to motivate their sales representatives. Other problematic provisions in the 2005 measures include onerous and vague requirements to establish fixed location "service centers" in each urban district where direct sellers operate; a three-year experience requirement that only applies to foreign enterprises, not domestic ones; restrictions on the cross-border supply of direct selling services; limited product categories permitted for direct sales; and high capital requirements that may limit smaller direct sellers' access to the market. The measures also impose burdensome education and certification requirements for salespersons and trainers, forbidding foreigners from working in either capacity.

In September 2006, China issued implementing rules governing the establishment of direct selling service centers. These rules, while clarifying some aspects of the earlier measures, also include vague provisions that could lead to undue local requirements being placed on service centers. The rules should streamline service center requirements at the national level.

Under the 2005 measures, a direct selling company must receive approvals from both MOFCOM and SAIC before beginning operations. MOFCOM issued its first direct selling license approval under the 2005 measures in February 2006 and had approved 15 licenses to Chinese and foreign companies by the end of 2006. Despite this progress, the MOFCOM licensing process has been characterized by a lack of transparency and significant delays. The 2005 measures establish a 90-day license approval process, but most of the MOFCOM approvals took between 4 months and 11 months. In addition, according to U.S. industry, more than 20 companies that applied for direct selling licenses in early 2006 are still awaiting approval, with little clarity on timing or process. The scope of licenses approved by MOFCOM has also been limited, with only three companies approved to conduct direct selling in more than one province in China. Meanwhile, few companies have received the SAIC approval necessary to begin operations.

Express Delivery Services

Beginning in December 2001, the State Postal Bureau (together with MOFTEC and MII) issued restrictive measures that could have jeopardized market access that foreign express delivery firms (which were then required to operate as joint ventures with Chinese partners) enjoyed prior to China's accession. These measures threatened to curtail the scope of operations of foreign express delivery firms licensed prior to China's accession to the WTO, despite China's horizontal commitment on acquired rights. Specifically, a measure issued in December 2001 required firms wishing to deliver letters to apply for entrustment with China Post. A second measure, issued in February 2002, extended China Post's monopoly on letters by creating weight and rate restrictions on letter deliveries by private firms. Following high-level U.S. interventions, in September 2002, a third measure eliminated the weight and rate restrictions on letter deliveries and streamlined the entrustment application procedure. Two major

U.S. express delivery firms subsequently applied for and obtained entrustment certificates from China Post.

In July 2003, however, China circulated draft amendments to its Postal Law that generated two immediate concerns among U.S. companies. First, the draft amendments purported to give China Post a monopoly over the delivery of letters under 500 grams, which would have constituted a new restriction on the scope of activities of existing foreign-invested express delivery companies, raising concerns in light of China's horizontal acquired rights commitment. Second, the draft amendments did not address the need for an independent regulator.

In September, October and November 2003, China circulated new sets of draft Postal Law amendments. While each set of draft amendments included a different definition of the China Post monopoly, the most recent draft amendments continued to provide China Post with a monopoly on letters weighing less than 500 grams. They also included other problematic provisions. For example, they appeared to create a new, more burdensome licensing process, and they seemed to require express couriers to pay a percentage of their revenue from the delivery of letters into a universal service fund.

In April 2004, following high-level U.S. engagement urging China not to cut back on the scope of activities that foreign-invested express delivery companies had been licensed to provide prior to China's WTO accession, Vice Premier Wu Yi committed that old problems, like the weight restriction, would not resurface as new problems. In July 2004, however, the State Council circulated another set of draft amendments to the postal services law. Despite Vice Premier Wu's commitment, these draft amendments continued to include a weight restriction, now reduced from 500 grams to 350 grams and did little to address other U.S. concerns.

In April 2006, as more reports began to surface of problematic provisions in subsequent drafts of the Postal Law, Vice Premier Wu Yi reiterated China's commitment that the regulatory environment for express delivery services by foreign companies would not be negatively impacted by the issuance of new rules, including the Postal Law. Later in 2006, however, China began to circulate an "eighth" draft of the Postal Law among Chinese stakeholders, and this draft continued to generate serious concerns. Although this draft has not been officially released, it reportedly would impose a minimum weight restriction on addressed letters weighing less than 150 grams, exclude foreign service providers from the domestic express delivery market and impose a tax to fund universal mail service in China. When the United States raised concerns about this "eighth" draft both bilaterally and at the WTO in October 2006 and November 2006, Chinese government officials responded that the draft is undergoing major revisions.

Meanwhile, in August 2006, the State Council began implementing its July 2005 plan to separate China's postal operations from the administrative function of regulating China's postal system, with the State Postal Administration (SPA) to serve as the regulator and a new state-owned enterprise – the China Post Group Corporation – to be set up to conduct postal business. Although the July 2005 plan has still not been released to the public, SPA announced the establishment of 31 provincial-level Postal Management Bureaus to assist in the regulatory effort in September 2006. The China Post Group Corporation was established in January 2007.

Construction, Engineering, Architectural and Contracting Services

Prior to China's WTO accession, U.S. construction, engineering and architectural firms and U.S. contractors enjoyed a relatively cooperative and open relationship with the Chinese government. These firms operated in the Chinese market through joint venture arrangements and were less affected by regulatory problems than other service sectors. Nevertheless, they also faced restrictions. It was difficult for foreign firms to obtain licenses to perform services except on a project-by-project basis. Foreign firms also faced severe partnering and bidding restrictions.

In September 2002, the Ministry of Construction and MOFTEC jointly issued Decrees 113 and 114, which opened up construction and related construction design services to joint ventures with majority foreign ownership and, two years ahead of schedule, wholly foreign-owned enterprises. At the same time, however, these decrees created concerns for U.S. and other foreign firms by imposing new and more restrictive conditions than existed prior to China's WTO accession, when they were permitted to work in China on a project-by-project basis pursuant to Ministry of Construction rules. In particular, these decrees for the first time required foreign firms to obtain qualification certificates, effective October 2003. In addition, these decrees for the first time required foreign-invested firms supplying construction services to incorporate in China, and they imposed high minimum registered capital requirements and foreign personnel residency requirements that are difficult for many foreign firms to satisfy. In consultation with

U.S. industry, the United States, in a high-level intervention, pressed its concerns about Decrees 113 and 114 and sought a delay before the decrees' problematic requirements would become effective. In September 2003, the Ministry of Construction agreed to extend the implementation date from October 2003 until April 2004 so the concerns of foreign firms could be analyzed further.

In April 2004, Decree 113 went into effect. However, in September 2004, the Ministry of Construction and MOFCOM issued Circular 159, which permitted foreign providers of construction services and related construction engineering design services to continue operating on a project by-project basis until July 2005, effectively extending the effective date of the incorporation-related requirements.

Decree 114 implementing rules were released and became effective in January 2007. These rules allow the Chinese authorities to begin accepting applications from foreign-invested enterprises, including wholly foreign-owned enterprises, seeking to provide engineering, integrated engineering and architectural services. The rules also make several positive regulatory changes, including the temporary lifting of foreign personnel staffing and residency requirements for foreign-invested design companies.

Meanwhile, in November 2004, the Ministry of Construction issued the Provisional Measures for Construction Project Management (known as Decree 200), which became effective in December 2004. Among other things, Decree 200 appears to preclude the same company from providing construction services and related construction engineering design services if it also provides project management services on the same project. This aspect of the decree raises concerns because U.S. companies often provide all of these services in combination when working on a project in a foreign market. No implementing regulations for Decree 200 have been issued.

Transportation and Logistics Services

The transportation and logistics sector has in the past faced severe regulatory restrictions, high costs, dominance by government-invested agents and limitations on permitted activities. The multiple government bodies responsible for this sector include the Ministry of Communications, the Ministry of Railways, MOFCOM, NDRC and the Civil Aviation Administration of China. Overlapping jurisdictions, multiple sets of approval requirements and opaque regulations hinder market access. In some areas, domestic firms have also used government connections and investments to monopolize the sector.

Nevertheless, like China's own reform policies, China's WTO commitments support a broad opening of the transportation and logistics sector to foreign service providers, to be phased in over time. Foreign firms should be able to invest freely in warehousing, road freight transport, rail freight transport and freight forwarding companies within three years to six years after WTO accession, depending on the sector.

In July 2002, MOFCOM's predecessor, MOFTEC, issued a Notice on Establishing Foreign-Invested Logistics Companies in Trial Regions. This notice allows foreign-invested logistics companies (with up to 50 percent foreign ownership and registered capital of $5 million) to establish in several designated cities. U.S. firms have expressed concern about the high capital requirement and the 50 percent cap on foreign ownership, which may conflict with China's WTO commitments for certain types of logistics services.

In November 2002, China issued regulations allowing majority foreign ownership of road transportation firms, as it was required to do within one year of its WTO accession. China was also obligated to issue regulations allowing majority foreign-owned joint ventures to enter the fields of packaging services, storage and warehousing, and freight forwarding one year after its accession; it issued timely regulations allowing 75 percent foreign-owned joint ventures in these fields.

China took a significant step in July 2004 to increase market access for U.S. passenger and cargo carriers by signing a landmark amendment to the aviation agreement with the United States. The amended agreement will more than double the number of U.S. airlines operating in China and will increase by five times the number of flights providing passenger and cargo services between the two countries over the next six years. The agreement also allows each country's carriers to serve any city in the other country, provides for unlimited code-sharing between them, expands opportunities for charter operators, and eliminates government regulation of pricing as of 2008. U.S. passenger and cargo carriers have since obtained additional routes and increased flight frequencies, as envisioned by the agreement. Meanwhile, an important commitment enshrined in the July 2004 agreement calls for the commencement of negotiations toward further liberalization through a bilateral Open Skies Agreement. The first round of these negotiations took place in April 2006. However, China subsequently postponed the second round of negotiations. In December 2006, at the inaugural meeting of U.S.-China Strategic Economic Dialogue (SED) in Beijing, the United States and China agreed to resume work toward liberalization of the aviation relationship with the mutually agreed goal of making meaningful progress in time for the second SED meeting, tentatively scheduled for May 2007. U.S. and Chinese civil aviation delegations resumed negotiations in January 2007.

In 2003, China took steps to liberalize the maritime services sector despite having made limited WTO commitments. The United States and China signed a far-reaching, five-year bilateral maritime agreement, which gave U.S.-registered companies the legal flexibility to perform an extensive range of additional shipping and logistics activities in China. U.S. shipping and container transport services companies, along with their subsidiaries, affiliates and joint ventures are also able to establish branch offices in China without geographic limitation.

In April 2005, AQSIQ issued the Criteria for the Classification and Assessment of Logistics Firms. Under this measure, AQSIQ uses a firm's business and financial situation, equipment, operating infrastructure, management, services provided and human resource information as of the time of its business license application in order to classify the firm into one of three broad categories: transport, warehouse or multi-service, for regulatory purposes. Some firms have criticized this measure as creating "hastily formulated standards" that inappropriately restrict the business scope of logistics firms and have also complained about unnecessary and burdensome requirements. In addition, freight forwarding firms are concerned about not being included in one of the three logistics business categories, particularly because it may prevent their participation in relevant standards-setting activities.

Telecommunications

In its WTO accession agreement, China made important commitments in the area of telecommunications services. It agreed to permit foreign suppliers to provide a broad range of services through joint ventures with Chinese companies, including domestic and international wired services, mobile voice and data services, value-added services, such as electronic mail, voice mail and on-line information and database retrieval, and paging services. The foreign stake permitted in the joint ventures is to increase over time, reaching a maximum of 49 percent for most types of services. In addition, China agreed to eliminate all geographical restrictions within two to six years after its WTO accession, depending on the particular service sector.

Importantly, when it acceded to the WTO, China also accepted key regulatory principles from the WTO Reference Paper. As a result, China became obligated to separate the regulatory and operating functions of MII (which had been both the telecommunications regulatory agency in China and the operator of China Telecom) upon its accession and to implement its regulations in an impartial manner. Since China's accession, MII has spun-off China Telecom, which now competes in the market with other telecommunications operators. While the formal separation of regulator and operator has occurred, evidence of continued MII influence over operational decisions of the telecommunications operators (e.g., relating to personnel, corporate organization and standards) suggests that regulatory independence may be far from complete. The current regulator, MII, is not structured as an independent entity as it still bears the responsibility to help develop China's information technology and telecommunications manufacturing industries.

China is also obligated to adopt pro-competitive regulatory principles, such as transparent licensing, cost-based pricing and the right of interconnection, which are necessary for foreign-invested joint ventures to compete against established operators. China appears laggard in implementing these commitments, however. For example, there is no sign that "major suppliers" in China have made their interconnection arrangements public. With practically no foreign participation in the market, it has been difficult to assess compliance with such commitments. This very lack of foreign participation, however, is indicative of a licensing regime that has not been conducive to foreign investment, in part due to a lack of transparency.

China's Regulations on Foreign-Invested Telecommunications Enterprises went into effect in January 2002. These regulations define registered-capital requirements, equity caps, requirements for Chinese and foreign partners, and licensing procedures. The regulations stipulate that foreign-invested telecommunications enterprises can undertake either basic or value-added telecommunications services. Foreign ownership may not exceed 49 percent in the case of basic telecommunications services (excluding wireless paging) and 50 percent in the case of value-added services (including wireless paging, which is otherwise categorized as a basic service). While China committed to giving foreign applicants freedom to choose potential joint venture partners, it appears that MII is interpreting requirements regarding technical qualifications to effectively exclude all but incumbent operators, foreclosing additional competition in the market. For foreign operators interested in offering international services, requirements to use a gateway operated by a state-owned operator appear excessive and unjustified. The capitalization requirement established for new entrants, which exceeds \$240 million, is another major impediment to market access. There appears to be no justification for such a requirement, particularly for companies interested in leasing, rather than building facilities, while specific licensing terms for resale-based operators do not appear to exist. Meanwhile, MII continues to process applications very slowly for the few foreign-invested telecommunications enterprises that have attempted to satisfy MII's licensing requirements. The results have been predictable: no new joint ventures appear to have been formed in the basic telecommunications sector since China introduced the January 2002 regulations.

At times, MII has also changed applicable rules without notice and without transparency. For example, in February 2003, MII announced a reclassification of certain basic and value-added telecommunications services effective in April 2003. No public comment period was provided. This move limited the ability of U.S. firms to access China's telecommunications market because basic services are on a slower liberalization schedule and are subject to lower foreign equity limits and higher capitalization requirements.

Little progress has been made in opening the market for value-added services, such as Internet service and content providers. MII announced moves toward convergence in voice, video and data services in 2000, but China considers information content sensitive, so foreign companies face significant barriers in the Internet services sector. Although more foreign companies are registering ".com.cn" websites in China, these sites are still often blocked, which hinders companies' abilities to maintain a stable Internet presence. The requirement that Internet service providers (ISPs) must provide user login information and transaction records to authorities upon request, without clear guidelines as to the circumstances and situations that warrant such actions, raises concerns about consumer privacy and prevention of data misuse. Meanwhile, even though China has now completed its fifth year of WTO membership, the United States is aware of only one application for a license to provide value-added services that has completed the MII licensing process. That license was awarded to a Chinese-Korean joint venture in 2005.

Foreign equity investment limitations for ISPs and Internet content providers (ICPs) mirror the timetable for value-added services in China's WTO accession agreement (30 percent upon accession, 49 percent within one year after accession and 50 percent within two years after accession). However, ICPs must still win the approval of MII and/or local telecommunications administrations depending on the geographic coverage of their services before they can receive foreign capital, cooperate with foreign businesses, or attempt domestic or overseas stock listings. Their services, including even simple commercial websites, are also subject to excessive capitalization requirements that bear little relation to any legitimate licensing goals.

In 2004, a draft of the long-awaited Telecommunications Law began to circulate among Chinese ministries and agencies. If China takes the initiative, this law could be a vehicle for addressing existing market access barriers and other problematic aspects of China's current telecommunications regime. The current status and content of this legislation is unclear, despite repeated U.S. efforts to obtain this information.

Meanwhile, even though China committed in its WTO accession agreement that further liberalization of this sector would be discussed in the current round of WTO negotiations, China has yet to make an improved services offer. With the modest telecommunications commitments made by China in its WTO accession agreement having so far failed to facilitate effective market entry for foreign firms, further liberalization, bound through the current round of WTO negotiations, appears critical to improving market access prospects for this sector.

At the April 2006 JCCT meeting, China committed to make appropriate adjustments to its registered capital requirements for telecommunications service providers. However, to date, Chinese regulators have taken no steps to adjust capitalization levels, nor have they provided any information on the timing, scope or level of any planned adjustments. China's continued imposition of excessive capital requirements, taken together with MII's reclassification of value-added services as basic services and MII's slow license application process, has kept in place formidable barriers to market entry for foreign enterprises.

On-Line Services

China operates the world's most comprehensive and technologically advanced Internet filtering regime. Chinese authorities routinely filter Internet traffic entering China, focusing primarily on the content they deem objectionable on political, social or religious grounds. In 2002, China lifted filters on most major western news sites. Nevertheless, since then, foreign news websites have periodically been blocked, as happened, for example, for several weeks during the 16th National Congress of the Communist Party of China in 2003. More generally, according to a Harvard University study published in 2002, China had still blocked 19,032 sites on multiple occasions. This study was updated in 2005, and identified routinely blocked sites that relate to Taiwan, the Falun Gong spiritual movement, Tibet, the Tiananmen Square incident and Chinese opposition political parties. The updated study also identified routinely blocked sites that relate to various political topics including "boycott," "human rights," "pro-democracy" and "opposition."

Changes to Internet filtering can occur without warning or public explanation. For example, the popular Internet search engine Google was blocked completely in China for a few weeks starting in late August 2002. When Google became available again in September 2002, its "cached pages" feature remained blocked; that feature had previously allowed users in China to access "snapshots" of some web pages that were otherwise blocked in China.

While all of these practices remain prevalent, the updated study found that China's filtering regime had become more targeted and fine-tuned than in 2002. For example, sites relating to specific topics such as Falun Gong and the Tiananmen Square incident were less accessible in 2005 while sites relating vaguely to topics such as revolution and Taiwan were more accessible. Few, if any, websites related strictly to economic and business matters, however, are blocked.

China's Internet regulation regime is exceedingly complex. Internet content restrictions for ICPs, electronic commerce sites and application service providers located in China are governed by a number of measures, not all of which are public. Since 2000, these measures have increased greatly, and it is reported that at least 12 government entities have authority over Internet access and content. Some of these measures restrict who may report news and place limits on what exactly may constitute news. The most important of these measures was issued in September 2000 and updated in September 2005. In addition to interfering with news reporting in the traditional sense, this measure may provide a basis for Chinese authorities to interfere with the normal business reporting operations of non-news organizations, such as multinational corporations, if they use the Internet to keep clients, members, their headquarters and other interested parties informed about events in China.

In March 2002, the Internet Society of China established a "Public Pledge on Self-Discipline for the China Internet Industry." This group is nominally private but is affiliated with China's Ministry of Information Industry and currently has more than 200 members. Signatories commit to "refrain from producing, posting or disseminating pernicious information that may jeopardize state security and disrupt social stability, contravene laws and regulations and spread superstition and obscenity." Reportedly, 130 major Internet portals have since signed the pledge.

Audio-Visual Services

Shortly after acceding to the WTO in December 2001, China issued the Regulations on the Administration of Audio-Visual Products and the Regulations on the Management of Film, both of which went into effect on February 1, 2002. These regulations were designed to bring more order and transparency to the audio-visual and film industries, with the objective of moving toward greater commercial efficiency in accordance with domestic reform efforts and China's WTO commitments.

Despite these positive moves and various subsequently issued regulations that provided incrementally more market access, China's desire to protect the revenues earned by the state-owned movie and print media importers and distributors, and China's concerns about politically sensitive materials, result in continued restrictions on foreign providers of audio-visual services. For example, importation and distribution of sound recordings, videos, films, books and journals remain highly restricted. Inconsistent and subjective application of censorship regulations further impedes market growth for foreign providers.

In July 2004, the State Administration for Radio, Film and TV (SARFT) issued the Rules for the Administration of China-Foreign Cooperation in Filmmaking. These rules cover filmmaking and provide for joint Chinese-foreign filmmaking cooperatives, with licenses required for both the cooperative and the Chinese partner. In October 2004, SARFT and MOFCOM issued the Provisional Rules on the Access Requirements for Film. These rules cover film production, distribution, screening and imports by domestic firms, and film production and screenings involving foreign firms. All firms engaged in these businesses are subject to SARFT licensing. Foreign firms are allowed to form joint ventures and cooperative firms engaged in film production, technology and equipment. Joint ventures or cooperative firms must have at least RMB5 million ($625,000) of registered capital, and foreign capital cannot make up more than 49 percent of the total share.

The Chinese government limits the number of foreign films allowed to enter China each year on a revenue-sharing basis. China currently allows in 20 foreign films per year (up from ten foreign films per year through much of the 1990s) on a revenue-sharing basis pursuant to a commitment that it made upon acceding to the WTO. However, China treats its WTO commitment as a ceiling, rather than a floor, which artificially increases demand for pirated products. Furthermore, lengthy censorship reviews by Chinese authorities at times can delay the arrival of legitimately imported foreign films on Chinese movie screens. When the films do make it through the censorship process, they have sometimes been subject to blackout viewing periods during national holidays and other times. China's large black market for foreign DVDs and other home entertainment video products continues to grow because these market access restrictions create a demand for pirated goods in the absence of legitimately licensed home entertainment. When legitimate products are blocked from the market by Chinese legal restrictions, demand is satisfied almost entirely by pirates. Rampant piracy also diminishes the incentive for foreign investment in movie theaters (which is currently limited to a minority stake). Some progress was achieved in 2004, when MOFCOM approved a U.S.-invested film distribution joint venture and took steps to shorten the time required to bring films to market.

In October 2004, SARFT and MOFCOM issued the Provisional Rules on the Administration of China-Foreign Joint Venture and Cooperative TV Program Production Firms. These rules establish a minimum registered capital requirement of RMB2 million ($250,000) for joint ventures and cooperative firms and mandate a share of no less than 51 percent for domestic partners. In February 2005, SARFT issued a circular placing further restrictions on foreign partners and requiring two-thirds of the programs of a joint venture or cooperative firm to have Chinese themes.

China is reportedly in the process of formulating a policy to support its weak cartoon industry. According to several reports, in June 2005, SARFT began circulating a draft measure providing that only domestically-produced cartoons could be broadcast during prime-time viewing hours and that advertisements shown during this period should be used to finance the production of domestic cartoons. The draft measure also reportedly forbids the introduction of foreign cartoons under the disguise of domestic cartoons as well as cartoons that are jointly made with foreigners. SARFT issued the final version of this measure in August 2006, and it became effective in September 2006.

Finally, in August 2005, the State Council issued a directive stating that non-public capital cannot be used to establish or operate a news agency, newspaper, publishing house, radio station or TV station. The directive also stated that radio and television signal broadcasting and relay station, satellite and backbone networks are closed to non-public capital.

Tourism and Travel Services

Since its accession to the WTO in December 2001, China has relaxed some of its restrictions on foreign operators to improve the competitiveness of its tourism and travel industries. China has also taken steps to implement its WTO commitments.

Immediately following its WTO accession, the State Council issued new travel agency regulations, the Regulations on the Administration of Travel Agencies. These regulations were designed to better enable large foreign travel and tourism service providers to participate as minority partners in operating full-service joint venture travel agencies handling foreign inbound tourism.

The China National Tourism Administration (CNTA) and MOFCOM subsequently issued the Provisional Measures for the Establishment of Foreign-Controlled and Wholly Foreign-Funded Travel Agencies, effective July 2003, which for the first time expressly allowed both foreign-controlled joint ventures and wholly foreign-owned enterprises in its travel industry. Under this measure, these travel agencies were allowed to engage in foreign inbound tourism through the establishment of offices in five major foreign tourist destinations in China (Beijing, Shanghai, Guangzhou, Shenzhen and Xian). Furthermore, the measures stipulated that foreign-controlled travel agencies must have an annual worldwide turnover in excess of $40 million, and wholly foreign-funded travel agencies must have an annual worldwide turnover in excess of $500 million. Both types of travel agencies were also subject to a local registered capital requirement of RMB4 million (approximately $500,000).

In February 2005, CNTA and MOFCOM issued a measure lowering the minimum registered capital requirement for foreign-controlled and wholly foreign-owned travel agencies from RMB4 million (approximately $500,000) to RMB2.5 million (approximately $312,500), which had been required as of December 2004 by its WTO accession agreement. It also lifted all remaining geographical restrictions on the establishment of foreign-controlled and wholly foreign-owned travel agencies, nearly three years in advance of the schedule set forth in its WTO accession agreement.

Recently, it was reported that CNTA would further ease its restrictions on foreign travel agencies operating in China beginning in July 2007. Among other proposed measures, CNTA will reportedly remove controls on the subsidiaries of foreign travel agencies and lower the capital requirements for foreign travel agencies to the same level as domestic travel agencies.

Foreign entry into China's tourism and travel industry continues to grow. In November 2003, Germany's Touristic Union International (TUI) signed a letter of intent with the China Tourism Agency to form the first foreign-controlled joint venture travel agency since China's WTO accession. Japan Airlines subsequently established the first wholly foreign-owned travel agency. By the end of 2006, China had approved the operations of 25 foreign-controlled joint venture travel agencies and wholly foreign-owned travel agencies.

The growth in China's travel and tourism industry is strong. In 2006, China hosted 22 million foreign tourists, representing an increase of 8.5 percent over the previous year. China also generated $33.5 billion in tourism revenues, making it the sixth-largest market globally. The World Tourism Council (WTC) estimates that, in 2006, growth in China's tourism and travel industry ranked second globally. The WTC also predicts sustained long-term growth in demand for China's tourism and travel industry at 8.7 percent per year (in real terms) between 2007 and 2016.

While notable improvements have been made by China, foreign firms continue to be restricted from competing under the same conditions as Chinese firms. For example, with regard to the outbound tourist market, wholly foreign-owned enterprises and Chinese-foreign joint ventures continue to be restricted in selling outbound airline tickets. In addition, China requires all travel agents, airlines and other booking entities to use or connect into China's nationally owned and operated computer reservation system when booking airline tickets. Meanwhile, holders of official Chinese passports are required to use China's state-owned airlines or their code-share partners. Nearly 23,000 holders of official Chinese passports were issued U.S. visas (in 2004), and most of them were employees of state-owned enterprises, who would not be considered government employees in most countries. This represents a significant loss of business for U.S. airlines.

At the same time, the United States has increased its visa options to Chinese nationals visiting the United States. Beginning in January 2005, eligible Chinese nationals wishing to visit the United States temporarily for business (B-1) or tourism (B-2) could be issued visas that were valid for 12 months and multiple entries. The previous maximum length of visas issued for these purposes was six months and multiple entries. Additionally, since November 2006, U.S.-bound tour parties from seven Chinese travel agencies have been allowed to apply for group visas as opposed to previously required business visas.

Education and Training Services

China faces a shortage of qualified teachers and clearly needs educators in inland regions. However, the Ministry of Education (MOE) continues to restrict participation by foreign educators and trainers. China permits only non-profit educational activities that do not compete with the MOE-supervised nine years of compulsory education, thereby inhibiting much-needed foreign investment in the education sector. In April 2000, MOE also banned foreign companies and organizations from offering educational services via satellite networks.

In June 2004, the Ministry of Education issued the Implementing Rules for China-Foreign Cooperative Education Projects. Although formulated to implement the Regulations on China-Foreign Cooperation in Running Schools, issued in September 2003, the rules allow foreign educators to participate only in certain activities, including education offering academic certificates, supplementary education and preschool education. These activities cannot take the form of activities at actual educational institutions.

Foreign universities may set up non-profit operations. However, they must have a Chinese university host and partner to ensure that programs bar subversive content and localize imported information.

Meanwhile, China's training market is unregulated, which discourages potential investors from entering the market.

Legal Services

Prior to its WTO accession, China maintained various restrictions in the area of legal services. It prohibited representative offices of foreign law firms from practicing Chinese law or engaging in profit-making activities with regard to non-Chinese law. It also imposed restrictions on foreign law firms' formal affiliation with Chinese law firms, limited foreign law firms to one representative office and maintained geographic restrictions. Chinese law firms, on the other hand, have been able to open offices freely throughout China since 1996.

As part of its WTO accession, China agreed to lift quantitative and geographical restrictions on the establishment of representative offices by foreign law firms within one year after accession. In addition, foreign representative offices are to be able to engage in profit-making business, to advise clients on foreign legal matters and to provide information on the impact of the Chinese legal environment, among other things. They also are to be able to maintain long-term "entrustment" relationships with Chinese law firms and to instruct lawyers in the Chinese law firm as agreed between the two law firms.

The State Council issued the Regulations on the Administration of Foreign Law Firm Representative Offices in December 2001, and the Ministry of Justice issued implementing rules in July 2002. While these measures removed some market access barriers, they also generated concern among foreign law firms doing business in China. In many areas, these measures were ambiguous. For example, it appeared that these measures created an economic needs test for foreign law firms that want to establish offices in China, which would raise concerns regarding China's compliance with its GATS commitments. The measures also seemed to take an overly restrictive view of the types of legal services that foreign law firms may provide. In addition, the procedures for establishing a new office or an additional office were unnecessarily time-consuming. For example, a foreign law firm may not establish an additional representative office until its most recently established representative office has been in practice for three consecutive years. Foreign attorneys also may not take China's bar examination, and they may not hire registered members of the Chinese bar as attorneys.

Although a number of U.S. and other foreign law firms have been able to open a second office in China, little progress has been made on the other problematic aspects of these measures, particularly the economic needs test, the unreasonable restrictions on the types of legal services that can be provided and the unnecessary delays that must be endured when seeking to establish new offices. These obstacles continue to prevent foreign law firms from participating fully in China's legal market.

Accounting and Management Consultancy Services

Prior to China's accession to the WTO, foreign accounting firms could not choose their own Chinese joint venture partners freely or enter into contractual agreements that could fully integrate these joint ventures. Upon its accession to the WTO, China agreed to allow foreign accounting firms to partner with any Chinese entity of their choice. China also agreed to abandon the prohibition on foreign accounting firms' representative offices engaging in profit-making activities. In addition, China agreed that foreign accounting firms could engage in taxation and management consulting services, without having to satisfy the more restrictive requirements on form of establishment applicable to new entities seeking to provide those services separately.

The Chinese Institute of Certified Public Accountants, a government body under MOF, has made progress in modernizing accounting in China. Since China's WTO accession, MOF has released four newly revised auditing statements covering inter-bank confirmation, capital verification, accounting estimates and the audit of commercial bank financial statements. Furthermore, MOF has been active in standardizing accounting procedures across a wide range of topics including investments, inventories, cash flow statements and fixed assets. CSRC, meanwhile, requires a listed company to appoint a certified international CPA firm to conduct audits on prospectuses and annual reports in accordance with international standards.

Despite these positive changes, pervasive problems remain. Differing accounting regulations limit the comparability of data, and the accounting practices followed by many domestic firms do not meet international conventions.

Advertising Services

Prior to China's accession to the WTO, foreign advertising firms had been restricted to representative offices or minority ownership of joint ventures. In its WTO accession agreement, however, China agreed to allow majority foreign ownership of joint venture advertising companies by December 11, 2003, and wholly foreign-owned subsidiaries by December 11, 2005.

In March 2004, SAIC and MOFCOM issued rules governing joint venture, cooperative and wholly foreign-owned advertising firms. To establish branches, a firm must have paid in full its registered capital and have at least RMB20 million ($2.5 million) in annual advertising revenue. Foreign firms are currently limited to a 70 percent share of joint venture and cooperative firms. Implementing rules, effective January 1, 2005, subsequently allowed wholly foreign-owned advertising firms to conduct business in China.

Advertising in China is still governed by China's 1995 Advertising Law, which is enforced by SAIC. Among other things, the law bans messages "hindering the public or violating social customs." The law is also subject to interpretation by SAIC, which must approve all advertising campaigns. One additional difficulty for foreign advertising firms, as well as foreign manufacturers, is that China has strict regulations prohibiting comparative advertising as well as any advertising with claims about the relative superiority of one brand over another. Marketing strategies that are successful in some other countries are therefore illegal in China.

Movement of Professionals

Generally, there are no special entry restrictions placed on U.S. professionals who wish to work in China, such as doctors or engineers. However, like other foreign professionals, they must receive approval from the Foreign Experts Bureau. Prior to arrival, a prospective American job applicant may be asked to provide notarized copies of his or her professional credentials and a summary of past work experience. The credentials will be used by the employer to file for a "foreign experts residency permit" for the American employee. Once the "foreign expert" permit is authorized, the prospective employee can request a work visa (a "Z" visa) from a Chinese embassy or consulate. If the prospective employee arrives in China on a visitors' visa (an "L" visa) prior to commencing employment, the prospective employee is usually asked to depart China prior to starting work, and to apply for the appropriate work visa from a foreign entry point (usually Hong Kong). Local employers are responsible for all employment or income tax and other withholdings for these "foreign experts" while they are employed in China. The government has liberalized access somewhat by issuing "permanent resident" visas to longtime foreign residents of China, which replace the additional "resident cards" previously required.

INVESTMENT BARRIERS

The volume of foreign investment in China remained high in 2006 despite the introduction of significant new investment barriers. According to the United Nations Conference on Trade and Development, China received $72.4 billion in FDI in 2006, 3 percent less than in 2005. China was the world's third-largest investment destination, after the United States and the United Kingdom. Foreign investors also continued to earn high rates of return in 2006, indicating that China remains an attractive market in which to invest despite the continuing challenges of doing business there. The World Bank Doing Business Report gave China a global ranking for "ease of doing business" of 93 in 2006. Although this ranking was an improvement over China's 108 ranking in 2005, faster progress toward removing investment barriers and reducing government intervention in companies' investment decisions could open new markets to U.S. and other foreign firms, especially in the services sector. In 2006, investors continued to face a lack of transparency, inconsistently enforced laws and regulations, weak IPR protection, corruption and an unreliable legal system incapable of enforcing contracts and judgments.

While China's leadership has repeatedly affirmed its commitment to further open China to foreign investment, China adopted a series of more restrictive foreign investment policies in 2006. These policies indicated that China would be more selective in encouraging foreign investment, more actively targeting higher value-added sectors (including high technology research and development, advanced manufacturing, energy efficiency and modern agriculture and services) rather than basic manufacturing. It also appeared that China would be seeking to spread the benefits of foreign investment beyond China's comparatively wealthy coastal area by encouraging multinationals to establish regional headquarters and operations in Central, Western and Northeast China.

While the United States supports the liberalization of China's investment regime, the United States is concerned about the recent increase in proposed and adopted measures that restrict investment. Often, these restrictions are accompanied by other problematic industrial policies, such as the increased use of subsidies, preferences for using domestic rather than imported goods and the development of China-specific standards. Many of these developments appear to represent protectionist tools by industrial planners to shield inefficient or monopolistic enterprises from competition, counter to the market-oriented principles that have been the basis for much of China's economic success.

Investment Requirements

Upon its accession to the WTO, China assumed the obligations of the Agreement on Trade-Related Investment Measures (TRIMS Agreement), which prohibits investment measures that violate GATT Article III obligations to treat imports no less favorably than domestic products or the GATT Article XI obligation not to impose quantitative restrictions on imports. The TRIMS Agreement thus expressly requires elimination of measures such as those that require or provide benefits for the incorporation of local inputs (known as local content requirements) in the manufacturing process, or measures that restrict a firm's imports to an amount related to its exports or related to the amount of foreign exchange a firm earns (known as trade balancing requirements). In its WTO accession agreement, China also specifically agreed to eliminate export performance, local content and foreign exchange balancing requirements from its laws, regulations and other measures, and not to enforce the terms of any contracts imposing these requirements. In addition, China agreed that it would no longer condition importation or investment approvals on these requirements or on requirements such as technology transfer and offsets.

Although China has revised many laws and regulations to conform to its WTO investment commitments, some of the revised laws and regulations continue to "encourage" technology transfer, without formally requiring it. U.S. companies remain concerned that this "encouragement" in practice can amount to a "requirement" in many cases, particularly in light of the high degree of discretion provided to Chinese government officials when reviewing investment applications. Similarly, some laws and regulations "encourage" exportation or the use of local content. Moreover, according to U.S. companies, some Chinese government officials in 2006 – even in the absence of encouraging language in a law or regulation – still consider factors such as export performance and local content when deciding whether to approve an investment or to recommend approval of a loan from a Chinese policy bank, which is often essential to the success of an investment project.

Investment Guidelines

Foreign Investment Catalogue

China's foreign investment objectives are primarily defined through its Foreign Investment Catalogue, which is revised every few years and supplemented by directives from various government agencies. Revisions to the catalogue and contradictions between it and other pronouncements have confused investors and added to the perception that the investment guidelines do not provide a stable basis for business planning. The resulting uncertainty as to which industries are being promoted as investment targets and for how long undermines confidence in the stability of the investment climate.

China's most recent revisions to the catalogue took effect January 1, 2005. Investment in unlisted sectors is considered "permitted," while China "encourages" investment in sectors where it believes it benefits from foreign assistance or technology transfers. Furthermore, investment is "restricted" in sectors that do not meet "the needs of China's national economic development." In these instances, foreign firms must form joint ventures with Chinese firms and restrict their equity ownership to a minority share if they want to invest in China.

China "prohibits" foreign investment in sectors that it views as key to its national security, such as news agencies, radio and television broadcasting stations and networks, radio and television programming, film production and screening, and the publication, importation and wholesale distribution of press and audiovisual products. The production of arms and the mining and processing of certain minerals by foreign investors are also prohibited. In addition, U.S. investors have expressed concern about China's prohibition of investment in the production and development of biotechnology plant seeds.

Since 2004, provincial governments have enjoyed expanded authority to directly approve many foreign investment projects. Currently, in "encouraged" and "permitted" sectors, proposed foreign investments valued above $500 million require NDRC review and State Council approval. Furthermore, foreign projects in "restricted" sectors valued above $50 million require similar central government review and approval.

China uses a variety of incentives to encourage foreign investment in targeted sectors, like high technology industries, such as duty-free import of capital equipment and VAT rebates on inputs. Foreign investors in targeted regions and special economic zones and in certain industries, such as machinery and construction, also benefit from reduced income taxes, although in December 2006 the National People's Congress began considering a draft enterprise income tax law that could eliminate many of these tax advantages.

Administrative Measures to Restrict Investment

In 2006, Chinese regulators announced several measures that limit the ability of foreign firms to participate in investment in China's market.

For example, in June 2006, the State Council issued the Opinions on the Revitalization of the Industrial Machinery Manufacturing Industries, which calls for China to expand the market share of domestic companies involved in 16 types of equipment manufacturing, including large equipment for clean and efficient power generation, critical semiconductor manufacturing equipment, civilian aircraft and aircraft engines, pollution control equipment, textiles machinery and large excavators. This measure advocates a variety of policy supports, such as preferential import duties on parts needed for research and development, encouraging domestic procurement of major technical equipment, a dedicated capital market financing fund for domestic firms and strict review of imports. This measure also suggests that China will implement controls on foreign investments in the industrial machinery manufacturing industries, including a requirement for administrative approval when foreign entities seek majority ownership or control of leading domestic firms.

In August 2006, MOFCOM and five other government agencies issued the Provisions of Acquisition of Domestic Enterprises by Foreign Investment, which became effective September 2006. This measure revised existing rules for mergers and acquisitions involving foreign investors and, among other things, established a legal basis for a "national economic security" review process that can block proposed transactions. Under the new rules, foreign mergers and acquisitions of domestic enterprises that would result in "actual control" of a domestic enterprise in a "key industry" with "potential impact on national economic security" or that would alter control of a famous Chinese trademark or brand require MOFCOM approval. The new rules also place MOFCOM in the role of determining if the domestic acquisition target has been appropriately valued and allow MOFCOM to initiate an anti-monopoly investigation if "large market shares" are involved or if market competition is "materially" affected. Although implementing measures have not yet been issued, foreign investors have already found that they face greater difficulties purchasing controlling stakes in prominent Chinese firms, and several proposed transactions have stalled. In one positive development, the new rules do now permit the use of foreign shares as consideration for the acquisition of Chinese companies, a change that could facilitate foreign investment in China.

Subsequently, in November 2006, the NDRC released a Five-Year Plan on foreign investment, which promised greater scrutiny over foreign capital utilization. The plan calls for the realization of a "fundamental shift" from "quantity" to "quality" in foreign investment during the period from 2006 to 2010. The state's focus would change from shoring up domestic capital and foreign exchange shortfalls to introducing advanced technology, management expertise and talent. In addition, more attention would be paid to ecology, environment and energy efficiency. The plan also demands tighter tax supervision of foreign enterprises, and it seeks to restrict foreign firms' acquisition of "dragon head" enterprises, to prevent the "emergence or expansion of foreign capital monopolies," to protect national economic security and to prevent the "abuse of intellectual property."

In December 2006, the State Assets Supervision and Administration Commission (SASAC) issued the Guiding Opinion Concerning the Advancement of Adjustments of State Capital and the Restructuring of State-Owned Enterprises, which identified an expansive list of sectors deemed critical to the national economy. This measure explained that "pillar" and "backbone" industries such as automotive, chemical, construction, electronic information, equipment manufacturing, iron and steel, non-ferrous metal, science and technology, and survey and design must maintain relatively strong state control. Reportedly, SASAC officials also identified a separate set of seven strategic sectors in which state capital must play a leading role, including aviation, coal, defense, electric power and grid, oil and petrochemicals, shipping, and telecommunications. It remains unclear how SASAC will implement these policies.

In 2006, China also continued to employ various sector-specific measures designed to impose new requirements on foreign investors. Measures affecting foreign investment in the automotive and steel sectors are discussed above in the section on Import Substitution Policies.

Other Investment Issues

Venture Capital

In March 2003, new regulations took effect permitting the establishment of foreign-invested venture capital firms, including wholly foreign-owned enterprises, aimed at funding high technology and new technology startups in industries open to foreign investment. These regulations lowered capital requirements, allowed foreign-invested firms to manage funds directly invested from overseas, and offered the option of establishing venture capital firms in a form similar to the limited liability partnerships used in other countries.

Meanwhile, regulations that took effect in April 2001 permitted foreign private equity firms subject to limits on corporate structure, share issuance and transfers, and investment exit options. These same regulations, however, bar all domestic and foreign securities firms from the private equity business.

Investment exit problems, especially the difficulty of listing on China's stock exchanges, coupled with the bureaucratic approvals required to list overseas, have limited interest in establishing China-based venture capital and private equity investment. As a result, most foreign venture capital and private equity investments in China are actually housed in offshore investment entities, which, as with other offshore FDI, can be transferred without Chinese government approval.

The Chinese government issued new regulations for domestic venture capital firms in the fall of 2005, and implementing rules went into effect on March 1, 2006. It is unclear if foreign firms choosing to operate onshore will be allowed to take advantage of the incentives offered to domestic firms.

Holding Companies

China has relaxed some restrictions on the scope and operations of holding companies, although minimum capital requirements normally make the establishment of a holding company suitable only for corporations with several large investments. Holding companies may manage human resources across their affiliates and also provide certain market research and other services. However, some restrictions on services provided by holding companies and on holding companies' financial operations and the ability to balance foreign exchange internally remain in place. Profit and loss consolidation within holding companies also remains prohibited.

China has begun to open its domestic equity markets to investments from foreign firms. Through the Qualified Foreign Institutional Investor (QFII) program, foreign securities firms may apply for QFII status, which permits limited access to the RMB-denominated A-share market. As of October 2006, China had granted QFII status to 50 foreign entities, 41 of which had obtained quotas totaling $8.2 billion.

Access to Capital Markets

Foreign-invested firms in China are often unable to access domestic and international stock markets, to sell corporate bonds and equity, or to engage in normal merger, acquisition and divestment activity. In addition, foreign exchange transactions on China's capital account can be concluded only with case-bycase official review, and approvals are tightly regulated. However, recent regulations permitting greater capital outflows and pronouncements by Chinese government officials encouraging Chinese firms to invest abroad suggest that China now recognizes that continued large capital inflows are not sustainable. To date, foreign firms remain generally satisfied because they are able to repatriate profits. At the same time, most major foreign firms prefer to reinvest their profits, not exit the Chinese market.

GOVERNMENT PROCUREMENT

The WTO Agreement on Government Procurement (GPA) is a plurilateral agreement and currently covers the United States and 39 other WTO Members that have joined it. The GPA applies to the procurement of goods and services by central and sub-central government entities listed by each party, subject to thresholds and certain exceptions. It requires GPA parties to provide MFN and national treatment to the goods, services and suppliers of other GPA parties and to apply detailed procedures designed to ensure fairness and predictability in the procurement process.

At present, China is not a party to the GPA. It committed to become an observer to the GPA upon its WTO accession, and in February 2002, it became an observer to the WTO Committee on Government Procurement. China also committed, in its WTO accession agreement, to initiate negotiations for accession to the GPA "as soon as possible." Following sustained U.S. engagement, China agreed at the April 2006 JCCT meeting that it would initiate GPA negotiations by no later than December 2007.

Until it joins the GPA, China has committed in its WTO accession agreement that all of its central and local government entities will conduct their procurements in a transparent manner. China also agreed that, if it opened a procurement to foreign suppliers, it would provide MFN treatment by allowing all foreign suppliers an equal opportunity to participate in the bidding process.

In June 2002, China adopted its Government Procurement Law, which became effective in January 2003. This law attempts to follow the spirit of the GPA and incorporates provisions from the United Nations Model Law on Procurement of Goods. The law also directs central and sub-central government entities to give priority to "local" goods and services, with limited exceptions, as China is permitted to do, because it is not yet a party to the GPA. China envisions that this law will improve transparency, reduce corruption and lower government costs. This law is also seen as a necessary step toward reforming China's government procurement system in preparation for China eventually becoming a party to the GPA. It is notable, however, that the Government Procurement Law does not cover tendering and bidding for public works projects, which represent at least one-half of China's government procurement market. Those projects are subject to a different regulatory regime, which will have to be brought into compliance with the GPA before China accedes to the GPA.

China began the process of drafting regulations implementing the Government Procurement Law soon after its issuance in June 2002. MOF issued these regulations – the Measures on the Administration of Bidding for Government-Procured Goods and Services – in August 2004. They set out detailed procedures for the solicitation, submission and evaluation of bids for government contracts relating to goods and services and help to clarify the scope and coverage of the Government Procurement Law. MOF also issued several sets of implementing rules, including measures relating to the announcement of government procurements and the handling of complaints by suppliers relating to government procurement.

Meanwhile, beginning in 2003, U.S. companies expressed concerns about implementing rules on government software procurement being drafted by MOF. At a time when China's already large software market was projected to grow by more than 50 percent annually, the initial draft of these rules reportedly contained guidelines mandating that central and local governments – the largest purchasers of software in China – purchase only software developed in China to the extent possible. In response, the United States organized an industry roundtable to inform the relevant Chinese ministries of the views and concerns of interested U.S. trade associations. U.S. industry officials explained that the creation of a domestic software industry cut off from global standards would lead to inefficiencies and would limit, rather than promote, the development of China's software industry. Working closely with U.S. industry, the United States also submitted written comments on the software procurement proposal and followed up by strongly reiterating its concerns with China during a series of bilateral meetings. The United States was concerned not only about U.S. software exporters continuing access to China's large and growing market for packaged and custom software – $7.5 billion in 2004 – but also about the precedent that could be established for other sectors if China proceeded with MOF's proposed restrictions on the purchase of foreign software by central and local governments. At the July 2005 JCCT meeting, China took note of the United States' strong concerns and indicated that it would indefinitely suspend the drafting of implementing rules on government software procurement.

Soon afterwards, however, the issue of preferences for the purchase of domestic goods again appeared, when the State Council issued China's Medium to Long Term Science and Technology Master Plan in early 2006. The NDRC and several other ministries and agencies are in charge of developing regulations to implement this strategy, which includes preferences for the purchase of domestic goods as an important industrial policy tool. The United States is concerned that these regulations may unfairly discriminate against U.S. firms and is therefore closely monitoring developments in this area.

A similar issue arose in December 2005, when China issued a measure announcing that products incorporating the WAPI standards should be given preference in government procurement. This measure is discussed above in the "Standards, Technical Regulations and Conformity Assessment Procedures" section.

Electronic Commerce

China has experienced dramatic growth in Internet usage since 1999. According to the 19th Internet survey recently published by the China Internet Network Information Center (CNNIC), the number of Internet users in China reached approximately 137 million at the end of 2006, representing an increase of 23 percent over the previous year, second only to the United States in terms of total users. Falling personal computer prices and the arrival of devices tailored for the Chinese market will further expand Internet access.

China has also experienced a dramatic increase in the number of domain names established. By the end of 2006, there were more than 4.1 million registered domain names in China. Of this total, there were more than 1.8 million domain names registered under ".cn", representing a 64 percent increase over the previous year. However, despite these developments, CNNIC reported that only 24 percent of surveyed Chinese Internet users frequently use the Internet for online shopping services. Nevertheless, China is experiencing the rapid development of online businesses such as search engines, network education, online advertisements, audio-video service, paid e-mail, short message, online job hunting, Internet consulting, e-trading and online gaming.

The Chinese government recognizes the potential of electronic commerce to promote exports and increase competitiveness and has made some progress toward establishing a viable commercial environment. However, some Chinese ministries with responsibility for electronic commerce have excessively regulated the Internet, thereby stifling the free flow of information and the consumer privacy needed for electronic commerce to flourish. Content is still controlled and encryption regulated, as discussed more fully above (in the "Online Services" section).

A number of technical problems also inhibit the growth of electronic commerce in China. Rates charged by government-approved Internet service providers make Internet access expensive for most Chinese citizens. Slow connection speeds are another problem, although this is changing quickly as broadband connections become more readily available. By the end of 2006, nearly 76 percent of China's Internet users had broadband connections, representing an increase of 18 percentage points over 2005, and China Telecom is now reportedly the world's largest digital subscriber line, or DSL, operator. There are now 104 million broadband subscribers in China. China surpassed Japan in 2004 as the country with the second most broadband lines after the United States. At the same time, Internet penetration remains relatively low in China, and there is a large urban/rural divide in penetration rates (the urban penetration rate is six times higher than the rural penetration rate as of July 2006), so there is still significant room for growth.

Other impediments to Chinese businesses and consumers conducting online transactions include the paucity of credit payment systems, consumer reluctance to trust online merchants, the lack of secure online payment systems and inefficient delivery systems. China has also yet to develop a legal framework conducive to the rapid growth of electronic commerce. Laws recognizing the validity of "econtracting" tools and stressing the importance of online privacy and security have been proposed, but not yet issued. Despite these obstacles, however, a large and growing percentage of Chinese Internet users reportedly have made online purchases.

In August 2004, China passed its first electronic commerce legislation, which addressed, among other things, e-signatures. China is reportedly drafting data privacy legislation and regulations that will address online transactions and payments.

ANTICOMPETITIVE PRACTICES

Competition Policy Laws and Regulations

China maintains many laws and regulations in the competition policy area. China's principal law is the Anti-Unfair Competition Law, enacted by the National People's Congress (NPC) in 1993. This law addresses a variety of matters, as it (a) prohibits firms from using a trademark, name or packaging without a license, as well as false advertising and other practices intended to confuse consumers; (b) outlaws bribery, the purchase or sale of business secrets, and predatory pricing; (c) restricts a firm's ability to tie the sale of one product to another or impose "unreasonable conditions" on purchases; (d) bans collusion and outlaws "spreading false facts" that damage a competitor; and (e) in theory, limits the business practices of legally-authorized monopolies and restricts the government's ability to require that private firms engage in certain commercial transactions with state-owned enterprises.

China maintains some laws and regulations that limit competition. For example, the national government has legislated that production in certain sectors be concentrated in monopolies, near monopolies or authorized oligopolies. As in some other countries, these enterprises are concentrated in capital intensive sectors, like electricity and transportation, or in industries such as fixed-line telephony and postal services, in which this approach may be used to ensure national coverage. Some of the key laws and regulations include the Law on Electricity (1996), Civil Aviation Law (1995), Regulations on Telecommunication (2000), Postal Law (1986), Railroad Law (1991) and Commercial Bank Law (amended in 2003), among others. The enforcement of these laws and regulations is uneven as a result of the challenges inherent in attempting to coordinate their implementation nationally and as a result of inconsistent local and provincial enforcement. As China further reforms its economy, it is expected that many of these laws will be revised.

More troubling are efforts by government authorities at all levels in China to regulate competition with specific firms, often state-owned enterprises. Official statements often suggest that these efforts are tied primarily to employment concerns. However, the ultimate beneficiaries of the resulting protectionist measures are often unclear. In addition, local governments frequently enact rules that restrict interprovincial trade. Because the central government has difficulty enforcing its own competition policy measures at the local level, these local government rules continue to restrict market access for certain imported products, raise production costs and limit market opportunities for foreign-invested enterprises.

In June 2006, the NPC conducted the first of the three required readings of a draft Anti-Monopoly Law, which has been in development for nearly 15 years. The United States is carefully following the progress of the draft law, which, among other things, would strengthen the central government's ability to tackle locally authorized monopolies. In bilateral meetings, the United States has raised concerns with particular aspects of the draft law, including legal standards for determining whether a firm has a dominant market position and whether it is abusing that position, notification obligations for foreign mergers and acquisitions, the coverage of state enterprises and disciplines on administrative monopolies. The United States has also raised concerns about the proper relationship between intellectual property rights and antimonopoly enforcement, urging that the mere ownership of an intellectual property right not be considered proof of a dominant market position and that a patent owner's simple refusal to license its technology not be viewed as an antimonopoly violation. A second NPC reading has not yet been scheduled.

Measures Restricting Inward Investment

In 2006, China began to revise its policies toward inward investment. While insisting that it remains open to foreign investment, China adopted policies that restrict inward investment in a range of "strategic" sectors, which appear designed to shield domestic enterprises from foreign competition.

As discussed above in the Investment Barriers section, these policies include the State Council's June 2006 Opinions on the Revitalization of the Industrial Machinery Manufacturing Industries, which calls for China to expand the market share of domestic companies in 16 equipment manufacturing industries. In August 2006, the Ministry of Commerce and five other agencies issued revised rules for foreign mergers and acquisitions, which, among other things, establish a vague "national economic security" basis for rejecting proposed deals as well as an anti-monopoly review that can block deals. In November 2006, the NDRC issued a Five-Year Plan on foreign investment that seeks to restrict foreign acquisitions of leading Chinese enterprises, prevent the emergence of foreign capital monopolies, protect industrial security and prevent abuse of intellectual property. Finally, in December 2006, SASAC published an expansive list of "critical economic sectors" in which China should restrict foreign participation.

Some of these measures maintain or create conflicts of interest by assigning regulatory power to agencies that administer state-owned enterprises competing in the same sectors. In addition, key terms in the new policies, such as "national economic security," remain undefined. The opaque standards and ill-defined processes in these measures have introduced additional ambiguity into China's competition policy.

OTHER BARRIERS

Transparency

In its WTO accession agreement, China committed to publish all laws, regulations and other measures that relate to trade matters, including those that affect imports, and generally to provide a reasonable period for commenting on them before implementation. China also agreed to establish or designate an official journal for the publication of these trade-related measures. In addition, China agreed to provide a copy of new trade-related laws, regulations and other measures to the WTO Secretariat in Geneva, translated into one or more of the WTO's official languages (English, French and Spanish) no later than 90 days after implementation. China further agreed to create various enquiry points for its WTO trading partners and foreign businesses to obtain information about these measures.

Various government-owned specialty newspapers routinely carry the texts of government regulations, implementing rules, circulars and announcements. Many government ministries also publish digests or gazettes containing the texts of these measures, both in written form and on their websites. In addition, there has been a proliferation of online news and information services that routinely offer up-to-date news about, and texts of, new laws and regulations. Some services even provide legal-quality English translations by subscription. However, many measures that do not rise to the level of ministry-issued regulations or implementing rules continue to remain unavailable to the public. China's ministries routinely implement policies based on internal "guidance" or "opinions" that are not available to foreign firms. In addition, experimental or informal policies and draft regulations are regarded as internal matters and public access is tightly controlled.

While positive in some respects, the sheer number of outlets through which trade-related measures are published complicates the ability of interested parties to track their development and issuance. In late 2002, China designated the China Foreign Economic and Trade Gazette as the official journal for this purpose. Published by MOFCOM, it came out on a trial basis in October 2002 and as an official publication in January 2003. However, this journal does not carry draft measures for public comment, nor does it consistently carry trade-related measures developed by ministries and agencies other than MOFCOM. The establishment or designation of a single comprehensive journal would enhance the ability of WTO Members to track the drafting, issuance and implementation of trade-related measures. Furthermore, the use of a single journal to request comments on proposed trade-related measures, as envisioned in China's WTO accession agreement, would facilitate the timely notification of comment periods and submission of comments. In March 2006, the State Council issued a notice directing all central, provincial and local government entities to begin sending copies of all of their trade-related measures to MOFCOM for immediate publication in the MOFCOM Gazette. The United States has been monitoring the effectiveness of this notice, both to assess whether all government entities regularly publish their trade-related measures in the MOFCOM Gazette and whether all types of measures are being published. So far, adherence to the State Council's notice is far from complete.

In December 2001, the State Council issued regulations explicitly allowing comment periods and hearings. However, many of China's ministries and agencies continued to follow the practice prior to China's accession to the WTO. The ministry or agency responsible for drafting a new or revised law or regulation will normally consult with and submit drafts to other ministries and agencies, Chinese experts and affected Chinese companies. At times, the responsible ministry or agency will also consult with select foreign companies, although it will not necessarily share drafts with them. As a result, only a small proportion of new or revised laws and regulations have been issued after a period for public comment, and even in these cases the amount of time provided for public comment has generally been short.

In 2004, some improvements took place, particularly on the part of MOFCOM, which began following the rules set forth in its Provisional Regulations on Administrative Transparency, issued in November 2003. Those rules could potentially serve as a model for other ministries and agencies seeking to improve their transparency. Nevertheless, basic compliance with China's notice-and-comment commitment has continued to be uneven. In the area of intellectual property rights, for example, several ministries and agencies circulated proposed measures for public comment in 2005 and 2006. The National People's Congress also circulated a proposed Labor Contract Law for public comment in March 2006. However, China did not provide for public comment on major trade-related laws and regulations, such as the April 2005 Measures on the Importation of Parts for Entire Automobiles, which has since given rise to a WTO dispute brought by the United States, the EC and Canada, CIRC's December 2005 Regulations on the Administration of the Reinsurance Business, August 2006 merger and acquisition regulations, or Xinhua's September 2006 Administrative Measures on News and Information Release by Foreign News Agencies within China. In addition, China did not seek public input on new rules on telecommunications value-added services issued by MII in July 2006, or new rules on qualification requirements for senior managers of insurance companies issued by CIRC in July 2006. The United States and other WTO Members have also been seeking the opportunity to comment on a number of significant new measures, such as the draft Postal Law and the draft Telecommunications Law, so far without success.

Meanwhile, China's ministries and agencies continue to have a much better record when it comes to making new or revised laws and regulations available to the public. In accordance with State Council regulations issued in December 2001, which require the publication of new or amended regulations 30 days before their implementation, almost all new or revised laws and regulations have been available (in Chinese) soon after issuance and prior to their effective date, an improvement over pre-WTO accession practice. Indeed, these laws and regulations are often published not only in official journals, but also on the Internet. At the same time, however, China continues to lag behind in providing translations of these laws and regulations.

U.S. industry continues to report instances where Chinese regulators provide Chinese companies unofficial guidance, which is usually unavailable to foreign entities. In some cases, Chinese officials have provided unpublished documents to interested parties, but this dissemination has been *ad hoc* and based more on personal connections than formal procedures.

In late 2001, MOFCOM's predecessor, MOFTEC, established an enquiry point to provide information on new trade and investment laws, regulations and other measures. Other ministries and agencies have also established formal or informal, subject-specific enquiry points. Since the creation of these various enquiry points, U.S. companies have generally found them to be responsive and helpful, and have generally received timely replies.

Legal Framework

Laws and Regulations

Laws and regulations in China tend to be more general and ambiguous than in other countries. While this approach allows the Chinese authorities to apply laws and regulations flexibly, it also results in inconsistency and confusion in application. Companies often have difficulty determining whether their activities contravene a particular law or regulation.

In China, regulations are also promulgated by a host of different ministries and governments at the central, provincial and local levels, and it is not unusual for the resulting regulations to be at odds with each other. Even though finalized regulations are now routinely published in China, they often leave room for discretionary application and inconsistencies, either through honest misunderstanding or by design. Indeed, government bureaucracies have sometimes been accused of selectively applying regulations. China has many strict rules that are often ignored in practice until a person or entity falls out of official favor. Governmental authorities can wield their discretionary power to crack down on foreign or disfavored investors or make special demands on them simply by threatening to crack down.

This lack of a clear and consistent framework of laws and regulations can be a barrier to the participation of foreign firms in the Chinese domestic market. A comprehensive legal framework, coupled with adequate prior notice of proposed changes to laws and regulations and an opportunity to comment on those changes, would greatly enhance business conditions, promote commerce and reduce opportunities for corruption. The U.S. Government has provided technical assistance, at the central, provincial and local levels of government in China, in an effort to promote improvements in China's legislative and regulatory drafting process. In its WTO accession agreement, China committed to establish tribunals for the review of all administrative actions relating to the implementation of trade-related laws, regulations, judicial decisions and administrative rulings. These tribunals must be impartial and independent of the government authorities entrusted with the administrative enforcement in question, and their review procedures must include the right of appeal. To date, little information is publicly available regarding the frequency or outcomes of review before these tribunals.

China also committed, at all levels of government, to apply, implement and administer all of its laws, regulations and other measures relating to trade in goods and services in a uniform and impartial manner throughout China, including in special economic areas. In connection with this commitment, in 2002, China also established an internal review mechanism, now overseen by MOFCOM's Department of WTO Affairs, to handle cases of non-uniform application of laws. The actual workings of this mechanism remain unclear, however.

Commercial Dispute Resolution

Both foreign and domestic companies often avoid seeking resolution of commercial disputes through the Chinese courts, as skepticism about the independence and professionalism of China's court system and the enforceability of court judgments and awards remains high. There is a widespread perception that judges, particularly outside of China's big cities, are subject to influence by local political or business pressures. Most judges are not trained in the law and/or lack higher education, although this problem decreases at the higher levels of the judiciary.

At the same time, the Chinese government is moving to establish consistent and reliable mechanisms for dispute resolution through the adoption of improved codes of ethics for judges and lawyers and increased emphasis on the consistent and predictable application of laws. The Judges' Law, issued by the Standing Committee of the National People's Congress in 1995, requires judges to have degrees in law or in other subjects where they have acquired specialized legal knowledge, and permits judges appointed before the law's implementation who do not meet these standards to undergo necessary training. In 1999, the Supreme People's Court began requiring judges to be appointed based on merit and educational background and experience, rather than through politics or favoritism. In 2002, the Supreme People's Court issued rules designating certain higher-level courts to hear cases involving administrative agency decisions relating to international trade in goods or services or intellectual property rights. According to the Supreme People's Court, China's more experienced judges sit on the designated courts, and the geographic area under the jurisdiction of each of these designated courts has been broadened in an attempt to minimize local protectionism. The rules provide that foreign or Chinese enterprises and individuals may bring cases in the designated courts raising challenges under the Administrative Litigation Law to decisions made by China's administrative agencies relating to international trade matters. The rules also state that when there is more than one reasonable interpretation of a law or regulation, the courts should choose an interpretation that is consistent with the provisions of international agreements to which China has committed, such as the WTO rules.

Despite initial enthusiasm, foreign observers have grown increasingly skeptical of the China International Economic and Trade Arbitration Commission (CIETAC) as a forum for the arbitration of trade disputes. Some foreign firms have obtained satisfactory rulings from CIETAC but other firms and legal professionals have raised concerns about restrictions on the selection of arbitrators and inadequacies in procedural rules necessary to ensure thorough, orderly and fair management of cases.

Finally, in cases where the judiciary or arbitration panels have issued judgments in favor of foreign-invested enterprises, enforcement of the judgments has often been difficult. Officials responsible for enforcement are often beholden to local interests and unwilling to enforce court judgments against locally powerful companies or individuals.

Labor Issues

In recent years, China has expanded the scope of its national labor laws and regulations so they now cover most, though not all, key labor areas. Even with these changes, China does not adhere to certain internationally recognized labor standards, such as the rights of freedom of association and collective bargaining. There are many reports indicating that China does not enforce its laws and regulations concerning minimum wages, hours of work and occupational safety and health. There are also persistent concerns about the use of prison labor and child labor. In addition, labor laws and regulations are applied inconsistently between Chinese-owned enterprises and foreign-invested enterprises.

The Chinese government is slowly developing nationwide pension, unemployment insurance, medical insurance and workplace injury insurance systems that require substantial employer contributions. These systems are still rudimentary and characterized by serious funding shortfalls, in part due to widespread non-compliance among domestic firms. A Chinese government audit report published in November 2006 reveals that more than RMB7 billion ($875 million) of China's RMB2 trillion ($250 billion) social security funds had been misappropriated. This revelation has made social security the primary concern for many Chinese citizens, according to a subsequent survey.

The cost of labor, especially unskilled labor, is low in much of China. The existence of a large pool of surplus rural workers, many of whom seek work in urban areas, helps to keep unskilled wages low. Some companies offering substandard wages and working conditions have experienced shortages of unskilled labor. Where competition for workers is intense and the supply limited, as in the case of technical, managerial and professional staff in China's coastal areas, wages can be higher. However, restrictions on labor mobility distort labor costs. China is gradually easing restrictions under the country's household registration system, which has traditionally limited the movement of workers within the country, in part due to the recognition that labor mobility is essential to the continued growth of the economy. Reportedly, wages for many migrant workers, especially construction workers, are not paid on a monthly basis as required by China's national labor laws and regulations, but rather at year end. These workers also remain vulnerable to wage arrearages.

In 2005, the China National Textile and Apparel Council established the Committee for the Promotion of Corporate Social Accountability System for Chinese Textile Enterprises (CSC-9000T). Reportedly, increasing numbers of Chinese firms have realized the importance of social accountability but remain confused about the various foreign corporate social accountability standards and certifications bodies that exist. The council formed CSC-9000T to formulate Chinese corporate social responsibility standards to promote among Chinese firms. The standards are based on relevant Chinese legislation and regulations and reference international practices. More than 300 council members have adopted these standards. CSC-9000T is designed as a capacity building program to train members on best practices for complying with Chinese legal standards, rather than an accreditation or audit-based system. Ten members participated in the pilot phase of the CSC-9000T project in 2006, and the organization is now preparing to expand the pilot project to 100 members. The pilot project consists of surveying standards implementation and providing follow-up training for participating companies. CSC-9000T is also working with international Corporate Social Responsibility organizations and buyers to refine the program and publicize its existence.

Corruption

Many people expected that China's entry into the WTO, which mandated a significant reduction in tariffs, would in turn reduce incentives for smuggling-related corruption. While WTO membership has increased China's exposure to international best practices and resulted in some overall improvements in transparency, corruption remains endemic. Chinese officials themselves admit that corruption is one of the most serious problems the country faces, and China's new leadership has called for an acceleration of the country's anti-corruption drive with a focus on closer monitoring of provincial-level officials. According to Chinese state media sources, from January 2003 to August 2006, more than 67,500 government officials were punished for corruption, with approximately 17,000 of those officials being punished for corruption between January 2006 and August 2006. China also launched an anti-corruption campaign in 2006 targeting Communist Party of China officials. According to the Xinhua News Agency, more than 97,000 party officials were punished in 2006.

In July 2004, China implemented a new Administrative Licensing Law. This law is designed to increase transparency in the licensing process, an area that has long served as a source of official corruption. This law seeks to ensure the reasonable use of administrative licensing powers to protect the interests of corporations and individuals and to promote efficient administrative management by requiring government agencies to set up special offices for issuing licenses and to respond to applications within 20 days. Since its 2004 implementation, the law has increased transparency in the licensing process, while reducing procedural obstacles and strengthening the legal environment for domestic and foreign enterprises.

China issued its first law on unfair competition in 1993, and the central government continues to call for improved self-discipline and anti-corruption initiatives at all levels of government. While the central government in recent years has pledged to begin awarding contracts solely on the basis of commercial criteria, it is unclear how quickly and to what extent the government will be able to follow through on this commitment. U.S. suppliers complain that the widespread existence of unfair bidding practices in China puts them at a competitive disadvantage. This dilemma is less severe in sectors where the United States holds clear technological or cost advantages. Corruption nevertheless undermines the long-term competitiveness of both foreign and domestic entities in the Chinese market.

Land Issues

China's constitution specifies that all land is owned in common by all the people. In practice, agricultural collectives, under the firm control of local Communist Party chairmen, distribute agricultural land to the rural poor, while city governments distribute land for residential and industrial use. The State and collectives can either "grant" or "allocate" land use rights to enterprises in return for the payment of fees. Enterprises granted land-use rights are guaranteed compensation if the State asserts eminent domain over the land, while those with allocated rights are not. Granted land-use rights cost more, not surprisingly, than allocated rights. However, the law does not define standards for compensation when eminent domain supersedes granted land-use rights. This situation creates considerable uncertainty when foreign investors are ordered to vacate. The absence of public hearings on planned public projects, moreover, can give affected parties, including foreign investors, little advance warning.

The time limit for land-use rights acquired by foreign investors for both industrial and commercial enterprises is 50 years. A major problem for foreign investors is the array of regulations that govern their ability to acquire land-use rights. Local implementation of these regulations may vary from central government standards, and prohibited practices may occur in one area while they are enforced in another. Most wholly-owned foreign enterprises seek granted land-use rights to state-owned urban land as the most reliable protection for their operations. Chinese-foreign joint ventures usually attempt to acquire granted land-use rights through lease or contribution arrangements with the local partners.

China's current rural land law, which took effect in 2003, gives peasants fixed contracts for periods of 30 years to 50 years and permits peasants to exchange or rent out their land-use rights while their use contract remains in force. There is no immediate prospect for changing from land-use rights to direct ownership of rural land. However, since 2004, China's leadership has pressed for sturdier land rights for farmers along with stricter controls over the legal process for converting farmland from agricultural to industrial or residential use. Local governments are no longer supposed to expropriate land for commercial use, as farmers are now supposed to be able to negotiate a compensation price for land directly with commercial users. However, implementation of these provisions lags.

China's National People's Congress passed a Property Rights Law on March 16, 2007, the first comprehensive legal protection to private property since the founding of the People's Republic in 1949. The property law, which generated years of controversy in the Chinese government but was never published in draft form, reportedly grants equal legal protection to private, state, and collectively owned property. This protection would cover the "means of production," such as factories, but agricultural land would remain a collective possession subject to 30-year leases. It is unclear at this time how the law will be implemented.

In: China: Economic, Political and Social Issues
Editors: J. M. Phillips and L. J. Moore

ISBN: 978-60456-727-4

Chapter 3

DYNAMIC LINKAGES BETWEEN U.S. PORTFOLIO EQUITY FLOWS AND EQUITY RETURNS IN CHINA AND INDIA

Joseph J. French*
School of Finance and Quantitative Methods, Kenneth W. Monfort College of Business
University of Northern Colorado, Campus Box 128, Greely, CO 80639, USA
Atsuyuki Naka†
Department of Economics and Finance, College of Business Administration
University of New Orleans, Lakefront, New Orleans, LA70148, USA

ABSTRACT

Asia presents one of the most vibrant economic environments in the world. China and India have emerged as the leaders in the Asian region due to their rapid growth and market size. Consequently, equity markets in both China and India have significantly developed following liberalization in the early 1990s. The rapid growth of these economies coupled with the development of their financial markets has attracted significant portfolio investment from U.S. investors. For example, U.S. equity portfolio flows have increased from 0.63 billion to 7.14 billion in China and from 0.5 to 11 billion in India between 1994 and 2005.

This research examines the dynamic nature of the relationship between U.S. portfolio equity flows and equity returns in China and India. To understand the linkages between equity flows, market returns, and other variables we dissect our empirical findings as follows: first, we examine the correlations between stock market returns and portfolio flows; second, we decompose flows into expected and unexpected components to analyze how returns are influenced by different flow components; and third, we explore the dynamic relationships among flows, returns, and related variables. Our findings show that flows are 'pulled' into China and India by returns greater than U.S. market returns.

* Email: joseph.french@unco.edu
† Email: anaka@uno.edu

Additionally, we find that the Indian equity index is influenced by U.S. investment activity and dividend yields, whereas the Chinese equity index is statistically unaffected by foreign investor behavior and fundamental determinates of value. This supports the ideas espoused in the popular press that the Chinese government still plays a major role in determining equity prices. A unique finding of this research is that the variance of the flow sequence in both China and India is better explained by shock to fundamentals vs. shocks to returns. This indicates that large American investors are making portfolio allocation decisions not simply on the basis of simple 'return chasing', but are at least partially informed about the markets of China and India. We anticipate that the strong relationship between equity flows and fundamentals should strengthen in the future as information asymmetries decline and U.S. investors continue to develop more sophisticated methods of assessing underlying value in these markets.

1. INTRODUCTION

China and India have recently emerged as the leaders in the Asian region due to their rapid growth and market size. China's economic growth in the past 20 years has been close to 8% per year, while India's annual GDP growth between 1999 and 2004 averaged approximately 6%. Consequently, equity markets in both China and India have significantly developed following liberalization in the early 1990s. The rapid growth of these economies, coupled with the development of their financial markets has attracted significant portfolio investment from U.S. investors. For example, U.S. institutional equity portfolio flows have increased from 0.63 billion to 7.14 billion in China and from 0.5 to 11 billion in India between 1994 and 2005.[1]

Portfolio flows have often been referred to as 'hot money', and are more volatile compared to other forms of capital flows (Kim and Ying, 2001). Investors have been known to reverse portfolio investments at the slightest hint of trouble in the host country or neighboring countries, often leading to disastrous economic consequences. Portfolio flows have been blamed for exacerbating small economic problems in a country by making large concentrated withdrawals at the first sign of economic weakness. Portfolio flows have also been held responsible for spreading financial crisis and causing contagion in international financial markets.[2]

This chapter examines the dynamic nature of the relationships between U.S. portfolio equity flows and equity returns in China and India. Equity flows represent cross-border portfolio flows of investors living abroad. These flows are comprised of inflows, the flows originating in the 'home' country and flowing into a foreign market; outflows, the flows originating in the 'foreign' country and flowing to the home market; and net flows (inflow-outflow). The broad purpose of this study is to understand the relationship between portfolio equity flows and equity returns in China and India. Do U.S. institutional flows affect asset returns? Do equity returns influence flows? These questions have been of recurrent interest to economists, investors, and policy makers, and are posed with greater urgency during times of financial upheaval or changes in the distribution of capital flows. The answers to the above

[1] Figures calculated using US treasury department data.

[2] Evidence is provided by the actions of portfolio investors in Malaysia during the 1997 Asian Financial Crisis. Maroney, Naka, and Wansi (2004) provide detailed discussion on the 1997 Asian Financial Crisis.

questions have often cast foreign investors in a negative light. It is often argued that foreign equity flows lead to price overreaction and can result in a contagion effect. An alternative efficient markets view is that equity flows are merely the process by which information is incorporated into asset prices

While there are numerous and strongly competing views, there is surprisingly little information on the behavior of international portfolio flows and their relation to asset returns, particularly in China and India. The large concentration of flows being channeled to China and India makes understanding the nature of the relationship between equity returns and flows in these countries of particular interest between equity flows and financial markets has not been extensively considered. The fact that China and India are special economies with huge market potentials and growth rates, coupled with the unique financial market in China, makes understanding how equity flows affect these financial markets particularly important.

International equity flows have emerged as an important policy issue in China and India (Tian, 2001). The danger of a 'Thailand-style' abrupt and sudden withdrawal of equity flows and the destabilizing effects on equity markets are of concern. While concerns about the negative impacts of sudden reversals of equity flows may have merits comparatively less attention has been paid to analyzing the actual equity flow data, to understand the key relationships between these flows and equity markets. A proper understanding of the influence of equity flows on equity markets and vice versa is essential to have a consequential debate about their effect.

To examine the dynamic relationship between U.S. cross-border equity flows of institutional investors and equity markets, we first look at the key features of equity flows, and then study the relationship between equity flows and stock markets with a key objective of determining causality or more generally forecastability. Secondly, we investigate the nature of the relationship between portfolio equity flows, equity markets, and related variables to uncover if U.S. portfolio investors act as informed investors. To address the emerging debate in the literature over the equality of information between foreign and domestic investors, we examine the response of U.S. equity flows to unexpected shocks in both market prices and fundamental determinants of equity prices. The majority of academic research argues that local (i.e., Chinese or Indian) investors in emerging markets naturally have an information advantage over foreigners (i.e., U.S.), while a new line of research suggests that foreign investors may perform better than domestic investors in their selection and timing of emerging market investments.[3]

The primary empirical method employed is vector autoregression (VAR) model. This method has been widely used by researchers to analyze the dynamic relationships as a reduced form of a system of simultaneous equations. The attractive feature of VAR is that the model allows for each variable in the system to be treated endogenously. The relationship between flows and returns is not well established, and neither variable is known to be exogenous. A VAR analysis allows for the estimation impulse response functions (IRF) and variance decompositions. IRFs provide the time path of the short-run dynamics that result from a shock in one variable to all of the variables in the system, while the variance decompositions provide the forecast error variance explained by variations in the variables in the system.

---

[3] See Brennan and Cao (1997), Seasholes (2004), Brennan, Cao, Strong and Wu (2005), Dvorak (2003).

The findings of this chapter show that flows are 'pulled' into China by returns greater than U.S. market returns. Results in India are less conclusive, but indicate a similar influence of returns on flows. Overall, this result implies that U.S. investors funnel investment funds to foreign markets in an attempt to take advantage of higher returns. This finding is consistent with return chasing behavior, suggested by Bohn and Tesar (1996), and has been documented in other countries. There is stronger evidence of return chasing in China than in India. This suggests that agents are relying more on past return realizations to forecast future returns in China, and indicates that information asymmetries are larger for US investors in China than in India.

The second major finding of this research is that the variance of the Indian equity index is influenced by U.S. investment activity and dividend yields, whereas the Chinese equity index is statistically unaffected by U.S. investor behavior and fundamental determinates of value. This supports the ideas espoused in current academic literature that the Chinese government still plays a major role in determining equity prices.[4] The results indicate that the Chinese market does not view increases in U.S. equity purchases as signaling information because the time path of the market is unaffected by this behavior. On the other hand, Indian market participants consider changes in the purchasing behavior of large U.S. investors as signaling information. The variance of the Indian equity market is influenced by the investment decisions of U.S. portfolio investors. This finding provides evidence that U.S. institutional investors are playing a major role in the Indian market. Further, we find that when returns are decomposed, flows tend to be better explained by fundamental shocks as opposed to price shocks. These results indicate that U.S. investors are reacting to fundamentals in both the Chinese and Indian markets, which suggests that U.S. institutional investors are not informationally deficient.

The reminder of this chapter will be structured as follows: Section 2 discusses capital flows to China and India and the equity markets of these nations, Section 3 discusses the literature, Section 4 describes our methodology and data, Section 5 reports our empirical results and Section 6 concludes this chapter.

2. Capital Flows and Equity Markets

2.1. FDI and Portfolio Flows in China and India

Capital flows are comprised of foreign direct investment flows (FDI) and portfolio flows (bond flows and equity flows). International portfolio flows are, as opposed to foreign direct investment, liquid in nature and are motivated by international portfolio diversification benefits for individual and institutional investors. Institutional investors, such as pension funds and mutual funds, initiate the majority of cross-border equity flows and bond flows.[5] According to Table 1, there is a positive correlation between FDI and portfolio investment in both China and India. This indicates that many of the factors that make a country a desirable place to acquire fixed assets also make it a desirable place to invest portfolio monies. China has become a magnet for foreign direct investment, overtaking the United States in 2003 as

[4] See Tian (2001) and Allen et al (2006).

[5] Treasury International Capital System Notes (TIC).

the number one destination of FDI (Prasad and Shang-Jin, 2005). FDI makes up the majority of U.S. investment in China (www.bea.gov), while in India portfolio investments are equally important.

Table 1. Correlation between US Institutional Equity Flows and Foreign Direct Investment Flows (FDI)

	FDI (CHINA)	FDI (INDIA)	E(CHINA)	E(India)
FDI (CHINA)	1			
FDI (INDIA)	0.87	1		
Equity(CHINA)	0.63	0.39	1	
Equity(India)	0.57	0.54	0.66	1

Source: Bureau of Economic Analysis (BEA). Date from 1994-2005.

One of the primary theoretical reasons to invest in countries such as China and India is the diversification benefits. Erb, Harvey and Viskanta (1996) found that from 1985 to 1993, China had a correlation of 5% with the world market, and for the period from 1979 to 1993, India had a negative correlation of 5% with the world market. These findings imply that, at least theoretically, India and China are naturally attractive to international portfolio investors. Beginning in early 1992, the Chinese and Indian markets that were previously closed to foreign investors began to liberalize, making portfolio investments possible, and equity investments started to pour into the region. As the consequence, the correlation has increased. Chinese equity market return is now correlated with the U.S. market at 14.97% and India is correlated with the U.S. market at 24.72% for the period January 1994 to May 2006. Besides diversification benefits of investing in these markets, China and India's rapid growth, market size, and increasing global competitiveness make these two economies the leaders in the Asian region (Griffith-Jones, 2004). Table 2 presents net portfolio equity flows to emerging markets, including China and India, from the developed countries. As Table 2 illustrates, China and India are becoming the major destinations for portfolio investment, accounting for about 67% of total portfolio equity flows to developing countries in 2004.

Table 2. Net Equity Flows to Developing Countries: China and India

	1996	1997	1999	2000	2001	2002	2003	2004
Developing Countries	32.9	22.6	12.7	12.4	6.0	5.8	24.8	26.8
China	1.9	5.7	0.6	6.9	0.8	2.2	7.7	10.5
India	4.0	2.6	2.3	2.5	3.0	1.1	8.2	7.5
As a proportion of net equity flows to developing countries (%)								
China	5.8	25.2	4.7	55.6	13.3	37.9	31.0	39.2
India	12.2	11.5	18.1	20.2	50.0	19.0	33.0	28.0
China and India	18.0	36.7	22.8	75.8	63.3	56.9	64.0	67.2

Source: Global Development Finance 2005, all numbers in USD billions.

Graphs 1 and 2 show monthly portfolio equity inflows into China and India from the United States. The data, from the Treasury Department of the United States, provides further evidence of the importance of studying portfolio flows to China and India. As these pictures clearly illustrate, inflows to China and India from the United States have increased substantially from 2000 to 2005, and we expect that equity flows to the region should continue. Noteworthy spikes have occurred in both countries. In China, the spike in equity inflows occurred in the month immediately following the appreciation of the Chinese Yuan (RMB). In India, the spike in equity flows occurred around the time of increased public interest in Indian equities, evidenced by an investment of 100 million dollars by Goldman Sacs in the month the spike occurs and a corresponding visit by President George W. Bush on November 2005.

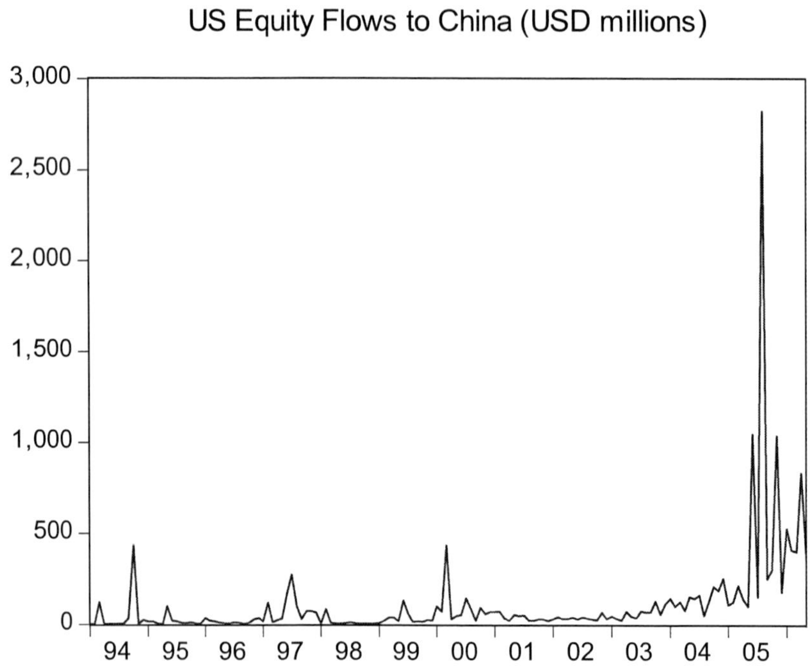

Graph 1. Monthly Equity Flows from the U.S. to China.

Another key aspect of the Chinese and Indian markets which makes them attractive to portfolio investors is the large reserve that both countries have built-up over the period of 2000 to 2004. These high reserves serve the purpose of protecting against instability in financial markets and help to mitigate undesirable appreciation of the Rupee and Yuan, which could undermine their international competitiveness (Griffith-Jones, 2004). Table 3 shows just how rapidly these two countries built-up foreign exchange reserves from 2000 to 2004. Most of these reserves have been invested in U.S. assets, and have helped to finance the U.S.'s large and growing current account deficit and Government debt (Rogoff, 2003).

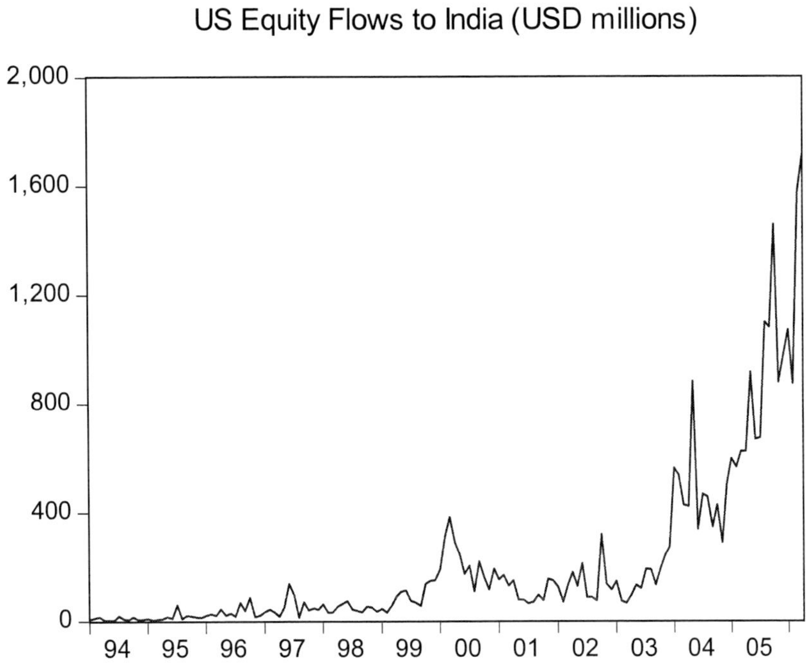

Graph 2. Monthly Equity Flows from the U.S. to India.

Table 3. Foreign Exchange Reserves of China and India

	2000	2001	2002	2003	2004
China	165.6	212.2	286.4	403.3	610.0
India	37.3	45.3	67.0	97.6	125.5

Source: Global Development Finance 2005. All number in USD billions.

Although China's trade surplus with the United States has been growing, its overall trade surplus is modest because it is running a growing trade deficit with Asia-Pacific countries; in large part offsetting its trade surplus with the U.S. China has accumulated substantial foreign exchange reserves that exceed its annual imports. There is little doubt that China's growing exports to countries outside of Asia has generated equally rapid growth in imports by China from other Asian and Pacific countries. According to Perez (2002), Japan's current economic recovery is being driven by a surge in exports to China. Australia's healthy economy is being kept that way by Chinese investments in liquid natural gas products. China is now also South Korea's largest trading partner. Although India is the largest market in South Asia, it has yet to have a major impact on the trade of its neighbors in South Asia despite of the creation of the South Asian Preferential Trade Area (SAPTA) in 1997. Prasad and Shang-Jin (2005) point out the recent increase in the pace of reserve accumulation in China is potentially related to "hot money' (i.e. bond and equity flows) rather than trade surplus or FDI flows. The evolution of Indian reserves is similar to what is occurring in China. India had reserves of around \$98 billion at the end of 2003, exceeding by a substantial margin imports of \$60 billion.

The issue of the appropriate level of reserves is unsettled (Griffith-Jones, 2004). Any attempt to determine the appropriate level of reserves has to be based on an analysis of the exchange rate regime for each country, and the related issue of whether the benefits from integration with the global financial markets outweigh the costs. Rogoff (2003) discusses these issues in the context of China and India, and concludes that for the most part China and India are getting to the point where the lost opportunity cost of building up reserves is beginning to outweigh the benefits of the reduction of the risk of exchange rate appreciation. The Indian exchange rate regime is one of managed float, and it does allow some flexibility. China, on the other hand, is maintaining a fixed exchange rate system. China also faces serious problems in the financial sector, in particular the overhang of nonperforming loans, and an immediate revaluation might worsen the problem.

2.2. Chinese Equity Markets

China's stock markets were not open to foreign equity portfolio investment until 1992, but since then the markets have been growing very rapidly. Despite the fast growth of the Chinese stock markets, they are not efficient in the traditional sense compared with more developed exchange markets (Tian, 2001). In general, prices and domestic investor's behavior do not reflect fundamental values of listed firms (Allen et al, 2006). Table 4 shows that the ranking of different exchange markets in terms of number of transactions. Shanghai Stock Exchange (SHSE) ranked fourth and the Shenzhen Stock Exchange (SZSE) ranked eighth in 2003 and 2004.

One distinctive characteristic of the Chinese equity markets is that the shares are of two primary types.[6] Class A and B shares are listed in either SHSE or SZSE. Class A shares are issued to domestic Chinese investors and class B shares to foreign investors, including who are overseas Chinese. The restriction on holding class A shares by foreigners was relaxed in 2002 (Lin et al, 2005). The A shares of each listed company are divided into three categories; state owned shares, legal person shares, and tradable shares. The first two types of shares are held by the government, government agencies, state owned enterprises, or other enterprises. They were not tradable on the stock exchanges until very recently when the government started the process of gradually making all shares tradable (Allen et al, 2006)

Shirai (2002) and Chen, Lee and Rui (2001) find a significant price discount for Class B shares held by foreigners, as compared to Class A shares held by Chinese. Tian (2001) finds that firm value is negatively affected by government ownership, and that B shares move more closely with fundamentals than A shares. Two major differences that academic literature has shown to be unique to the Chinese equity market are the separation of three types of shares (a non-tradable A tradable, and B tradable) and the dominant role of the government.[7] The separation of three different types of shares has its costs in terms of low market efficiency and corporate governance. When state owned shares are not tradable, the largest shareholder is often the government. This gives the government the dominant position in the corporation.

---

[6] Another issue associated with the Chinese equity markets is that many of the larger companies are listed overseas or in Hong Kong, which leave the domestic market with primarily small firms and has been blamed for the Chinese markets volatile first fifteen years.

[7] See Allen, Qian and Qian (2006) for a summary of this literature.

Even if the government prefers to reduce its dominant position, it cannot sell shares easily because they are not fully tradable on the stock market.

Table 4. Largest Exchanges by Number of Transactions

Index	2001	2002	2003	2004
NASDAQ	1	1	1	1
NYSE	2	2	2	2
NSE	4	3	3	3
SHSE	3	5	4	4
BSE	8	7	5	5
Korea	6	4	7	6
Taiwan	7	6	6	7
SZSE	5	8	8	8
Germany	9	9	9	9
London	14	12	11	10

Source: http:/indiabudget.nic.in

Another significant factor affecting the development of the Chinese equity market is the fact that there are very few stocks that would fit the definition of "blue-chip" trading on China's mainland exchanges (Gao, 2002). Whereas most developed markets are dominated by a limited number of large-cap stocks,[8] China's market has a disproportionate number of small-cap stocks. This feature allows for increased speculation and higher turnover. Another factor that has influenced speculation is that the Chinese market is a retail market, e.g., expansion through the issuance of new shares rather than the appreciation in value of existing stocks (Chen et al, 2003). There is also very stringent regulation of IPO's in China. The government sets the quota for new listings each year and selects the qualified companies based on provincial and sector allocations. Under current laws in China, no company is allowed to list without three years of continuous profitability, which has been cited as a law that favors state owned companies (Gao, 2002).

2.3. Indian Equity Markets

The Bombay Stock Exchange (BSE), established in 1875, has a long history. India hosts the largest number of listed companies after the United States and investors are increasing turning to India (Griffith-Jones, 2004). As of early 2006, there were about 3,500 Indian companies listed with the stock exchange, accounting for over 90% of the total market capitalization in India. The average value of transactions in India is small, but at the same time India has a very high volume of transactions that are required to be implemented by commensurately large, yet low-cost IT systems (Padmanabhan, 2005). The number of BSE

[8] An example is Nokia in the Finnish market which accounts for roughly 70% of Finland's total market value. In China, the top fifteen companies account for only about 11% of market capitalization.

transactions ranked among the world's top five in 2003 and 2004 (see Table 4). India officially opened its stock markets to foreign investors in September 1992 and has since received a considerable amount of portfolio investment in equities from Foreign Institutional Investors. In January of 1993, foreign brokerage firms were also allowed to begin operating in India. This has become one of the main channels of international portfolio investment in India for foreigners (Padmanabhan, 2005). During the liberalization period of 1992-1993, the gates to the Indian stock market was the scene of a series of major fraudulent transactions that resulted in regulators being blamed for inexperience, laxity, and outright corruption (Rao, 2002). However, as scandals have decreased, the number of registered foreign institutional investors has risen substantially. The total amount of foreign institutional investment in terms of market capitalization has steadily climbed to about 9% of the total market capitalization of the BSE with U.S.-based institutions accounting for over 41% of total equity flows (World Bank, 2005).

The growing sophistication of the market is evidenced by numerous and very large recent stock issues. The mean IPO size increased twenty fold over the period 2001-2004 (BSE). The success of these large issues has dispelled earlier doubts about the feasibility of billion-dollar offerings on the Indian market. Another major development is the introduction of the Indian primary market. It has been introduced as "screen based book building", where securities are auctioned through an anonymous screen-based system, and the price at which securities are sold is discovered on the screen. This eliminates the delays, risks, and implementation difficulties associated with traditional procedures. Despite considerable skepticism about the extent to which computers could replace the services of skilled investment bankers, it is reported that resource mobilization through book building rose steadily from 25 percent of public equity offerings in 2001 to 53 percent in 2002, 64 percent in 2003, and 99 percent in 2004 (Padmanabhan, 2005).

Just as in the case of China, the markets in India have unique structure of note. The Indian market, unlike the U.S., has widespread retail participation that spans the country. With households directly owing the bulk of securities, the shareholding pattern in India is not conducive to market to discipline. Given the high promoter stakes, hostile takeover bids are unlikely to succeed. In fact, there have been very few such bids in India, and even these turned out to be attempts at making fast money rather than seeking management control to improve performance of the target firm (Rao, 2002). There is also evidence that corporate governance may be improving, with insider trading laws have been enacted in 1992 and the first conviction under these laws occurring in 1998 (Rao, 2002).

3. Literature Review and Common Hypotheses

Existing evidence indicates a strong relationship between inflows of foreign capital and market returns. Griffin, Nardari, and Stulz (2004) have confirmed this result in their studies on emerging Asian equity markets, although China and India were not included. What is unsettled is the interpretation of this relationship and implications for the role of foreign investors in emerging markets. There are several competing hypotheses to explain the relationship. One such hypothesis is that the participation of foreign investors in the market brings about a demand shift and hence a permanent price change.

In support of this hypothesis, Merton (1987) demonstrates that if investors were able to invest in all equities, the standard capital asset pricing model pricing relations would hold. However, with segmentation restrictions or a restricted investor base, the expected return on a market will be higher than its unrestricted return by a risk premium. Merton's model predicts that the greater the number of informed investors the lower the required rate of return. This hypothesis is often referred to as the base broadening hypothesis. Berkaert, Harvey and Lumsdaine (2002) apply this idea to show that equity flows should lower the cost of capital in many countries, and facilitate the flow of capital to firms and countries that have the best investment opportunities irrespective of their location. In their empirical work, Berkaert et al (2002) use dividend yield to proxy the cost of capital, and find a negative relationship between equity flows and dividend yields, implying that as investor base increases, the cost of capital declines, which in turn increases equity prices.

The converse of the base broadening theory was tested in the context of aggregate mutual fund flows by Warther (1995) and in the context of exchange rates by Hau, Massa and Peress (2005). Warther (1995) develops a theory in the context of aggregate mutual fund flows which is referred to as the price pressure hypothesis, suggesting that a rise in prices associated with inflow surges are due to temporary illiquidity. This theory then predicts that inflow induced price increases will be reversed. Shleifer (1986) presents evidence that increases in stock prices resulting from the announcement of inclusion of individual stocks in the Standard and Poor's 500 are at least partially reversed over the subsequent 30-60 trading days.

The most commonly found characteristic of the relationship between equity flows and returns is return chasing or the fact that U.S. purchases are positively correlated with both current and lagged stock returns. The seminal paper that developed the return chasing hypothesis in the context of equity flows was by Bohn and Tesar (1996). The return chasing hypothesis implies that investors chase high returns into equity markets. The empirical implication is that flows should be correlated with lagged returns, and therefore flows should be able to be predicted from lagged returns.

Froot, O'Connell and Seasholes (2001) find that the majority of co-movement of flows and returns is actually due to returns predicting future flows, which would be supportive of the return chasing behavior of international investors. They also find some ability for international inflows to forecast returns. A number of papers have documented a similar phenomenon, which has also been termed positive feedback trading. Choe, Kho and Stulz (1999) detect strong positive feedback activity in Korea before the Asian financial crisis, but not during the crisis. They find that foreign sales do not lead to negative abnormal returns, which implies that there is no evidence that foreign investment is destabilizing. Dahlquist and Robertsson (2004) also document a similar feedback trading behavior in the Swedish market, showing that such behavior may not be just a characteristic of emerging markets. However, the return chasing hypothesis is not without challenge. Portes and Rey (2005), for example, fail to find evidence of return chasing in a large panel study.

One consistent finding in the literature of equity flows is that foreign investors build up positions slowly, which leads to autocorrelation in equity flows. These results have been taken to suggest cross-border heterogeneity in information endowments because autocorrelation in equity flows reflects a learning process and may suggest informationally deficient foreign investors.[9] Brennan and Cao (1997) postulate that one reason for the

[9] See Brennan and Cao (1997), Griffen et al (2004), Brennan, Strong and Xu (2005), Kim and Ying (2001)

autocorrelation of equity flows is that foreign investors are less informed about local markets than are domestic investors. The crux of their argument is that if domestic investors are better informed than foreign investors, they will hold more domestic shares on average. Foreign investors discount share prices relative to domestic investors since domestic investors tend to sell if they have adverse information that is not incorporated in asset prices. This implies that foreign investors do not take advantage of the complete benefits of diversification as they would if information were symmetric.

The home bias resulting from information asymmetries implies that the cost of capital in the domestic country is higher than it would be in the absence of these asymmetries. Therefore, as flows leave the country due to bad news, equity prices decline because domestic investors have to hold more domestic shares, and hence bear more risk (Brennan and Cao, 1997). Inflows have the opposite effect; prices should increase to reflect the lower risk bore by domestic investors. Kang and Stulz (1997) argue that the ideal setting to further test the hypothesis of information asymmetry would be to see if foreign investors favor large firms. Japan is one of the few countries besides the U.S. where the data on holdings of equity by foreign investors is easily available at the firm level. Kang and Stulz (1997) demonstrate that foreign investors have a considerable bias toward large firm stocks in Japan.

Dvorak (2003) and Seasholes (2004) suggest that there is a strong possibility that foreign investors may be well informed. If one assumes that foreign institutional investors are informed, this could explain the observed autocorrelation in flows. For example, if a US institution were able to gain an informational advantage, they would want to hide or conceal this informational advantage. The attempt to conceal this information would lead to rationing behavior in an attempt to minimize the price impact of their purchases.

Further motivation for the idea that U.S. investors may not have inferior information endowments reflects the nature of the economies of China and India. China and India are countries that export many products and services to the United States. Alfaro, Kalemali-Ozen and Volosovych (2005) mention that several factors tend to reduce information asymmetries between countries. The first one is the rapidly growing economy, i.e., as GDP increases, informational asymmetries decline. The second factor which reduces differences in information is an increase in trade between nations or regions. The fact that China and India are expanding, coupled with the increase in trade with the U.S., indicates that informational asymmetries have likely declined. The decline in information asymmetries combined with China and India's suboptimal financial systems makes it entirely possible that economists in the U.S. can be better at analyzing some companies in China and India than are Chinese and Indian economists.

Empirically, Seasholes (2004) finds evidence that foreign investors are better informed than domestic investors. He also finds that the amount that foreigners hold or trade in an underlying stock is a good proxy for profitability. Froot and Ramadori (2005) agree with Seasholds and find that foreign investors act informed. Hamao and Mei (2001) also argue that foreign investors are more sophisticated than domestic investors in Japan and tend to be long term contrarians; additionally Grinblatt and Keloharju (2000) suggest that foreign institutional investors are the most sophisticated investor class in Finland.

4. Methodology and Data

4.1. Motivations and Empirical Methods

To motivate for our variable selection, we begin with a simple model of stock prices given as:[10]

$$P_{t+1} = E_t\left[\sum_{j=1}^{K}\left(\frac{1}{1+R_t}\right)^j D_{t+j}\right] + E_t\left[\left(\frac{1}{1+R_t}\right)^K P_{t+K}\right], \qquad (1)$$

where P_{t+1} is the stock price level, D_{t+j} is the dividend, E_t is the conditional expectations operator based on information available to market participants, and K is the investor's time horizon. As K increases the second term on the right approaches zero, leaving the familiar Gordon growth model. R_t is the rate of return used by market participants to discount future value. R_t is a decreasing function of the number of foreign investors. To understand why R_t is decreasing in the number of foreign investors, we appeal to a model developed by Merton (1987), who present the base-broadening hypothesis in the context of capital market equilibrium with incomplete information.

The basic argument is best summarized by Merton's (1987) comparative statics, shown below:

$$\frac{\partial V_k}{\partial q_k} = V_k \delta x_k \sigma_k^2 / q_k^2 > 0, \qquad (2)$$

where V_k is market value of firm k (or market k), δ is a non-negative parameter in the utility function, q_k is the fraction of all investors who know about security *k*, x_k is the fraction of the market portfolio invested in security k, σ_k^2 is the standard deviation of security *k*. The result directly shows that as the number of investors increases, the value of the firm increases. His model has very appealing implications for studying the relationships between equity market prices and net equity flows. If one considers the q in Merton's model to be the number of foreign investors, then increases in purchases of foreign investors should increase the value of the market or firm. It has been empirically found that foreign portfolio flows as a percentage market capitalization will increase as relatively positive information is released about a foreign market (Henry, 2000).

Researchers have found that as markets are liberalized and more foreign investors enter the equity market, the cost of capital declines. Bekaert, Harvey and Lumsdaine (2002) find that the higher firm value is a result of a permanent reduction in the cost of capital by using dividend yield to proxy the cost of capital. This result could also be expected based on the

---

[10] discussed by Campbell and Lo, MacKinlay (1997)

nature of portfolio equity flows found in previous literature. Since portfolio equity flows are autocorrelated, after a positive shock to flows, rational foreign and domestic investors would expect greater demand from foreign investors in the future. This would cause prices to be bid higher following the flow shock.

A vector autoregression (VAR) model is useful for forecasting systems of interrelated time-series variables and testing causality among these endogenous variables. Let a VAR be expressed as:

$$Z_t = \mu + \Gamma_1 Z_{t-1} + \ldots + \Gamma_p Z_{t-p} + \varepsilon_t, \tag{3}$$

where $Z_t = [R_{it}, f_{it}]'$ and R_{it} and f_{it} are returns of market i and inflows from the U.S. to either China or India for a case of the bivariate VAR. μ is a parameter vector and Γ's are the matrices of the parameters estimated, and ε_t is the residual vector. The lag length is determined by the Akaike information criterion (AIC). VAR with an exogenous variables is also estimated (VARX), where the exogenous variable is a dummy variable for extreme observations on equity flows. Block exogeneity or Granger causality tests are used to examine whether or not the lagged values of other endogenous variables have forecasting power for a variable in the system. The variance decomposition and impulse response functions (IRF) are constructed to illustrate the responses of all variables given a shock in one variable. In order to control for other endogenous factors, we estimate a three variable and a four variable VAR. Griffen et al (2004) suggest the inclusion of industrial production as additional endogenous variable. Fama and French (1992) and Dvorak (2003) provide theoretical motivation for the consideration of dividend yields as endogenously related to equity returns and equity flows.

4.2. Data Description

The data for our empirical investigation consists of equity flows, industrial production, dividend yields, market capitalization, and returns on global market indices. The source for monthly data on equity flows is the U.S Treasury International Capital System (TIC) reporting system.[11] U.S. net purchases of securities are defined as gross purchases (inflows) of foreign securities by U.S. residents from the host country minus gross sales (outflows) of foreign securities from U.S. residents to the host country. We note that the data on equity flows is limited to bilateral portfolio flows into and out of the United States, and does not include other countries' investment in China and India. We use the International Financial Corporations Emerging Market Database (EMDB) for U.S. dollar returns for Global market indices, market capitalization, and dividend yields for China and India. Industrial production is taken from the International Financial Statistics database (IFS). Table 5 summarizes the definitions of the variables used in our empirical analysis.

[11] See Tesar and Werner (1994, 1995) for a complete description and analysis of this data.

Table 5. Variable Definitions

Variable	Definition
INFLOW	US purchases of Chinese/Indian equities
OUTFLOW	US sales of Chinese/Indian equities
NETFLOW	Inflows-Outflows
NIFLOWUS	Inflow divided by market capitalization in USD
NOFLOWUS	Outflow divided by market capitalization in USD
NNFLOWUS	Outflow divided by market capitalization in USD
EIFLOW	Expected inflows
UIFLOW	Unexpected inflows
FOREX	Exchange rate
DIV1	Log of dividend yield
INDEXUS, INDEXLC	Index level in USD and index level in local currency
LNIP	Log difference industrial production
RUSD, RLC	Return in USD and return in local currency
ERUSD	Indian or Chinese equity market return minus US equity market return in USD

Equity flow data is from the TIC database, equity prices, returns, market capitalization and dividends are from the EMDB, and industrial production is from IFS.

The sample period for this study is from January 1994 to May 2006 for both China and India. The reason this sample period is chosen is to allow for a significant time for the effects of liberalization to taper out. Henry (2000) and Berkaert et al (2002) show that equity flows follow a distinctively different pattern surrounding liberalization. Henry (2000) examines at the impact of stock market liberalization on 12 emerging markets. He finds that on average aggregate equity price index experiences a positive abnormal return of 3.3% after a country's government allows foreigners to purchase shares. Kim and Singal (2002) also find that emerging market stock returns are abnormally high in the months leading up to liberalization. Additionally, Berkaert and Harvey (2000) show that aggregate dividend yields decline after liberalization, which is evidence of a lower cost of capital after liberalization. The timeline that contains only post liberalization data with a significantly long time-series will make this research one of the first to look at the relationships between equity flows and returns for China and India without the contamination of liberalization.

Table 6 Panels A and B report the summary statistics for China and India, respectively. The average monthly inflow (INFLOW) from U.S. institutional investors into China over the sample period was about 109.5 million (USD), which represents approximately 0.1019% of market capitalization. While this number may seem insignificant, over the course of a year about 1.2% of the market capitalization of China flows to the country from the U.S. Net equity flows (NETFLOW) had a positive mean of 55.32 million over the sample period. This implies that U.S. institutional investors are increasing their portfolio weights in the Chinese equity market. In contrast, the average monthly equity flow from U.S. institutional investors to India was 268.72 million (USD), accounting for approximately 1% of market capitalization. Similar to China, India also had a positive mean net equity flow, indicating that

U.S. investors are building up portfolio investments in India.[12] Monthly returns (RUSD) in China averaged roughly 1% over the sample period, which is very close to the average return on the Indian market of 0.98%. Excess dollar returns (ERUSD) in both Chinese and Indian equity markets averaged above the U.S market by approximately 0.3% in China and 0.28% in India per month. [13]

Table 6. Summary Statistics

Panel A: China

	Obs	Mean	S.D	Min	Max
INFLOW	149	109.50	274.65	1.00	2823.00
OUTLFOW	149	54.17	70.44	0.00	395.00
NETFLOW	149	55.32	251.13	-265.00	2660.00
NIFLOWUS	149	0.0011	0.0023	0.0004	0.0210
NOFLOWUS	149	0.0005	0.0005	0.00	0.0041
NNFLOWUS	149	0.0006	0.0022	-0.0030	0.0208
LNIP	149	0.0081	0.5369	-0.2004	0.2148
DIV1	149	0.0022	0.0012	0.0002	0.0626
INDEXUS	149	134.15	43.99	37.59	218.91
ERUSD	149	0.0035	0.1174	-0.2361	0.9597
RUSD	149	0.0111	0.1161	-0.2046	0.9973

Panel B: India

	Obs	Mean	S.D	Min	Max
INFLOW	149	268.72	379.49	7.00	2962.00
OUTLFOW	149	220.88	330.03	2.00	1717.00
NETFLOW	149	47.85	156.21	-604.00	1245.00
NIFLOWUS	149	0.0102	0.0145	0.0003	0.1168
NOFLOWUS	149	0.0083	0.0124	0.0008	0.0677
NNFLOWUS	149	0.0019	0.0062	-0.0238	0.0491
LNIP	149	0.0050	0.0501	-0.1479	0.1141
DIV1	149	0.0162	0.0052	0.0063	0.0295
INDEXUS	149	525.66	259.37	281.40	1566.86
ERUSD	149	0.0022	0.0805	-0.1930	0.2198
RUSD	149	0.0099	0.0803	-0.1726	0.2267

Means, standard deviations and extreme values for data equity flow and return data are reported in the tables above for the period of January 1994 to June 2006.

[12] In equity flow, accounting inflows are reported as flows into a foreign country from the domestic country. Hence, an inflow would be a flow out of the US into to China or India. Accounting out flows are the exact opposite. Net flows are inflows minus outflows, where a positive net flow indicates that more equity has exited the US than entered.

[13] Following Bekaert, Harvey and Lumsdaine (2002), NIFLOWS, NOFLOWS and NNFLOWS are standardized by market capitalization.

Graph 3A. Chinese Global Index Level.

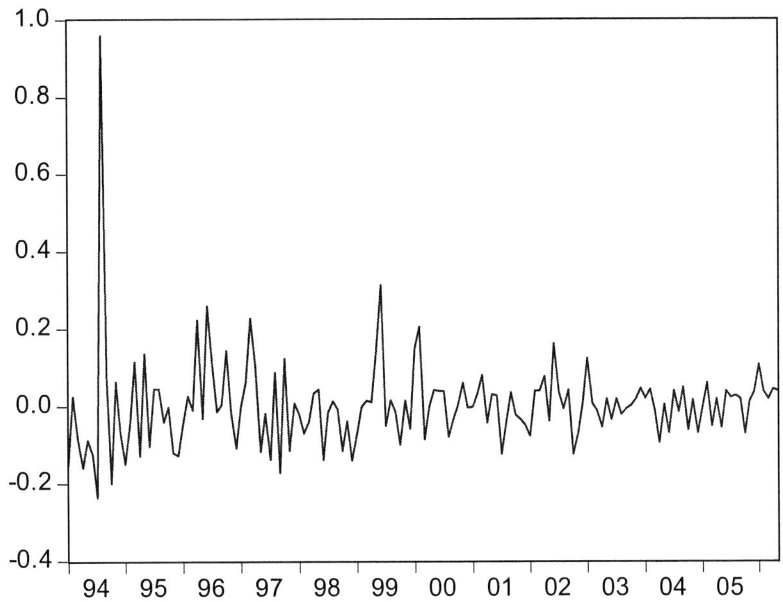

Graph 3B. Excess Return (Chinese return-U.S. return, in USD).

Graphs 3A and 3B illustrate the time series of the Chinese stock index and the excess returns over the U.S. returns. Also, Graphs 4A and 4B illustrate the Indian stock index and Indian excess returns. We observe that the Chinese stock index shows a steady upward trend over time, but that the Indian stock index remains relatively flat until 2002 when it then shows substantial upward movement.

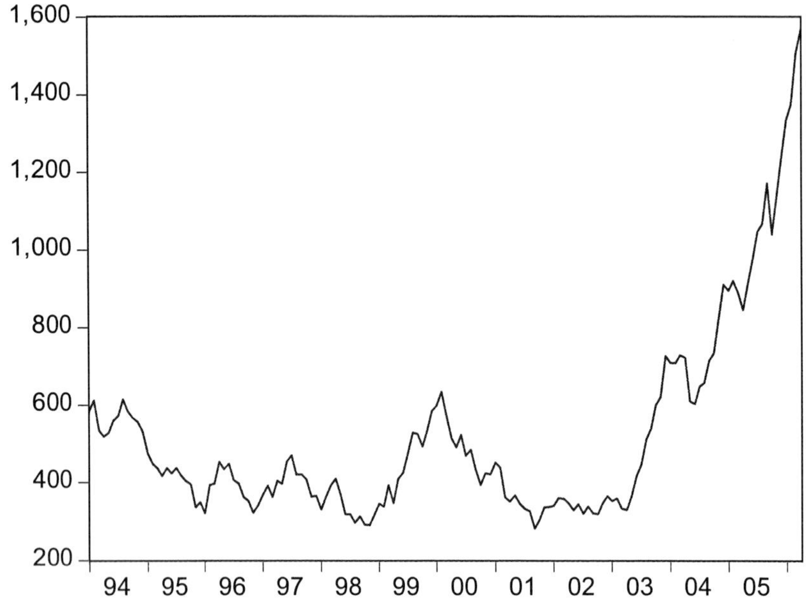

Graph 4A. Indian Global Index Level.

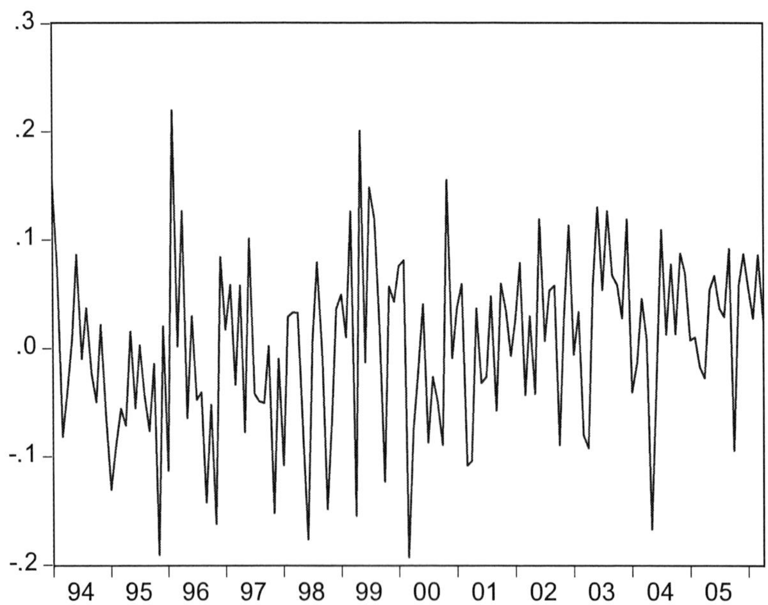

Graph 4B: Excess Return (Indian return-USA return, in USD).

Table 7 Panels A and B report the contemporaneous correlations between variables used in this study for China and India, respectively. The correlation between dividend yield and index level in both China and India are negative at -49% in China and at -34% in India. This finding is consistent with the notion that rapidly growing economies reinvest earnings rather than paying out dividends, and could indicate that future growth is expected. There is also a small negative correlation between equity flows and dividend yields, which is consistent with the base broadening hypothesis as adapted by Bekaert, Harvey and Lumsdaine (2002). If one uses dividend yield to proxy the cost of capital, then one would expect, according the base-broadening hypothesis that as inflows increase the cost capital should decline. There is a strongly positive correlation between inflows and outflows. Tesar and Werner (1995) first pointed out that international capital markets are characterized by large turnovers and show that turnover of foreign equity holdings is roughly twice that of domestic holdings.

Table 7. Correlation Matrixes of Variables

Panel A: China

	INDEXUS	RUSD	DIV1	IN-FLOW	OUT-FLOW	NET-FLOW	NI-FLOWUS	NO-FLOWUS
INDEXUS	1							
RUSD	0.071	1						
DIV1	-0.491	-0.020	1					
INFLOW	0.267	0.023	-0.004	1				
OUTFLOW	0.576	0.041	-0.142	0.448	1			
NETFLOW	0.127	0.013	0.036	0.968	0.209	1		
NIFLOWUS	0.009	-0.085	0.003	0.688	0.165	0.706	1	
NOFLOWUS	0.396	0.025	-0.187	0.254	0.784	0.058	0.131	1
NNFLOWUS	-0.070	-0.090	0.040	0.641	0.009	0.699	0.980	-0.069

Panel B: India

	INDEXUS	RUSD	DIV1	IN-FLOW	OUT-FLOW	NET-FLOW	NI-FLOWUS	NO-FLOWUS
INDEXUS	1							
RUSD	0.238	1						
DIV1	-0.344	-0.070	1					
INFLOW	0.891	0.104	-0.059	1				
OUTFLOW	0.860	0.147	-0.093	0.906	1			
NETFLOW	0.221	0.136	-0.098	0.108	0.520	1		
NIFLOWUS	0.860	0.147	-0.093	0.906	0.975	0.520	1	
NOFLOWUS	0.891	0.104	-0.059	0.894	0.906	0.108	0.906	1
NNFLOWUS	0.221	0.136	-0.098	0.108	0.520	0.933	0.520	0.108

Correlations between major variable used in this study are reported in the tables above for the period January, 1994 to June 2006.

If we measure excess flows as the difference between total flows (outflows + inflows) and the absolute value of net flows, then total flows are huge compared to net flows. In China net flows account for about 33% of total flows and in India net flows account for only about 10% of total flows on average. The large size of total flows compared to net flows, particularly in India, suggests that turnover is high and demonstrates that U.S. investors are constantly altering positions based on the changing investment environment. In China, the evidence is not so strong, with net flows being roughly equal to outflow. Further, gross inflows and outflows are positively correlated at over 45% in China and at 90% in India. This appears to indicate that investors, particularly in India, are adjusting or rebalancing their portfolios within a given month among different stocks. In India, the small positive correlation between flows and returns is consistent with the findings of previous literature (i.e., Froot et al, 2001). China, on the other hand, appears to demonstrate a small negative correlation between flows and returns.

5. Empirical Results

5.1. Behavior of Portfolio Equity Flows

In this section we address the following questions: How are returns and flows related? Do flows forecast returns or vice versa? The first evidence is simply visual. As shown in Graphs 1, 2, 3 and 4 flows and prices move together at low frequencies. The co-movement could be ascribed to a variety of factors, including overreaction, information shocks, or demand shocks. Following the spirit of Froot et al (2001), we estimate correlations between flows and returns over four month lags and decompose the correlation structure between net and gross flows and returns. The correlation between lagged returns and flows may provide preliminary evidence of return chasing. The correlation between contemporaneous returns and flows will give some indication about the relevance of the information story of Brennan and Cao (1997). The correlation between future returns and flows will give us ideas about the predictability of returns from flows. For example, if future returns are positively correlated with contemporaneous flows, then flows could be a useful factor in predicting future equity returns. One the other hand, if returns are negatively correlated with contemporaneous flows, then this would provide preliminary evidence of the price pressure hypothesis.

Table 8 reports the results of correlation between excess returns and normalized net flows and inflows. Column 1 reports the correlation between flows and lagged excess returns (ERUSD) for four months. Column 2 reports the contemporaneous correlation between ERUSD and flows, and the final column reports the correlation between flows and four month future ERUSD. The correlation between lagged excess returns and flows is strongly positive in both countries indicating that flows appear to follow returns. If flows are correlated with lagged returns, then it indicates that excess returns have some predictive power as to the purchasing behavior of U.S. institutional investors. Contemporaneously, flows are positively correlated in India and negatively correlated in China. The model developed by Brennan and Cao (1997) demonstrates that if domestic investors have net information advantage, then flows and returns should be positively correlated. We find that this holds in the case of India, but in the case of China, we see the opposite effect. This could be because of a number of reasons related to the degree of regulation in the Chinese market. As far as the predictability of future returns from current flows, again we find opposite results in China and India. In China, flows are negatively correlated with future returns, but in India, inflows are positively correlated with future returns. The result indicate that price pressure is be present in India, as U.S. investors make up 41% of foreign equity flows to the nation.

Table 8. Monthly Correlation Structure

	Flows and lagged returns (4 months)	Contemporaneous correlation	Flows and future returns (4 months)
China (net flows)	0.405	-0.113	-0.188
China (inflows)	0.403	-0.106	-0.194
India (net flows)	0.204	0.180	-0.093
India (inflows)	0.754	0.144	0.581

Reported are correlations between monthly Chinese and Indian stock market index returns (in USD) and inflows and net flows from the US to China and India.

Table 9 presents the results of the correlations between unexpected inflows (UIFLOW) and ERUSD. Following Warther (1995), we estimate an autoregressive model to predict one-step-ahead values of inflows and to obtain both an expected and an unexpected inflow series, where the unanticipated flows are based on the residuals. The results show that lagged ERUSD appear to be positively correlated to unexpected inflows. This is consistent with the logic of Warther (1995) and Clark and Berko (1997). For example, our findings imply that after the Chinese or Indian equity market outperforms the U.S. markets, U.S. institutional investors increase their purchases of equities in China and India more than anticipated. Contemporaneously, there is also a positive relationship between excess returns and flows in the case of India and only a slightly negative correlation in China. Also in China, high unexpected flows are negatively correlated with future excess returns, and in India future excess returns are positively correlated with unexpected flows.

Table 9. Monthly Correlation Structure: Unanticipated Inflows

	Flows and lagged returns (4 months)	Contemporaneous correlation	Flows and future returns (4 months)
China (uiflows)	0.280	-0.023	-0.230
India (uiflows)	0.256	0.128	-0.194

Unanticipated inflows are calculated as the residual of an AR(2) model similar to Warther (1995).

5.2. Causality and Impulse Response Functions

We estimated several sets of the bivariate VARs with excess returns and different measures of equity flows (i.e., inflows, outflows, net flow, and unexpected inflows, etc) in order to check the robustness of the results. The results are similar for each, mostly likely due to most likely the high correlation between different flow components in both countries. Additionally we note that the results of our VAR estimation are generally unaffected by the ordering of variables, which is consistent with the findings by Bekarert et al (2002) and Dahlquist and Robertsson (2004). We select the lag length of two based on the AIC for all VARs estimated.

Table 10 reports the summary of the Granger causality tests for three different VAR configurations. The first column of Table 10 reports the results of the causality between excess returns (ERUSD) and normalized inflows (NIFLOWUS). From Panel A, we find that lagged excess returns are statistically significant in predicting future inflows, but inflows do not have statistically significant predictive power on ERUD in China. It appears that the results support the return chasing behavior in China.[14] There is no significant causality between excess returns and flows in India from Panel B. These results indicate that foreign investors are involved in positive feedback trading in China but not in India.

The second VAR model are estimated is a bivariant model of unexpected inflows (UIFLOW) and ERUSD, and the results are reported in Column 2. Excess returns are found to cause unexpected flows in China but not visa versa, and there is no significant causality for India as found in the first column. The contrasting results between China and India with respect to unanticipated inflows and returns can be partially explained by the fact that 41% of portfolio equity inflow to India is from the U.S., while only about 1% of portfolio flows to China are from American institutional investors.

Column 3 of Table 10 reports the results of Granger causality tests of VARX, including an exogenous dummy variable to control for extreme values.[15] The motivation for including a dummy variable for extreme observations can be given in, for example, Graphs 1A and 2A. It is clearly evident that there are a few significant outliners in both countries, and in order to uncover the general nature of the relationship between flows and returns, spikes should be controlled out. Panel A reports the results of the causality test for China, and they are consistent with results found in Column 1 and 2. This provides further support for the ERUSD as a predictive factor in equity flows for China. According to Panel B, lagged returns are now significant in predicting flows at the 5% significant level.

Graphs 5A and 5B illustrate the impulse response functions constructed with ERUSD and NIFLOWUS in China and India, respectively. We observe that in China, one standard deviation shock to excess returns causes a significant increase in inflows over the next two to four months but returns do not respond to a shock in inflows.[16] We observe that in Inida, neither inflows nor returns respond to a shock in another variable. The impulse response functions basically agree with the results found in Table 10. Graphs 6A and 6B present the IRFs with ERUSD and UIFLOW in China and India. In both China and India, a shock to unexpected flows negatively predicts future unexpected flows after an initial increase. This pattern indicates that temporary distortions to the unexpected inflow series are transient and then partially reversed over a short forecasting period. U.S. investors may incorporate information on equity flows quickly into their future purchasing behavior. The response of UFLOWS to an unexpected ERUSD shock is significant in China, where one standard deviation shock to ERUSD leads to a 1.2% increase in equity inflows by the third month. Again the results in India do not show any clear relationships between ERUSD and UIFLOW.

[14] Similar Granger causality results are found with net flows (not reported).

[15] Extreme values are observations two standard deviations or more from the mean.

[16] Standard errors for impulse response functions are calculated using Monte Carlo Simulation and the bands represent 90% confidence levels. Note that the lower bound of 90% confidence crosses the middle line.

Table 10. Summary of Granger Causality Tests

	VAR 1	VAR 2	VARX
Panel A: China			
Flows Causing Returns	0.58	1.06	0.23
Returns Causing Flows	55.95***	60.14***	42.84***
Panel B: India			
Flows Causing Returns	3.30	3.82	3.33
Returns Causing Flows	3.21	1.00	8.38**

The table above summarizes the results of the Granger causality tests for three different VAR specifications. VAR1 is based on ERUSD and INFLOWUS. VAR2 is based on ERUSD and UIFOW. VARX is based on ERUSD, INFLOWUS with an exogenous dummy for extreme observations of inflows. Test statistics are distributed as a Chi-square with two degrees of freedom. *** indicates significance at 1% and ** indicates significance at 5%. Significance levels are calculated using Chi-square statistics with 2 degrees of freedom.

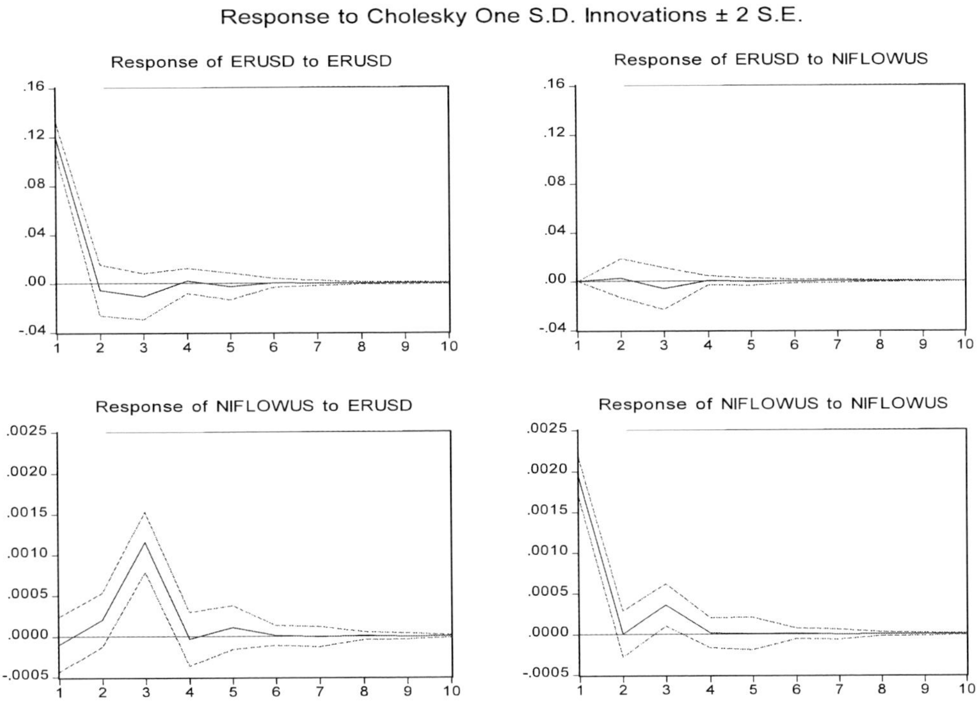

Graph 5A. Impulse Response Functions of China: VAR [ERUSD, NIFLOWUS].

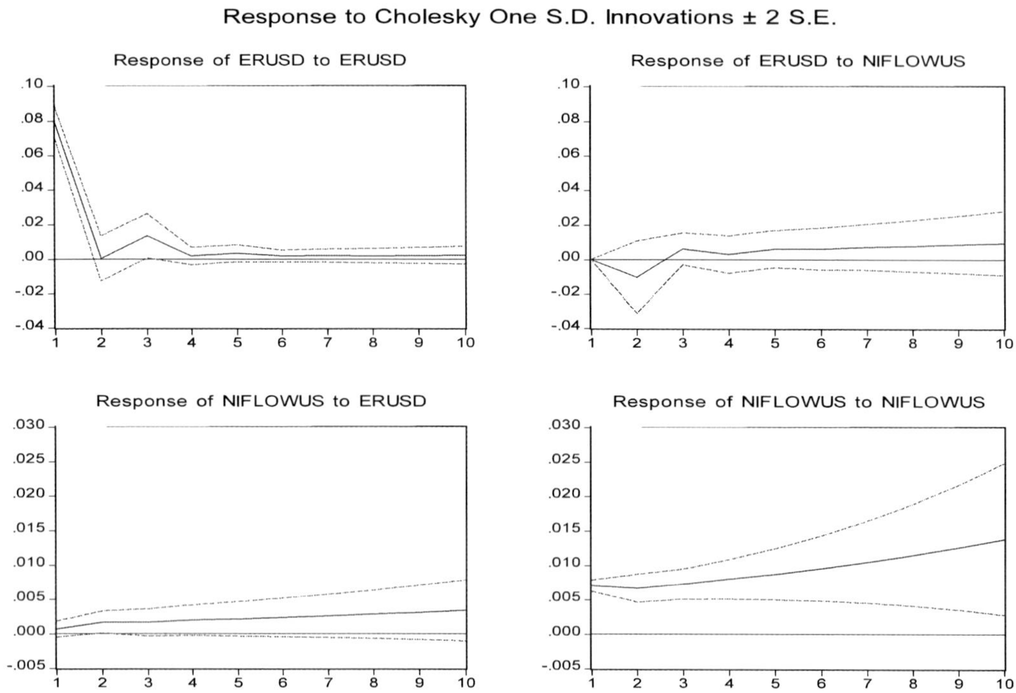

Graph 5B. Impulse response functions in India: VAR [ERUSD, NIFLOWUS].

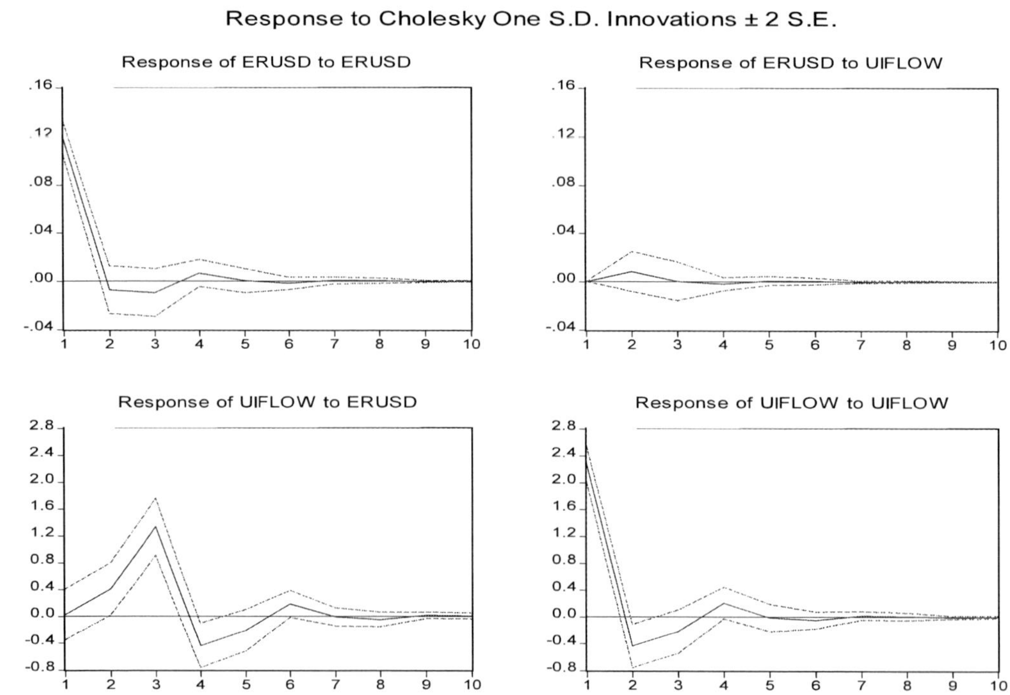

Graph 6A. Impulse response functions in China: VAR [ERUSD, UIFLOW].

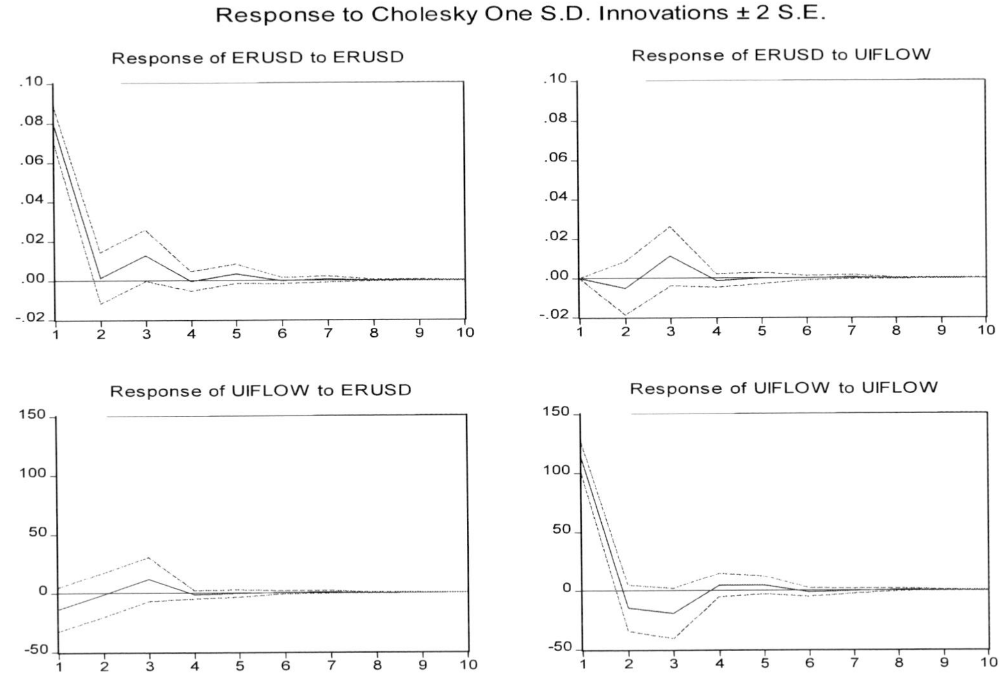

Graph 6B. Impulse response functions in India: VAR [ERUSD, UIFLOW].

In sum, it appears that there is strong evidence of returns forecasting flows positively in China, but the evidence of returns forecasting flows is rather ambiguous in India. Froot et al (2001) find positive forecastability of capital flows from returns in emerging markets. However, in more developed markets the forecastablity of flows from returns is ambiguous, as our findings suggest for India. If we interpret these findings in terms of relative information asymmetry between the U.S. and China, and the U.S. and India, it could be conjectured that information asymmetry is more acute in China due to two possible reasons. First, equity flows to India are over two times greater than flows to China, and this relatively larger amount of equity flowing to India implies that U.S. investors are likely more informed about the Indian equity market than the Chinese market. As Alfaro et al (2005) point out, information asymmetries decline as trade increases. The second evidence for relatively greater information asymmetry between the U.S. and China comes from the strong relationship between returns and flows in China. The strong relationship could be a result of the U.S. investors relying on previous realizations of the return sequence to forecast future returns due to lack of detailed information on fundamentals. On the other hand, there is relatively more information available for investors to forecast future market performance in India as developed countries, and hence returns may not be as important in forecasting future purchases.

5.3. Additional Variables in VAR and Variance Decompositions

We investigate the trivariate and four-variable VAR for China and India to see if the previous findings hold after adding other endogenous variables in a VAR. For example, there may be a positive relationship between current equity flows and lagged equity returns, but part of this correlation may come indirectly through the effect of industrial production and other fundamental variable such as dividend on equity returns. In the literature, dividend yield is frequently hypothesized to be an important factor in determining equity prices, and possibly the investor decision making process. Panel A and Panel B of Table 11 report the results of the block exogeneity tests (Granger causality for more than two variables) in China and India, respectively. We find that returns are causing inflows in China but not for India. The results are consistent with the previous findings in Table 10. Interestingly, there is no causality running between dividend yields and returns in China. This is in contrast to the case of India shown in Panel B. In India, dividends appear to have predictive power for forecasting returns and this is consistent with the finding of developed markets. These contrasting findings in the cases of China and India further lend credence to the idea that the Chinese market is not operating efficiently (Tian, 2001). We also observe that returns on the Indian market as well as dividend yields are significant for forecasting future industrial production. This, again, is consistent with the findings in developed markets that equity markets lead real markets. Since expectations are built into equity market and returns, firms make dividend policy decisions based on estimated future productivity.

Table 11. Summary of Granger Causality Tests

	ERUSD	Inflows	DIV	IP
Panel A: China				
ERUSD causing	n/a	74.34***	0.04	1.02
Inflows causing	0.45	n/a	0.8	0.04
Dividends Causing	0.55	0.12	n/a	0.33
IP causing	0.42	0.11	0.07	n/a
Panel B: India				
ERUSD causing	n/a	1.43	1.61	7.83**
Inflows causing	3.49	n/a	0.34	0.16
Dividends Causing	6.84**	2.66	n/a	6.45**
IP causing	0.34	0.01	1.04	n/a

The table above summarizes the results of the Granger causality tests for a VAR that includes ERUSD, INFLOWUS, DIV, and IP. *** indicates significance at 1% and ** indicates significance at 5%. Significance levels are calculated using Chi-square statistics with 6 degrees of freedom.

Panels A and B of Table 12 report variance decompositions based on shocks in returns, dividends and inflows over ten periods for China and India, respectively. In China, the contribution of dividend shocks to the variance of returns is negligible at only 0.28% and the results support the notion that equity markets in China are basically controlled by the government. In contrast, between 20% and 24% of the variance in the return sequence is explained by shocks to dividends for India. A particularly interesting finding in the context of this study comes from the decomposition of the flows sequences. We observe that between about 27% and 21% of the variance in the flows sequences are explained by dividend shocks in China and India, respectively. These results indicate that the behavior of U.S. institutional investors might be influenced more by fundamental determinants (i.e., dividend shocks) than price shocks or flow shocks. The findings support a model developed by Dvorak (2003).

Table 12. Variance decomposition [ERUSD, dividend, Inflow]

	ERUSD Shock	Div. Shock	Flow Shock
		Panel A: China	
Variance Decomposition RUSD			
Period			
1	100	0	0
2	99.67	0.29	0.04
3	99.42	0.28	0.3
4	99.41	0.28	0.3
5	99.41	0.28	0.3
6	99.41	0.28	0.3
7	99.41	0.28	0.3
8	99.41	0.28	0.3
9	99.41	0.28	0.3
10	99.41	0.28	0.3
Variance Decomposition Dividend			
Period			
1	0.12	99.88	0
2	0.06	99.94	0
3	0.05	99.58	0.37
4	0.04	99.37	0.59
5	0.15	99.05	0.79
6	0.23	98.84	0.93
7	0.3	98.68	1.02
8	0.34	98.58	1.08
9	0.37	98.51	1.12
10	0.39	98.46	1.15
Variance Decomposition Flows			
1	20.05	0.24	79.72
2	20.19	1.33	78.48
3	20.14	26.63	53.22
4	20.2	26.63	53.17
5	20.2	26.8	53.01
6	20.2	26.8	53
7	20.2	26.8	53
8	20.2	26.8	53
9	20.2	26.8	53
10	20.2	26.8	53

Table 12. (Continued)

	ERUSD Shock	Div. Shock	Flow Shock
		Panel B: India	
Variance Decomposition RUSD			
Period			
1	100	0	0
2	69.22	20.16	10.62
3	68.39	20.93	10.68
4	67.66	21.62	10.72
5	66.99	22.3	10.71
6	66.46	22.83	10.71
7	66.02	23.27	10.71
8	65.68	23.61	10.71
9	65.41	23.88	10.7
10	65.2	24.1	10.7
Variance Decomposition Dividend			
Period			
1	17.79	82.21	0
2	16.12	83.55	0.32
3	18.19	81.3	0.52
4	18.93	80.14	0.92
5	19.52	79.12	1.36
6	19.77	78.31	1.91
7	19.85	77.58	2.57
8	19.78	76.85	3.38
9	19.58	76.07	4.35
10	19.29	75.19	5.52
Variance Decomposition Flows			
Period			
1	0.31	20.03	79.66
2	2.1	20.5	77.41
3	7.23	20.8	71.96
4	7.83	20.99	71.18
5	8.35	21.05	70.6
6	8.42	21.08	70.5
7	8.46	21.09	70.45
8	8.46	21.1	70.44
9	8.47	21.1	70.43
10	8.47	21.1	70.43

Table 12 presents the variance decomposition based on VAR with ERUSD, Dividend and NIFLOWUS. Each value indicates how much each shock affects others in percentage over 10 future periods.

To gauge the stability of the relationship found in the previous section, we estimate the VAR using sub-samples, and the results (not reported) are basically similar to those reported in Tables 10 and 11. The results for China appear to be consistent for periods before 2003, but they differ somewhat after 2003. This could be due in part to the fact that foreign investors were allowed to invest in both A and B shares after 2002.

6. CONCLUSION

This research has uncovered several important aspects of the Chinese and Indian equity markets and the influences of U.S. institutional equity portfolio investment on these two emerging giants. The results indicate that U.S. institutional investors are chasing returns into China, but that similar results are not found in India. Some evidence is found that U.S. investors' behavior might be influencing the Indian equity market, while no evidence supports U.S. equity flows influencing the Chinese market. In China, returns appear to forecast future inflows positively; in India, the results are more ambiguous. The results of the variance decomposition demonstrate that the variance of the Indian equity market is influenced by foreign activity and dividend yields, whereas the Chinese equity markets is unaffected by foreign investor behavior and fundamental determinates of value. This supports the ideas espoused in the financial press that the Chinese government still plays a major role in determining the markets. In both markets, fundamental shocks have a stronger influence than excess return shocks. This finding points toward the conclusion that foreign investors are responding to real information rather than simply to returns, which are likely noisy proxies for underlying value, and demonstrates that U.S. investors are reacting more strongly to shocks in fundamentals in both markets. These findings are in contrast to much of the literature that assumes that domestic investors are better informed than foreign investors.

REFERENCES

Alfaro, L., & Kalemli-Ozcan, S., & Volosovych, V. (2005). Capital Flows in a Globalized World: The Role of Policies and Institutions. *NBER Working Papers.*

Allen, F., & Quin, J., & Quin, M., (2006). Law, Finance and Economic Growth in China. *Financial Institutions Center of Wharton School of Business Working Paper,* University of Pennsylvania.

Bekaert, G., & Harvey, C. (2000). Foreign Speculators and Emerging Equity Markets. *Journal of Finance, 55*, 565-613.

Bekaert, G., & Harvey, C., & Lumsdaine, C. (2002). The Dynamics of Emerging Market Equity Flows. *Journal of International Money and Finance, 21*, 295-350.

Bohn, H., & Tesar, L.L. (1996). US equity investment in foreign markets: Portfolio rebalancing or return chasing? *American Economic Review 86*, 77–81.

Brennan, M.J., & Cao, H., & Strong, N., & Xu, X. (2005). The dynamics of international equity expectations. *Journal of Financial Economics, 77,* 257-288.

Brennan, M. J., & Cao, H., (1997). International Portfolio Flows. *Journal of Finance, 52*, 1851–1880.

Campbell, J., & Andrew W. Lo., & MacKinlay, A. (1997), *The Econometrics of Financial Markets*. Princeton University Press.

Chen, G., & Lee, B., & Rui, O. (2001). Foreign ownership restriction and market segmentation in China's stock markets. *Journal of Financial Research, 24*, 133-155.

Chen, G., & Lee, B., & Rui, O., & Wu, W. (2003). Revisiting B-share Discounts in the Chinese Stock Market. *Working Paper,* University of Houston.

Choe, H., & Kho, B.-C., & Stulz, R. (1999). Do foreign investors destabilize stock markets? The Korean experience in 1997. *Journal of Financial Economics, 54*, 227-264.

Clark, J., & Berko, E. (1997). Foreign investment fluctuations and emerging market stock returns: The case of Mexico. *Sta. report 24, Federal Reserve Bank,* New York, NY.

Dahlquist, M., & Robertsson, G. (2004). A note on foreigners' trading and price effects across firms. *Journal of Banking and Finance, 28*, 615-632.

Dvorak, T. (2003). Gross Capital Flows and asymmetric information. *Journal of International Money and Finance, 22*, 835-864.

Erb, C., & Harvey, C., & Viskanta, T. (1996). Expected Returns and Volatility in 135 Countries. *Journal of Portfolio Management, 22*, 46-58.

Fama, Eugene F., & French, K. (1992). The cross-section of expected stock returns. *Journal of Finance, 47*, 427-465.

Froot, K., & O'Connell, P., & Seasholes, M. (2001). The Portfolio Flows of International Investors. *Journal of Financial Economics*, *59*, 151-193.

Froot, K., & Ramadorai, T. (2005). Currency Returns, Intrinsic Value, and Institutional Investor Flows. *Journal of Finance*, *60*, 03, 1535-1566.

Gao, S. (2002). China Stock Market in a Global Perspective. *Dow Jones Indexes.*

Global Development Finance. (2005). *Statistical Appendix.*

Grinblatt, M., & Keloharj. M. (2000). The Investment Behavior and Performance of Various Investor Types: A Study of Finland's Unique Data Set. *Journal of Financial Economics, 55*, 43-67.

Griffith-Jones. S. (2004). Asian Drivers: international financial and macro-economic implications globally and for developing countries. Paper prepared for the First Asian Drivers' workshop held in November 2004 at IDS, Sussex.

Griffin J., & Nardari, F., & Stulz, R., (2004). Daily Cross-Border Equity Flows: Pushed or Pulled? *Review of Economics and Statistics*, *86*, 641-657.

Hamao, Y. & Mei, J. (2001). Living with the "enemy": An analysis of foreign investment in the Japanese equity market. *Journal of International Money and* Finance, *20*, 715–735.

Hau, H., & Massa, M., & Peress, J. (2005). Do Demand Curves for Currencies Slope Down? Evidence from the MSCI Global Index Change. *CEPR Discussion Papers* 4862, C.E.P.R. Discussion Papers.

Henry, P.B. (2000b). Stock market liberalization, economic reform, and emerging market equity prices. *Journal of Finance,* 55, 529–564.

Kang, J., & . Stulz, R., (1997). Why is there home bias? An analysis of foreign portfolio equity ownership in Japan. *Journal of Financial Economics.*

Kim, E. H., & Singal, V. (2002). Stock market openings: Experience of emerging economies. *Journal of Business, 73*, 25-66.

Kim, Y. & Ying, T. (2001). An Empirical Analysis on Capital Flows: The Case of Korea and Mexico. *Southern Economic Journal*, *67*, No4, 954-968.

Lin, K., & Menkveld, A., & Yang, Z. (2005). China and the World Equity Markets: A Review of the First Decade. *Working paper,* Portland State University.

Maroney, N., & Naka., A., & Wansi, T. (2004). Changing Risk, Return, and Leverage: The 1997 Asian Financial Crisis. *Journal of Financial and Quantitative Analysis, 39*,143-66.

Merton, R, C. (1987). A Simple Model of Capital Market Equilibrium with Incomplete Information. *Journal of Finance, 42*,483-510.

Padmanabhan, P. (2005). Operationalising Capital Account Liberalization: The Indian Experience. *BIS paper, 15.*

Perez, C. (2002). *Technological Revolutions and Financial Capital: The Dynamics of Bubbles and Golden Ages.* Cheltenham:Edward Elgar.

Portes R., & Rey, H. (2005). The Determinants of Cross-Border Equity Flows. *Journal of International Economics, 65*, 269-296.

Prasad, E., & Shang-Jin, W., (2005). The Chinese approach to Capital Inflows: Patterns and Possible Explanations. *NBER Working Paper.*

Rao, K.S., & Chalapati. (2002). An Overview of the Indian Stock Market with Emphasis on Ownership Pattern of Listed Companies. *Alternative Economic Survey.*

Rogoff, K. (2003). Globalization and Global Disinflation. *Federal Reserve Bank of Kansas City, Monetary Policy and Uncertainty: Adapting to a Changing Economy*, 2003. (Paper presented at a symposium sponsored by the Federal Reserve Bank of Kansas City, at Jackson Hole, WY, August 28-30.

Seasholes, M. S. (2004). Smart foreign traders in emerging markets. *Working paper, Harvard University*, Cambridge, MA.

Shirai., S. (2002). Is the Equity market really developed in the People republic of China? *Working Paper,* Keio University.

Shleifer, A. (1986). Do demand curves for stocks slope down? *Journal of Finance* 41, 579-590.

Tesar, L., & Werner, I.. (1994). International equity transactions and U.S. portfolio choice. *In: Frankel, J. (Ed.), The Internationalization of Equity Markets.* University of Chicago Press, Chicago, IL, 185–215.

Tesar, L., & Werner, I. (1995). U.S. equity investment in emerging stock markets. *World Bank Economic Review, 9*, 109–130.

Tian., G. L. (2001). State Shareholding and the Value of Chin's firms. *Working paper,* London Business School.

Warther, V.A.(1995). Aggregate mutual fund flows and security returns. *Journal of Financial Economics, 39*, 209–235.

World Bank. (2005). *Private Capital flows to Developing Countries.*

In: China: Economic, Political and Social Issues
Editors: J. M. Phillips and L. J. Moore
ISBN: 978-60456-727-4

Chapter 4

THE IMPACT OF FAMILY STRUCTURE ON OEDIPAL FORMS IN AN ORIENTAL CULTURE: A CASE STUDY OF LITERARY DATA IN CHINA'S GREATEST CLASSICAL NOVEL[1]

Ming Dong Gu
University of Texas at Dallas

ABSTRACT

Oriental cultures differ from white, Christian cultures in the structure by which the family is organized and the way children are brought up. The formal representation of the Oedipus complex in Confucian Chinese society shows a distinct difference from that of white, Christian, Western societies. The classic oedipal situation as described by Freud seldom, if ever, exists in pre-modern Chinese literary works, but variant forms do appear even in classical Chinese literature. In this chapter, I attempt to explore to what extent the Oedipus complex as the "fate of all of us" is true of other cultures. I am going to make my inquiry, however, not by conducting a case study of social data collected in a non-Western culture, but by analyzing textual data contained in a literary masterpiece in an approach adopted by Freud when he formulated his initial idea of the Oedipus complex. The literary text is China's greatest classical novel, the *Hongloumeng*, authored by Cao Xueqin, which has two complete English translations: *A Dream of Red Mansions* and *The Story of the Stone*. This masterpiece offers an encyclopedic representation of traditional Chinese family life and narrates deeply hidden oedipal themes. Although their formal structure is very different from the triadic structure of the classical Freudian concept, it still falls within what Ernest Jones calls "the nuclear family complex." My case study will be conducted in relation to various debates on the Oedipus complex in the West.

[1] I wish to thank Professor Peter Rudnytsky, editor of the American Imago and formerly director of the Institute of Psychological Studies of Arts at the University of Florida, who read my paper and offered valuable comments. I am also grateful to Professor Norman Holland, president of the International Association of Literature and Psychology, for his advice on psychoanalytic theory.

INTRODUCTION

At an international conference of psychoanalysis and literature, I struck up a conversation with a Hungary psychoanalytic critic. Seeing that I am Chinese, he told me that he had a Chinese student who argued that there is no Oedipus Complex in Chinese culture. His remarks reminded me of some other Chinese scholars who believed that the Oedipus complex is an alien concept imported from the West and can only be found in modern Chinese literature. Indeed, in the existing Chinese studies of oedipal themes in literature, we cannot find any analysis of pre-modern cases (Wang Ning 1991 and 1992; Yu Fenggao 1987). As a result, scholars frequently invoke the lack of oedipal themes in pre-modern Chinese literature as evidence to challenge the universality of the Oedipus complex. The challenge is quite similar to the calling into question the universality of the Oedipus complex in the famous debate between Ernest Jones and Bronislaw Malinowski in the 1920s. Jones defended Freud's conception of the complex as intrinsic to the human condition, and even inherited. Malinowski (1929) disagreed with Freud's claim of the universality of the complex by citing the example of Trobriand islanders who had only mothers and did not know the facts of fatherhood. He argued that people in such a society could not have an Oedipus complex. Jones counter-argued that the mother's brother, who assumed the role of the father in the family, served as the target of a child's oedipal projections, and Malinowski's observation of a boy's incestuous attraction to his sister was but superficial displacement of the "nuclear family complex" (145-73). Since then, the Oedipus complex has stood up to a series of challenges and revisions, which include the radical anti-Oedipus familialism of Gilles Deleuze and Felix Guattari (1972), the idiosyncratic theory of "mimetism" of René Girard (1972), the deconstructionist reading of *Oedipus the King* by Sandor Goodhart (1978), the socio-political anti-familialism of feminist critique, and the psycholinguistic revision by Jacques Lacan (1977). With the rise of postcolonial criticism and the call for decolonialization of Western ideas, the Chinese scholars' view represents another challenge from non-western cultures.

The debate between Malinowski and Jones set forth some theoretical differences between psychoanalysis and anthropology. However, as Peter Rudnytsky notes in his book *Freud and Oedipus*, "the fundamental terms have not changed very much since the early part of the twentieth century" when the Malinowski-Jones debate took place (358). In 1970, Anne Parsons updated the Jones-Malinowski debate by looking at the matter from a combined perspective of psychology and anthropology (331-341). In 1979, André Green reasserted the universality of the psychoanalytic position but at the same time took note of both determining factors: the primary human constants and the secondary cultural determinants (232-36). I find convincing Parson's synthesis that the form of the Oedipus complex may vary from culture to culture, but the complex itself is universal; and I also find forceful Green's statement that "only the secondary determinations are susceptible to the influence of time, or the historico-social context." Parson's synthesis and Green's restatement find support in psychoanalytic study of the specific forms of the Oedipus complex. Fenichel points out: "There are determining factors which ensure the development of the Oedipus complex and of castration anxiety; their occurrence is predestined. But the mode in which they occur--that is, the factors which realize them--depends on the actual events of the individual's life and his reaction to them; and this, again, depends on his constitution and his whole previous experience" (208).

This flexible approach is not only appropriate to white, Christian societies, but also pertinent to non-Western cultures.

Oriental cultures differ from white, Christian cultures in the structure by which the family is organized and the way children are brought up. The formal representation of the Oedipus complex in Confucian Chinese society shows a distinct difference from that of white, Christian, Western societies. The classic oedipal situation as described by Freud seldom, if ever, exists in pre-modern Chinese literary works, but variant forms do appear even in classical Chinese literature. In this article, I attempt to explore to what extent the Oedipus complex as the "fate of all of us" is true of other cultures. I am going to make my inquiry, however, not by conducting a case study of social data collected in a non-Western culture, but by analyzing textual data contained in a literary masterpiece in an approach adopted by Freud himself when he formulated his initial ideas concerning the Oedipus complex. The literary text is China's greatest classical nove, the *Hongloumeng* authored by Cao Xueqin, which has two complete English versions: *A Dream of Red Mansions*, and *The Story of the Stone*. This masterpiece offers an encyclopedic representation of traditional Chinese family life, which reveals diffused oedipal themes. Although the formal structure is very different from the triadic structure of the classical Freudian concept, it still falls within what Jones called "the nuclear family complex" (169). In the novel, the oedipal hostility is not overtly or covertly directed against the father because of deeply entrenched Confucian values of filial piety, but against the Confucian system which the father upholds and represents. And the male protagonist Jia Bao-yu's incestuous desires are not oriented to his mother, but to his sister and surrogate sisters. Again because of the formidable moral inhibition, his incestuous desires are desexualized and reemerge as an adoration of the gender his sister possesses, while his sexual libido is diverted towards persons who possess some of his sister's qualities, and toward objects that can provide him oral gratifications. The defense mechanism in his mind compels him to choose between two options: to refuse to grow up so as to have the company of his sister or sister surrogates or to flee the human world so as to return to the primal mother. Since the Confucian social structure makes the first option impossible, Bao-yu is forced to desert the world of Red Dust and become a Buddhist and Taoist convert. In addition to the sibling complex in Bao-yu's story, the novel features other themes of sibling love.

Myth and Sibling Love

The story of Bao-yu has the quality of a myth. The novel, structured on a mythological frame, is saturated with supernatural elements, such as Nü Wa's creation of the stone, the stone's incarnation in Bao-yu, the Land of Illusion, the magic mirror, and the story of the twelve girls of Jingling. These supernatural elements contain beneath their conventional facade of popular folklore and superstition, karma and retribution, a universality that has been confirmed by anthropological studies and psychological observations. It seems that these mythological elements and supernatural ingredients are not to be construed as reflecting the author's intention to cater to the popular taste for myth, legends and Buddhist and Taoist stories. In his "Creative Writers and Daydreaming," Freud makes the famous remark that myths, legends, and fairy-tales are "distorted vestiges of the wishful phantasies of whole nations, the secular dreams of youthful humanity" (Freud Reader, 442). In a way, *A Dream of Red Mansions* can be considered a reworked myth of the Chinese nation. The mythic qualities are due not simply to the author's ample use of ready-made materials from the popular treasure-house of the Chinese tradition. They come from the author's creative use of ready-made materials. The materials at hand, when woven into a realistically-oriented narrative mode and coupled with psychological insights, reveal a great deal that may be said to belong to the deepest mental structure of mankind in general and the Chinese nation in particular. His refashioning of the familiar Chinese myths, legends and folk-tales, while evincing a great amount of creative independence, gives the novel a quality that makes it worthy of the name of myth in the sense that it tells some underlying truths about a deep dimension of the Chinese mentality.

The novel opens with Nü Wa's creation of the protagonist as a stone, continues with the incarnation of the stone in human form and its vicissitudes as the male protagonist in the human world in close association with the fate of the stone, and ends with the stone's return to its original place. Andrew Plaks, an eminent scholar of the novel, observes that "the novel may be described as the story of the sexual initiation of the rainbow-stone, from the puberty rites of Chapters 5 and 6 to the conjunction of marriage and death in Chapter 97" (83). He seems to say that the novel is a narrative in Chinese form of the archetypal pattern of the existential process from birth thorough growth to death, the inalterable human journey in a condensed form. Although I agree with his view, I wish to point out that the novel does not end in Bao-yu's death. The archetypal journey seems to miss an important link. If I were to draw a trajectory of the journey undertaken by the stone (and Bao-yu), it would be something like this: the creation of the stone by Nü Wa, the incredible Crags of the Great Fable Mountains, the stone's incarnation into Bao-yu in Jia's family, Bao-yu's growth and development in the Total Vision Garden, his adventure in the Confucian world, Bao-yu's escape from the Red Dust, and the stone's return to its place of origin through the Buddhist monk and Taoist priest. This trajectory may be understood to represent a journey, but it looks more like a circle. In a way, the circular movement of the stone may be construed to embody a universal and hidden dimension of human beings: the unconscious and fearful infantile wish of every human being to return to the mother's womb. In other words, Bao-yu's escape from the world of Red Dust to the Incredible Crags of the Great Fable Mountain is a symbolic return to the primal mother. By incorporating the Nü Wa myth into its mythological frame, the novelist touches upon an aspect of the deep structure of the Chinese mind. The novel opens with Nü Wa in her role as repairer of the broken heaven. Bao-yu is the odd stone left unused for the colossal task. The Goddess appears very briefly and then recedes into the background, only to return to the foreground towards the end of the novel. Such an opening and ending are not simply intended as a frame of reference for the various supernatural elements ingeniously placed throughout the novel, eventually bringing it to an end with Bao-yu's exit from the madding crowd. It serves as the larger background for the novel, which forms a facet of what C. G. Jung described as the "collective unconscious." In this sense, the novel may be viewed as a newly created myth of the Chinese nation.

The various mythological sources about Nü Wa do not seem to have much interrelation with one another and may lead to the conclusion that they represent independent traditions with no intrinsic connection. Andrew Plaks argues, however, that "the various sources fall together into a more meaningful cluster when we consider Nü-Kwa [Nü Wa] not as an independent entity, but as one term of a dual mythical construction in which she and Fu-Hsi [Fu Xi] are intimately joined" (33). Plaks documents the relationship between Nü Wa as an assistant or successor to Fu Xi in his work, hence her appellation Nu-huang, but many sources grant them a more intimate link as brother and sister. This trait of consanguinity is indicated by the variants P'ao-Kwa and Nü-Xi for Nü Wa's name, as well as by a common surname Feng, and a similar physical description consisting of a snake's body and a human head. Another scholar cited by Plaks suggested that the "nü" of Nü Wa is a surname, and that she is in fact a male relative of Fu Xi with the given name "Wa" (34). Lu Tong, a Tang poet, depicts Nü Wa as the wife of Fu Xi. This view is confirmed by the stone relief in the Mausoleum of Wu-liang Tombs from the East Han period, silk painting (in color) from Astana Mausoleum at the ancient site of Gao-chang of the Sui period, and the stone relief from the East Han period. All the above-mentioned pictorial representations of Nü Wa and Fu Xi portray them as two deities, one male, the other female standing side by side in stately robes with serpentine tails intertwined. The intertwining of their tails signifies more than brother-sister affection, and attests to the conjugal relation of the two figures. The overlapping of the roles of sibling and spouse seems to hint at an important feature in the Chinese mythological tradition. The Tang collection of *Duyi zhi* tells of Nü Wa and Fu Xi as universal progenitors of human races:

> In high antiquity, when the universe was first formed, there were no people under heaven except Nü Wa and her brother, who lived on Mount Kunlun. They discussed becoming man and wife, but felt ashamed by themselves. So the brother and sister climbed up Mount Kunlun and prayed: "If Heaven permits us brother and sister to become man and wife, then the smoke will be intertwined. If not, the smoke will disperse." After so saying, the smoke was indeed intertwined, and the sister cleaved onto his brother (Li, 2:19).

The same mythical theme persists in other Chinese folktales. For example, Rui Yifu, a Chinese anthropologist, documented a cycle of folktales in various regions in South and Southwest China among both Han and non-Han ethnic groups (1972). In north and central China, where Han is the dominant ethnic group and where Confucian morality is predominant, the same theme of brother and sister as spouses is more deeply hidden and more drastically distorted. With the exception of Nü Wa-Fu Xi legend, the motif of brother and sister as spouses are almost non-existent in the mythology and legends of the Han nationality. Even the exception was cast in an uncertain light. While some versions state that Nü Wa and Fu Xi were brother and sister who were married, other versions only confirm the sibling relation without mentioning the marital relation. The narrative summarized from various sources of Chinese mythology about Nü Wa and Fu Xi runs like this: in the ancient past, a brother and sister disobeyed their father's order and gave aid to the thunder-dragon. When a deluge wrought by the enraged Lord of Thunder swept the earth, all people perished except the brother and sister, who were rescued by a magic gourd-boat. After the flood receded, they had to repopulate the surface of the earth (Yuan 42). Another version of this motif has it that Nü Wa and Fu Xi got married after the Deluge and produced a strange formless offspring. They wrapped the formless flesh in a cloth and carried it up a "ladder of Heaven," when it suddenly fell to the ground, smashing into myriad fragments, which miraculously became human beings (Yuan, 45).

Otto Rank, a renowned psychoanalyst of Freud's circle, documented an extensive list of sibling incest motif in the myths and legends of other cultures, ranging from the Egyptian legend of Osiris, the Greek myth of Cronus and Zeus, and the Nordic saga of sigmund's union with his twin sister to the Japanese legend of Izanami and Izanagi, the creation myth of the

Eskimos, and the sun-moon myth of the American Indians (363-381). By contrast, Chinese myths and legends are truly poor in this respect. Apart from the Nü Wa-Fu Xi myth, the only legend with a sibling incest motif is the story of Emperor Yang-Di of the Sui dynasty who attempted to marry his sister. But the legend is condemnatory in its tenor: Yang-Di was described as a notorious ruler who indulged in women's beauty. Fed up with women in his palace, he wanted to marry his sister, who, on hearing the news, committed suicide. She turned into a rare flower which lured Yang-Di out of his capital. Rebellion arose all over China. Yang-Di was killed by his soldiers and the dynasty fell. The connection between a dynasty's fall and sibling incest in the folk story anticipates the total lack of sibling incest motif in Chinese literature in contrast to the abundance of it the literature of other cultures.

Talking about unconscious desires as the larger background of fiction, D. H. Lawrence says that great writers like Sophocles, Shakespeare and Tolstoi are always "setting behind the small action of his protagonists the terrific action of unfathomed nature; setting a smaller system of morality, the one grasped and formulated by the human consciousness within the vast, uncomprehended and incomprehensible morality of nature or of life itself, surpassing human consciousness" (419). In the Chinese novel, the Nü Wa myth serves as such a large background. The Nü Wa and Fu Xi myth is a clue to the repressed wish of the Chinese nation in remote times. My analysis of the myth is not concerned with the origin of the Chinese race but with the repressed collective spirit of the Chinese nation. In terms of depth psychology, it is not far wrong to deduce from the myth that in the deep structure of the Chinese mentality, the incestuous desires defined by the Freudian oedipal theory are not directed to the mother, but to the sibling of the opposite sex. This facet of the collective unconscious represents the larger background of the novel and at the same time constitutes one of its major themes. I suggest that against the large background of the Nü Wa myth, the novel presents a hidden motif of Bao-yu's longing for the mother displaced to his sister and sister-surrogates, and sublimated into an adoration of the fair sex.

FATHER-SON CONFLICT

The Goddess Nü Wa has several roles in her career in Chinese mythology, among them, those of the repairer of the heaven and of creator of human beings. The author of the novel combines the two roles of Nü Wa's career into one with the mythological frame. Bao-yu is created by her, yet he is special and extraordinary in that he, unlike other stones, is not used to repair Heaven. This seems to imply that his function is not to repair the broken social fabric and that he would be a square peg in the round hole of Confucian society.

Freud says: "The chief part in the mental lives of all children who later become psychoneurotic is played by their parents. Being in love with one parent and hating the other are among the essential constituents of the stock of psychical impulses which is formed at that time and which is of such importance in determining the symptoms of the later neurosis" (1965, 294). In many ways, Bao-yu's parents are largely responsible for his eccentric personality. In his infancy, they adopt a laisez-faire policy and put the burden of parenting on to the shoulder of others. When Bao-yu has formed his eccentric personality, they try to force him out of it to take on his social responsibilities. As he cannot do this, he has to rebel or flee. His rebellion is oedipal in nature, but the oedipal theme is a diffused one because of Bao-yu's upbringing and strong social inhibition. Bao-yu's primary caretakers are several: a wet-nurse, his sister Yuan-chun and some maid-servants. His mother does not care for him; she only dotes on him, like the grandmother. It seems to me that Bao-yu does not care for his mother as much as he cares for his sister, and his female cousin Dai-yu, and other girls. His sister was sent to the imperial palace and died there. His cousin died of broken heart because she is unable to be married to him. Other girls were dispersed in all directions. All the female persons with whom he could identify were taken away from him. He becomes literally "friendless and alone."

Scholars of the novel all agree that it is autobiographical in nature. They have developed various hypotheses with regard to its genesis. One view has it that the novel is a moving account of Cao Xue-qin's love for his cousin. They were brought up together from childhood, and when they grew up, vowed to marry no one else. However, his cousin was forced to become a royal concubine. They plotted together to poison the emperor. When the aim was achieved, his cousin poisoned herself to show her faithful love for him. Left behind brokenhearted, Cao spent ten years turning their love story into a novel as a monument to their devotion and a hidden condemnation of the depravity of the emperor. It is impossible to verify this account, but it has some relevance to the novel, in which the cousin is obviously Dai-yu, who died brokenhearted because she could not marry Bao-yu. There is a major splitting of personality involved. Dai-yu was not selected to be a royal concubine. Instead, it is Bao-yu's sister Yuan-chun who became a royal concubine and died in the imperial palace due to her melancholic depression resulting from her separation from her family. We cannot account for this difference unless there is a splitting of roles here. According to the oedipal structure, Bao-yu's incestuous desires should be directed towards Yuan-chun, who brought him up and treated him like a mother. This is out of question because of the incest taboo. By means of splitting, Bao-yu's affectionate current is directed to Yuan-chun while his sensual current is reserved for Dai-yu. Consciously or unconsciously, the splitting reveals one facet of the deep structure of the Chinese culture.

Although the splitting succeeds in hiding the incestuous desires, a remnant can still be felt in the relationship between Bao-yu and Dai-yu. They are first cousin, with Dai-yu's mother being Bao-yu's father's sister. Their names provide another hint; both have the character "jade" to their names, as Bao-yu means "precious jade," while Dai-yu means "black jade." The names may be an hint that they belong to the same family. There are other hints as to their brother and sister relationship. In Chapter 3, when Dai-yu comes to live with the Jia Clan, she and Bao-yu meet for the first time in their lives. Strangely enough, both of them seem to know each other so well that they feel that they have met before: "Dai-yu looked at him with astonishment. How strange! How very strange! It was as though she had seen him somewhere before, he was so extraordinarily familiar" (1:101). Bao-yu cherishes the same impression:

> Having completed his survey [of Dai-yu], Bao-yu gave a laugh.
> 'I have seen this cousin before.'
> 'Nonsense!' said Grandmother Jia. 'How could you possibly have done?'
> 'Well, perhaps not,' said Bao-yu, 'but her face seems so familiar that I have the impression of meeting her again after a long separation.'
> 'All the better,' said Grandmother Jia. 'That means that you should get on well together' (1:103).

The point here is not about children's fantasizing, nor even about the authorial hint at the supernatural element of love karma. It seems to me that the impression they share of having met each other before is an oblique suggestion that they are meant to be brother and sister.

According to psychoanalytic theory, the resolution of the Oedipus complex has a lot to do with castration anxiety: if the boy persists in choosing the mother as the object of love, he runs the risk of being physically harmed by the father. As a result of castration anxiety, the boy represses his incestuous desire for the mother and his hostility for the father, and the Oedipus complex disappears. In the Chinese novel, Bao-yu's castration anxiety takes the form of fear for his life. In the novel, his father Jia Zheng literally intends to put him to death. Jia Zheng's attitude towards Bao-yu is saturated with unconscious infanticidal strivings. From the time of Bao-yu's birth, Jia Zheng has ill feelings towards the infant, as he himself tells us towards the end of the novel: "Bao-yu came into the world with his jade, and there was always something strange about it. I knew it for an ill omen. But because his grandmother doted on him so, we nurtured him and brought him up until now" (5:360). His words imply that had the grandmother not taken to the infant, Jia Zheng would long ago have disposed of his son in some way. Because of this confession, we have reason to believe that from the day of Bao-yu's birth, the father nursed the secret desire to remove him, in the same way that Laius felt towards Oedipus in the Greek tragedy. Thus, from the very beginning, the father-son relationship is characterized by a hidden oedipal antagonism. As Bao-yu grows old enough to understand human relationships, he instinctively feels that his father dislikes him. So he tries, as much as he can, to stay out of his way. When his father's presence cannot be avoided, Bao-yu is always filled with anxiety and trepidation.

The father-son conflict comes to a head in a climactic episode in which Jia Zheng almost beats Bao-yu to death. There are several precipitating incidents leading to the beating. The major factor that infuriates Jia Zheng is the misinformation that Bao-yu attempted to rape one of his mother's maidservants. The maidservant reportedly resisted and Bao-yu gave her a beating. Humiliated, the maidservant committed suicide by drowning herself. The truth is that Bao-yu had nothing to do with the girl's death. Without any investigation of the report, Jia Zheng flies into a rage and orders his son to be beaten to death. It seems that he has at last found an opportunity to dispose of him. Fearing any interference with his aim from his mother and wife, he makes sure that the door is locked and no one is to disclose the order:

> "Jia Zheng turned a pair of wild and blood-shot eyes on him as he entered. Forgetting the 'riotous and dissipated conduct abroad leading to the unseemly bestowal of impudicities on a theatrical performer' and the 'neglect of proper pursuits and studies at home culminating in the attempted violation of a parent's maidservant [the original Chinese is "mother's maidservant"] and all the other high-sounding charges he had been preparing to hurl against him, he shouted two brief orders to the pages".
>
> 'Gag his mouth. Beat him to death.'(148)

What infuriates Jia Zheng most seems to be Bao-yu's alleged attempt to rape his mother's maidservant. His rage betrays an oedipal fear shared by Laius towards Oedipus. Jia Zheng must have suspected that Bao-yu chose his object by a way of displacement. Since the mother is a fond impossibility, the maidservant who is close to the mother is a good substitute for that which he fears to have. It is perhaps this unconscious fantasy in Jia Zheng's mind that throws him into an uncontrollable rage and makes him resolve to dispose of his son. Otherwise, it is rather unthinkable that Jia Zheng, a cool-headed, calculating Confucian scholar would believe in unproved gossip, without any investigation.

Throwing overboard his usual benevolent facade of a Confucian scholar, Jia Zheng, not satisfied because the executioner of his order does not hit hard enough, kicks the servant impatiently aside, wrests the bamboo from his hands, and gritting his teeth, strikes his son with the "utmost savagery." When his literary colleague tries to intervene, he responds: “Ask him what he has done and then tell me if you think I should spare him,' he said. 'It is the encouragement of people like you that has corrupted him; now, when things have come to this pass, you intercede for him. I suppose you would like me to wait until he commits parricide, or worse. Would you still intercede for him then?” (2:148) Thus the fear of parricide has been on Jia Zheng's mind. His worst fear may allude to the boy's incestuous desires, which find proof in Jia Zheng's strong reaction to his wife's appearance and pleading. His renewed savagery may have been prompted by his recollection of his wife's pampering of his son. But it may also have been provoked by his oedipal jealousy, which reveals itself in the following passage:

> "Don't try that sort of talk with me!' said Jia Zheng bitterly. 'Merely by fathering a monster like this I have proved myself an unfilial son; yet whenever in the past I have tried to discipline him, the rest of you have all conspired against me to protect him. Now that I have the opportunity at last, I may as well finish off what I have begun and put him down, like the vermin he is, before he can do any more damage”.
>
> So saying, he took up a rope and would have put his threat into execution, had not Lady Wang held her arms around him to prevent it (149).

Jia Zheng is very angry with his wife's interference with his purpose. The narration bears a close resemblance to Laius's attempted infanticide. The difference is that Laius wants to kill Oedipus in his infancy, whereas Jia Zheng wants to kill Bao-yu in his adolescence. It is worth noting that all in the family agree that Jia Zheng has overdone his disciplinary job as a father. Even if Bao-yu had done something wrong, even if he had raped the maidservant, he should not have incurred such savage beating, still less a threat on his life. After all, who among the male members of this official family is not a rake indulging in sensual pleasure? Jia Zheng's over-reaction to an alleged rape only testifies to his oedipal aggressivity towards his son.

There is more to the confrontation between the father and son. The savage beating of Bao-yu channels his libido in another direction. In psychoanalytic theory, the fear of castration forces the boy to give up the mother as a love object and to find another female as his life's companion. Bao-yu's fear of his father suppresses his unconscious strivings towards the mother and his hatred for his father. He consequently turns to his siblings as love objects as they are close at hand.

While displacing his desire for the mother onto his sister and sister-surrogates, Bao-yu transfers his hatred for the father to Confucianism. Bao-yu is never on good terms with his father, nor is his father fond of him. Throughout the novel, Bao-yu hates his father unconsciously, but the social morality forbids his hatred. So he has to displace his hatred on to something related to his father. Jia Zheng is a devout Confucian moralist who epitomizes Confucianism. Hence, in Bao-yu's heart, Confucianism becomes the substitute target of his hatred. From this point of view, it is not Jia Zheng who represents Confucianism, but Confucianism that takes the place of Jia Zheng in Bao-yu's mind. In feudalist China, to hate one's father is strictly taboo. Although it is also forbidden to hate things related to Confucianism, the restriction is relatively less formidable. In the novel, under no circumstances does Bao-yu express his hatred for Jia Zheng, even when Jia Zheng wants to put him to death. His repressed hatred has to find another target. It so happens that Jia Zheng not only represents Confucianism, but also forces Bao-yu to follow the Confucian road to an official career through civil service examinations. Since he cannot hate his father, Bao-yu turns to hating the things he represents: the Confucian classics and the Confucian order. While Confucianism regards women as inferior and treats them with contempt, Bao-yu considers women superior to men and treats them with reverence and respect. The Confucian order maintains a distance between master and servant, but Bao-yu befriends servants, especially maid-servants, and treats them as his equals. This burgeoning of democratic ideas goes directly against the tyrannical ideology his father upholds and embodies. By attacking Confucian learning and civil service examinations Bao-yu attains two purposes with one throw. This may explain why he openly expresses his dissatisfaction with and hatred for Confucianism and imperial examinations.

Problematic Upbringing and Problems of Sexuality

Scholars of the novel concur that the novel is a great love tragedy. Most of them agree that the root cause of the tragedy lies in the parental obstruction that prevents Bao-yu from marrying Dai-yu, whom he really loves. This is certainly true on the social plane, but the psychological dimension of the tragedy has so far been neglected. I think that, apart from the social obstacles, Bao-yu's tragedy is grounded in his neurotic personality fostered by problematic upbringing. In his contributions to the psychology of love, Freud describes the abnormal way neurotic persons behave in love, which may throw some light on the love tragedy of Bao-yu. Freud sums up a number of necessary preconditions for a neurotic person to fall in love with a particular object choice. First, there should be an injured third party; he shall choose as his love object a woman to whom another man can claim right of possession. Second, only a woman who is, in one way or other, of bad reputation sexually is likely to be raised to the status of a love object; a woman who is chaste and whose reputation is irreproachable never exercises sufficient attraction. Third, the woman must be of inferior social position, or he may suffer from psychical impotence. Fourth, there must be a confluence of the affectionate and sensual currents in his mind (1910, 165-168). The psychological origin of these preconditions is derived from the same source: the infantile fixation of tender feelings on the primary caretaker: "An incestuous fixation on mother or sister, which has never been surmounted, plays a prominent part in this pathogenic material and is its most universal content. In addition there is the influence to be considered of accidental distressing impressions connected with infantile sexual activity, and also those factors which in a general way reduce the libido that is to be directed on to the female sexual objects" (1912, 180).

I have pointed out earlier that Bao-yu's love of girls does not contain what is ordinarily called lust, nor does it aim at sexual consummation through genital contact. Although, technically, he is not an impotent male, Bao-yu has shown signs of psychical impotence: his lack of adult interest in Dai-yu and other eligible girls, his homosexual leanings in his friendship with Qin Zhong, his sense of inner inhibition and obstacles, and moreover his choice of sexual objects in his dreams. In the novel, he is surrounded by girls suitable as adult sexual objects, but, as the reader notices, he has sexual relations with only two girls: Aroma and Bao-chai. As a matter of fact, Bao-yu's only genital relation before his forced marriage with Bao-chai is with Aroma. On the occasion of waking up from his erotic dream of the Land of Illusion, he enacts the secret instructions in the act of love with Aroma. Aroma is the only girl whom he treats in a genital-oriented manner, all his other relations with girls being free from the lust in the common sense of the word. Of all girls, he loves Dai-yu most. His love for her, however, is sibling love, arising from their growing up together since early childhood: Bao-yu and Dai-yu "began to feel an affection for each other which far exceeded what they felt for any of the rest. Sharing each other's company every minute of the day and sleeping in the same room at night, they developed an understanding so intense that it was almost as if they had grown into a single person" (1:124). Although their affection in adolescence takes on an ostensibly sexual color, it is still sibling love in essence. I can cite one episode to support my argument. After his first sexual experience with Aroma, Bao-yu still does not view Dai-yu as a sexual object. In Chapter 19, there is a lengthy description of Bao-yu's intimate relationship with Dai-yu. Bao-yu goes to visit Dai-yu, who is having a midday nap. He insists on sleeping on the same bed, too. They recline on the bed, facing each other, at the opposite end of the bed. The point worth noting is not that they have already passed the age at which they should not be so intimately close to each other according to one Confucian commandment, "Boys and girls reaching seven shall not sit on the same mattress," but that Bao-yu does not show a jot of sexual interest in Dai-yu. We must bear in mind that this episode occurs when Bao-yu and Dai-yu are 14 and 13 respectively, and Bao-yu has already had a real sexual experience with Aroma.

Bao-yu's other real sexual experience is with Bao-chai, but the marriage proves to be the straw that breaks the camel's back. Bao-yu no longer can tolerate any encroachment upon his personality. He has to flee the world of the Red Dust. Hence his self-imposed exile. Oddly enough, neither Bao-chai nor Aroma satisfies him psychically, as they are unable to retain him through their sexual charm. He longs for the love of Dai-yu, even after her death. I suspect that even if Dai-yu were alive and he were allowed to marry her, the love tragedy would remain unchanged. He would escape the world of Red Dust, not simply because of the supernatural arrangement of love karma, but because Dai-yu is still wanting as an ideal love object who can unite his affectionate and sensual currents. This may account for Dai-yu's death at the time of Bao-yu's wedding. She is disposed of for the sake of psychical convenience. Her death is a hint at Bao-yu's inability to find a suitable love object.

Freud defines love as the confluence of "the affectionate and sensual currents" in the psyche. The former stems from infantile love for the mother, who, as the provider of nursing, is the target of affection. The latter does not come into being until the child reaches puberty. The affectionate current and sensual current are related, with the former being older than the latter. The affectionate current is formed on the basis of the self-preservative instinct and is directed to the members of the family and those who look after the child. From the outset, it carries along with it contributions from the sexual instinct--components of erotic interest. It corresponds to the child's primary object-choice. It persists throughout childhood and throughout life. It continually carries along with it an eroticism, which is diverted from its sexual aims. Then at the age of puberty it is joined by the powerful sensual current, which has as its aim genital contact (1912, 179-183).

Normal people are able to find another person of the opposite sex with whom the affectionate and sensual currents can be united. At first, however, the sensual current still follows the earlier paths by loving objects of primary infantile choice--members of the family. It, however, meets the obstacles erected by the barrier against incest. Consequently, it will make efforts to pass on from family members, who are unsuitable in reality, to other persons with whom a sexual life may be carried out. The new person will still be chosen on the model of the infantile ones, but in the course of time, persons unrelated in blood will attract to themselves the affection that was tied to the earlier ones. And then the person will leave his original infantile object and cleave unto a spouse on whom the affectionate and sensual currents are united. Some factors may obstruct the advance of libido along its socially accepted path of development. One of them is the strength of the attraction exercised by the infantile objects that have to be relinquished. Another factor is the amount of affection the person has invested during his childhood in those who cared for him. Still another factor is the power of social repression, which opposes the new object-choice and reduces its value for the person concerned. This simply means that there is no point in choosing when no choice is allowed or if there is no prospect of being able to choose suitable persons. If any of the factors is powerfully strong, the mechanism by which neuroses are formed comes into operation. The libido turns away from reality, is controlled by imaginative activity, strengthens the images of the first object choice and becomes fixated on them.

Generally, a child is nursed by one caretaker, usually his mother. But Bao-yu, as we have noted, was nursed by several female persons. His real mother, Madame Wang, who does not attend to Bao-yu's nursing and upbringing personally, is not as closely related to him as the other female figures. To a great extent, these female figures assume the maternal role of Madame Wang. Above all, his eldest sister Yuan-chun, assumes the role of a mother. One passage in Chapter 18 explains why Bao-yu is so close to his sister:

> The answer lies in Yuan-chun's special relationship with Bao-yu. Before Yuan-chun entered the Palace, she had been brought up mainly by Grandmother Jia; and when Bao-yu appeared on the scene (at a time when his mother was already middle-aged and unlikely to have any more children) she had lavished all her affection on his little brother who spent all his time with her at their grandmother's. When he was still a very little boy of only three or four and had not yet begun his schooling, she had taught him to recite several texts and to recognize several thousand characters. Although they were brother and sister, their relationship was more like that of a mother and son; and even after she entered the Palace, she was always writing letters to her father and her male cousins in which she expressed concern for the little boy who was so constantly in her thoughts. 'I beg you to be most careful in your handling of this child,' she once wrote. 'If you are not strict with him, he will never grow up into a proper man. But if you are too strict, you may endanger his health and cause Grandmother to be distressed (1:358).

The lengthy quotation reveals a number of significant points. First, Bao-yu's mother was too old to have the energy to nurse him when he was born. She had to relinquish her mother role to a wet-nurse and Bao-yu's sister. Second, the relationship between Bao-yu and his sister is one of mother and child, which is suggested by the novel and corroborated by Yuan-chun's letter home. The tone of her letter is one of motherly love rather than sisterly love. When Bao-yu is led to her presence on her visit home, Yuan-chun, "stretching out her arms, drew him to her bosom where she held him in a close embrace, stroking his hair and fondling the back of his neck" (1:363). Pleased to hear that Bao-yu can compose verses, she asks him to write an octet for each of the four places in the garden she likes best. Contrary to his quick wit and exuberant talent in the proceeding chapter, in which Jia Zheng had tested him for literary talent by ordering him to name the places in the garden, he becomes slow-witted and can hardly finish his task without the help of others. This dramatic change, I suspect, may be due to his contradictory emotions. He feels happy, seeing his sister, but at the same time sad, thinking her visit too short and brief and that he will not be able to see her again. This mixed feeling is subtly expressed in the first poem of the octet:

"The Phoenix Dance
Perfected now at last, this place is fit
For Bird of Paradise to enter it.
Each graceful wind lets fall a dewy tear;
Each glossy leaf breathes coolness on the air.
Through chinks of blind the incense thinly seeps.
Let none the checkered shade with violence rude
Disrupting, on the slumberer's dream intrude! "(1: 369)

The whole tenor of this poem is one of waiting, expecting, and longing, which characterize the feelings of anxiety lest the slumberer's dream might be disrupted by violent intrusion. In the second poem of the octet, there is a literary allusion. The mention of *san chun cao* "grass at spring" alludes to Meng Jiao's "A Departing Son's Lament": "Who would say that a small grass's longing/ could requite the radiance of spring." Menjiao's poetic line compares a son to a small grass and his mother's love to the warmth of spring, and expresses the impossibility of a son to repay the nurturing love of his mother. Bao-yu's allusion to the poetic line hints at his impossibility of repaying his sister's love. Of the four poems, three are composed by Bao-yu and the fourth by Dai-yu. Bao-yu's poem contrasts with Dai-yu's poem in tone and mood: the former is dominated by melancholic depression and anxious expectancy, while the latter is characterized by a joyful jubilance and carefree nonchalance. Perhaps Bao-yu expresses his unconscious desire to repay his sister for the kindness of her nursing and upbringing. Unfortunately, he will have no such chance, except by transference. In the novel, he seems to transfer much of his affection for his sister onto other young women in the family. This may be one of the reasons he loves girls so much.

Sibling Love and Sibling Complex

One of the consequences of infantile fixation is that the love objects are always mother-surrogates. In Bao-yu's case, things become complicated due to fact that his primary caretaker is not his mother but his sister. As a result, his love choice must be a woman who possesses more qualities than Freud enumerates in his study. She must be a sister-surrogate as well as a mother-surrogate, in addition to being able to meet the demands of moral repression. There are plenty of suitable girls for him to choose, but his investment of affection in his infantile object is so strong that he is unable to relinquish it. Because of the incest taboo, he has to split his affectionate and erotic currents and assign them to different persons. As we have seen, he directs his affectionate current to Dai-yu, who serves as a surrogate sister, while he reserves his sensual current for girls like Bao-chai and Aroma. Whether it is Dai-yu, Bao-chai, or Aroma, they are part objects in the sense that each of them can only fulfill part of his longing. Dai-yu is a sister surrogate, but she is no mother figure; nor is she a lowly person. The same is true of Bao-chai. Aroma meets Bao-yu's need for sensual pleasure to a certain extent: she is a sister surrogate, a social inferior, who does not recall incestuous figures forbidden to his desires. But she is inadequate in other ways: she is not married, and is no mother figure. On the whole, the girls in Bao-yu's entourage are without exception inadequate for various reasons. As a result, he is landed in an awkward position: where he loves he cannot desire due to inhibition; where he desires he cannot love due to lack of affection. In the deep recess of his mind, he is constantly engaged in a search for an ideal love object that can join his affectionate and sensual currents. This ideal person does not exist in reality. She lives only in his fantasy, in his dreams. This may explain why he dreams of having married Qin-shi in the Land of Illusion. And only in the world of fantasy is he able to find a fully satisfying love object. In his dream adventure in the Land of Illusion, he finds:

> To his intense surprise there was a fairy girl sitting in the middle of it. Her rose-fresh beauty reminded him strongly of Bao-chai; but there was something about her of Dai-yu's delicate charm. As he was pondering the meaning of this apparition, he suddenly became aware that Disenchantment was addressing him (1:145).

Fairy Disenchantment's lecture on the difference between love and lust may be said to reflect an intuitive understanding of the nature of human sexuality, and comes close to Freud's division of love into affectionate and erotic currents. The sex object she gives to Bao-yu meets the requirement of unifying the affectionate and sensual currents and is what Bao-yu has unconsciously desired. She is the fairy's little sister called "Two-in-one" (Jian-mei). Her name in Chinese means literally "having two kinds of beauties rolled into one." It refers to the two kinds of attractions Dai-yu and Bao-chai possess respectively: Bao-chai is plum, warm, and sensual, while Dai-yu is thin, delicate, and ethereal. The former may represent bodily sensuality, while the latter embodies ethereal charm. Each represents an attraction of a different order.

We are told that the fairy in Bao-yu's dream has another name, "Ke-qing," (homophone of "lovable"), which is the childhood name of Qin-shi, Bao-yu's nephew's wife. The reference to another name makes Bao-yu's love choice even more complicated. In the dream, Bao-yu loves Qin-shi with all his heart, being "locked in blissful tenderness with Ke-qin, murmuring sweet endearments in her ear and unable to tear himself away from her" (1: 147). At the end of the dream, Bao-yu falls into the Ford of Error and is being dragged down by monsters and demons. He bursts out crying, "Ke-qin! Save me!" and then wakes up in cold sweat. Just at this moment, Qin-shi is out in the courtyard supervising maid-servants. She is perplexed by Bao-yu calling her childhood name in his sleep: "'Ke-qin' was the name they called me back at home when I was a little girl. Nobody knows it. I wonder how he could have found it out?"(1:148) There is no realistic explanation to this surprise, but I think it may be a hint by the author that Ke-qin and Bao-yu are meant to be brother and sister, if not in reality, at least in spirit. That may explain why Bao-yu knows her childhood name while no one in the Jia clan knows it. At any rate, it is an indication that Bao-yu and Ke-qin share a special relationship. In Chapter 13, when the news of Qi-shi's death reaches Bao-yu, his response is surprisingly strong:

> During the last few days, since Dai-yu's return to her father had deprived him of her companionship, Bao-yu, far from seeking diversion in the company of the others, had kept to himself, going to bed early every night and sleeping disconsolately on his own. The news of Qin Shi's death came to him in the midst of his dreams, causing him to start up in bed with a jerk. A sudden stabbing pain shot through his heart. He retched involuntarily and spat out a mouthful of blood. Aroma and the maids clung to him, terrified, and asked him what was the matter (1: 258).

> Despite strong objection from Grandmother Jia, who thinks it bad both for his health and luck, Bao-yu insists on going to see the dead woman at once. By the side of Qin-shi's death-bed, Bao-yu weeps very bitterly for a long while. Bao-yu's heartbroken pain can be matched only by his cousin Jia Zhen, Qin-shi's father-in-law, who is believed by many critics to have had incestuous relations with Qin-shi. Yu Ping-bo, a renowned scholar of the novel, even claims that Bao-yu has had illicit sexual relations with Qin-shi, too. His comment reads: "It is very clearly delineated in the novel that Bao-yu and Qin-shi have had illicit affairs, but the author deliberately threw the reader of the track by saying it is an absurd story" (159-178). He cites six instances from the novel to support his argument, concluding: "Commenting on this chapter, previous critics consider Bao-yu's sex experience as his first one, but as a matter of fact, it is apt to say that it is his 'second experience (75).

I both agree and disagree with Yu's comments on this particular point. I agree with him that Jia Zhen has had incestuous affairs with Qin-shi, but I do not accept his suggestion that Bao-yu has had real sexual experience with Qin-shi. In my opinion, Bao-yu does have incestuous desire towards Qin-shi, but he is unable to carry it out. And his incestuous desire is of a different order. It is first of all only a wish. Its wishful nature can be seen from the way it is expressed. It is in his dream that Bao-yu has married Ke-qin. A dream, as Freud has argued, "is the fulfillment of a wish" (1965, 155-66). A dream represents what the dreamer longs to have, rather than what he has already had. The novel is replete with dreams. Although most of them are literary dreams, artificially designed by the author to convey his intentions, yet all have retained the basic characteristics of dreams, which are what Freud calls dream-work. Dreams and literature have much in common. Freud has argued convincingly about the relations between dream, fantasy, and creative writing: "Our dreams at night are nothing else than phantasies like these, as we can demonstrate from the interpretation of dreams. Language, in its unrivalled wisdom, long ago decided the question of the essential nature of dreams by giving the name of 'day-dreams' to the airy creation of phantasy" (Freud Reader 440). Like any other day-dreamer or creative writer, Cao Xue-qin had fantasies and wishes that he hoped to fulfill through his creative writing. He carefully concealed them because for many reasons. Hence his artistic distortion and manipulation of his fantasies, which make the novel obscure to the reader. Unconsciously or otherwise, he employed the techniques of dream-work -- distortion, condensation, displacement, splitting, projection, reversal, etc. The title of the novel implies that the whole book is a super-dream incorporating clusters of fantasies woven into a coherent system. We are, therefore, justified if we interpret incidents and dreams in accordance with the techniques of dream interpretation.

If Bao-yu did not have sexual relations with Qin-shi, the question arises as to why Qin-shi figures so importantly in Bao-yu's life. I suggest that Qin-shi represents the ideal love object in Bao-yu's psyche. She satisfies the different strands of Bao-yu's unconscious and conscious desires. First of all, she is a surrogate sister, for she is a sister figure in the novel.

She has a brother, Qin Zhong, with whom Bao-yu is on extraordinarily friendly terms. In many ways, he is Bao-yu's alter-ego. One critic reads his name as meaning "seed of love," an appropriate epithet for Bao-yu. He and Bao-yu have some prominent similarities:

> Qin Zhong's father, Qin Bang-ye, was one of the Secretaries in the Public Buildings Department of the Board of Works and a man in his middle sixties. He had lost his wife early, and finding himself still childless at the age of fifty, had adopted a boy and a girl from an orphanage. The boy had died, leaving only the girl Ke-er, or 'Ke-qin' as she was more elegantly renamed, who had grown up into an extremely charming and vivacious young woman and been married into the Jia family, with whom her adoptive father had long had a connection. Qin Bang-ye fathered Qin Zhong when he was fifty-three and the boy was now twelve years old (1:200).

There are some points of similarity here: (1) Like Bao-yu, Qin Zhong was born when his father was in his mid-age; (2) Qin Zhong has Qin-shi as his only sister, as Bao-yu has Yuan-chun as his sister; (3) Qin Zhong's brother died of illness at almost the same age as Bao-yu's brother, leaving his family with only a girl child; (4) Although Qin-shi is not his biological sister, Qin Zhong is on very good terms with his sister, who treats him like a son, in the same loving manner as Yuan-chun treats Bao-yu; (5) both Qin-shi's and Yuan-chun's marriages bring honor and privilege to their respective families. Qin Zhong's father is a junior official. Qin-shi's marriage into the Jia Clan brings social mobility for the Qin family. In a similar way, Bao-yu's sister Yuan-chun gains a great deal of fame and honor for the Jia Clan, when she is selected as an Imperial concubine. A final similarity is their age and life-span: Qin-shi and Yuan-chun are similar in age; both died after marriage, about the same time of the year. (Yuan-chun died at the beginning of spring, while Qin-shi died at when the winter ends and spring returns).

When I say Qin Zhong is Bao-yu's alter-ego, I mean that Bao-yu wants to put himself in the place of Qin Zhong. They can be said to resemble each other in outward appearance and inner temperament. Both are handsome boys with good looks and gentle demeanor. Both are delicate in body and hypersensitive in mind and feminine in behavior. In the episode in which they meet for the first time, Bao-yu's people cannot help comparing Qin Zhong with Bao-yu: they see Qin Zhong as "a youth who, though somewhat thinner than Bao-yu, was more than his equal in freshness and loveliness of feature, in delicacy of complexion, handsomeness of figure, and grace of deportment, but whose painful bashfulness created a somewhat girlish impression" (1:177). Wang Xi-feng' playful words to Bao-yu drive home a point: "You've met your match!" Bao-yu's own response on seeing Qin Zhong reveals the secret of his heart:

> When Bao-yu first set eyes on Qin Zhong it had been as though part of his soul had left him. For a while he stared blankly, oblivious to all around him, while a stream of idle fancies passed through his mind.
>
> How perfect he is! Who would have believed there could be such perfection? Now that I have seen him I know that I am just a pig wallowing in the mud, a mangy dog! Why, why did I have to be born in this pretentious aristocratic household? Why couldn't I have been born in the family of some poor scholar or low-grade clerk? Then I could have been near him and got to know him, and my life would have been worth living. Though I am so much richer and more nobly born than he, what use are my fine clothes but to cover up the dead and rotten wood beneath? What use the luxuries I eat and drink but to fill the cesspit and swell the stinking sewer of my inside? (1:178).

Bao-yu's idle fancies are quite perplexing. Even more so is his condemnation of rank and wealth. Ostensibly, he condemns wealth and rank because he views them as obstacles preventing him from being close to Qin Zhong--a manifestation of boyish homosexual longings on Bao-yu's part. Qin Zhong's reverie seems to attest to this: "No wonder my sister raves about him whenever his name is mentioned! Why did I have to be born in a poor respectable family? How I should have liked to get to know him; to have shared moments of warmth and affection with him! But it was not to be!"(178) Nevertheless, behind the facade of homosexual longings on both sides, Bao-yu has something else on his mind. His condemnation is, I think, the result of his envy of Qin Zhong's closeness to his sister Ke-qin, whom he can visit whenever he likes. Qin Zhong's sister marries above her social position, yet the marriage does not hinder her brother from visiting her. By contrast, Bao-yu's sister marries into the Imperial Palace, where she is locked like a prisoner, and Bao-yu is forbidden to visit her. Out of his longing to be close to his sister, Bao-yu envies Qin Zhong's lot. To satisfy his unconscious need, he wants to put himself in Qin Zhong's place. As it is impossible to be Qin Zhong, he resorts to an symbolic act of becoming Qin Zhong's brother, throwing overboard the social customs and family restrictions:

> Bao-yu had always been impatient of social conventions, preferring to let sentiment rather than convention dictate the terms of his relationships. It was this which now prompted him to make Qin Zhong the following proposal:
>
> 'You and I are schoolmates and pretty much the same age. Let us in future forget all this "uncle" "nephew" business and address each other exactly like friends or brothers!
>
> Qin Zhong was at first too timid to comply; but as Bao-yu persisted and went on calling him 'brother'...Qin Zhong himself gradually fell into the habit of addressing Bao-yu as an equal" (1:206).

With this move, Bao-yu becomes Qin Zhong's brother. This implies that he is Qin-shi's brother too. Now it becomes clearer why Bao-yu is related to Qin Zhong and, more important, how he is related to Qin-shi. By placing Bao-yu in the position of Qin Zhong, the author succeeds in producing another version of Bao-yu's hidden incestuous desire for his sister. It is not difficult to explain why he chooses to have a nap in Qin-shi's bedroom and why he has the erotic dream in which he takes Qin-shi as his bride. The little detail that Bao-yu addresses Qin-shi using her childhood name is a strategy to hint at the time when brother and sister used to call each other by their childhood names.

Now I shall attempt a detailed analysis of the episode leading to Bao-yu's erotic dream. On this occasion, Bao-yu is overcome with tiredness and wants to take an afternoon nap. Grandmother Jia asks him to go back to his own home, but Qin-shi proposes an alternative, much to Bao-yu's satisfaction. She suggests that Bao-yu be entrusted to her and she will get him comfortably settled at her house. This is the first time Bao-yu and Qin-shi come into direct contact in the novel. Her suggestion is the trigger that leads to Bao-yu's extraordinary dream journey in the Land of Illusion. Freud explains the process of dream formation by an analogy: "A daytime thought may very well play the part of entrepreneur for a dream; but the entrepreneur, who, as people say, has the idea and the initiative to carry it out, can do nothing without capital; he needs a capitalist who can afford the outlay, and the capitalist who provides the psychical outlay for the dream is invariably and indisputably, whatever may be the thoughts of the previous day, a wish from the unconscious" (1965, 599-600). He also points out that "a wish which is represented in a dream must be an infantile one" (592). Bao-yu's infantile wish, as I have tried to prove, is to possess his sister Yuan-chun. This incestuous desire is certainly forbidden to the conscious mind. Even in dreams, it has to be disguised so as to bypass the obstacle set up by the censor. Through a process known as displacement, the incestuous desire is shifted onto an object having similar qualities, which in this case means that the person must be a sister of another person with whom Bao-yu identifies. After the displacement, the incestuous idea becomes innocuous and acceptable to the censor in the dream, and to readers of the novel. The essential characteristics of the wish, however, remain unchanged. Qin-shi has the essential qualities of Yuan-chun. Besides being a sister, she is highly regarded by Grandmother Jia.

Qin-shi first conducts Bao-yu to a room at her house. Seeing a painting with the theme of Confucian scholarly diligence, Bao-yu is displeased. Qin-shi is quick to understand his displeasure, and offers to let him have her own bedroom, to the delight of Bao-yu, but to the dismay of his moral-minded nurses:

> A little smile played over Bao-yu's face and he nodded. The nurses were shocked.
> 'An uncle sleeps in the bedroom of his nephew's wife! Whoever heard of such a thing!'
> Qin-shi laughed again.
> 'He won't misbehave. Good gracious, he's only a little boy! We don't have to worry about that sort of thing yet! You know my little brother who came last month: he's the same age as Uncle Bao, but if you stood them side by side I shouldn't be a bit surprised if he wasn't the taller of the two.'
> 'Why haven't I seen your brother yet?' Bao-yu demanded. 'Bring him in and let me have a look at him!"(1:126)

Qin-shi's disclosure that she has a brother perhaps adds impetus to Bao-yu's incestuous phantasy. His impetuous demand reveals another reason he chooses Qin-shi as a love-object: she is a sister, too. Once inside Qin-shi's bedroom Bao-yu becomes aware of the erotic atmosphere of the room with its interior decorations: the whiff of delicious perfume, Qin-Guan's couplet with the innuendo of sexual love, Tang-yin's painting entitled "Spring Slumber." The detailed enumeration of items ranging from lascivious Empress Wu Ze-tian, Flying Swallow, An Lushan and Yang Gui-fei, Princess Shou-yang and Princess Tong-chang, all known for their sexual licentiousness or incestuous behavior reinforces the erotic tone of the episode and imparts the incestuous undertones of the episode. After Bao-yu falls asleep, he is led by Qin-shi, in his dream, to the Land of Illusion, where he has his sexual initiation. In a later episode, Bao-yu goes to visit Qin-shi in her fatal sickness. It recalls the earlier episode:

> Bao-yu had been studying the 'Spring Slumber' painting on Qin-shi's wall all this time and re-reading the couplet by Qin Guan on the scrolls at each side of it:
> The coldness of spring has imprisoned the soft buds in a wintry dream;
> The fragrance of wine has intoxicated the beholder with imagined flower-scents.
> As he did so, the memory returned of that earlier afternoon when he had slept in that very same room and dreamed about the Land of Illusion. He was musing on the contents of that dream when he suddenly become aware of the words that Qin-shi was saying [she is going to die]. They pierced his heart like the points of a thousand arrows. Great tears welled up in his eyes and rolled down his cheeks (1: 234).

To sum up, Qin-shi is an ideal love object that combines the qualities of mother, sister, and fallen woman. While being a surrogate sister, Qin-shi plays a role that Yuan-chun cannot fulfill. Yuan-chun represents the object only of Bao-yu's affectionate current. Qin-shi represents an ideal object of choice that unites his affectionate and sensual currents.

While the motif of brother-sister incest is deeply hidden and only obliquely alluded to in the description of Bao-yu (with whom the author and reader find it easy to identify), it manifests itself in a less hidden form in the portrayal of disreputable characters whom the reader is ready to condemn. Xue Pan's wife, Jin-gui, is such a character. In depicting this notorious woman married to a notorious husband, the author feels it less necessary to hide the incest motif in her case. Even in depicting her sexual licentiousness, however, the author still adopts measures to soften an otherwise blatant case of brother-sister incest by making her have a sexual relation with her adopted brother:

> Jin-gui's father was already dead, and the only surviving members of her family were her mother and her newly adopted brother, Xia San, a ne'er-do-well who had succeeded in squandering what remained of the family's resources. Now that they were living in town, he became a frequent visitor at the Xue household. Jin-gui was a fickle creature, little suited to the role of the faithful, pining wife. Her failure to entrap Xue Ke had left her ravenous for the slight morsel, and now even this adopted brother of hers seemed an acceptable means of assuaging her desire. Xia San, however, was a trifle on the slow side, and although he sensed her intentions soon enough, held back from steering his craft directly into her rapacious harbor. Jin-gui paid more and more frequent visits to her family, taking with her presents of money to pave the way for Xia San's eventual capitulation (5:84).

It is interesting to note that Jin-gui and Xia San stand as counterparts to Qin-shi and Qin-zhong: the relationship is that of adopted brother and sister. Jin Gui's family is of lower social status than the Xue family. By marrying Xue Pan, Jin Gui brings reputation and wealth to her family in the same way as Qin-shi does. They are also counterparts of Bao-yu and Yuan-chun, though even further removed.

Conclusion

Maud Bodkin argues for the validity of Jung's hypothesis that the emotional significance of great literary works is due to the "stirring in the reader's mind ... of unconscious forces or.. archetypes" (1). We may attribute a great deal of the literary appeal and lasting value of *A Dream of Red Mansions* to the characterization of Bao-yu. In many ways, he represents a facet of every Chinese youth who has, since ancient times, lived under the shadow of the father supposed to possess the right to dispose of his son as he pleases. Sun Lung-kee, a Chinese scholar who has studied the deep structure of Chinese culture in the framework of the Oedipus complex, advances the hypothesis that Chinese culture stays in an "infantile" stage without success in overturning the repression of the paternal figure who symbolically smothers his sons (174-186). The "family romance" in the novel seems to support his hypothesis. What I wish to add is that because of the formidable paternal obstacle and social repression, the Chinese son has to repress his unconscious desires for the mother and displace them onto his sister. In literary works, this sibling-complex undergoes further distortions. The brother-sister relation is either disguised as one between cousins or adoptive and step siblings, (as in this novel) or as that between sworn brothers and sisters, or between two beloved children who grow up together and address each other as brother and sister. In some other works, the ploy of mistaken identity is employed to realize the forbidden unconscious desire; characters who are brother and sister turn out to be born of different parents, who are not related by blood. When their true identities are revealed at the end of the story, the erstwhile brother and sister get married and live happily ever after. There are many stories with this motif. In popular songs and folk stories, the epithets of "brother" and "sister" are often addressed to the beloved. All this seems to point to a facet of the unconscious wish in Chinese culture: instead of the unconscious desires for the father or mother typically found in the white, Christian, Western culture, the unconscious strivings in the Chinese mind seem to have as their object of love a brother or a sister. This unconscious attraction to a sibling of the opposite sex is but one of the displaced forms of the original Oedipus complex in a culture where incest is strictly taboo and filial piety is emphasized as a paramount virtue.

REFERENCES

Bodkin, Maud. (1934). *Archetypal Patterns in Poetry*: *Psychological Studies in Imagination.* London, UK: Oxford UP.

Cao, Xueqin., and Gao, E. (1792). *Hongloumeng* (A Dream of Red Mansions). 3 vol.s Beijing, China: Renmin wenxue chubanshe, 1982.

Cao, Xueqin., and Gao, E. (1792). *The Story Of The Stone*. vols. 1-4. Trans. David Hawkes. Harmondsworth, England, UK: Penguin Books, 1973.

Cao, Xueqin., and Gao, E. (1792). *The Story Of The Stone*. vol. 5. Trans. John Minford. Harmondsworth, England, UK: Penguin Books, 1986.

Chodorow, Nancy. (1978). *The Reproduction of Mothering*. Berkley and London: U. of California Press.

Deleuze, Gilles., and Guattari, Felix. (1977). *Anti-Oedipus: Capitalism and Schizophrenia.* Trans. Robert Hurley, Mark Seem, and Helen R. Lane. New York, USA: Viking P.

Fenichel, Otto. (1953). *The Collected Papers of Otto Fenichel.* New York, USA: W.W. Norton.. (1931). "*Specific Forms of the Oedipus Complex*" In *Collected Papers of Otto Fechichel*. First Series. New York, USA: Norton, 1953. pp. 204-220

Foucault, Michel. (1976). *The History of Sexuality: An Introduction.* New York, USA: Vintage Books, 1980.

_________(1984). *The History of Sexuality: The Use of Pleasure*. New York, USA: Vintage Books, 1990.

_________ (1984). *The History of Sexuality: The Care of The Self.* New York, USA: Vintage Books, 1988.

Freud, Sigmund. (1953-1974). The Standard Edition of *the Complete Psychological Works of Sigmund Freud*. 24 vols. Eds. and trs. James Strachey *et al*. London, UK: Hogarth Press.

_________ (1908). "*Creative Writers and Daydreaming*". Standard Edition. 9: 142-153.

_________ (1900). *The Interpretation of Dreams*. Standard Edition. Vols. 4 and 5.

_________ (1912). "*On the Universal Tendency to Debasement in the Sphere of Love*". Standard Edition. Vol. 11, pp. 178-190.

_________ (1910) "*A Special Type of Choice of Object Made by Men.*" Standard Edition. Vol. 11, pp. 163-175.

Girard, René. (1977). *Violence and the Sacred.* Trans. Patrick Gregory. Baltimore, USA: Johns Hopkins UP.

Goodhart, Sandor. (1978). "*Lhstas Efaske: Oedipus and Laius' Many Murderers*". *Diacritics.* 8.1: 55-71.

Green, André. (1969). *The Tragic Effect: The Oedipus Complex in Tragedy.* Translated by Alan Sheridan. Cambridge, UK: Cambridge UP., 1979.

Johnson, Allen and Douglass Prince-Williams. Eds. (1996). *Oedipus Ubiquitous: The Family Complex in World Folk Literature.* Stanford, USA: Stanford University Press, 1996.

Jones, Ernest.(1964). "*Mother-Right and Sexual Ignorance of Savages*" in Essays in Applied Psychoanalysis. New York, USA: International UP. 2:145-73.

Klein, Melanie. (1946). "*The Oedipus Complex in the Light of Early Anxieties*" In *Love, Guilt and Reparation.* New York, USA: Dell, 1975. pp. 370-419.

Lacan, Jacques. (1966). *Écrits: A Selection.* Tr. Alan Sheridan. New York, USA: Norton, 1977.

Lawrence, D. H. (1964). *Phoenix: The Posthumous Papers of D. H. Lawrence.* New York, USA: Viking Press.(1913). *Sons and Lovers.* Eds. Helen Baron and Carl Baron. Cambridge, UK: Cambridge UP, 2002.

Li, Rong. (1965). "*Duyi zhi*" (Records of the Unique and Strange). In *Pai-hai.* Taipai, Taiwan.

Malinowski, Bronislaw. (1929). *The Sexual Life of Savages*, London, UK: Routledge.

Muensterberger. New York, USA: Taplinger Publishing Co.

Parsons, Anne. (1970). *"Is the Oedipus Complex Universal? The Jones-Malinowsky Debate Revisited and a South Italian 'Nuclear Complex'"* in *Man and His Culture.* Ed. W.

Ping-bo, Yu. (1923). "*On the Death of Qin Ke-qing*" In *Hongloumeng bian* (An Analysis of A Dream of Red Mansions). Appendix to vol. 2. Shanghai: Ya-Dong Library.

Plaks, Andréw. (1976). *Archetype and Allegory in the Dream of the Red Chamber.* Princeton, USA: Princeton UP.

Rank, Otto. (1992). *The Incest Theme in Literature and Legend.* Trans. Gregory C. Richter. Baltimore and London: The Johns Hopkins UP.

Rudnytsky, Peter. (1987). *Freud and Oedipus.* New York, USA: Columbia UP.

Rui Yifu. (1972). *Zhongguo minzu ji qi wenhua lungao* (Collected Essays on Chinese Ethnic Groups and Their Cultures). Taipei, Taiwan: Yiwen yinshuguan.

Sheridan, Tr. Alan. (1973). *The Four Fundamental Concepts of Psycho-Analysis.* Harmondsworth: Penguin, 1977.

Sophocles. (1949). *The Oedipus Cycle.* New York, USA: Harvester Press.

Sun, Lung-kee. (1983). *Zhongguo wenhua de shenceng jiegou* (The Deep Structure of Chinese Culture). Hong Kong, China: Jie-Xian Press.

The Freud Reader. Ed. Peter Gay. New York, USA: Norton, 1989.

The Interpretation of Dreams. New York, USA: Avon Books, 1965.

Wang, Ning. (1992). *Shenceng xinlixue yu wenxue piping* (Depth Psychology and Literary *Criticism*). Xi'an: Shanxi remin chubanshe.(1991). "*The Reception of Freudianism in Modern Chinese Literature*" *China Information.* 5.4: 58-71 and 6.1: 46-54.

Wang, Xiaolian. (1977). *Zhongguo de shenhua yu chuanshuo* (Chinese Myths and Legends). Taipei: Lianjing chuban shiye gongsi.

Yang, Xien-yi., and Gladys, Yang. trans. (1978). *A Dream of Red Mansion*. By Tsao Hsuen-chin and Kao Ngo. 3 vols. Beijing, China: Foreign Languages Press.

Yu, Fenggao. (1987). *Xinli fenxi yu Zhongguo xiandai xiaoshuo* (Psychoanalysis and Modern Chinese Fiction). Beijing: Shehui kexue chubanshe.

Yuan, Ke. (1960). *Zhongguo gudai shenhua* (Myths in Ancient China). Beijing, China: Shangwu yinshuguan.

Zilboorg, Gregory. (1973). "*Masculine and Feminine: Some Biological and Cultural Aspects*" In *Psychoanalysis and Women*. Ed. Jean Baker Miller. New York, USA: Penguin.

In: China: Economic, Political and Social Issues
Editors: J. M. Phillips and L. J. Moore
ISBN: 978-60456-727-4

Chapter 5

CHINESE BUSINESS CULTURE AND NEGOTIATING STYLE

Tony Fang
School of Business, Stockholm University, Stockholm, Sweden

INTRODUCTION

The purpose of this chapter is to present a framework for understanding Chinese business culture and negotiating style. I have had opportunities to discuss this topic with a large number of foreign executives. Many of them said they loved to negotiate and work with the Chinese. They perceived Chinese businesspeople as sincere business "gentlemen" who worked at a high level of mutual trust and respect. However, many others gave a diametrically different picture; they hated to negotiate with the Chinese and they were fed up with the tricky Chinese style of negotiating. In their eyes, the Chinese are "immoral" businesspeople who can "cheat", "lie", or just do whatever is necessary to knock you off balance at the negotiation table.

I was struck by this contradictory image and was myself very much a part of this Chinese phenomenon some years ago when I was negotiating (as a Chinese negotiator) with foreign businesspeople: the Chinese negotiator is a both sincere and deceptive negotiator. This chapter aims to decode the paradox of Chinese negotiating style. I will start by discussing the philosophical foundation of Chinese culture. Next I will present a model of Chinese business culture. The chapter will conclude with managerial implications about how to do business effectively in China. A case study of Chinese negotiation behavior will be presented in the Appendix.

PHILOSOPHICAL FOUNDATION OF CHINESE BEHAVIOR

To understand the richness and complexity of Chinese business culture we need to start with the image of Yin Yang, a Chinese philosophical principle of dualism and a cosmic symbol of primordial unity and harmony. Yin Yang is illustrated in a circle being equally divided by a curved line forming the black and white areas. Yin represents female energies/elements such as the moon, night, water, weakness, darkness, mystery, softness, passivity, etc., while Yang stands for male energies/elements such as the sun, day, fire, strength, brightness, clearness, hardness, activity, etc. Yin and Yang are not two absolute opposing forces but rather the paired nature of everything in the universe (Picture 1).

Picture 1. The Yin Yang Principle.

In the image of Yin Yang we see a dot of black in the white and also a dot of white in the black. The Yin Yang principle suggests that there exists neither absolute black nor absolute white. Opposites contain within them the seeds of the other and together form a dynamic unity (Chen, 2001). Yin and Yang depend on each other, exist within each other, give birth to each other, and succeed each other at different points in time. In other words, every universal phenomenon embraces contradiction, paradox and change.

The Chinese thought has been molded by three different philosophical traditions: Confucianism, Taoism, and Buddhism. Briefly, Confucianism deals with how to handle human relationships, Taoism deals with life in harmony with nature, and Buddhism deals with one's immortal world.

Whereas Confucianism teaches you how to do things, Taoism guides you how to do nothing (Wu Wei – both literally and strategically). Whereas Confucianism and Taoism are practical-oriented this-worldly philosophies, Buddhism with its doctrine of "reincarnation" opens an immortal world to the Chinese mind which allows Chinese people to see life in terms of the relationship between one's pre-life, present-life and after-life.

To most Chinese Confucianism, Taoism, and Buddhism are philosophical teachings instead of religions. Although these teachings "compete" and "contradict" with each other in many respects, Chinese people follow all of them, instead of sticking to just one of them, to enrich various aspects of their life. This makes Chinese behavior intensely practical, paradoxical, and embracing. Given different philosophical influences, the Chinese are morally able to play different roles in different situations and contexts. This is key to understanding the paradoxical and intensely flexible Chinese style of behaving and negotiating.

CHINESE BUSINESS CULTURE

In *Chinese Business Negotiating Style* (Fang, 1999), I have constructed a model of Chinese business culture to understand Chinese business negotiating style (Picture 2). The model captures the paradox of Chinese business culture through holding together three different yet interrelated driving forces: the PRC condition, Confucianism, and Chinese stratagems.

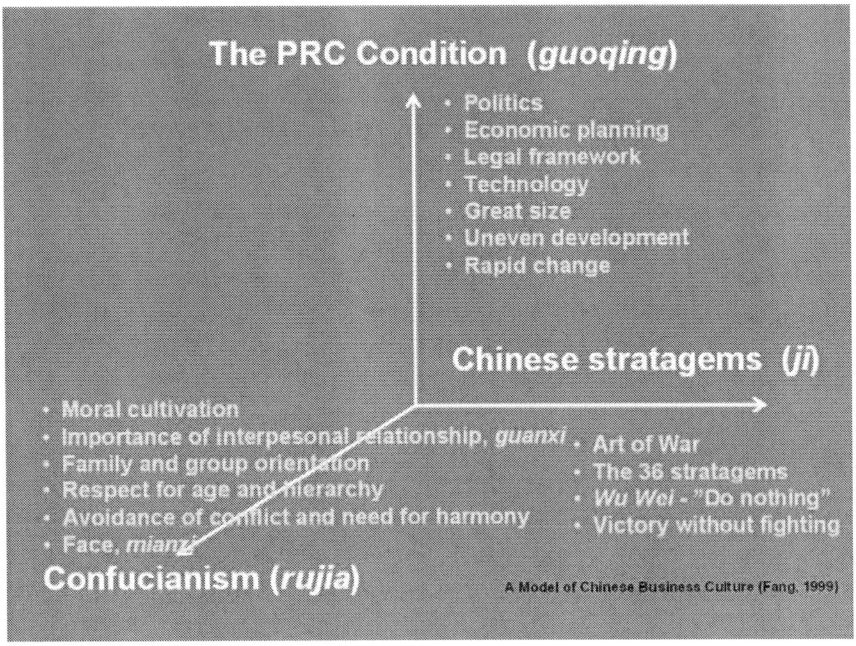

Source: Fang, 1999.

Picture 2. A Model of Chinese Business Culture.

The PRC Condition

The PRC condition (*Guoqing*) refers to the distinctive characteristics of contemporary social political system and conditions of the People's Republic of China (PRC). The PRC condition involves variables such as Chinese politics, China's socialist planned market economy, legal framework, technology development, great size, backwardness and uneven development and rapid change. The central theme under the PRC condition is Chinese bureaucracy, characterized by centralized decision making, internal bargaining, bureaucratic red tape but quick learning in the age of reform. Politics plays an important role in Chinese business life. China is a changing, dynamic, and competitive market with huge regional differences. Economic exchanges with foreign countries and utilization of new technology are at the core of Chinese development.

China is undergoing a dramatic transformation; the diversity and changing aspects of the PRC condition warrant serious attention such as the rise of non-state sectors, the emerging values (capitalism, individualism, material success, quality of life, and environmental concern) given the influence of globalization and foreign direct investment in China. Today some 500,000 foreign invested enterprises are operating on the Chinese soil and China is full of Western commercials. An increasing number of Chinese brands (e.g., Haier, Huawei, Lenovo, etc.) are also going global.

Confucianism

Confucianism (*Rujia*) is a fundamental philosophical tradition that has shaped Chinese culture for 2,500 years. Confucius (551–479 BC), a native of Qufu, Shandong province, is the founder of Confucian philosophy. Confucianism is a form of moral ethic and a practical philosophy of human relationship and conduct. Six Confucian values can be singled out to study Chinese business culture: moral cultivation, importance of interpersonal relationships (concepts of trust, *guanxi, renqing,* and *li*), family orientation, respect for age and hierarchy, avoidance of conflict and need for harmony, and concept of face. Guanxi means personal contacts and connections. Guanxi and family are important given the scarcity of resources and the lack of well-functioning legal and social welfare systems. The Chinese often make great efforts to avoid face-losing situations.

Confucianism sees the human world through the lens of the Five Cardinal Relationships (*Wulun*), i.e. the relationship between the ruler and subject, father and son, husband and wife, elder and younger brothers, and between senior and junior friends. Confucianism never defines any interorganizational relationship but rather views all types of relationships in human society from the interpersonal relationship perspective. The upshot is that the Chinese often do business with you as individual persons, not as organizations, which implies that in Chinese eyes, interfirm adaptations are essentially interpersonal adaptations.

All the five relationships defined by Confucianism feature "reciprocity". Confucianism demands the junior's loyalty, filial piety, obedience, and respect. Yet the senior must be self-righteous, benevolent, charismatic, and loving to enable the junior to become loyal, filial, obedient, and respectful. If not, the junior can disobey and even rise up to choose a better senior. Mencius (in Chan, 1963), a great Confucian philosopher second only to Confucius, writes: "If a ruler regards his ministers as his hands and feet, then his ministers will regard him as their heart and mind. If a ruler regards his ministers as dogs and horses, his ministers will regard him as any other man. If a ruler regards his ministers as dirt and grass, his ministers will regard him as a bandit and an enemy."

Yang (1957) elaborates on the Confucian notion of reciprocity by looking at the Chinese word "bao" (or "pao" in his original text), which possesses a wide range of meanings such as "to report", "to respond", "to repay" and "to retaliate". The center of this area of meanings is "response" or "return", which has served as one basis for social relations in China. The Chinese believe that reciprocity of actions (favor and hatred, reward and punishment) between man and man, and indeed between men and supernatural beings, should be as certain as a cause-and-effect relationship, and, therefore, when a Chinese acts, he normally anticipates a response or return. Favors done for others are often considered what may be termed "social investments", for which handsome returns are expected.

In traditional Chinese culture, relationship is a reciprocal, situational, and context-related concept. It is also through the rule of reciprocity that we see how Chinese stratagems (see the next section) work in Chinese negotiation processes. Chinese business people can be both sincere and deceptive when dealing with their counterparts by following the principle of reciprocity. The case study "If you honor me a foot, I will honor you ten feet in return" (in Appendix) illustrates this way of doing business from the traditional Chinese cultural perspective.

Chinese Stratagem

The Chinese stratagem (*Ji*) is a strategic component in Chinese culture. A Chinese proverb "The marketplace is a battlefield" reflects a deep-seated Chinese belief that the wisdom that guides the general commander in the battlefield is the same one that applies to business (Chu, 1991). Sun Tzu's *Art of War* is the best introduction to the strategic Chinese thinking or Chinese stratagems. Another widely read text is *The Thirty–Six Stratagems* which has crystallized the Chinese nation's wisdom in dealing with enemies and overcoming difficult and dangerous situations. Inherent in all Chinese stratagems lies Sun Tzu's (1982) admonition: "To win one hundred victories in one hundred battles is not the acme of skill. To subdue the enemy without fighting is the acme of skill."

Chinese stratagems assert the superiority of using human wisdom and indirect means rather than resorting to direct pitched battle to cope with various situations and to gain advantages over the opponent. The Chinese negotiator will typically not force you into accepting the Chinese terms but rather signals that your competitors are waiting next door preparing to present a better offer. All Chinese stratagems used by the Chinese negotiator at the negotiation table (Table 19.1) find their philosophical origins in the Yin Yang and Wu Wei ("do nothing") principles.

Table 19.1. The Thirty–Six Chinese Stratagems (Ji's)

Ji 1	Cross the sea without Heaven's knowledge (*Man Tian Guo Hai*) Deceive the Emperor ("Heaven") into sailing across the sea by inviting him into a seaside city which is in reality a huge camouflaged ship. Hide the deepest secrets in the most obvious situations.
Ji 2	Besiege Wei to rescue Zhao (*Wei Wei Jiu Zhao*) Save the state of Zhao by besieging the state of Wei, whose troops are out attacking Zhao. Avoid the strong to attack the weak.
Ji 3	Kill with a borrowed knife (*Jie Dao Sha Ren*) Make use of external resources for one's own gain.
Ji 4	Await leisurely the exhausted enemy (*Yi Yi Dai Lao*) Relax and preserve your strength while watching the enemy exhaust himself.
Ji 5	Loot a burning house (*Chen Huo Da Jie*) Take advantage of the opponent's trouble or crisis.
Ji 6	Clamor in the east but attack in the west (*Sheng Dong Ji Xi*) Devise a feint eastward but launch an attack westward.
Ji 7	Create something out of nothing (*Wu Zhong Sheng You*) Make the unreal seem real. Gain advantage by conjuring illusion.
Ji 8	Openly repair the walkway but secretly march to Chen Cang *(An Du Chen Cang)* Play overt, predictable, and public maneuvers (the walkway) against covert, surprising, and secretive ones (Chen Cang).
Ji 9	Watch the fire burning from across the river (*Ge An Guan Huo*) Master the art of delay. Wait for favorable conditions to emerge.
Ji 10	Hide a knife in a smile (*Xiao Li Cang Dao*) Hide a strong will under a compliant appearance, win the opponent's trust and act only after his guard is down.

Table 19.1. (Continued)

Ji 11	Let the plum tree wither in place of the peach tree (*Li Dai Tao Jiang*) Make a small sacrifice in order to gain a major profit.
Ji 12	Lead away a goat in passing (*Shun Shou Qian Yang*) Take advantage of opportunities when they appear.
Ji 13	Beat the grass to startle the snake (*Da Cao Jing She*) Use direct or indirect warning and agitation.
Ji 14	Borrow a corpse to return the soul (*Jie Shi Huan Hun*) According to a popular Chinese myth, the spirit of a deceased may finds reincarnation. Revive something "dead" by decorating or expressing it in a new face.
Ji 15	Lure the tiger to leave the mountains (*Diao Hu Li Shan*) Draw the opponent out of his natural environment from which his source of power comes to make him more vulnerable to attack.
Ji 16	In order to capture, first let it go (*Yu Qin Gu Zong*) The enemy should be given room to retreat so that he is not forced to act out of desperation.
Ji 17	Toss out a brick to attract a piece of jade (*Pao Zhuan Yin Yu)* Trade something of minor value for something of major value in exchange.
Ji 18	To capture bandits, first capture the ringleader (*Qin Zei Qin Wang*) Deal with the most important issues first.
Ji 19	Remove the firewood from under the cooking pot (*Fu Di Chou Xin*) Avoid confronting your opponent's strong points and remove the source of his strength.
Ji 20	Muddle the water to catch the fish (*Hun Shui Mo Yu*) Take advantage of the opponent's inability to resist when they are put in a difficult and complicated situation.
Ji 21	The golden cicada sheds its shell (*Jin Chan Tuo Qiao*) Create an illusion by appearing to present the original "shape" to the opponent while secretly withdrawing the real "body" from danger.
Ji 22	Shut the door to catch the thief (*Guan Men Zhuo Zei*) Create a favorable enveloping environment to encircle the opponent and close off all his escape routes.
Ji 23	Befriend the distant states while attacking the nearby ones (*Yuan Jiao Jin Gong*) Deal with the "enemies" one by one. After the neighboring state is conquered, one can then attack the distant state.
Ji 24	Borrow the road to conquer Guo (*Jia Dao Fa Guo*) Deal with the enemies one by one. Use the nearby state as a springboard to reach the distant state. Then remove the nearby state.
Ji 25	Steal the beams and change the pillars (*Tou Liang Huan Zhu*) In a broader sense the stratagem refers to the use of various replacement tactics to achieve one's masked purposes.
Ji 26	Point at the mulberry tree but curse the locust tree (*Zhi Sang Ma Huai*) Convey one's intention, opinions in an indirect way.
Ji 27	Play a sober-minded fool (*Jia Chi Bu Dian*) Hide one's ambition in order to win by total surprise.

Table 19.1. (Continued)

Ji 28	Lure the enemy onto the roof, then take away the ladder (*Shang Wu Chou Ti*) Lure the enemy into a trap and then cut off his escape route.
Ji 29	Flowers bloom in the tree (*Shu Shang Kai Hua*) One can decorate a flowerless tree with lifelike yet artificial flowers attached to it, so that it looks like a tree capable of bearing flowers. One who lacks internal strength may resort to external forces to achieve his goal.
Ji 30	The guest becomes the host (*Fan Ke Wei Zhu*) Turn one's defensive and passive position to an offensive and active one.
Ji 31	The beautiful woman stratagem (*Mei Ren Ji*) Use women, temptation and espionage to overpower the enemy; attach importance to espionage, intelligence and information collecting.
Ji 32	The empty city stratagem (*Kong Cheng Ji*) If you have absolutely no means of defense for your city and you openly display this vulnerable situation to your suspicious enemy by just opening the city gate, he is likely to assume the opposite. A deliberate display of weakness can conceal the true vulnerability and thus confuse the enemy. The stratagem can also be used to mean something with a grand exterior but a void interior.
Ji 33	The counter-espionage stratagem (*Fan Jian Ji*) When the enemy's spy is detected, do not "beat the grass to startle the snake", but furnish him with false information to sow discord in his camp. Maintain high intelligence and alertness.
Ji 34	The self-torture stratagem (*Ku Rou Ji*) Display one's own suffering in order to win sympathy from others.
Ji 35	The stratagem of interrelated stratagems (*Lian Huan Ji*) A stratagem combining various stratagems into one interconnected arrangement. Deliberately planning a series of stratagems.
Ji 36	Running away is the best stratagem (*Zou Wei Shang Ji*) Run away, when all else fails. Put up with temporary disgrace and losses to win ultimate victory. Running away to gain more bargaining power.

Source: Own work.

Sun Tzu's strategic thinking "victory without fighting" is often reflected in Chinese negotiating tactics. A common Chinese "ploy" is to conduct parallel negotiations with competing firms to play them off against each other. As mentioned earlier, a typical Chinese negotiator would not corner you to adjust your price level but rather signal that you are in a race and your competitors are to come to offer a better proposal so that you know how to modify your proposal automatically. This is a typical "Kill with a borrowed knife" stratagem (No. 3 in the list of The Thirty-Six Stratagems).

At the negotiation table your Chinese negotiation counterpart may appear absent-minded, not listening to you or silent as if he/she does not understand you to stimulate you to speak and promise more ("Play a sober-minded fool"; No. 27 in the list of The Thirty-Six Stratagems). Chinese hospitality and friendliness can be a double-edged sword, which can make it difficult for you to feel too business-minded. Much of the Chinese negotiating style is based on building up a mental guilt feeling which you are expected to be paid back in various ways. This tactic is illustrated in "Hide a knife in a smile" (No. 10 in the list of The Thirty-Six Stratagems) or "The beautiful woman stratagem" (No. 31).

What Is a Chinese Negotiating Style?

Given the impacts of different driving forces, a Chinese negotiator often plays paradoxical roles. The Chinese negotiator may be understood as a blend of "Maoist bureaucrat in learning", "Confucian gentleman"[1], and "Sun Tzu-like strategist".

"Maoist Bureaucrat in Learning"

As a Maoist bureaucrat, the Chinese negotiator follows his government's plans to do business. He gives first priority to China's national interest and never separates business from politics. He avoids taking initiatives, shuns responsibility, fears criticism, and has no final say. He lacked international business experience but is currently moving quickly upward on the steep learning curve. He is a shrewd negotiator because he is trained daily in Chinese bureaucracy in which bargaining is an integrated element. Given the changing PRC condition and the increasing impacts of foreign direct investment, the Chinese "communist" bureaucracy has started embracing the capitalist spirit. Entrepreneurial passion is often reflected in the behavior of Chinese negotiator even from a state-owned enterprise.

"Confucian Gentleman"

Being a Confucian gentleman, the Chinese negotiator behaves on the basis of mutual trust and benefit, seeking cooperation and "win-win" solutions. He shows a profound capacity to conclude business without negotiating. He simply does not like the word "negotiation"; he prefers to use the words "talk" or "discuss"(as a matter of fact, the Mandarin words for negotiation is *Tan Pan*, which literally translates as "Talk" and "Judge", respectively) because the Western notion of "negotiation" suggests somewhat disagreeable connotations of conflict, which must be avoided at all costs. He views contracting essentially as an ongoing relationship or problem-solving process rather than a one-off watertight legal package. He associates business with *guanxi*, friendship, and trust. He is group-oriented, self-restrained, conscious of face, age, hierarchy, and etiquette, and suspicious of "non-family" persons. He can be a daunting negotiator, for example, when he revisits old issues in the light of a changing market situation to seek mutual benefits and when he bargains toughly in the interests of his "family." His negotiation strategy is characterized basically by cooperation.

"Sun Tzu-Like Strategist"

As a Sun Tzu-like strategist, the Chinese negotiator views marketplace as a battlefield. He sets out to "win-lose" you. He is a skilful negotiator, endowed with a formidable variety of Chinese stratagems from his ancestors. At the heart of his bargaining technique lies Sun Tzu's secret: "To subdue the enemy without fighting." He seldom wages a physical war; rather, he is keen on a psychological wrestling of wit to manipulate you into doing business

[1] In this chapter, the words "gentleman" and "he", etc. are used for the sake of simplicity; they refer, however, to both genders.

his way. His actions tend to be deceitful and indirect. He often creates favorable situations to attain his objectives by utilizing external forces. His most favored negotiating tactic is "Kill with a borrowed knife" (Stratagem 3). He is always ready to withdraw from the bargaining table when all else fails, but this is only a Chinese stratagem for fighting back (Chiao, 1981). His negotiation strategy is characterized by competition. As such, Chinese negotiating style is intrinsically a paradox. For example, the Chinese negotiator values *face* when doing business as gentlemen. But the same person values "thick face and black heart" (suggesting "faceless", "merciless"; Chu, 1992) when doing business as a strategist.

As such, the Chinese negotiating style is flexible, situation-related and paradoxical in nature. The frequently heard Chinese phrase "Foreign guests first!" is not just a courtesy invitation but also a strategic consideration. The Chinese negotiator uses both the Confucian-style cooperation strategy and the Sun Tzu style competition strategy in negotiations – a strategic paradox which I call the "coop–comp" Chinese negotiation strategy. The term *coop–comp* suggests that Chinese negotiators negotiate both cooperatively and competitively, and both sincerely and deceptively because they are driven by cultural traits of both – cooperative and competitive qualities.

But when would the Chinese negotiator use a cooperation strategy and when would the same person use a competition strategy? It depends ultimately on *trust* between the negotiating parties.

When mutual trust is high, the Chinese negotiator negotiates as a Confucian gentleman; when mutual trust is low, the same person manipulates as a Sun Tzu-like strategist. Meeting you for the first time, even the Chinese themselves are not sure which roles they should play; all depends on how you act in your first moves. The Chinese negotiator routinely examines and evaluates the state of trust between the parties at the outset of negotiation, and then calibrates his negotiation strategies in dealing with the other party based on the Confucian principle of reciprocity.

THE CHANGING SUCCESS AND FAILURE FACTORS IN NEGOTIATIONS WITH THE PRC

A survey of Swedish firms was conducted in 2003 concerning the success and failure factors in business negotiations with China (Fang and Fann, 2003, see "This study" in Table 19.2, Table 19.3). The survey used a questionnaire which was adopted in two earlier studies, one in the 1980s and the other in the 1990s. Although the empirical bases of these three studies differ from each other (size of the firm, location, and industry), the general trend seems to be pointing to a more professional and competition-oriented business environment in Post–WTO China where technical competence plays an increasingly important role. At the same time, the impacts of some cultural factors cannot be underestimated (e.g., your sincerity in negotiation – an important step to building up trust in negotiations).

Table 19.2. Success Factors in Negotiating with the PRC – A Comparison Between Three Studies

Items	This study			Leung and Yeung (1995)			Stewart and Keown (1989)		
	Mean	SD	Ranking	Mean	SD	Ranking	Mean	SD	Ranking
Sincerity on the part of our team	6.26	1.00	1	3.68	1.72	18	5.78	X	8
Preparation by our team	5.94	0.91	2	4.46	1.54	11	5.72	X	10
Our firm's technical expertise	5.87	1.16	3	4.18	1.60	13	5.82	X	6
Patience on the part of our team	5.64	1.09	4	4.45	1.64	12	5.93	X	5
Our knowledge of PRC business practices	5.17	1.17	5	5.80	1.02	2	5.80	X	7
Good personal relationships	5.02	1.37	6	6.01	1.07	1	5.98	X	4
Our willingness to sell at a good price	4.70	1.41	7	4.82	1.32	9	5.69	X	11
Uniqueness of our product	4.68	1.14	8	5.11	1.39	6	6.81	X	1
Our ability to meet delivery requirements	4.49	1.40	9	3.98	1.54	14	5.31	X	13
PRC's need for our product	4.43	2.00	10	5.26	1.36	5	6.34	X	2
PRC's requirement being clear	4.13	1.57	11	5.31	1.24	3	5.73	X	9
Our familiarity with PRC social customs	4.04	1.16	12	3.94	1.51	15	5.05	X	15
Good interpreter on our side	3.81	2.17	13	2.80	1.37	20	3.85	X	18
Our knowledge of the PRC's political and economic situation	3.64	1.52	14	3.77	1.63	17	5.11	X	14
Our use of the "old friend" approach	3.30	1.78	15	5.29	1.64	4	4.57	X	16
Our firm's past reputation in selling to PRC	3.28	1.68	16	3.86	1.54	16	5.35	X	12
Our willingness to offer good financing	3.04	1.69	17	5.07	1.25	7	4.38	X	17
Our use of an intermediary/agent	2.96	1.69	18	3.29	1.50	19	3.21	X	20
PRC's foreign exchange availability	2.74	1.92	19	5.04	1.68	8	6.22	X	3
Gift and tour service	2.19	1.46	20	4.73	1.56	10	X	X	X
Our willingness to arrange counter trade (e.g. buyback)	1.42	1.01	21	2.75	1.25	21	3.42	X	19

Table 19.3. Failure Factors in Negotiating with the PRC: A Comparison Between the Three Studies

Items	This study			Leung and Yeung (1995)			Stewart and Keown (1989)		
	Mean	SD	Ranking	Mean	SD	Ranking	Mean	SD	Ranking
Our inability to lower price	6.18	1.67	1	3.80	1.39	13	5.21	X	8
Too many competitors offering the same product	5.68	1.07	2	3.68	1.41	15	5.64	X	5
Lack of preparation by our team	5.27	1.20	3	4.10	1.55	10	4.64	X	13
PRC insincerity	4.91	1.12	4	5.20	1.51	2	5.36	X	6
Disagreement on contractual terms	3.61	1.24	5	3.81	1.55	12	4.79	X	12
Our inability to meet delivery requirements	3.55	1.76	6	3.80	1.33	14	5.15	X	10
Different objectives	3.45	1.39	7	3.05	1.53	19	3.71	X	18
A breakdown in communication	3.25	1.57	8	4.77	1.72	4	5.93	X	3
Our unwillingness to meet financing demands	3.16	1.67	9	4.73	1.38	5	5.21	X	9
Difference in business practices	3.11	1.73	10	4.71	1.61	6	4.36	X	15
Lack of patience by our team	3.11	1.53	11	3.63	1.47	16	5.14	X	11
Not knowing any “old friends”	2.86	1.46	12	4.61	1.40	8	5.23	X	7
PRC did not really need our product	2.84	1.36	13	4.86	1.39	3	5.86	X	4
Differences in negotiation styles	2.82	1.04	14	3.20	1.64	18	4.31	X	16
Our firm’s lack of good reputation in PRC	2.77	1.46	15	3.85	1.45	11	4.64	X	14
PRC’s shortage of foreign exchange	2.68	1.55	16	4.34	1.50	9	6.93	X	1
PRC’s lack of budget	2.66	1.48	17	5.34	1.18	1	6.14	X	2
Difference in social customs	2.64	1.16	18	2.48	1.25	20	3.71	X	17
Not using an intermediary/agent	2.32	1.22	19	3.32	1.49	17	3.64	X	19
Language problems	2.00	1.56	20	2.37	1.24	21	3.62	X	20
Cannot cope with “stress” created by the PRC team	1.86	0.85	21	4.63	1.52	7	X	X	X

Managerial Implications

(1) Send Your Best Team to China

China is a demanding marketplace to which you need to send your best team. Your team leader should be a person with charismatic charm, a patient personality, credibility, and sufficient authority to make key decisions. If you need to send a young professional to China, you need to show that this young person is not every man or woman but a key person in your company who can make important decisions on behalf of the company. Technical and financial specialists must always be included on your team to be able to answer technical and financial questions raised by the Chinese counterparts, who are technology- and price-sensitive. Your lawyer, if participating in face-to-face meetings, should be well versed not only in Western laws but also in Chinese law and government regulations.

(2) Show Political Support

In China, the Chinese government is often found to be "the biggest boss" in many business projects. The all-pervasive influence of Chinese politics on Chinese business would imply that the Chinese may simply doubt your company's stability, reliability, and credibility if your government does not support your company. It is of crucial importance to show political support and governmental backing behind your important China missions especially when negotiating large industrial high-risk projects in China. Large business contracts can be secured and potential problems resolved if leaders of your government and your business community work hand in hand in doing business with China.

(3) Identify Real Chinese Negotiators

The real Chinese negotiators or final decision makers are often absent from formal negotiation sessions. High-ranking officials, private business owners and key profiles of certain interest groups and even their private networks can all drive the process of negotiations. Never miss the chance, if any, to meet directly with Chinese political and business leaders. By identifying and negotiating with the real Chinese negotiators, you can, as a Chinese proverb states, "get twice the result with half the effort."

(4) Take a People-Oriented Approach

There is a growing awareness of legalism in today's China. However, the traditional Confucian aversion to law still exists and many Chinese associate law and lawyers with coercion, troubles, and failure of the relationship. A cooperative spirit and trust are at least equally valued as formal contracts as the Chinese seldom expect one-off legal agreements to bring about an exactly planned outcome. Chinese business negotiation is distinctively people-oriented, and the Chinese do business with you as a person and not as a company. Many foreign firms have killed their negotiations in China before the negotiations even got started, because they did not give importance to "pre-negotiation" and "social talks" which would otherwise help build up trust (*xinren*) to open the door to formal negotiation processes.

(5) Local Presence

In the traditional Chinese culture trust is often high inside the family and low outside the family. Chinese negotiators tend to haggle "ruthlessly" when negotiations are held between parties who are strangers. Your local Chinese employees will be able to help you penetrate into "the Chinese family" and establish a trusting relationship with your Chinese customers and suppliers more effectively than would be the case otherwise. Chinese loyalty is not a universal notion but a highly reciprocal business, depending on how fair and trustful you are perceived in the eyes of your Chinese partners. A Chinese is your "friend for life" and behaves as a gentleman when you behave as a gentleman; he employs tricks and ploys when you play games. How to motivate, train, and retain your local Chinese human resources to contribute actively to your China market development strategies is an issue of strategic importance if you want to secure a long-standing foothold in the Chinese market.

(6) Maintain a Consistent Team

Maintaining the same team throughout the negotiation process is an essential means of gaining trust from the Chinese side. Chinese tend to do business with you as a person not as a company; your successor does not automatically inherit your personal networks. Trust which often takes time to build up may be undermined overnight if you frequently rotate members of your team. Therefore, it is important to retain a consistent team as much as possible when negotiating with the Chinese, allowing the same persons to deal with each other as long as business continues.

(7) Pad Your Price Culturally

Bargaining is a Chinese way of life, both politically and culturally. If the Chinese are not familiar with your culture and corporate practices, they tend to believe automatically that any price you quote must have some huge "water content" (*shuifen*). Chinese negotiators often set out automatically to squeeze out the water content. By doing so, a Chinese can not only gain face but also show that he/she is the "winner" in front of superiors. Therefore, it is often necessary to pad your price to a culturally reasonable level that allows you to give away some margin to the Chinese to help them gain face and satisfy their bureaucratic needs and wants. Today, foreign firms are bringing in new practices and new business culture. For example, although IKEA does not allow bargaining and price haggling in IKEA stores in China, the Chinese have accepted IKEA. China is a paradox and China is changing!

(8) Help Your Chinese Counterpart

The Chinese way of doing business is reciprocal. Favor (as well as disfavor) needs to be returned. For example, behind your Chinese negotiating counterpart often lies a complicated internal Chinese negotiation game. Helping your Chinese negotiating counterpart to avoid would-be criticism and punishment within Chinese systems would eventually help your negotiations.

(9) Invite the Chinese to Negotiate Abroad

Much has been written about how Westerners should adapt to the Chinese. Western firms can influence the Chinese as well. The Chinese are learning fast. Inviting the Chinese to visit your country for some of the negotiating sessions is a rewarding strategy. Even if you pay for the trip, the payment would be well worth the cost. A visit to your country, for example, would expose the Chinese to your culture and business ambience. The Chinese negotiators who come from a tradition in which bargaining is a way of life would probably alter their bargaining strategies to adapt to you. Moreover, access to high-ranking Chinese officials is far easier in your own country than in China.

(10) Design "8-Numbered" Products for China

Chinese society is shaped by a set of norms, rules, habits, symbols, and moral obligations different from those of Western societies. For example, number "8" is adored (whereas number "4" is disfavored) in Chinese culture. A careless unintentional violation of the Chinese codes of etiquette may risk losing business opportunities. Therefore, I use "Design 8-numbered products for China" as a metaphor to enunciate the importance of respecting and learning Chinese sociocultural traits. Your products should avoid a "4-numbered" identity when entering and operating in the Chinese market.

(11) Be Patient

From the perspective of the PRC condition, China is such a large country that problems of various types are bound to crop up. The formidable Chinese bureaucracy often invites marathon negotiations. From the perspective of Confucianism, China is a familistic society in which it takes time to build trust between non-family members. "The Chinese distrust fast talkers who want to make quick deals" (Pye, 1982). Remember that "Kung Fu" means essentially "time", "efforts" and "hard work" in Chinese. From the vantage point of Chinese stratagems, you need patience to deal with Chinese stratagems and strategists. By being patient, tolerant, calm, persistent, and honest in dealing with the Chinese, you will eventually win the Chinese heart and trust.

(12) Explode the Myth of Face

The Chinese are face conscious; they can go to great lengths to avoid saying the word "No" (in China, there are at least 16 ways of saying "no", including "yes"). However, respecting Chinese face and never saying "no" to a Chinese is advisable only within the domain of business relations between Confucian gentlemen or in an ideal Confucian working domain. The Chinese negotiators can, paradoxically, be both Confucian gentlemen and Sun Tzu-like strategists. Therefore, the advice that you should never say "no" to a Chinese could be dangerous when it is practiced in front of a Sun Tzu-like Chinese strategist. For example, your reluctance to say "no" can be taken advantage of by the Chinese strategist to suggest that you have agreed with the Chinese demand. Therefore, it is strategically important not to be shattered by the Chinese face. You must dare to explode the myth of face.

(13) Approach China as the "United States of China"

With a vast land area of 9.6 million square kilometers, a huge population of 1.3 billion inhabitants, and enormous ethnic, linguistic and subculture variations, China is a huge continent and may be called a "United States of China". Today more than 70% of all public spending is actually decided at the regional level instead of at the central level. Chinese regions are significantly different in purchasing power, attitudes, lifestyles, media use, consumption patterns, and customs and traditions. One of the reasons why many Western companies have failed to establish a firm foothold in China is their lack of a "regional approach" to the Chinese market (Cui and Liu, 2000). While various regions in China share common Chinese characteristics we discussed above, they also possess their unique regional features. For example, business style in Beijing, Shanghai, and Guangdong may be called relational, professional, and entrepreneurial, respectively (Fang, 2004).

APPENDIX

If You Honor Me a Foot, I Will Honor You Ten Feet in Return [218]

China is the world's third largest shipbuilding nation, after Korea and Japan. Scandinavian countries are among the world's leading shipping nations. The Chinese shipyard C brought home from Scandinavia three new building contracts to build chemical tankers of 8,300 to 13,600 deadweight tons (1 for N, 3 for D, and 1 for S), with the total contract value worth around USD 100 million. All the important negotiation sessions took place in Norway, Denmark, and Sweden. The first contract involving the construction of one chemical tanker was signed between C and N in June 1996. C won the contract in tough competition with the Japanese and the Koreans because of its more attractive ship design (an outsourced product from a leading Norwegian naval architecture consulting firm) and cheaper price. It was agreed that NOR classified the vessel.

[218] This case study was originally a part of the author's article "Culture as a Driving Force for Interfirm Adaptation: A Chinese Case", which was published in *Industrial Marketing Management*, 2001, Vol. 30.

The second contract, regarding three chemical tankers, was signed between C and D in August 1996. These three vessels were also of the Norwegian design that was outsourced by C. This time, whereas the design and price still remained a major competitive advantage for the Chinese in comparison with those of the Koreans and the Japanese, the positive word of mouth from N helped increase D's confidence in C's ability to build technology-intensive chemical tankers. These three Danish vessels were classified by LL instead of NOR.

The third contract the Chinese signed in their Scandinavian tour was that with the Swedish ship owner S in the autumn of 1996. The vessel was a sister vessel of the Norwegian vessel that the Chinese, at that time, already had started constructing in Shanghai. The negotiation between C and S was largely ceremonial – this was a result of the positive word of mouth from N and D, and almost exactly the same design as that of its Norwegian sister vessel. This time, it was agreed that the Swedish vessel would be constructed in conformity with the NOR's rules and regulations.

Picture 3 shows the actors in the scope of this case and their interactions. Shipbuilding is a complex and time-consuming process. For the ship owner, it usually takes five to six years to plan a new building project, negotiate the contract, supervise the construction processes, and finally take over the vessel from the shipyard and put it into operation. For the shipyard/shipbuilder, the shipbuilding negotiation involves not only negotiations of the contract and technical specifications with the ship owner but also those with the classification society, insurance company, and marine equipment suppliers from around the world who often are connected to one another in the whole shipbuilding project. A chemical tanker of the size discussed in this study would take two to three years to construct after the signing of the contract. After a classification standard (e.g., NOR, LL, or others) is selected by the shipyard, the selected classification society will send its site supervisors to the shipyard to approve the drawings and plans and supervise the whole construction processes. After the vessel has passed the final inspection, this classification society will issue a certificate to the ship owner to certify that the vessel is seaworthy and ready for delivery to the ship owner. The whole shipbuilding process suggests that the shipyard, ship owner, classification society, and other actors have to interact with, and adapt to each other intensively throughout the contract negotiation and shipbuilding construction processes. Three major adaptations that the Chinese shipyard has adopted during its negotiations with D and NOR are described in detail as follows.

Adaptation 1: The Chinese shipyard C agreed to the Danish ship owner D's request to change the main engine from the medium-speed type to a low-speed alternative even though the change would involve a great amount of work of a technological and management nature for C.

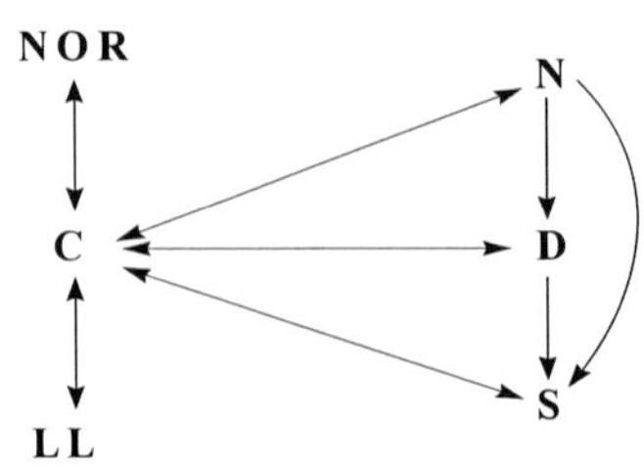

Picture 3. The Shipbuilding Case: Actors and Their Interactions.

Several months after C and D signed the shipbuilding contract (including the technical specification), D asked to modify the contract by changing the main engine from the agreed medium–speed type to a low–speed version (MAN/BandW 6S42MC). A more cost-effective vessel was the main reason behind D's desire to change the contract. The main engine of a vessel may be compared to the human heart. To change the main engine would cause a great amount of work of both a technological and management nature on the part of C. The Chinese negotiator, Mr. Q, detailed some of the major technical adjustments related to the change of the main engine. He said:

> "First, the weight of the vessel would be increased. Consider that the low-speed main engine body itself was heavier than the medium-speed main engine body by almost 50 tons. This means that the deadweight of the vessel would be decreased by 50 tons accordingly. Second, we would need to design some more daily fuel oil tanks if a low-speed main engine was adopted; this in turn would increase steel structures and space. Third, the low-speed main engine was greater in length. We would therefore need to calculate whether the engine room would be able to accommodate it [the new engine]. Fourth, a number of auxiliary systems were to be changed too. For example, the cooling system was to be expanded; oil heating equipment needed to be connected to the oil separating system, since heavy diesel oil would be used [for the proposed low-speed main engine]. Altogether, we had some 12 issues which needed to be discussed with the ship owner if it wanted to change [from the medium-speed main engine] to the low-speed main engine."

Despite all the foreseen and unforeseen difficulties, the Chinese agreed to D's request. When asked why they did so, Mr. Q replied:

> "This was, as we Chinese put it, 'If you honor me a foot, I will honor you ten feet in return.' Earlier I have said that M [D's vice president and technical director] had made a very good impression in our shipyard, P [D's sales and marketing director] too, in the whole of this project. In normal cases, a shipyard can refuse to accept such a request to change the type of main engine, as suggested by the Danish ship owner, because the contract has already been signed. The shipyard may simply say 'No', and you can do nothing about it. If your ship owner insisted that I make the change, I would say, 'OK, 2 million US dollars.' There is nothing to be discussed, because the contract was signed and binding. But we did not do business in this way, *because* 'If you honor me a foot, I will honor you ten feet in return.'"

As such, the Chinese adapted positively to the demand of the Danish ship owner simply because the latter had earlier made a good impression on the Chinese and helped them to solve their problems. In Chinese terms, D had previously honored C "a foot" and it was now C's turn to honor D "ten feet in return." When asked "How did they honor you a foot?", Mr. Q answered:

> "I always said that M was a very reasonable man. Take an example. By oversight, we had not discovered that the vessels' painting work, according to the specification, was a job that we would not be able to accomplish in reality. The specification prevented us from carrying out any welding work once the painting was finished. In other words, we were not permitted to paint the vessel before it had been completely constructed... Our shipyard lacked experience at that time; the person who was responsible for painting didn't realize this problem when proofreading the specification. I talked to M about my problem. Then, M said: 'OK, I agree to

change to [the method of] sectional painting, without price adjustment.' His short answer had helped solve a big problem for our shipyard, a problem that could not be solved otherwise. Any ship owner has the right to refuse to accept a vessel that is not built exactly to the technical specifications. You simply can't pass the inspection, because your painting is not done in accordance with the contract. So, when M wanted us to change to a low-speed main engine, we responded to him in a very cooperative and active way."

According to the Chinese, C and D had established a high level of rapport and a strong "cooperation spirit". This was because C had got a very good impression of M, D's vice president and technical director, who had previously helped C to solve its painting dilemma. In other words, D had previously agreed to C's request to modify the contract to make it easier for the latter to do the painting work.

Mr. Q also mentioned that M had once helped him "personally" in the negotiation of the Danish project. The story started with the negotiation between C and NOR regarding the classification of the Norwegian vessel.

"It was in June last year [1996] when we were negotiating the Norwegian vessel. The vessel was to be classified by NOR. As a matter of fact, NOR was the only classification society that was endorsed in the specification. When we discussed the price, NOR [Shanghai] insisted 'USD 240,000' [for this vessel of 8,300 DWT]. Since then, I have had many discussions with the NOR Shanghai Office. I told them that the price was too high. They asked for my expectation. I said USD 200,000 to 220,000, about 1% of the price of the vessel. LL gave me a 'USD 210,000' offer, but unfortunately we couldn't talk further about it... NOR's trump card was: 'You had already signed the specification in which NOR was the only recommended classification society, you couldn't escape.'"

Mr. Q continued:

"Then, I went to the NOR Shanghai Office, together with five other people from our shipyard, for the final meeting... Now all other parts of the commercial negotiations were finalized except for the price. 'This is the first time I do business with NOR,' I said to the NOR Shanghai representative, a Hong Kong Chinese, and to his assistant, a Shanghainese, 'You all know our Chinese customs. Today, I would be heartily grateful to get even the slightest discount from you. I would see it as your giving me a *mianzi* ["face"].' Then, we were all sitting in silence, face-to-face, with the shipyard's six people on one side and NOR's two people on the other side of the table. About 30 minutes passed like this. Then, he [the Hong Kong Chinese] broke the silence: 'USD 240,000. Not a dollar's discount!' I took out my pen gently and put my signature on the contract. 'I agree with you, USD 240,000,' I said. After signing the contract, they invited us to stay to have a dinner together. 'No,' I replied, 'I do not have time. I must go.' But I also said, 'I don't know if my colleagues would like to stay. I can ask them.' Remember: I was the team leader; if I wanted to go, who else would dare to stay to eat? We all left ... As such, I declined the dinner. When leaving, I told them [NOR managers] clearly: 'Your price is too high. It seems that we will not be able to have any chance to serve you in the future.'"

The Chinese felt they had lost face badly in their encounter with the NOR managers. The last sentence by the Chinese signaled that they did not want to do business with NOR in the future. The story went on.

Adaptation 2: The Chinese shipyard C stood firm, not accepting NOR as the vessels' classification standard, even though NOR's price was eventually reduced to the level lower than that of its competitor LL.

Now the time came for the Chinese shipyard C to negotiate the new building project with the Danish ship owner D. Which classification standard was to be adopted, NOR, LL, or others, was an issue that had to be agreed upon between C and D. Because the Chinese felt that NOR's representative had, in the Norwegian project, made them lose face – a terrible shame in Chinese culture – they decided to use LL, not NOR, this time. But this had to be realized by a proviso in the shipbuilding contract that allowed the shipyard to make a choice among various classification societies. Mr. Q recalled:

> "Then came the project of the three Danish new buildings in August last year [1996]. I was about to negotiate the shipbuilding contract with the Danish ship owner. NOR [Shanghai Office] got the news. The Shanghainese phoned me, asking if they could make an offer. 'Of course,' I said. And I described the general outline of the vessels. NOR said that because the ship owner was from Scandinavia, it was most likely that they would want to have their vessels classified by NOR. I asked them to make an offer first. In the meantime, I sent an inquiry to LL. Not long after, two offers arrived: NOR offered USD 380,000 and LL offered USD 210,000. This was the per vessel price for the three vessels. Then, [we] went to [Denmark to] negotiate with D. I talked to M about the vessels' classification issue. I told the story of NOR in [the negotiation of] Norwegian contract. I expressed my discontent with NOR. I said I had to modify the provision of the specification to the effect that a choice can be made [by the shipyard] between NOR, LL, or the equivalent, as the vessels' classification standard... Why was I so annoyed? Because NOR did not give me face. In other words, NOR utilized the fact that they were the only option in the specification to corner me into an indefensible position. This was not an issue of my own feeling but concerned my shipyard's feeling... I felt that NOR looked down upon the Chinese; they went too far. Lao M understood me very well. After I told the story, he said, 'No problem. NOR and LL mean the same to us. We can accept both.' As such, the specification was signed which allowed our shipyard to choose between NOR, LL, or the equivalent. Then, I sent a fax [to NOR]: 'Dear NOR, we have signed the agreement with the Danish ship owner. Now, it's high time to discuss one of the most important issues – classification. Your offer has already been received. Thank you very much. Would you please consider reducing your price because your price is higher than that of LL.'"

From the ship owner's point of view, NOR and LL meant pretty much the same. However, the shipbuilding contract between C and D, which allowed C "to choose between NOR, LL, or the equivalent" as a classification standard, provided C with an opportunity to take a handsome revenge upon NOR.

NOR managers approached the Chinese for the Danish project. But the Chinese had long set out to offend them. Mr. Q said:

> "Now, the NOR Shanghai Office was managed by a Norwegian who once was NOR's regional manager in Dalian. This general manager and his assistant, the same Shanghainese as before, came to our shipyard one day at about 11 o'clock. I was sitting in a meeting. When I was informed that the general manager of NOR Shanghai Office was looking for me, I realized immediately what it was about. I wanted to show my discontent. But out of *limao* ["courtesy"], I asked my colleague to tell them to wait 15 minutes or so because I was in the

middle of an important meeting. The two gentlemen were then left alone to cool their heels in the waiting room. In fact, I could have stayed away from the meeting, which was not as important as I told them. About 15 minutes later, I came out to meet the gentlemen. He [the Shanghainese] introduced his new boss to me and we exchanged a few courtesy words. They certainly felt I was fairly cold. They then asked me about the progress of the project, the agreement with the Danish ship owner, etc. I told them what was going on and said I was now handling four contracts, the first two of which were already concluded: the ship owner contract, the design contract, the ship classification contract, and the ship insurance contract. The last one, the ship insurance contract, was no panic; it was still not yet on the agenda. Then, the gentlemen said, 'How about going out to eat together?' I replied, 'Not necessary. If you talk business, we can do it right here.' 'Yes, we are here to talk business, but we can still eat and talk,' they persuaded me. Then I said, 'Let's do this way. You come to visit me; you are the guests and I am the host. Let me entertain you in our shipyard.'"

Mr. Q. continued:

"Then, I phoned the shipyard's general office, asking them to arrange three working luncheons for me. To be frank, I had never entertained my guests to a working luncheon before. Whenever I received guests, I always did it in decent restaurants, never in the works canteen ... This time, I would say, I intended to offend them. I placed them on a low-ranking shelf, and myself with them. We went to the works canteen. It was a canteen for site supervisors and service engineers from overseas. Many of them were dressed in rather oily working clothes. I was in casual clothes that day. But the two NOR gentlemen were both in suits. The working lunch standard was eight yuan per person: several dishes, a bowl of rice, a bowl of soup, and a bottle of Coke ... Looking around the pretty noisy and 'working clothes background,' the NOR general manager certainly realized that something was wrong. So did the Shanghainese assistant, who told me at once that NOR had not treated me well before, or something like that. To this, the Chinese did not say 'Forget it.' I said: 'Never mind.'"

He went on:

"Then, I told the Shanghainese: 'You are Chinese too. You know the Chinese seldom hate or love a person too much. What the Chinese do is *li shang wang lai* ["A gift needs to be reciprocated," "Courtesy demands reciprocity"]. You remember: *li shang wang lai*'. Here, the word *li* means not only "gift," but also something negative, an insulting action, disrespectful, or a blow from the opponent, to name a few examples. Then, they asked me about the price offered by LL. I said: 'Sorry, this is a commercial secret. You shouldn't ask such question and I am not in a position to answer this question either. I can let you know that the LL's price is on my office desk right now. You just do your best.' They whispered a while. Then, the Shanghainese said to me: 'USD 300,000,' looking straight into my eyes. I smiled. I said: 'What I need is not a verbal promise but a written one. You may say 300,000 today, but say "I forget it" tomorrow. To whom would I turn for help then? I must have your offer in writing.' ... After the lunch, we went to the shipyard's foreign guests' house to drink tea. I answered their questions one by one except for those about the LL's price. They certainly found me annoying. Finally, before leaving, the Shanghainese said: 'If USD 300,000 is still too high, would you give me a hint please. We can do USD 240,000.' I smiled without saying a word. I asked him to send me a written offer... That evening, he did send a fax to my home: USD 220,000 per vessel."

Now, NOR had substantially reduced its price from the previous USD 380,000 to USD 220,000 per vessel. This offer was very close to LL's USD 210,000. But the Chinese stood firm. Mr. Q recalled:

"Yes, very close. But I told him [NOR manager] that I have almost decided to use LL. Then, he asked me how much LL had offered. I said: 'I can tell you now, USD 210,000 per vessel.' Three days later, he sent a fax to me again, offering USD 210,000 for the first vessel, and USD 180,000 for each of the two sister vessels. They also invited me to their office. I went to the NOR office, this time together with almost the same group of people as the last time. Before going, I told my colleagues that I would not sign any contract with them [NOR] on that day. I asked them not to make any preparations, because I would use LL this time. At the NOR Shanghai Office, the NOR people told us that it would be best to use the NOR classification, since NOR was already used for an earlier [the Norwegian] vessel at our shipyard. This allowed them to be able to offer very cheap prices for the rest of the vessels. And this was also why the price for the Norwegian vessel was relatively high and those for the Danish vessels were relatively low. They had clearly prepared for the meeting and put forth many reasons. They also admitted that several paragraphs in the Norwegian contract were not very fair to the shipyard. For example, the shipyard had to pay extra salary for the NOR supervisors' overtime work at the shipyard... The general manager told me frankly that they knew they had made a big mistake [regarding the Norwegian vessel]. But the contract was signed, he had no mandate to adjust the price. The only thing he could do at this moment, however, was to cancel those two 'overtime salary' paragraphs. Then, he cancelled the paragraphs and we both initialed the contracts. The general manager said: 'This is the only compensation I am able to make.'"

Mr. Q continued:

"Now I felt the need to say a few words, in English, to the general manager. But I changed my mind, because few of my colleagues understood English. I told the Shanghainese: 'I will speak Chinese and you help translate.' I said: 'Indeed, our cooperation for the first vessel was very unpleasant. I had never met a person who treated me so poorly. I viewed the matter not from the perspective of my personal *mianzi*, but from the perspective of the shipyard's *mianzi*. My feeling was when NOR was in an overwhelming negotiation position, it could give an unmerciful blow to its counterpart. This was what I did not understand most. The Chinese attach great importance to the word *li*. But I had not experienced it from you. I can tell you definitely that I will use LL this time, even though your price is lower.' Then, the Shanghainese wondered why I decided to use LL instead of NOR and how I could justify my decision. I replied: 'I can say that your price is lower but your service is worse than that of LL... You may make a report to the shipyard director, complaining about me selecting LL even though its price is higher than yours. But I believe if you did so, you would lose our shipyard for good... This time, what I want is to give you a lesson about how to deal with Chinese shipyards, and how to deal with the Chinese. You [the Shanghainese] are a Chinese; you should help them [Western people] to deal with the Chinese, not just to make money on the Chinese. I hope you translate my words over [to the general manager].' He did the English translation word for word from my original words. [I knew] because I understood English. The general manager looked very awkward. He apologized again and again. He said: 'I am so sorry. Mr. KK [the former NOR representative in Shanghai] made an unforgivable mistake... I have lived in Dalian for three years and I know how to do business with the Chinese. Had I been the person to negotiate with you that day, I would never have done it that way... I would try to give you face.'"

Mr. Q went on:

> "That evening, NOR invited us to dinner and we all attended. We ate although we did not reach any agreement with NOR. I did not make a secret of my point; the reason why I did not sign the contract this time was simply because you pushed me too hard the last time. I took revenge on you. This was *yi ya huan ya* ["a tooth for a tooth"]."

Interestingly, the last time, they reached the agreement (on the Norwegian project) at the negotiation table, but could not get together at the dinner table. By contrast, this time, they did not reach any agreement (for the Danish project) at the negotiation table, but they could get together at the dinner table. At this moment, the Chinese began to recognize and accept NOR's sincerity. Rapport and trust were beginning to be built. This was a welcome sign for the future cooperation between C and NOR.

Adaptation 3: The Chinese shipyard C chose to use NOR's classification standard and did not bargain over the price at all, even though it was likely to be lowered considerably.

Now, the Chinese shipyard C was going to sign the shipbuilding contract with the Swedish ship owner S. Mr. Q recalled how he decided to let NOR do this business in their third encounter. He said:

> "Then the new building project for the Swedish ship owner started. First, this was a sister ship to the Norwegian vessel. Second, I did not want to go too far. If I insisted on the wording 'LL, NOR, or the equivalent' [but finally chose LL], I believed the Swedish ship owner would 100% agree with me. But, I did not act in this way. Before I went to visit Sweden, I phoned NOR. It was that Shanghainese who answered the phone. I said I was going to Sweden to sign the contract. The vessel was of the 8,300 DWT type [the Norwegian vessel type]. My feeling was to use NOR, not LL, this time. Because this was about a sister vessel. 'Would you please consider giving me an offer to increase my confidence in making this decision?' I asked. He understood my meaning immediately... I was to leave for Sweden in a week. I hoped to receive their fax before my departure. I told him that LL had contacted me a number of times. But I had not said OK yet. This time, I might also put LL on it [the specification] but I thought I would use NOR anyway. Taking revenge should not go too far. Once you have let him know your strength, you should try to get along with him. What I tended to employ was *en wei bin shi* ["Apply the carrot and stick judiciously"], or in other words, [the tactic of] using the carrot plus the stick. One must never chase one's opponent to nowhere."

He continued:

> "I received the offer from NOR before my departure: USD 180,000. I believed I could further reduce the price to the USD 160,000 level. A normal situation would allow a 60% discount for sister vessels. But if various kinds of costs were included, USD 120,000 for the second vessel would be reasonable. But consider this time, the ship owner was new, although the vessel was of the same type. So, the ship owner might regard the vessel as a new vessel anyway. That's why I said USD 160,000 would work. But I did not haggle over the price with NOR. I knew that if I used LL, the price would certainly be around USD 210,000, because this was a new vessel for LL. LL had to examine and approve all the drawings from the beginning. So, my method was to give you a *mianzi* and make you feel comfortable. I knew I couldn't give this business to LL anyway, and I did beat you too hard the last time. I must let you be comfortable in order to thaw our relationship. The bottom line was your Norwegian vessel was being built in our shipyard; if you really became too upset and made trouble for the

shipyard in the supervision process, we would have an even harder time. So, whatever style was adopted, *en* ["carrot"] or *wei* ["stick"], the purpose was *he wei gui* ["peace and harmony"]. This was my ultimate purpose."

Finally, the dinner was arranged and the contract was signed between C and NOR in a harmonious atmosphere. The parties have since had a very good business relationship. Mr. Q said: "After I came back from Sweden, the NOR general manager and the Shanghainese invited me out to dinner to welcome me back. I informed them of the changes that would be made on the vessel, etc. The previous [Norwegian] contract could be used almost at once after the change of price to USD 180,000. 'OK,' I said, 'I will not counter your price. I believe I can lower your price by USD 20,000–30,000, but I won't do that. What I have wanted to do is to let you understand how to deal with the Chinese. What is the most important is *guanxi* ["relationship"], *xianghu zunzhong* ["mutual respect"], and *xianghu peihe* ["mutual collaboration"].' Finally, the contract was signed at the NOR Shanghai office. Our very good relationship has been maintained to date."

REFERENCES

Chen, M. J. 2001. "*Inside Chinese Business: A Guide for Managers Worldwide.*" Boston: Harvard Business School Press.

Chiao, C. 1981. "Chinese Strategic Behaviors: A Preliminary List." In *Proceedings of the International Conference on Sinology*, Taipei, August 15–17, 1980, Taipei, Academia Sinica, 429–440.

Chu, C. N. 1991. "*The Asian Mind Game.*" New York: Rawson Associates.

Chu, C. N. 1992. "*Thick Face Black Heart: The Path to Thriving, Winning and Succeeding.*" Beaverton: AMC Publishing.

Cui, G., and Liu, Q. 2000. "Regional Market Segments of China: Opportunities and Barriers in a Big Emerging Market." *Journal of Consumer Marketing*, 17(1): 55–72.

Fang, T. 1999. "*Chinese Business Negotiating Style.*" Thousand Oaks: Sage Publications.

Fang, T. 2004. "Chinese Business Style: A Regional Approach." In Macbean, A. and Brown, D. (eds): "*Challenges for China's Development: An Enterprise Perspective.*" London: Routledge, 156–172.

Fang, T., and Fann, T. T. 2003. "Changing Success and Failure Factors in Negotiating with the PRC." *Competitive paper presented at The Annual EAMSA Conference*, Stockholm, October 22–24.

Pye, L. W. 1982. "*Chinese Commercial Negotiating Style.*" Cambridge, MA: Oelgeschlager, Gunn and Hain.

Sun Tzu. 1982. "*Sun Tzu: The Art of War.*" Translated by Samuel B. Griffith. London: Oxford University Press.

Chan, W. T. 1963. "*A Source Book in Chinese Philosophy.*" Princeton, NJ: Princeton University Press.

Yang, L. S. 1957. "The Concept of 'Pao' as a Basis for Social Relations in China." In Fairbank, J. K. (ed): "*Chinese Thought and Institutions.*" Chicago: The University of Chicago Press, 291–309.

In: China: Economic, Political and Social Issues
Editors: J. M. Phillips and L. J. Moore
ISBN: 978-60456-727-4

Chapter 6

CHILD PHYSICAL ABUSE IN A PREDOMINANTLY CHINESE COMMUNITY

Anselm Chi-wai Lee,* Chak-ho Li and Kwan-tong So
Department of Paediatrics and Adolescent Medicine, Tuen Mun Hospital, New Territories, Hong Kong Special Administrative Region, Peoples' Republic of China

ABSTRACT

The modern concept of child abuse as a public health concern originates from Western societies. The various forms of child maltreatment have been extensively studied in the past 40 years. However, studies of child abuse among Chinese communities are extremely limited. The purpose of this study is to examine the clinical characteristics of child physical abuse seen in a regional hospital that provides acute and ambulatory care to one-sixth of the childhood population in Hong Kong. Children admitted into the hospital from January 1998 to June 2004 for management of suspected physical abuse were included. They were examined by one of the designated paediatricians, Medical Coordinators on Child Abuse, and were managed according to a hospital protocol and a set of inter-professional procedures. The management included medical and health evaluation, injury documentation, nursing observations, and a social enquiry into the family background and functioning, and the child's academic and behavioural problems at school. Seven hundred and twenty children had been evaluated for suspected physical abuse during the study period. An increasing annual incidence was seen and the number of cases had been rising by an average of 20% per year. Boys (392, 54%) outnumbered girls (328, 46%). The mean and median ages were both 8.8 years. A sharp rise in the number of cases was seen after the age of 6 years, the time when children started their primary school education. The male predominance was also evident only during the pre-primary and primary education ages. The highest number of cases was seen during May and June each year, the time when most students were preparing for their year-end examination. 568 (79%) cases were eventually substantiated as child abuse. The more

* Correspondence : Dr Anselm Lee, M.B., B.S.; F.H.K.A.M. Senior Medical Officer, Department of Paediatrics and Adolescent Medicine, Tuen Mun Hospital, New Territories, Hong Kong Special Administrative Region, Peoples' Republic of China ; Tel: 852-2468-5392; Fax: 852_2456-9111; Email: aclee@graduate.hku.hk

severe injuries included intracranial bleeding (n=7), fractures (n=17), poisoning (n=16), burns (n=12), and soft tissue lacerations (n=41). Two children died, one from shaken baby syndrome and the other from carbon monoxide poisoning. Family dysfunction, including dependency on social security (48%), parental conflicts (30%) and single-parenthood (29%), was prevalent. Genuine behavioural problems (14%) and problems in studying (12%) of the child concerned were less frequently seen. Hence, the pattern of physical abuse and vulnerabilities in families revealed in this study are comparable to those of the Western culture. The bias in the age and gender of the battered children may reflect the traditional and higher expectation on the male offspring to excel academically, and the culturally fostered practice of corporal punishment under such circumstances.

INTRODUCTION

Although Hong Kong has once been under British rule for more than one and a half century, the history of *Child Abuse and Neglect* as a matter of public concern is short. In October 1978, a 10-year-old girl hit the local headlines, when she stumbled into a police station in a badly injured state (Lui-Tsang, 1986). After years of battering and neglect at home, she was found to be severely emaciated, her body covered with bruises and burns from head to toes, hairs ripped off, and two ribs were fractured. In the following year, a non-government organization was formed to provide a hotline service for detection of child abuse. It was not until then that the community at large was awakened to the fact that harsh discipline or neglect on children by their parents could be viewed as child maltreatment. In 1981, the Social Welfare Department of the Government published the first Procedural Guidelines for Handling Child Abuse Cases and distributed it to various professionals (Lui-Tsang, 1986). A subsequent review of the child abuse management led to the establishment of the Child Protective Services Unit in 1983 (Mulvey, 1997). This specialized government unit under the Social Welfare Department, now renamed as Family and Child Protective Services Unit (FCPSU), has since been charged with the responsibility of co-coordinating the management of child abuse cases in the whole territory.

The procedures governing the management of *Child Abuse and Neglect* in Hong Kong follow closely those in the United Kingdom (Home Office, Department of Health, Department of Education and Science, Welsh Office, 1991). Reporting of child abuse is not mandatory. Professionals like social workers, doctors, teacher, and other childcare workers are strongly encouraged to bring the children whom maltreatment is suspected to the attention of the FCPSU or the Hong Kong Police. A caseworker, a social worker from either the Government or non-government organizations, will be assigned to conduct a social enquiry. The enquiry will include the family structure and functioning, childcare arrangement and discipline patterns, and the child's development and progress in the school. A multi-disciplinary case conference will be called in which the caseworker, other social workers, doctors, police, teachers, and other childcare workers who have been working with the child or the family are invited to participate. At the case conference, the professionals will share their information about the case, determine the case nature and subsequent risk of maltreatment, and formulate action plans for treatment and follow-up services. Although the police officer is often present, the information exchanged and the decisions made in the case conference are only meant for welfare planning. Criminal investigation, if deemed necessary, will be conducted separately from the social enquiry and the case conference (Social Welfare Department, 1999).

At the end of the case conference, a child victim whose maltreatment has been substantiated or, if the case of child abuse has not been established but the child is considered to be at risk (or of great concern) for subsequent abuse, the child's name will be placed in the Child Protection Registry operated by the Social Welfare Department. A key worker, most of the time a social worker from the FCPSU, will be assigned to follow up the child victim and the family concerned. If needed, the Director of Social Welfare may invoke a statutory Child Protection Order from the court to safeguard the best interest of the child victim (Social Welfare Department, 1999). Thus, social workers, especially those from the Government departments, play an important role in the initial handling, registration and deregistration, and subsequent follow-up of the child abuse cases.

A child who has been suspected of physical abuse is often brought to the medical attention. Because of the lack of a well-structured primary care service and a lack of interest of general practitioners in participating in the management of child abuse cases, victims of child abuse are often brought to the public hospitals where comprehensive evaluation and treatment are available at minimal and affordable charges. Over the last two decades, hospitals with paediatric departments have gradually developed the expertise in the management of child maltreatment and an advocacy for child protection. Our hospital serves Tuen Mun and Yuen Long Districts, two of the eighteen geographic districts in the Hong Kong Special Administrative Region. At the last census in 2001, 937,901 (14.0%) of the total population (6,708,389) lived in either of these districts (Census and Statistics Department, 2001b). As one of the major child abuse management centers in Hong Kong, our experience in the handling of child physical abuse will be studied in retrospect. This is preceded first by a review of the published data on physical abuse in Chinese communities, and then a discussion of the traditional concept of child discipline and filial piety.

PUBLISHED DATA OF CHILD ABUSE IN HONG KONG

Published information on the incidence, prevalence, and severity of *Child Abuse and Neglect* in Hong Kong is very limited. Three sources of information are identified: (1) regular official figures from the Child Protection Registry (CPR) released by the FCPSU, (2) occasional reports from individual hospitals, and (3) occasional reports from community surveys.

Child Protection Registry (CPR)

CPR became fully computerized in 1994 and the FCPSU has been publishing the number of new cases and the number of active cases remaining in the registry annually. Prior to that time, the CPR gave only the active cases that remained in the registry and studies based on such cases were often unrepresentative of the reality (Lau & Donnan, 1987). The annual statistical reports show the types of abuse and the basic demographic data of the victims and the perpetrators. With the exception of the year 1996 (Social Welfare Department, 1997), physical abuse represents the commonest type of childhood maltreatment. As a whole, the annual reports give a clear idea as to the incidence and general category of child abuse cases seen in the community. The figures from the CPR, however, only reflect the prevailing interests and focus of the frontline child protection workers, and perhaps the resources and support available to them. For instance, child sexual abuse suddenly became the major type of child maltreatment in 1996 when frontline social workers and police officers had to undergo specific training in relation to a change in legislation (Social Welfare Department, 1997). Child abandonment and children being left alone at home are not usually put into the CPR. Fatal child abuses are never included in the CPR because the registry only includes children who are considered to be at risk for subsequent maltreatment. Hence, the CPR depicts the prevailing trends and types of child maltreatment but gives no ideas as to the details and severity of the injuries.

Case Series from Individual Organizations

A review of the international and local literature identifies three published series of child physical abuse from various institutions in Hong Kong. Lieh-Mak, Chung & Liu (1983) reported the first series of child battering occurring between 1979 and 1980. Thirty-seven subjects were identified of which 20 cases were seen by the ACA and the other 17 children were admitted to a regional hospital in which the authors were working. There were 20 boys and 17 girls, and their median age was 5 years, ranging from 6 months to 13 years. Cutaneous injuries including five cases of burns were found in 28 subjects. Three children (8%) had fractures, and one (3%) was remarked to have injury to the internal organs. In 32 cases, the abuser was the victim's natural mother. Most of the parent abusers were found to be suffering from psychiatric disorders. That the victim was the outcome of an unwanted pregnancy and an early separation of the victim from the parents were identified as risk factors to the abuse.

Lau & Davies (1993) reported a second series of children seen in another regional hospital between 1984 and 1987. Thirty-eight subjects were found. All except one patient were physically abused. About three-quarters of the subjects were girls. Fractures were found in two (5%) of the children, and the injuries were considered serious and life-threatening in four cases (10%). These included two children presenting with intracranial bleeding and the other two children suffered extensive scalds. The victim's natural father or mother was the perpetrator in 15 and 16 cases, respectively. Again, prolonged separation of the child from the parents during early childhood was a common feature in one-quarter of the cases.

The last report was jointly published by a group of paediatricians looking at all cases of child abuse admitted to public hospitals during a two-year period from 1997 to 1999 (Hong Kong Medical Coordinators on Child Abuse, 2003). 592 cases were collected and maltreatment was ascertained in 320 children. Physical abuse accounted for 87% of the cases. Seven children (1.1%) died from the abuse.

Cases seen in the hospital are biased because child abuse other than physical abuse is under-represented. However, hospital series give a better picture of how bad children are injured. In addition to the three studies that look at child abuse in general, there are also specific case series and case reports that examine particular forms of physical maltreatment of children. These reports include shaken baby syndrome (Lee, So, Fong & Luk, 1999), abusive head injury in the older child (Lee, Ou, So & Fong, 2003), non-accidental poisoning with carbon monoxide (Lee, Ou, Lam, So & Kam, 2002) and methadone (Lee & Lam, 2002), penetrating injury (Lee, So, Wong & Lau, 1998), and Munchausen syndrome by proxy (Ip, 1996).

Community Surveys

Various community surveys conducted by different organizations with different methodologies and targeting at different subjects have been carried out at different times. The International Year of the Child Coordinating Committee (1979) carried out the first comprehensive study of child abuse by collecting retrospective data obtained from 23 agencies of the government departments and various social services providers from September 1978 to February 1979. 358 cases of child abuse under 14 years of age were identified. There were more boys (56%) than girls (44%) and over 72% of the cases were aged 7-12 years. The commonest forms of maltreatment were found to be mental neglect (80.7%), unreasonable bodily harm (56.1%), and physical neglect (41.6%). The majority (64%) of the abusers were mothers who were currently married or cohabiting. Most of these children were attending the agencies for reasons other than child abuse, and the sample was therefore heavily biased towards the disadvantaged families. Samuda (1988) surveyed 100 university students and found that physical punishment was practised in 95% of the respondents' families. Tang (1996) surveyed a similar sample of 375 students in another university and found that 62% experienced verbal abuse, 13% minor physical violence, and 8% severe physical violence by their parents during the past year. A random telephone survey of 1,019 households carried out by the same author (Tang, 1998) revealed that minor physical violence happened to 526 per 1,000 children and severe physical violence affected 461 per 1,000 children during the study year. Children aged 3-6 years were the most frequent victims. Lau, Liu, Cheung, Yu & Wong (1999) conducted a questionnaire survey 3,355 secondary school students in Kwai Ching District about their experience of corporal punishment in the past three months. 4.9%, 2.0%, and 1.1% responded that they had experienced corporal punishment, beating without an obvious reason, and beating resulting in injury, respectively. Compared with the older teenagers, children of 15-16 years of age were more likely to have experienced corporal punishment and injurious beating. In another similar study (Lau, Chan, Lam, Choi & Lai, 2003) done in Shatin area, 489 Form 2 (12-14 years old) students were recruited. 4.5% and 10.9% reported that they had experienced corporal punishment and beating without an obvious reason, respectively, in the preceding 6 months. 10.4% said that they had been beaten to injury by family members before.

As a whole, community surveys focus more on interpersonal aggressions rather than the occurrence of non-accidental injury. Responding parents are unlikely to admit that they have used socially unacceptable weapons such as knives or sharps (Tang, 1998) when compared with adolescent respondents (Tang, 1996). Either parents or children respondents may under-estimate the abusive nature of the interactions unless specific criteria are laid down. Direct comparisons between the community studies should be taken with caution because of the different backgrounds. For instance, samples taken from social services providers are probably different from randomly chosen community subjects. Subjects' responses at different times may have been influenced by the prevailing concept of corporal punishment or child abuse. All studies, however, come to a conclusion that corporal punishment is a common, though not universal, practice in Hong Kong, and injury resulting from corporal punishment is not uncommon.

PUBLISHED DATE OF CHILD ABUSE IN OTHER CHINESE COMMUNITIES

Statistics on child abuse in mainland China is distinctively lacking (Korbin, 1981), although recent attention to child sexual abuse (Chen, Han & Dunne, 2004) and neglect (Yang & Pan, 2003) is emerging. In Taiwan, both child neglect and physical abuse represent the commonest form of childhood maltreatment (Yu, 1996). Of the 977 cases handled by the China's Children Fund in 1993, 40% and 29% were classified as neglect and physical abuse, respectively. The child protection services in the same year handled 1,927 children, among which 29% and 26% of cases were classified as physical abuse and neglect, respectively. However, the morbidity and mortality of child physical abuse in Taiwan and systematic study on child abuse are not available from the medical literature. Because of the difference in sociopolitical systems, it is likely that child abuse would not be of the same priority in the public health agenda in China, Taiwan and Hong Kong, even though the peoples are of the same ethnic and cultural origin.

CHILD DISCIPLINE, CORPORAL PUNISHMENT, AND THE TRADITIONAL CHINESE CULTURE

With the few exceptions in which a murderous intent is clearly shown (Lee, Ou, Lam, So & Kam, 2002; Lee, Ou & Fong, 2003), the great majority of child physical abuse cases involve the element of child discipline, or an execution of corporal punishment as a consequence of the child's failure to meet the parents' expectations. Indeed, child discipline, corporal punishment, and filial piety are deep-seated, intertwined beliefs within the Chinese culture that can be traced up to the Zhou Dynasty. Parallel to these beliefs, children, especially boys, are expected to learn from their elders in order to excel themselves as a prerequisite to establish their own character, their own families, their own states, and the whole country. Such a combination of concepts and doctrines are best exemplified in Confucian teachings that prevail in the Chinese community in the past two and a half millenniums.

The Confucian philosophy originated from the beginning of the Zhou Dynasty when feudalism was first implemented throughout China (Qu Tongzu, 2003). Zhou Gong, brother of the first emperor, set the laws and rules that governed the relationships between the emperor and the states, peoples among the different social classes, members within a family, and the lineage of inheritance. These laws and rules were collectively known as *li*. Indeed, Confucius (551-479 B.C.) regarded Zhou Gong as a saint and Confucianism based heavily on *li*. The relationship of a son towards his father was described as *xiao* or filial piety (*wei ren zi, zhi yu xiao*), which had been concisely stipulated in *Da Xue* edited by Zhu Xi (1130-1200 When a son failed to respect or follow the expectations of his father, he was not filial uld be liable to punishments. In the book *Shang Shu*, Confucius had clearly illustrated this relationship with the following story. When Boqin and Shukang went to visit their father, Zhou Gong, they were whipped and spanked and sent away. They were so scared after the third time that they went to see Shangshu for advice. Shangshu told them to go to Nanshan to examine *qiao* and *zi*. *Qiao* was a tree that stood tall and stern. *Zi* was a plant that crawled on the ground. Boqin and Shukang then understood *qiao* stood for father and *zi* meant sons. When they visited their father again and threw themselves onto the floor to greet him with respect, Zhou Gong was pleased. *Qiao-zi* has since been a reference term used to describe a model father-son relationship.

In the book *Xiao Jing* (The Scripture of Filial Piety), Confucius saw filial piety as the first stepping-stone for life-long personal success. Personal excellence was achieved through his ability to serve the king, which in turn was based on his fulfillment of his parents' needs (*shi yu shi qin, zhong yu shi jun, zhong yu li shen*). On the other hand, Confucius regarded the failure to observe filial piety as the greatest sin. Of the 3,000 crimes that were liable to the five punishments, none was as serious as being not filial (*wu xing zhi shu san qian, er zui mo da yu bu xiao*). In the Ming Dynasty (1368-1644 A.D.), the use of spanking as a way of punishment extended to the imperial office. According to the Laws of Punishment, part III, in *Ming Shi* (History of Ming Dynasty), Zhu Yuanzhang, the first emperor, enacted a law of *ting zhang* (imperial spanking) to allow the emperor to punish an official if he did or said something to displease the emperor. This political move was believed to have reinforced and legitimized the use of corporal punishment in families. For centuries, child discipline became an integral part of parental responsibilities (or rights) and corporal punishment is generally regarded as broadly equivalent to child discipline.

Cautionary Notes on Corporal Punishment

The use of corporal punishment has rarely been criticized by the Confucians. Yan Zhitui (531-590 AD) said in his famous parenting handbook *Yanshi Jia Xun* that corporal punishment should be prescribed to the misbehaving child like medicine or acupuncture to the ailed person. However, he also remarked that it could be avoided by early and effective teachings. Confucius also realized the adverse consequences of corporal punishment. In another Confucian writing, *Kongzi Jia Yu* (The Family Dialogue of Confucius), Zeng Shen and his father Zeng Xi were both beloved students of Confucius. One day Zeng Shen was knocked out by his father with a club because he ruined the crops carelessly. When Confucius knew that, he reprimanded Zeng Shen because a filial son would only accept mild punishments and should fled from heavy blows (*xiao zhang ze shou*; *da zhang ze zou*). By exposing himself to serious corporal punishment, a son would be regarded as treacherous to his father because his father would regret upon his acts.

Corporal Punishment and Adversity

Parallel to the parental use of corporal punishment as child discipline, children were taught to be obedient and to accept adversity. Confucians often emphasized the positive value of adversity and reinforced a person's capacity to overcome it, a belief that is still widely held in local Chinese (Shek, 2004). Mencius (372-289 B.C.), the most prominent Confucian after

Confucius, said, "So when heaven is about to place great responsibility upon a man, it will first temper his heart and mind, fatigue his bones and muscles with toil, starve him, reduce him to utter destitution and frustrate him in all his attempts so as to stir him up, strengthen his character and develop his capabilities… Then we come to know that one survives in worries and miseries, and perish in ease and comfort." (Mencius; *Gaozi*, part B) Child discipline, in the form of corporal punishment, was naturally an adversity well suited in this manner to stir up a misbehaving child, to strengthen his character and to develop his capabilities. After all, as stipulated in the classic Confucian text, *Lun Yu*, a filial son should observe his obedience with respect and never complained about the hardship (*you jing bu wei, lao er bu yuan*) even though his parents might not be right.

Childhood Teachings on Filial Piety

As filial piety towards parents and elders had been regarded as fundamental to the parent-child relationship, legends and stories modeling filial persons were told and compiled into chapters or books throughout the last millennium. Wu (1981) examined the two chapters of a compilation, *Tai Ping Yu Lan*, comprising 89 short stories edited during the Song Dynasty (960-1278 A.D.) and classified the filial behaviours into the following nine categories:

1. Sacrifice of one's own life or one's child's life for the parents' sake;
2. Mourning in excess of the normal rites;
3. To accomplish an impossible task or to suffer self-inflicted bodily pain in fulfillment of a parent's wishes or demands;
4. To attend sick parents or to seek medicine or a cure through extraordinary behaviour or miracles;
5. To provide parents with a proper, decent burial;
6. Extreme bravery in protecting a parent or a parent's corpse from harm or damage;
7. Attachment to parents through extrasensory or supernatural communication;
8. To avenge a father's death;
9. To support parents despite difficult circumstances or through self-sacrifice.

From these acts, Wu further deduced the following moral and cultural doctrines that were conveyed to Chinese children from centuries to centuries. (1) From a very young age, children were expected to show great devotion to their parents. (2) The parent's welfare comes before that of a son or the son's wife or children. A son should not be happy when his parents were not happy. (3) At the loss of a parent, one was expected to express one's grief openly. Those whose mourning behaviour exceeded that prescribed by the rites were considered filial. The most filial would rather die than continue to live without the parent's company. (4) No matter how unreasonable a parent's demands, or how harsh the treatment inflicted by a parent, a son or a daughter should obey and endure and make sure that the parent's wishes were fulfilled. Children's submissiveness to a stepmother's maltreatment was to be praised.

Even though the last empire state in China had been overturned for almost a century, e stories and doctrines are still told and taught unchallenged among Chinese communities. following story, extracted from *Ershisi Xiao* (Twenty-four Deeds of Filial Piety) compiled by Guo Jujing during the Yuan Dynasty (1279-1368 A.D.), is still a popular lesson and was taught during the authors' school years with omission of the first line, however. Wang Chang's stepmother had been unkind to him. His stepmother was fond of eating fresh fish. In order to please her, Wang Chang went outside during winter, took off his clothes and laid himself upon the ice on the lake. With the warmth of his body, the ice broke and two carps jumped into his hands. Wang Chang's story, though brief, has well illustrated most of Wu's deductions.

Although the use of corporal punishment remains a controversial subject in most Western countries, academic debates (DeAngelis, 1997; Ellimen & Lynch, 2000), empirical researches (Durrant, 1999), public consultations and discussions (Bailey, 2003; Department of Health, 2000), and guidance from learned societies (American Academy of Pediatrics, 1998; Canadian Paediatric Society, 2004) have helped to delineate its limitations, negative effects, and alternatives. In Hong Kong, the movements towards child protection in the last 25 years, however, have made corporal punishment by parents a potential crime punishable by the laws (Social Welfare Department, 1999). In 1991, corporal punishment in the schools was officially banned, and teachers found guilty for maltreating their students often hit the newspaper headlines (Chu, 1999). Corporal punishment behind closed doors is still pervasive. Studies on the adverse consequences of corporal punishment in Chinese societies are emerging (Kong, Wong, Goh, Lam, Chua & Kok, 1988; Lau, Chan, Lam, Choi & Lai, 2003; Lau, Liu, Cheung, Yu & Wong, 1999). Formal debates and discussions are largely unknown and probably difficult in Chinese communities. Any disputes on corporal punishment would inevitably challenge not only parental rights, but also the Confucian doctrine of filial piety. Nonetheless, the immediate and often alarming features of child discipline and physical abuse in Chinese communities deserve detailed discussion.

PATIENTS AND METHODS

The study was carried out in a regional general hospital that provides medical care to Yuen Long and Tuen Mun districts of the western New Territories in the Hong Kong Special Administrative Region. It is the only hospital that provides acute and ambulatory paediatric services, including intensive care and neurosurgery, to the population served. At the last census in 2001, the childhood population served by the hospital was 228,495, representing 16.6% of the total population under 18 years in Hong Kong (Census and Statistics Department, 2001a).

Children with suspected child abuse or neglect may be admitted to the hospital in one of the following manners: (1) attendance at the accident and emergency department or ambulatory centre for abuse- or non-abuse-related health problems, (2) referral from general practitioners or family physicians, (3) referral from social workers from government or non-government organisations. Once abuse or neglect is suspected, the child's name is enrolled in a departmental registry prospectively, which forms the basis of this study.

The initial management of suspected *Child Abuse and Neglect* follows the multi-disciplinary guidelines compiled by the Social Welfare Department (1999) and a hospital protocol devised by the authors that specifies the logistics of management and types of investigations needed according to the clinical information (Lee, Lee, Ou & So, 2000). As a result, the paediatrtician will obtain the child's medical and developmental history, examine the health and growth status, document the injuries, investigate for associated complications, exclude alternative diagnosis, and plan for follow-up assessment. The nurse will evaluate the child's behaviours and the parent-child interactions. The roles of the social worker, the police, and other workers and the subsequent management have been detailed in the introductory section.

The present study examines the children who had been enrolled in the departmental registry of child abuse between January 1998 and June 2004. Only patients who were admitted with an initial suspicion of child physical abuse were included. Their sex, age at the time of admission, the suspected perpetrator, mechanisms of injury, severity of injury, final diagnosis, enrolment into the Child Protection Registry were described. The occurrence of the cases was further enumerated according to the calendar years, calendar months (excluding cases in 2004), and different age groups. A limited number of risk factors, including the child's academic performance, behavioural problems, prior record of child abuse, and parental factors such as unemployment, single parenthood, conjugal conflicts, and reliance on social security, that were collected on a prospective basis were also described.

RESULTS

Within the six and a half years, 720 children were evaluated in our hospital for suspected child physical abuse. The annual incidence rose from 65 cases in 1998 to 154 cases in 2003, an average of 20% increase per annum (Figure 1). In the first six months of 2004, 101 children had already been admitted for physical abuse evaluation. When the number of cases was analyzed according to the month of admission (excluding figures in 2004), the peak incidence occurred in May and June, while the lowest figures were seen in July and August (Figure 2).

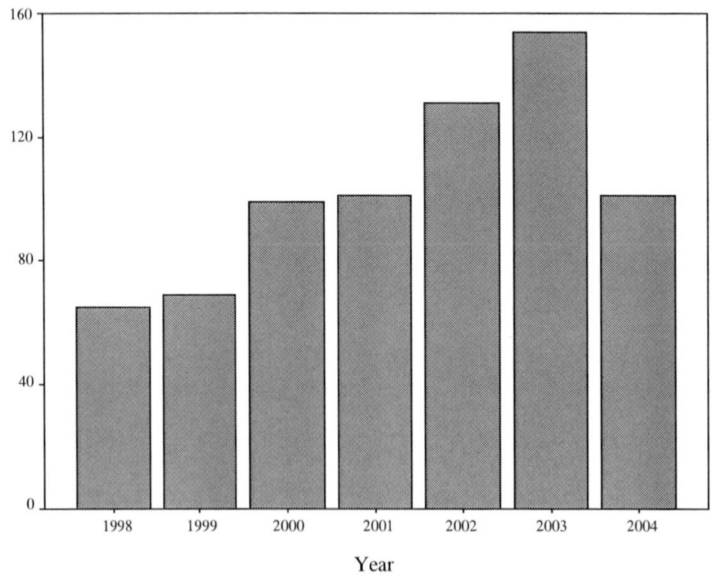

Figure 1. The number of suspected physical abuse cases according to years.

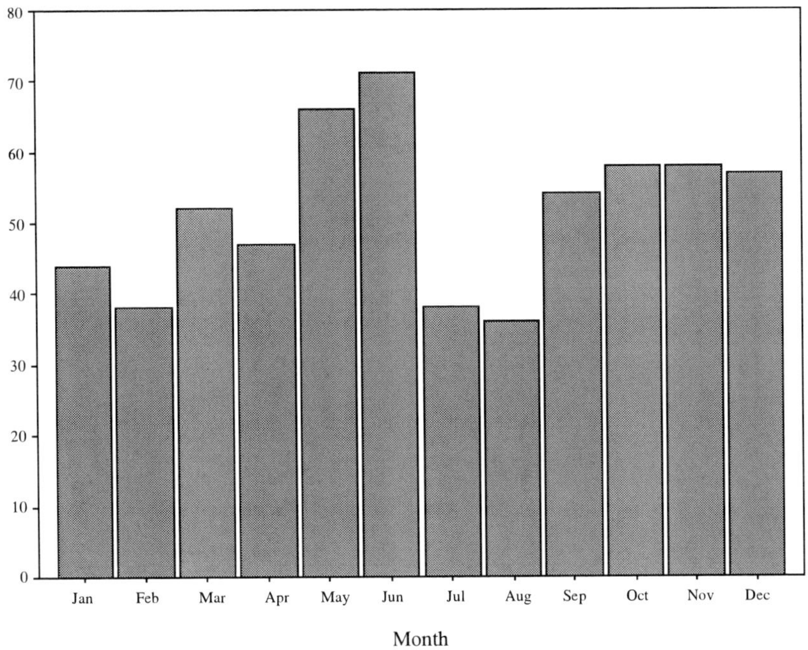

Figure 2. The number of suspected child abuse cases according to the months of presentation (excluding figures from 2004).

An excess of male victims was seen during the study period with 392 boys (54%) and 328 girls (46%). Their mean and median ages were both 8.8 years, ranging from 1 day to 17.9 years. When the number of cases was analyzed according to the age groups, the highest numbers were seen in the 6- to 13.9-year-old children. An abrupt increase of incidence was seen between the pre-school (4-5.9 years old) children and the primary school (6-11.9 years old) children. A gradual decrease in the number of cases was seen as children became more mature into adolescence (Figure 3).

When the number of cases was analyzed according to sex and age groups, the male predominance was seen only during the pre-school and primary school (4-11.9 years old) children. On the contrary, a female predominance was seen during late adolescence from 14 to 17.9 years of age (Figure 4).

Injuries were arbitrarily classified as "severe" if they fell into any the following categories: internal bleeding including intracranial bleeding, laceration of the skin or other soft tissues, fractures, burns or scalds, poisoning, and strangulation or smothering. The types of severe injuries were listed in Table 1. Thirty (4.2%) children experienced potentially life-threatening forms of injuries, of which two died from the injuries. The fatalities included a 1.4-year-old girl who died from inflicted head trauma (shaken baby syndrome) and a 7-year-old boy who died from carbon monoxide and zopiclone poisoning. The latter case occurred in the setting of an attempted homicide-suicide when a young woman tried to poison her two children with sleeping pills and to kill the three of them together by burning charcoal in an enclosed flat. The child died on arrival at the hospital while the other two were rescued from the scene. Both fatal cases have been reported previously (Lee, Hau & Fong, 2001; Lee, Ou,

Lam, So & Kam, 2002). In 12 (1.7%) children, significant injury to the central nervous system or psychosocial deprivation led to early signs of neurodevelopmental impairments.

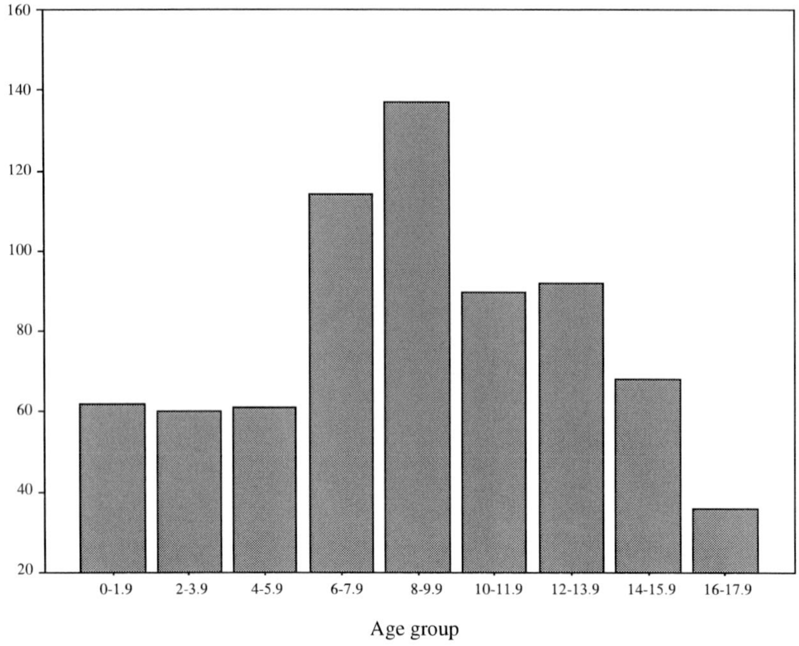

Figure 3. Number of suspected physical abuse cases according to victims' age groups.

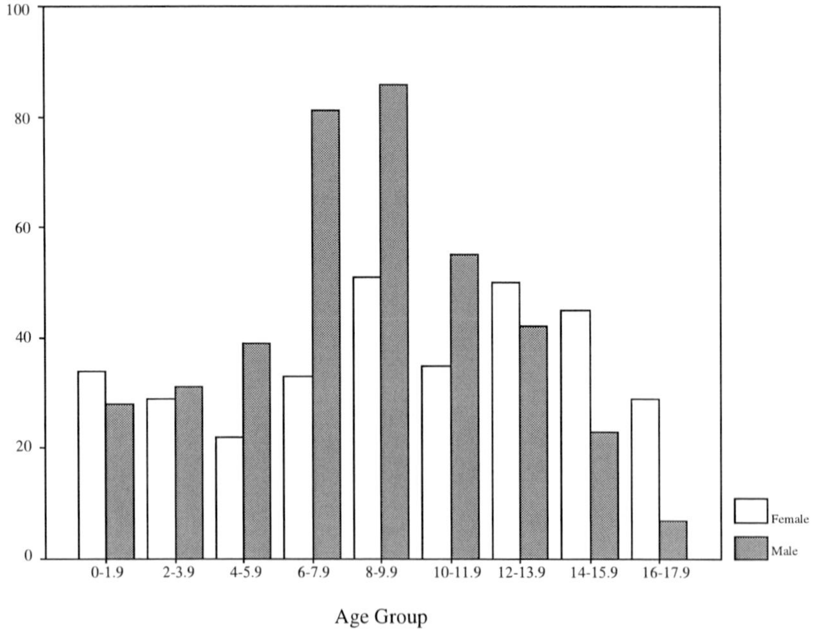

Figure 4. Number of suspected physical abuse cases according to victims' sex and age groups.

Table 1. Severe cases of abusive injuries among the 720 children

Type of injuries	Number of children (percent)
Potentially life threatening	
Intracranial bleeding	8 (1.1)
Poisoning	18 (2.5)
Strangulation/smothering	4 (0.6)
Signs of significant trauma	
Fractures	21 (2.9)
Burns and scalds	20 (2.8)
Lacerations, skin or other soft tissues	48 (6.7)
Subgaleal bleeding	1 (0.1)
Total	120 (16.7)

In another 90 (12.5%) children, significant trauma occurred in the forms of laceration of the skin or other soft tissues (such as tendon, frenulum, and the tympanic membranes), fractures of bones, burns or scalds, and other forms of internal bleeding. As a whole, one in every six children admitted for evaluation of physical abuse presented with severe forms of injury.

After medical and social evaluation, 568 (79%) of the 720 children were ascertained to be victim of child abuse. Among the 568 children, physical abuse, alone or in combination of other forms of maltreatment, was confirmed in over 95% of the cases. In a small proportion of cases, the original suspicion of physical abuse was not substantiated, but it led to the recognition of other forms of maltreatment. The final diagnosis was listed in Table 2. 592 (82%) children were registered to the Child Protection Registry. Among them, 504 children were put into the "abused" category while the other 88 children were registered as "at risk" cases.

Table 2. Final diagnosis of the 720 children

Final diagnosis	Number (percent)
Physical abuse alone	456 (80.3)
Physical abuse combined with other forms of maltreatment	86 (15.1)
+ neglect	26 (4.6)
+ sexual abuse	2 (0.4)
+ psychological abuse	56 (9.9)
+ sexual abuse and neglect	1 (0.2)
+ psychological abuse and neglect	1 (0.2)
Other forms of maltreatment (but not physical abuse)	26 (4.6)
Neglect	13 (2.3)
Sexual abuse	1 (0.2)
Psychological abuse	11 (1.9)
Psychological abuse and neglect	1 (0.2)
Total	568
Not abuse	152

Table 3 listed the persons who brought the victims' concern to the attention of the child protection services. Teachers and social workers from the school settings formed the most frequent source of referrals. As the existing guidelines instructed teachers to consult the school social workers when a disclosure of child abuse was received, it was impossible to tell in retrospect if it was the teacher or the social worker who initiated the referrals. The non-abusing parents were the second largest group of reporters. Medical practitioners and social workers outside schools were next on the list of frequent reporters. Almost 80% of the cases were brought into the child protection process by these four groups of people. Only 2% of cases were reported by neighbours that included reports made through anonymous hotlines.

Table 3. Persons who made the report of suspected child abuse

The reporting persons	Number (percent)
Teachers or social workers from schools	203 (28.2)
Social workers elsewhere	84 (11.7)
Non-abusing parents	167 (23.2)
Medical practitioners	122 (16.9)
Neighbours	15 (2.1)
Relatives	26 (3.6)
Self	44 (6.1)
Police	33 (4.6)
Others	26 (3.6)
Total	720

Table 4. Relationship of the perpetrators to the victims

Perpetrators	Number (percent)
Father	244 (43.0)
Mother	202 (35.6)
Both parents	24 (4.2)
Stepfather	4 (0.7)
Stepmother	7 (1.2)
Father substitute*	11 (1.9)
Mother substitute*	12 (2.1)
Sibling	14 (2.5)
Grandparent	1 (0.2)
Uncle/aunt	8 (1.4)
Maid	16 (2.8)
Childminder	1 (0.2)
Teacher	6 (1.1)
Others	6 (1.1)
Unknown/not identified	9 (1.6)
Total	568

* Parent substitute includes boyfriends, girlfriends, cohabitants who has an intimate relationship to a biological parent; it also includes foster parent.

Among the 568 ascertained cases of child physical abuse, the same rate of male predominance was seen (males, 318; females, 250). The relationship of the perpetrators to the victims was listed in Table 4. 89% of the perpetrators were parent figures, of which the great majority were biological parents. Half of the remaining cases were either abused by a maid or by a sibling.

When the instruments used for abusing a child or the modes of injury were examined (Table 5), no instruments were described in 182 (32%) of the incidents. Of these 182 incidents, slapping was the commonest mode of beating (26% of the cases). Rattan sticks (12.3%) and coat hangers (9.9%) were the commonest instruments used for beating up a child in this cohort of patients.

Table 5. Instruments used/mode of injury for child physical abuse

Instruments/mode of injury	Frequency (percent)
Slapping	47 (8.3)
Shaking	9 (1.6)
Biting	9 (1.6)
Pinching	8 (1.4)
Kicking/stamping	16 (2.8)
Unspecified beatings	93 (16.4)
Rattan sticks	70 (12.3)
Feather dusters	7 (1.2)
Brooms/mops	14 (2.5)
Wooden/plastic sticks or rods	55 (9.7)
Metal rods or pipes/umbrellas	26 (4.7)
Coat hangers	56 (9.9)
Hoses, cords, or belts	20 (3.5)
Chopsticks, spatulas or rulers	15 (2.6)
Slippers or shoes	12 (2.1)
Chairs or stools	11 (1.9)
Hammers	4 (0.7)
Flying/dropping objects	8 (1.4)
Knives, pencils or other sharps	26 (4.4)
Burns or scalds	21 (3.7)
Poisoning	17 (3.1)
Smothering/strangulation	7 (1.2)
Others	17 (3.1)
Total	568

Of the few risk factors examined in this study (Table 6), child-related factors such as behavioural problems or poor academic performance were relatively infrequent when compared with parental factors. Parental conflicts, single-parent families, and families relying on social security were much more prevalent in this cohort of patients.

Table 6. Risk factors associated with child physical abuse

Risk factors	Number examined	Frequency (percent)
Poor school performance	567	67 (11.8)
Behavioural problems	567	77 (13.6)
Previous abuse	567	42 (7.4)
Parental conflicts	567	172 (30.3)
Single-parent families	567	164 (28.9)
Parental unemployment	567	153 (27.0)
Family on social security	164	79 (48.2)

DISCUSSION

According to the interdisciplinary procedures on the handling of child abuse in Hong Kong (Social Welfare Department, 1999), child physical abuse is defined as a physical injury or suffering to a child, or failure to prevent physical injury or suffering to a child (including non-accidental use of force, deliberate poisoning, suffocation, burning or Munchausen syndrome by proxy), where there is a definite knowledge, or a reasonable suspicion that the injury has been inflicted non-accidentally or knowingly not prevented. It is the commonest form of childhood victimization according to the government registries and hospital surveillance. According to the statistics reports of the CPR, physical abuse accounts for 38% to 57% of the newly registered cases every year (Social Welfare Department, 1997 & 2002). From hospital surveillance, physical abuse represents 87% of the total caseload (Hong Kong Medical Coordinators on Child Abuse, 2003). This differs from other Western countries where child neglect is the predominant form of maltreatment (US Department of Health and Human Services, Administration on Children, Youths and Families, 2003). This difference either suggests that there are ethnic or cultural discrepancies between the Chinese and Western communities, or just because physical abuse can be identified without much training compared with other forms of maltreatment.

The Victims

The male to female ratio of 5:4 found in this study is surprisingly similar to earlier reports of child abuse (International Year of the Child Coordinating Committee, 1979; Samuda, 1988) and telephone survey for severe violence (Tang, 1998), but differs from that reported by Lau & Davies (1993) where more girls were affected compared with boys. Primary school and early secondary school children of ages between 6 and 14 years represent the majority of the victims, and late adolescent victims are less affected compared with early teenagers. These age trends agree with the previous observations made by Samuda (1988), Hong Kong Medical Coordinators on Child Abuse (2003), and Tang (1996), but are older than those of an earlier hospital series described by Lieh-Mak, Chung & Liu (1983) and a community sample surveyed by Tang (1998).

However, the gender difference is only meaningful when examined by the victims' age groups. The male predominance is seen only between the ages of 4 and 12 years, representing the stage of preschool-and primary school-aged children. As discussed in a subsequent section, physical abuse or severe corporal punishment is closely related with the parental expectation on the children's academic performance. The male predominance probably suggests that parents in general have a higher expectation on male children.

The Abusers

Almost 90% of the abusers in the ascertained cases of physical abuse in this series are parent figures. Over 90% of the parent-figured abusers are the children's biological parents, and the father to mother ratio was approximately 6 to 5. This contrasts remarkably with earlier series (International Year of the Child Coordinating Committee, 1979; Lieh-Mak, Chung & Liu, 1983) in which mothers were the usual abusers, and is in line with more recent findings by Tang & Davis (1996). This change probably reflects the increasing proportion of families with working couples (Samuda, 1988) and hence the proportion of fathers participating in child care and discipline.

Besides parent figures, maids (or domestic helper) and siblings represent the next commonest group of abusers. Our anecdotal experience indicates that parents readily report to the child protection services if an injury is inflicted by a maid, but they are reluctant to report or cooperate with investigation if the suspected abuser happens to be the victim's brother or sister. Hence, the rate of sibling abusers in this series is likely an underestimate.

Trends and Seasonal Variations

The increasing trend of child physical abuse described in this series, with an average annual increase of 20% of cases, is alarming. Population expansion is partially responsible for this increase. The combined population of Tuen Mun and Yuen Long districts in 1996 was 804,733, and was 937,901 in 2001 (Census and Statistics Department, 2001b). The 16.5% increase during this 5-year period, however, can hardly account for the alarming rate of increase observed in this series of physical abuse cases.

Tuen Mun and Yuen Long districts represent one of the few areas in Hong Kong in which a higher than average rate of families are dependent on social security and social services (Lee & So, 2004). The districts also contain the highest number of spouse abuse in the whole territory (Social Welfare Department, 2004). The high prevalence of parental conflict, single-parent family, parental unemployment, and reliance on social security seen in this series of cases is therefore not surprising. A perception of lack of social support and inadequacy in problem-solving are important risk factors that add to the parenting stress (Lam, 1999).

The clustering of cases in May and June and the relatively peaceful period of July and August seen in this report has not been previously observed, although it is a common anecdotal impression shared by most frontline child protection workers. The phenomenon is indeed congruent with the previously discussed features in the victims' gender and age. In essence, all students have to prepare for their final examination that is usually scheduled in June, the end of the academic year. After that, they enjoy their summer holidays in July and August before they return to the school in September. Only a small proportion of children in this series have genuine problems in their study, but parents in general have high, sometimes unrealistic, expectation on their children's study. Traditionally, in order to seek knowledge and cultivate a passion for persistent learning, a man is expected to foster diligence, endure hardship, and should feel shame for lack of desire to learn (Li, 2002). This is best summarized by the popular verses from the poems of Wang Zhu who lived in the Song Dynasty. He said that generals and ministers were not born into their posts, which belonged to the men who worked themselves hard (*jiang xiang ben wu zhong, nan er dang zi qiang*), and nothing was as superb as the scholar who studied hard (*wan guan jie xia pin, wei you du shu gao*). On the other hand, parents often place high expectations on their children's success in academic endeavours because failure to do so implies parental inadequacies (Kwok & Wong, 2000). The marked increase in physical abuse cases in May and June is therefore conceivable.

The Forms and Modes of Injury

The case series display a myriad of physical injuries with superficial non-specific and pattern bruises being the commonest manifestations. Of particular concern are the one-sixth of the cases that present with more serious injuries that included soft tissue lacerations, skeletal fractures, brain injuries, poisoning, and other life-threatening harms such as smothering or suffocation. The shaken baby syndrome represents the commonest cause of fatality among abused children (Lee, So, Fong & Luk, 1999), and accounts for one of the two cases of death in this series. Abusive head trauma is not limited to the young children, and we have observed a pattern of depressed skull fractures in older children with an apparent murderous intent (Lee, Ou & Fong, 2003). Non-accidental carbon monoxide poisoning in the setting of planned combined homicide-suicide accounts for the other case of mortality, and appears to be a new form of childhood victimization in our locality (Lee, Ou, Lam, So & Kam, 2002; Lee & So, 2004). Given the variety of physical injuries, the potentially crippling and life-threatening nature of the acts, and the small but significant proportion of homicidal cases, child protection workers should adopt various strategies and take appropriate measures to safeguard the best interest of the child victim according to the circumstances. Experienced workers are needed to foster expertise in this field where management of highly charged and emotive scenes is often needed (Lee & So, 2004).

The modes of injury and the weapons used for beating a child in this series concur with common experience. Most children are slapped or beaten in a non-specified manner. When an instrument is used, the rattan stick and the coat hanger are the most popular items. The rattan stick can be described as a standard instrument meant only for child discipline in Hong Kong. It is cylindrical in shape and measures 60 cm long and 0.8 cm in diameter. It was practically used in every household during the authors' childhood, and is still widely used to date and readily available in the market and grocery stores at a price of USD 0.13. The list of things used for child discipline or maltreatment seems inexhaustible, and is limited only by their accessibility and handiness rather than their harmfulness or lethality.

Persons Reporting Child Abuse

Over 80% of the cases in this series have been reported by the professionals and the non-abusing parents. Only 2% of the cases are notified by a neighbour or via service hotlines. This is partly related to the traditional concept that family matters should be handled behind closed doors, and partly because the conceptualization and awareness of child abuse in the general public differs from that of official definitions. In a telephone survey of a randomly chosen community sample, respondents seldom categorized mild injurious acts as maltreatment, and only 40% of the respondents would report to the authority even if they encountered an abusive situation (Lau, Liu, Yu & Wong, 1999). The enmeshed concept of child discipline and corporal punishment, and thus parental rights, probably exerts a significant influence on the attitude and behaviour of the general public.

Summary and Implications

Child physical abuse occurs at a remarkable frequency in Hong Kong. It is an important cause of childhood injury, chronic disability, and mortality. Chronic physical abuse contributes to behavioural and psychiatric problems in adolescence and adulthood. The occurrence of physical abuse is closely associated with the parental concept of child discipline and parental expectation on a child's developmental and academic excellence. The use of corporal punishment is deeply embedded, together with the Confucian doctrines of childrearing and filial piety, in the traditional Chinese culture. More discussions, both among the professionals and in the community, are needed to redress the issues of childrearing, child discipline, and the immediate and long-term consequences of serious or chronic corporal punishment. More thoughts are needed to educate the society at large on alternative and effective means of discipline that would better suit the needs of modern families (Save the Children Alliance, 2003).

References

American Academy of Pediatrics. (1998). Guidance for effective discipline. *Pediatrics, 101*, 723-728.

Bailey, M. (2003). The corporal punishment debate in Canada. *Family Court Review, 41*, 508-516.

Canadian Paediatric Society. (2004). Effective discipline for children. *Paediatric & Child Health, 9*, 37-41.

Census and Statistics Department. (1996). *1996 Population by-census: main report.* Hong Kong: Government Printer.

Census and Statistics Department. (2001a). *2001 Population census: basic tables for District Council districts*. Hong Kong: Printing Department.

Census and Statistics Department. (2001b). *2001 Population census: summary results*. Hong Kong: Printing Department.

Chen, J.Q., Han, P. & Dunne, M.P. (2004). Child sexual abuse: a study among 892 female students of a medical school. *Zhonghua Erke Zazhi, 42*, 39-43.

Chu, J. (1999). *Boys beaten over homework.* Hong Kong: Hong Kong Standard (1/21/1999).

DeAngelis, C.D. (1997). Research on discipline: the state of the art, deficits, and implications. *Archives of Pediatrics & Adolescent Medicine, 151*, 758-760.

Department of Health. (2000). *Protecting children, supporting parents: a consultation document on the physical punishment of children*. London: Department of Health.

Durrant, J.E. (1999). Evaluating the success of Sweden's corporal punishment ban. *Child Abuse & Neglect*, *23*, 435-448.

Ellimen, D. & Lynch, M.A. (2000). The physical punishment of children. *Archives of Diseases in Childhood*, *83*, 196-198.

Home Office, Department of Health, Department of Education and Science, Welsh Office. (1991). *Working together under the Children Act 1989*. London: Her Majesty Stationery Office.

Hong Kong Medical Coordinators on Child Abuse. Management of child abuse in Hong Kong: results of a territory-wide inter-hospital prospective surveillance. *Hong Kong Medical Journal*, *9*, 6-9.

International Year of the Child Coordinating Committee. (1979). *Report on study on child abuse cases*. Hong Kong: Hong Kong Council of Social Service.

Ip, P. (1996). Fever of the imagination – a case of Munchausen syndrome by proxy. *Hong Kong Journal of Paediatrics (New Series)*, *1*, 189-191.

Kong, D.S.G., Wong, S.T., Goh, C.W., Lam, S.L., Chua, K.L. & Kok, L.P. (1988). Child-rearing practices of Chinese parents and their relationship to behavioural problems in toddlers. *Acta Psychiatrica Scandinavia Supplement*, *344*, 127-132.

Korbin, J.E. (1981). "Very few cases": *Child Abuse and Neglect* in the People's Republic of China. In: J.E. Korbin (Ed.), *Child abuse and neglect: cross-cultural perspectives*. Berkeley: University of California Press, pp. 166-185.

Kwok, S. & Wong, D. (2000). Mental health of parents with young children in Hong Kong: the roles of parenting stress and parenting self-efficacy. *Child & Family Social Work*, *5*, 57-65.

Lam, D. (1999). Parenting stress and anger: the Hong Kong experience. *Child & Family Social Work*, *4*, 337-346.

Lau, E.M.C. & Donnan, S.P.B. (1987). Maternal and child factors for reported child abuse among Chinese in Hong Kong. *Social Science & Medicine*, *24*, 449-452.

Lau, I.K. & Davies, D.P. (1993). Non-accidental injury to children in Hong Kong: a 3-year hospital experience. *Child Abuse & Neglect*, *17*, 423-428.

Lau, J.T.F., Chan, K.K., Lam, P.K.W., Choi, P.Y.W. & Lai, K.Y.C. (2003). Psychological correlates of physical abuse in Hong Kong Chinese adolescents. *Child Abuse & Neglect*, *27*, 63-75.

Lau, J.T.F., Liu, J.L.Y., Cheung, J.C.K., Yu, A. & Wong, C.K. (1999). Prevalence and correlates of physical abuse in Hong Kong Chinese adolescents: a population-based approach. *Child Abuse & Neglect*, *23*, 549-557.

Lau, J.F.T., Liu, J.L.Y., Yu, A. & Wong, C.K. (1999). Conceptualization, reporting and underreporting of child abuse in Hong Kong. *Child Abuse & Neglect*, *11*, 1159-74.

Lee, A.C.W., Hau, K.L. & Fong, D. (2001). CT findings in hyperacute non-accidental brain injury. *Pediatric Radiology*, *31*, 673-4.

Lee, A.C.W. & Lam, S.Y. (2002). Nonaccidental methadone poisoning. *Clinical Pediatrics (Philadelphia)*, *41*, 365-366.

Lee, A.C.W., Lee, W., Ou, Y. & So, K.T. (2000). *Child Abuse and Neglect* tackling – hospital interdisciplinary team (CANT-HIT): a coordinated effort of handling child victims in a general hospital. *Proceedings of ISPCAN 5th Asian Conference on Child Protection,*

Hong Kong, November 25-27, 1999. Hong Kong: Federation of Medical Societies of Hong Kong, pp. 290-295.

Lee, A.C.W., Ou, Y. & Fong, D. (2003). Depressed skull fractures: a pattern of abusive head injury in three older children. *Child Abuse & Neglect, 27*, 1323-1329.

Lee, A.C.W., Ou, Y., Lam, S.Y., So, K.T. & Kam, C.W. (2002). Non-accidental carbon monoxide poisoning from burning charcoal in attempted combined homicide-suicide. *Journal of Paediatrics & Child Health, 38*, 465-468.

Lee, A.C.W. & So, K.T. (2004). *Responding to the review of family service in Tin Shui Wai/Yuen Long District with respect to domestic violence*. Hong Kong: Tuen Mun Hospital.

Lee, A.C.W., So, K.T., Fong, D. & Luk, S.H. (1999). The shaken baby syndrome: review of 10 cases. *Hong Kong Medical Journal, 5*, 337-341.

Lee, A.C.W., So, K.T., Wong, H.L. & Lau, S. (1998). Penetrating pencil injury: an unusual case of child abuse. *Child Abuse & Neglect, 22*, 749-752.

Li, J. (2002). A cultural model of learning: Chinese "heart and mind for wanting to learn". *Journal of Cross-Cultural Psychology, 33*, 248-69.

Lieh-Mak, F., Chung, S.Y. & Liu, Y.W. (1983). Characteristics of child battering in Hong Kong: a controlled study. *British Journal of Psychiatry, 142*, 89-94.

Lui-Tsang, S.K.P. (1986). Child abuse – trends and issues. In: Khoo, T.P. (Ed.) *Mental health in Hong Kong 1986*. Hong Kong: Sam Man Printing Press Co., pp. 120-126.

Mulvey, T. (1997). Historical overview: developments in child protection services and procedures. In: C. O'Brian, C.C. Ling, N. Rhind (Eds.), *Responding to child abuse: procedures and practice for child protection in Hong Kong*. Hong Kong: Hong Kong University Press, pp. 3-15.

Qu Tongzu (2003). *Feudalism in China*. Shanghai: Century Publishing Group of Shanghai.

Samuda, G.M. (1988). Child discipline and abuse in Hong Kong. *Child Abuse & Neglect, 12*, 283-287.

Save the Children Alliance. (2003). *Position on corporal punishment*. London: International Save the Children Alliance.

Shek, D.T.L. (2004). Chinese cultural beliefs about adversity: its relationship to psychological well-being, school adjustment and problem behaviour in Hong Kong adolescents with and without economic disadvantage. *Childhood, 11*, 63-80.

Social Welfare Department. (1997). *Child Protection Registry statistical report 1996*. Hong Kong: Printing Department.

Social Welfare Department. (1999). *Procedures for handling child abuse cases* – revised 1998. Hong Kong: Social Welfare Department.

Social Welfare Department. (2002). *Child Protection Registry statistical report 2001*. Hong Kong: Printing Department.

Social Welfare Department. (2004). *2004-2005 Strategic planning seminar for social service of the Yuen Long District*. Hong Kong: Social Welfare Department.

Tang, C.S.K. (1996). Adolescent child abuse in Chinese families. *Child Abuse & Neglect, 20*, 873-878.

Tang, C.S.K. (1998). The rate of physical child abuse in Chinese families: a community survey in Hong Kong. *Child Abuse & Neglect, 22*, 381-391.

Tang, C.S.K. & Davis, C. (1996). Child abuse in Hong Kong revisited after 15 years: characteristics of victims and abusers. *Child Abuse Neglect, 20*, 1213-1218.

US Department of Health and Human Services, Administration on Children, Youths and Families. (2003). *Child maltreatment 2001*. Washington, DC: US Government Printing Office.

Wu, D.Y.H. (1981). Child abuse in Taiwan. In: J.E. Korbin (Ed.), *Child abuse and neglect: cross-cultural perspectives*. Berkeley: University of California Press, pp. 139-165.

Yang, Z.N. & Pan, J.P. (2003). Investigation and analysis of child neglect in 1163 urban children aged 3-5 years. *Zhonghua Erke Zazhi*, *41*, 501-507.

Yu, H.Y. (1996). *Child abuse: review and re-examination*. Taipei: Chuliu Publishers.

In: China: Economic, Political and Social Issues
Editors: J. M. Phillips and L. J. Moore

ISBN: 978-60456-727-4

Chapter 7

MONEY PROFILE AND UNETHICAL BEHAVIOR: A STUDY OF FULL-TIME EMPLOYEES AND UNIVERSITY STUDENTS IN CHINA

***Du Linzhi*[*1], *Thomas Li-Ping Tang*[2†] *and Yang Dongtao*[3‡]**

[1]Department of Social Psychology, School of Zhou En'lai Government Management, Nankai University, Tianjin, 300071, People's Republic of China

[2]Department of Management and Marketing, Jennings A. Jones College of Business Middle Tennessee State University, Murfreesboro, TN 37132, U.S.A

[3]Business School of Nanjing University, Nanjing 210093, People's Republic of China

ABSTRACT

With two questionnaires named Money Ethics Scale (MES) and Propensity to Engage in Unethical Behavior Scale (PEUBS), which are designed by ourselves, this study investigates randomly 204 managerial staffs and 395 university students, to analyze their money profiles, and the relation between money profiles and unethical activity. The results show that Achieving Money Worshiper and Careless Money Admirer have more possibility to involve unethical activity than Apathetic Money Handler and Money Repeller when they are faced with work stress, but Apathetic Money Handler and Money Repeller have more possibility to involve unethical activity than Achieving Money Worshiper when they are faced with unethical organizational context; university students have more possibility to involve unethical activity than managerial staffs when they are faced with work stress, conformity and organizational context.

Keywords: managerial staffs and university students, money profiles, unethical activity

[*] E-mail:lzd6613_nj@163.com
[†] E-mail:ttang@mtsu.edu
[‡] E-mail: yangdt@nju.edu.cn

INTRODUCTION

There are more and more fake, inferior, non-genuine, and bastard products in China today than ever before. Business ethics is a major concern due to the lack of ethical culture at the organizational and individual level in the society. Most unethical behaviors performed by various organizations and employees are related to the desire to make more money. In this paper, we examine unethical behaviors among full-time employees and university students in China from people's money attitude perspective. More specifically, we apply cluster analysis and develop four money profiles based on people's endorsement of the Money Ethic Scales (Luna-Arocas and Tang, 2004) and then examine the differences in the propensity to engage in unethical behavior across these four money profiles.

THEORY AND HYPOTHESES

We trace the inspiration to study the love of money construct to the oldest references in the literature: "Poverty consists, not in the decrease of one's possessions, but in the increase of one's greed" (Plato, 427-347 BC). "People who want to get rich fall into temptation and a trap and into many foolish and harmful desires that plunge men into ruin and destruction. For the love of money is a root of all kinds of evil" (http://www.biblegateway.com, 1 Timothy, 6: 9-10, New International Version). These quotes suggest that "wanting to be rich" or "being rich" may be related to "the love of money" and that the love of money may be related to "evil".

There is a dearth of empirical research concerning *the love of money* and *evil*. Many researchers and lay people may consider this issue as a *taboo*, a religious/controversial issue, not a scientific/academic issue, and to be excessively value-laden, thereby, may have shown great *reluctance* to study this taboo (e.g., Vardi and Weitz, 2004; Vardi and Wiener, 1996). While sociologist, psychologists, criminologists, and anthropologists have studied it for many years, many management scholars, however, have largely "ignored misbehavior in organizations" (Ivancevich et al., 2005, p. 247). Thereby, the construct of unethical behavior is an under-represented area of research in the management field and deserves further attention.

Money has been used *universally* around the world. *The meaning of money*, however, is "in the eye of the beholder" (Tang, 1992). There are many measures of money attitudes in the literature (e.g., see Furnham and Argyle, 1998). Tang and his associates have developed several versions of the multidimensional Money Ethic Scale or MES (Tang, 1992; Tang et al., 2000) and the Love of Money Scale or LOMS that is a subset of the MES (Du and Tang, 2005; Tang and Chiu, 2003). Mitchell and Mickel (1999) considered "the Money Ethic Scale" (Tang, 1992) as one of the most "well-developed" and systematically used measures of money attitude (p. 571). MES and LOMS have been cited and published in Chinese, English, French, Italian, Spanish, Romanian, Russian, and many other languages (see Luna-Arocas & Tang, 2004).

People have different attitudes toward money (i.e., positive, indifferent, and negative). Due to individual differences in money attitudes, researchers have classified people into money profiles using cluster analysis based on their scores on the Money Ethic Scale (e.g., Tang, 1992, 1995; Tang & Tang, 2002; Tang, Luna-Arocas, & Whiteside, 2003). People in different money profiles may have different demographic variables, income, and other work-related attitudes and behaviors (e.g., Du & Tang, 2003; Du, Xu, & Tang, 2004; Luna-Arocas & Tang, 2004; Tang, Tillery, Lazarevski, & Luna-Arocas, 2004). We will briefly summarize relevant studies below.

Luna-Arocas and Tang (2004) identified four money profiles among university professors in the US and Spain. They used cluster analysis and Factors Budget, Evil, Equity, Success, and Motivator of the 15-item Money Ethic Scale and identified (1) Achieving Money Worshipers (37.6% of the sample), (2) Careless Money Admirers (19.9%), (3) Apathetic Money Managers (16.1%), and (4) Money Repellent Individuals (26.4%). We will briefly present these four money profiles below.

Achieving Money Worshipers have the most positive attitudes toward money. They worship money as their Success and Budget money carefully. Money Repellent Individuals have the most negative attitudes toward money. They consider that money is Evil and is not Success. The other two clusters of people fall between these two. Careless Money Admirers value Success but do not Budget money carefully. Apathetic Money Managers have somewhat indifferent attitudes toward money. They think that money is neither Evil nor a Motivator and tend to have high intrinsic job satisfaction and life satisfaction. American Business professors have the highest income among all different colleges. Further, most of Business professors (75%) are in the Achieving Money Worshiper cluster. Thus, high-income professors have the most positive attitudes toward money and the highest satisfaction with pay and pay administration. They also tend to have the highest work ethic and the longest work experiences. Money Repellent Individuals have the most negative attitudes toward money, the lowest income, the lowest work ethic, and the lowest satisfaction with pay administration.

Later, Tang, Tillery, Lazarevski, and Luna-Arocas (2004) investigated university students and small business owners in Macedonia. The same four money profiles were also identified in the Macedonian sample using the same 15-item Money Ethic Scale (Luna-Arocas & Tang, 2004): Achieving Money Worshipers (33.7%), Careless Money Admirers (21.3%), Apathetic Money Managers (15.7%), and Money Repellent Individuals (29.2%). The largest cluster for business owners is Achieving Money Worshiper (45.0%) and the smallest one is Apathetic Money Manager (6.7%). For students, the largest money profile is Money Repellent Individual (53.6%). Those who have money tend to have the most positive attitudes toward money and are Achieving Money Worshipers. Four money profiles can be consistently identified in different populations and cultures using the 15-item Money Ethic Scale.

More recently, Tang, Tang, and Luna-Arocas (2005) selected the original 30-item-6-factor Money Ethic Scale (Tang, 1992) and revealed four money profiles in a sample of 564 university students in the US: Achieving Money Worshipers (23.22%), Careless Money Admirers (30.16%), Apathetic Money Managers (31.08%), and Money Repellent Individuals (15.54%). It can be concluded that similar clusters can be identified using several versions of the Money Ethic Scale among different samples in several countries. The major attributes of the four clusters are similar across these studies and the percentage of people in each of these four clusters does vary from one sample to the next.

The main purpose of the present study is to investigate the money profiles using a different Money Ethic Scale and apply that to a sample of full-time employees and a sample of university students in People's Republic of China. Our focus is on people's propensity to engage in unethical behavior.

Hypotheses 1: Achieving Money Worshiper and Careless Money Admirer have a high propensity to engage in unethical behavior.

Achieving Money Worshipers tend to have the most positive money attitude. They worship money as their Success and Budget their money carefully. They have the highest competitive and winning attitude, high tendency to take actions and relatively high external locus of control. Although they are not the slave of money, they are still highly motivated by money. They, too, are very vulnerable to external pressures and opportunities. Careless Money Admirers also value Success, they exert effort trying to succeed and want to be millionaire, but they do not budget their money carefully, so they always feel lack of money. Otherwise, they tend to have high Work Ethic endorsement, the highest external locus of control, the highest tendency to take actions and be involved as a leader, but low intrinsic job satisfaction, pay satisfaction, and life satisfaction and the lowest fear of success (Tang, T. L. P., Luna-Arocas, R.and Sutarso, T. ,2005). So it is reasonable to expect that those people, whose are either Achieving Money Worshipers or Careless Money Admirers, will have a higher propensity to perform unethical behavior.

Hypotheses 2: Apathetic Money Handler and Money Repeller have a low propensity to engage in unethical behavior.

Money Repeller tend to have the most negative attitudes toward money, they negate all positive character of money (e.g. good, success, rich, respect, etc). To them money is not a power of motivation, (Lawler, 1971), but a kind of health protection (Herzberg et al., 1959), they have a low level of protestant work ethic endorsement, the highest fear of success, high internal locus of control, and low in winning attitude and involved as a leader. Apathetic Money Handlers think that money is not Evil and is not a Motivator and tend to have the highest intrinsic job satisfaction and life satisfaction. They would not work hard to make money and budget their money carefully, they have the highest internal locus of control, and the lowest degree of work devotion. So the power of money to attract, keep and promote them is quite weak, money is only a tool for them to sustain their lives. So it is reasonable to expect that Apathetic Money Handlers and Money Repeller may have a low propensity to engage in unethical behavior.

METHOD

Participants

Data were collected from 204 full-time employees in different locations (Nanjing, Shanghai, and Xining) and 395 university students at Hohai University in China. The mean age of employees was 31.57, and the mean age of university students was 20.9.

Table 1. Results of exploratory factor analysis (EFA) for the 42-Item Money Ethic[2] Scale

	Component									
	1	2	3	4	5	6	7	8	9	10
1	**.785**	.245E-02	.260	-.034	.103	-.077	.848E-02	-.024	.503E-02	.249E-02
2	**.759**	.068E-02	.233	-.002	.100	-.082	.879E-02	.279E-02	.136	.113
3	**.712**	-.007	.286	-.026	.841E-02	-.108	.119	.237E-02	.518E-02	.144
4	**.689**	.118	.164	-.077	.208	.192E-02	.133	-.040	.711E-02	.117
5	**.608**	.926E-02	.217	-.064	.293	.117	.898E-02	-.047	.113E-02	.769E-02
6	.961E-02	**.804**	.983E-02	-.036	-.037	-.026	.992E-02	.884E-02	.267E-02	.937E-02
7	.372E-02	**.794**	.536E-03	-.009	-.002	-.084	-.035	.368E-02	-.032	.001E-02
8	.905E-02	**.782**	.859E-02	-.009	-.071	-.028	.666E-02	.338E-03	-.025	.662E-02
9	-.164	**.675**	.232E-02	.790E-02	.128	.103	.153	.808E-02	.231E-02	.457E-02
10	.897E-02	**.596**	.064E-02	-.083	.342E-02	.147	.675E-02	.130	.133	-.052
11	.158	**.543**	-.040	-.009	-.014	-.017	.119	.209E-02	.518E-02	-.063
12	.198	.917E-02	**.779**	.628E-02	.832E-02	.513E-02	.101	.772E-02	-.010	.122
13	.173	.498E-03	**.752**	-.059	.106	-.100	.623E-02	-.034	.949E-02	.397E-02
14	.175	-.021	**.723**	-.045	.374E-02	-.046	.652E-02	-.057	.180	.755E-02
15	.156	.047E-02	**.701**	.102	.035E-02	.421E-03	.128E-02	.925E-02	-.041	.888E-02
16	.254	.234E-02	**.637**	.120E-03	.212	.116	.623E-02	-.028	.676E-02	.608E-03
17	.074E-02	-.100	-.018	**.784**	-.100	.790E-02	.298E-02	-.020	.562E-03	.331E-02
18	-.106	.807E-02	.504E-02	**.736**	-.007	.019E-02	.136E-02	.246E-02	.470E-02	-.063
19	-.152	-.042	.358E-03	**.734**	-.158	-.013	-.004	-.063	.875E-02	.133
20	.206E-02	-.046	-.030	**.727**	.879E-02	-.057	.197	.139	-.162	-.041
21	.821E-02	.967E-04	.656E-02	**.718**	.293E-02	.555E-02	.185	.214	-.111	-.150
22	.161	.324E-02	.179	-.037	**.828**	-.001	.283E-02	-.034	.162	.259
23	.190	.264E-02	.120	-.022	**.815**	-.012	.023E-02	.166E-02	.109	.219
24	.246	-.032	.180	-.086	**.765**	.708E-02	-.009	-.098	.150	.190
25	.045E-02	.299E-02	.451E-03	-.064	-.009	**.817**	.620E-03	-.024	.468E-02	.030E-02
26	.163E-02	.888E-02	.863E-03	.869E-02	.952E-02	**.815**	-.023	.439E-02	.574E-02	.128
27	-.138	-.114	.113	.866E-02	.464E-02	**.700**	.692E-03	.524E-02	.597E-02	.809E-03
28	.047E-02	.135	-.176	-.025	-.052	**.583**	-.124	.109	.359E-04	-.036
29	.130	.923E-02	.315E-02	.168	-.027	.621E-03	**.801**	.149	.421E-02	-.015
30	.237	.519E-02	.107	.133	.154E-02	-.054	**.780**	.859E-02	.049E-02	.146E-02
31	.234	.129	.202	.203E-02	-.041	-.072	**.611**	.072E-02	.002E-02	.126
32	-.077	.186	.361E-03	.296E-02	.121	-.025	**.604**	.054E-02	.848E-03	-.003
33	-.139	.848E-02	-.024	.323E-02	-.026	.148E-02	.586E-02	**.830**	.780E-02	.845E-03
34	-.173	.439E-02	.128E-02	-.043	-.119	.942E-03	.931E-02	**.711**	-.012	.133
35	.116	.597E-02	-.023	.153	.878E-02	.769E-02	.136	**.706**	.146	-.074
36	.256	.281E-02	.766E-02	.183	.477E-02	.154	.125	**.560**	.488E-02	-.176
37	.822E-02	.103	.595E-02	-.073	.105	.148	.042E-02	.773E-02	**.814**	.354E-02
38	.179	.130	.593E-02	.950E-02	.915E-02	.354E-02	.129E-03	.103	**.791**	.125
39	.332E-02	.698E-02	.326E-02	-.097	.224	-.022	.114	.976E-02	**.701**	-.003
40	.248	.977E-02	.130	-.010	.203	-.018	.205E-02	.170E-03	.606E-02	**.814**
41	.254	.386E-02	.110	-.025	.236	-.017	.534E-03	-.063	.831E-02	**.788**
42	.180E-02	-.044	.312E-02	-.012	.231	.290	.822E-02	.209E-02	.487E-02	**.594**

Extraction Method: Principal Component Analysis.
Rotation Method: Varimax with Kaiser Normalization.
a. Rotation converged in 7 iterations.

Table 2. Results of Exploratory Factor Analysis for the 15-Item Unethical Behavior Unethical Behavior Context Questionnaire[a]

	Component				
	1	2	3	4	5
1	**.745**	-.092	.226	.150	7.714E-02
2	**.713**	-.105	.351	2.010E-02	3.562E-02
3	**.669**	.240	7.688E-03	.136	-.027
4	**.663**	-.067	.138	.295	.104
5	**.656**	.269	7.137E-02	.244	-.040
6	**.644**	.126	8.028E-02	.142	-.020
7	**.621**	.341	2.407E-02	-.043	-.132
8	5.775E-02	**.828**	8.167E-02	7.136E-02	7.266E-02
9	.205	**.803**	5.227E-02	8.212E-02	.150
10	.147	.106	**.856**	.121	-.020
11	.246	4.483E-02	**.852**	1.426E-02	1.779E-02
12	.164	9.089E-02	.121	**.848**	-.032
13	.309	6.859E-02	4.931E-03	**.817**	1.536E-02
14	-.012	-.044	9.569E-02	-.006	**.855**
15	9.393E-03	.339	-.124	-.009	**.773**

Extraction Method: Principal Component Analysis.
Rotation Method: Varimax with Kaiser Normalization.
a. Rotation converged in 6 iterations.

Measure

The Money Ethic Scale (MES)

In the present study, we employed the Money Ethic Scale with (1) *disagree strongly*, (3) *neutral*, and (5) *agree strongly* as anchors (e.g., Tang and Tang, 2002; Tang and Chiu, 2003; Luna-Arocas and Tang, 2004; Du & Tang, 2005; Tang, Luna-Arocas, and Sutarso, 2005). Results of exploratory factor analysis (EFA) based on the whole sample are reported.

From the Exploratory Factor Analysis, there are ten factors: Rich (from item 1 to 5 in MES), Budget Money (from item 6 to 11 in MES), Good (from item 12 to 16 in MES), Evil (from item 17 to 20 in MES), Success (from item 21 to 23 in MES), Equity (from item 24 to 26 in MES), Charitable Giving (from item 27 to 30 in MES), Respect (from item 31 to 33 in MES), Motivator (from item 34 to 38 in MES), and Make Money (from item 39 to 42 in MES), which explain 62.34% total Variance. The coefficient alphas of Cronbach of them are: Total (0.8442), Good (0.8275), Evil (0.7636), Rich (0.8564), Success (0.8825), Equity 0.7391), Motivator (0.8084), Respect (0.7465), Budget Money (0.8048), Make Money (0.7426), Charitable Giving (0.7302).

Propensity to Engage in Unethical Behavior Scale (PEUBS)

We adopted the 15-item Propensity to Engage in Unethical Behavior Scale (Chen and Tang, in press; Tang and Chiu, 2003; Tang and Chen, 2006). Results of exploratory factor analysis (EFA) based on the whole sample are reported.

From the Exploratory Factor Analysis, there are five factors: Opportunity Context (from item 1 to 7 in PEUBS), Stressful Context (from item 8 to 9 in PEUBS), Non-master Feeling (from item 10 to 11 in PEUBS), Conformity (from item 12 to 13 in PEUBS), Unethical Organizational Context (from item 14 to 15 in PEUBS), which explain 66.16% total variance. The coefficient alphas of Cronbach of them are: Total (0.6372), Opportunity Context (0.8046), Stressful Context (0.7042), Non-master Feeling (0.7462), Conformity (0.6976), Unethical Organizational Context (0.5739).

RESULTS

Money Profiles Using the Money Ethic Scale

Using cluster analysis and discriminant analysis based on factors of the Money Ethic Scale, this study identified four money profiles using the 42-item, 10-factor Money Ethic Scale. The four money profiles are listed as follows: Achieving Money Worshiper (23.88% of participants in that sample), Careless Money Admirer (29.1%), Apathetic Money Handler (28.73%), and Money Repellent Individual (18.28%).

Table 3. Means (and Standard Deviations) of the Money Ethic Scale for the Four Clusters

Variable *n*=536 %	Cluster 1 Achieving Money Worshipers 128 23.88	Cluster 2 Money Repellent Individuals 98 18.28	Cluster 3 Apathetic Money Managers 154 28.73	Cluster 4 Careless Money Admirers 156 29.1	排序
Rich	4.29(0.55)	3.00(0.70)	3.57(0.61)	3.87(0.57)	1>4>3>2
Budget Money	3.66(0.71)	3.13(0.74)	3.56(0.62)	3.37(0.64)	1>3>4>2
Good	4.46(0.49)	3.54(0.63)	3.89(0.49)	4.09(0.55)	1>4>3>2
Motivator	1.85(0.70)	2.14(0.86)	1.56(0.52)	2.83(0.66)	4>2>1>3
Success	3.87(0.64)	2.21(0.70)	2.26(0.64)	3.16(0.75)	1>4>3>2
Evil	2.75(1.01)	2.87(0.75)	2.80(0.78)	2.55 (0.79)	2>3>1>4
Make Money	4.35(0.50)	3.45(0.74)	4.05(0.49)	3.61(0.58)	1>3>4>2
Charitable	3.44(0.64)	3.15(0.72)	3.68(0.56)	3.10(0.54)	3>1>2>4
Giving	3.92(0.76)	2.10(0.66)	3.20(0.68)	3.11(0.76)	1>3>4>2
Equity Respect	3.42(0.80)	2.24(0.70)	2.23(0.64)	2.96(0.67)	1>4>2,3

Note: The data which are out bracket are Mean, and the data which are in bracket are Standard deviation.

Achieving Money Worshipers tend to have the most positive money attitudes (the highest score on Factors Good, Budget, Make Money, Success, Respect, Rich, Equity, and low score on Factor Evil). Careless Money Admirers have the highest score on Factors Motivator, high score on Success, good, Rich and Respect, but the lowest score on Factors Charitable Giving and Evil. Apathetic Money Handlers have the highest score on Factors Charitable Giving, and the lowest score on Factors Motivator. Money Repellent Individuals tend to have the most negative attitudes toward money (the highest score on Factor Evil and the lowest score on Factors Good, Rich, Equity, Budget, Success, and Make Money).

The Differences of Unethical Behavior Among Four Money Profiles

We examine the differences of unethical behavior among four Money Profiles (Achieving Money Worshiper, Careless Money Admirer, Apathetic Money Handler and Money Repellent Individual) and two groups of participants (employees and university students) in a Univariate Analysis of Variance. Results of Univariate and Post Hoc Tests (LSD) suggested that there were significant differences among four money profiles in two unethical contexts such as Stress and Organization, that is: Achieving Money Worshiper and Careless Money Admirer have higher propensity to engage in unethical behavior than Apathetic Money Handler and Money Repellent Individual when they face unethical stressful context, but Apathetic Money Handler and Money Repellent Individual have higher propensity to engage in unethical behavior than Achieving Money Worshiper when they are face with unethical organizational context.

Furthermore, there were significant differences between Employees and University Students in three unethical contexts such as Stressful Context, Conformity and Unethical Organizational Context. University students had higher propensity to engage in unethical behavior than employees.

Table 4. Univariate Analysis of Variance of Stressful Context Among Money Profiles

Source	Type III Sum of Squares	df	Mean Square	F	Sig.	Observed Power
Corrected Model	1.489	4	0.372	11.786	0.000	1.000
Intercept	30.635	1	30.635	970.11	0.000	1.000
Money Type	0.933	3	0.311	9.849	0.000	0.998
id	0.635	1	0.635	20.117	0.000	0.994
Error	16.737	530	0.032			
Total	69.327	535				
Corrected Total	18.225	534				

Table 5. Univariate Analysis of Variance of Conformity Context Among Money Profiles

Source	Type III Sum of Squares	df	Mean Square	F	Sig.	Observed Power
Corrected Model	9.971	4	2.493	3.021	0.018	0.802
Intercept	1440.776	1	1440.776	1746.257	0.000	1.000
Money Type	3.379	3	1.126	1.365	0.253	0.365
id	3.235	1	3.235	3.921	0.048	0.507
Error	433.984	526	0.825			
Total	2636.5	531				
Corrected Total	443.956	530				

Table 6. Univariate Analysis of Variance of Unethical Organization Context Among Money Profiles

Source	Type III Sum of Squares	df	Mean Square	F	Sig.	Observed Power
Corrected Model	87.541	4	21.885	32.884	0.000	1.000
Intercept	1762.546	1	1762.546	2648.371	0.000	1.000
Money Type	12.512	3	4.171	6.267	0.000	0.965
id	53.801	1	53.801	80.841	0.000	1.000
Error	348.733	524	0.666			
Total	3497.25	529				
Corrected Total	436.274	528				

DISCUSSION

Different people have different money profiles. The way of people to deal with unethical context also varies with different attitude they have towards money. To classify people's money profiles can deepen our understanding of their behavior and attitude towards work. Using the Money Ethic Scale which includes ten factors (Good, Evil, Success, Rich, Equity, Respect, Motivator, Budget Money, Make Money, Charitable Giving), this study identified four types of money profiles: Achieving Money Worshipers, Money Repellent Individuals, Apathetic Money Handlers and Careless Money Admirers.

This study examined a sample of managerial staffs and university students generally and found that when faced with the "Stressful Context", Achieving Money Worshipers and Careless Money Admirers have a higher propensity to engage in unethical behavior than Apathetic Money Handlers and Money Repellent Individuals. Hypotheses 1 was fully supported here. From the results we can see that Achieving Money Worshipers think highly about the value of money, they view money as a symbol of success and a means of winning respect and keeping an affluent life. Careless Money Admirers may have negative attitude towards money to some extent, but they usually feel lack of money most strongly. This is because they are relatively weak in the ability to make money and they do not budget their money carefully. So the attraction of money to them would be the strongest. The motivating power of money is also the strongest to them. Therefore, Achieving Money Worshipers and Careless Money Admirers are more likely to conduct unethical behavior to make personal profits when they are faced with Stressful Context. According to Professor Tang T. L. P.'s research, Careless Money Admirers are usually young and they are lack of work experience, have low income and low job and life satisfaction. They worship money, but do not have money. The great contrast between low income and high expectation of money brought them oppressive psychological pressure. There are two behavioral possibilities of such kind of employees: on one hand, they will work hard to make money, sometimes may take on work load beyond their capability; on the other hand, their utmost desire for money and failing to budget money carefully may easily leads them to behave illegally to get money. To managers, Careless Money Admirers are the employees easiest to be motivated by money and the most active ones, but the managers must pay attention to keep them away from engaging in unethical or illegal behavior.

The study also found that Apathetic Money Handlers and Money Repellent Individuals are more likely to engage in unethical behavior than the others when faced with Unethical Organizational Context. This result corresponds with hypotheses 2. Apathetic Money Handlers and Money Repellent Individuals all have negative attitude towards money; they never view money as success or a means of winning respect and never think money is the root of self value. Money is only external things besides the body to them and never be regard as motivator. They will not use unfair methods to gain financial advantages or take risk to do unethical or illegal things. According to Professor Tang T. L. P.'s research, although Apathetic Money Handlers get low incomes and make few job-hopping, they have high job satisfaction and life satisfaction and they can gain intrinsic self satisfaction from their work and life. They can never become slave of money, they are poor but happy. But in the Unethical Organizational Context, each member of the organization is using unfair method to make money, Apathetic Money Handlers and Money Repellent Individuals may also follow them to engage in unethical behavior, while Achieving Money Worshipers are more likely to restrain themselves from doing unethical behavior in such a context. According to Professor Tang T. L. P.'s research, Achieving Money Worshipers are the ones who get high income, plenty experience of work, older age, more diligent spirit and high life satisfaction. In addition, people's money profiles are also influenced by cultural value orientation and this orientation can restrict unethical behavior. The author's another research indicated that Achieving Money Worshipers have more remarkable sense of masculine superiority, self-protection and tendency of independent self-care than Apathetic Money Handlers, Careless Money Admirers and Money Repellent Individuals (Du Linzhi, 2005). This difference may implied that the Achieving Money Worshipers may intentionally restrain themselves from engaging in unethical behavior in order to keep their self image and well protect themselves. However, further and scientific analysis of this conclusion still depends on future studies.

The present study still reveals that university students are more inclined to engage in unethical behavior than managerial staffs when they are faced with Stressful Context, Conformity and Unethical Organizational Context. This result should be thought deeply. University students are the managers in the future; they are the main driven power for the development of society and economy of China in the future. It is uneasy to imagine the future picture of the national economy and society if our university students are all lack of trust and honesty. However, Professor Tang has pointed out that the money profile of individual will vary with the increase of experience and the change of income. But some other research indicated that money profile formed in the early period of childhood. It would go on to adulthood (Kirkcaldy & Furnham, 1993) and varies more or less to the change of experience of development and social and economic environment (Bruner & Goodman, 1947). While university students have more negative attitude towards money, the full-time employees hold more positive attitude towards money, this may implied that the university students will appreciate money when they get into the society, and when they begin to work hard to make money and become self-consumptive. The direct experience of money will change their money profiles. Relative studies show that people get high income tend to view money as not evil (Tang, 1992). The importance of demands of people and satisfaction of life (Tang & West, 1997) and money profiles may change with the increase of income (Furnham & Argyle, 1998). There is a process for the development from the lack of physical demands to the psycho needs. Therefore, as long as we emphasize the money profile education on one hand, and build a healthy business environment of honesty in our society on the other hand, along with strict and standardized system of trust supervision, the national economy and society will keep developing stably, healthily and orderly.

APPENDIX 1

Money Ethics Scale (MES)

1. Having a lot of money (being rich) is good.
2. I want to be rich
3. It would be nice to be rich.
4. Money is a motivator.
5. My life will be more enjoyable, if I am rich and have more money.

6. I use my money very carefully.
7. I spend my money based on a budget.
8. I budget my money very well.
9. I am proud of my ability to save money.
10. I save money for the future.
11. I pay my bills immediately.
12. Money is important.
13. Money is valuable.
14. Money is good.
15. Money is an important factor in the lives of all of us.
16. Money is attractive.
17. Money is a major cause of people's unethical and evil acts.
18. Money motivates people to perform unethically.
19. Money undermines one's ethical norms and standards.
20. The love of money is the root of all evil.
21. Money represents my achievement.
22. Money is power.
23. Money is a symbol of my success.
24. More money should be paid to people with more talent.
25. More money should be paid to people with higher merit (performance).
26. More money should be paid to higher-level jobs with more responsibilities.
27. I give generously to charitable organizations.
28. I believe in charitable giving.
29. I give money to the Church (religious organization(s)).
30. I give money to the Hoping Program.
31. Money helps me gain respect.
32. Money makes people respect me in the community.
33. Money allows me to express myself.
34. Money does NOT enhance the "love" of my job.
35. Money offers less excitement than achievement on my job.
36. Money is less important than recognition and achievement.
37. Money does NOT make my job exciting, interesting, and challenging.
38. Money does not increase my enjoyment of my work.
39. I find smarter and better ways of making money.
40. I am proud of my ability to make money.
41. I look for new and legal ways to make money.
42. I use (invest) my money to make more money.

Propensity to Engage in Unethical Behavior Scale (PEUBS)

1. Take merchandise and/or cash home.
2. Borrow $20 from a register overnight without asking.
3. Reveal company secrets when a person offers several million dollars.
4. Abuse the company expense accounts and falsify accounting records (time cards).
5. Accept money, gift, and kickback from others.

6. Overcharge customers to increase sales and to earn higher bonus.
7. Sabotage the company to get even due to unfair treatment.
8. Manager in my company often engages in behaviors that I consider being unethical.
9. In order to succeed in my company, it is often necessary to compromise one's ethics.
10. Take no action for employees who steal cash/merchandise.
11. Take no action for shoplifting by customers.
12. Use office supplies (paper, pen), Xerox machine, and stamps for personal purpose.
13. Make personal long-distance (mobile phone) calls at work.
14. If a manager in my company is discovered to have engaged in unethical behaviors that result primarily in *corporate gain* (rather than personal gain), he or she will be promptly reprimanded.
15. Top management in my company has let it be known in no uncertain terms that unethical behaviors will not be tolerated.

About the Authors

Du Linzhi (Ph.D., Nankai University) is an Associate Professor in the Department of Social Psychology, School of Zhou En'lai Government Management, Nankai University, Tianjin, People's Republic of China. Currently, he is conducting his post-doctoral research at Nanjing University in Nanjing, PRC. His primary research interests are in the areas of organizational behavior, money attitudes, and social psychology. He has published more than 20 journal articles and presented many papers at several international conferences around the world. He received the First Place Award of Research Excellence from the Ministry of Personnel, China (2004).

Thomas Li-Ping Tang (Ph.D., Case Western Reserve University) is a Full Professor of Management in the Department of Management and Marketing, Jennings A. Jones College of Business, Middle Tennessee State University (MTSU) in Murfreesboro, TN USA. He has taught Industrial and Organizational Psychology at National Taiwan University and at MTSU. His primary research interests are in organizational behavior, the love of money, unethical behaviors in the financial domain, work motivation, compensation decisions, satisfaction, turnover, OCB, and cross-cultural issues. He has published more than 93 journal articles (e.g., Journal of Applied Psychology, Personnel Psychology, Human Relations, Journal of Organizational Behavior, Journal of Management, Journal of Business Ethics, etc.), presented more than 160 papers in many countries, and reviewed papers for 24 journals around the world. He has received two Outstanding Research Awards (1991, 1999) and the Distinguished International Service Award (1999) at MTSU and the Best Reviewer Award from the International Management Division of the Academy of Management in Seattle, WA (2003).

Yang Dongtao (Ph.D., Nanjing University) is a Full Professor of Management in the Department of Management, School of Business, Nanjing University in Nanjing, Jiangsu Province, PRC. She has taught human resource management, operate management at Nanjing University. Her primary research interests are in human resource management, operate management and organizational behavior. She has published more than 50 journal articles and presented many papers at several international conferences around the world.

REFERENCES

Bruner, J. S., & Goodman, C. C. (1947).Value and needs as organizing factors in perception. Journal of Abnormal and Social Psychology, 42, 33-44.

Chen, Y. J., & Tang, T. L. P. (2006). Attitude toward and propensity to engage in unethical behavior: Measurement invariance across major among university students. *Journal of Business Ethics*, in press.

Du Linzhi (2005, August).A Study about the Relation between Money Profiles and Cultural Tendency of University Students in China. Paper presented at the 2005 Conference of China's Social Psychology Association. Tianyuan, China.

Du, L.Z., & Tang, T. L.P. (2005). Measurement invariance across gender and major: The Love of Money among university students in People's Republic of China. *Journal of Business Ethics*, 59, 281-293

Du, L. Z., Xu, X. S. & Tang, T. L. P. (2004). Endorsement of Money Ethics and Work Stress: the Case of Full-Time Employees in China. *Journal of Hohai University* (Philosophy and Social Sciences), 6(2), 65-69.

Herzberg, F., Mausner, B., & Snyderman, B.(1959). *The motivation to work.* New York: John Wiley & Sons.

Ivancevich, J. M., Konopaske, R., & Matteson, M. T. (2005). *Organizational behavior and management* (7th ed.). Boston: McGraw-Hill Irwin.

Kirkcaldy, B., & Furnham, A. (1993). Predictors of belief about money. *Psychological Report*, 73, 1079-1082.

Lawler, E. E. (1971). *Pay and organizational effectiveness: A psychological view*. New York: McGraw-Hill.

Luna-Arocas, R., & Tang, T. L. P. (2004). The love of money, satisfaction, and the Protestant Work Ethic: Money profiles among university professors in the USA and Spain. *Journal of Business Ethics*, 50 (4), 329-354.

Luna-Arocas, R., & Tang, T. L. P. (2005). The use of cluster analysis to segment clients of a sport cent in Spain. *European Sport Management Quarterly,* 5 (4), 381-413.

Tang, T. L. P. (1992). The meaning of money revisited. *Journal of Organizational Behavior*, 13, 197-202.

Tang, T. L. P.(1995). The Development of a Short Money Ethic Scale: Attitudes Toward Money and Pay Satisfaction revisted. *Personality and Individual Differences*, 19, 809–817.

Tang, T. L. P. & Tang, T. L. N. (2002). The Money Ethic Scale and Money Attitude in the USA. Paper presented at the XXV International Congress of Applied Psychology (Singapore), July, 7–12.

Tang, T. L. P., & Chiu, R. K. (2003). Income, Money Ethic, pay satisfaction, commitment, and unethical behavior: Is the love of money the root of evil for Hong Kong employees? *Journal of Business Ethics*, 46,13-30.

Tang, T. L. P., Tillery, K. R., Lazarevski, B., & Luna-Arocas, R. (2004). The love of money and work-related attitudes: Money profiles in Macedonia. *Journal of Managerial Psychology*, 19 (5), 542-548.

Tang, T. L. P., Tang, D. S. H., & Luna-Arocas, R. (2005). Money profiles: The love of money, attitudes, and needs. *Personnel Review*, 34 (5), 603-618.

In: China: Economic, Political and Social Issues
Editors: J. M. Phillips and L. J. Moore
ISBN: 978-60456-727-4

Chapter 8

GRASSROOTS POLITICAL REFORMS IN RURAL CHINA

Björn Alpermann
Department of East Asian Studies,
University of Cologne
Cologne, Germany

INTRODUCTION

Contrary to the expectations of many outside observers at the beginning of the 1990s the political system of the People's Republic of China (PRC) experienced remarkably little transformation during the last decade of the twentieth century. The Chinese Communist Party (CCP) weathered the aftermath of the bloody repression of the Tiananmen democracy movement of 1989 as well as the demise of other Communist Party dictatorships in Russia and Eastern Europe. Neither the transition of authority from the late Deng Xiaoping to Jiang Zemin nor the passing of the helm from the latter to Hu Jintao at the Sixteenth Party Congress convened in Beijing in November 2002 have ushered in large-scale elite in-fighting or a systemic succession crisis disabling the functioning of the political system. Against this backdrop of stability, it has been the more subtle changes to that system on which most authors have pinned their hopes for a political transformation. These include *inter alia* the building of the rule of law, a more independent role for people's congresses at different levels of the political hierarchy, changing state-society relations and new intellectual trends.[1] However, one of the aspects receiving most attention in recent years has been ongoing political reform in the Chinese countryside. The very dearth of other eye-catching reforms in the political realm has made the adoption of direct elections at the basic-level of a Leninist

[1]See for example Pei Minxin, "China's Evolution Toward Soft Authoritarianism," in *What if China Doesn't Democratize? Implications for War and Peace*, ed. Edward Friedman and Barrett L. McCormick (Armonk: M. E. Sharpe, 2000), 74-98; Zhao Dingxin, "China's Prolonged Stability and Political Future: Same Political System, Different Policies and Methods," *Journal of Contemporary China* 10, no. 28 (2001): 427-444; and more general: Richard Baum and Alexei Shevchenko, "The 'State of the State'," in *The Paradox of China's Post-Mao Reforms*, ed. Merle Goldman and Roderick MacFarquhar (Cambridge: Harvard University Press, 1999), 333-360.

Party-state seems even more spectacular. These elections pertain to villagers' committees (VCs), the executive body at the rural grassroots-level which was instituted with the demise of collective farming and the people's commune system in the early 1980s. Only after a special law was passed in 1987 did these elections begin to resemble democratic procedures and during the 1990s the spread of these was still quite uneven. Yet, problems of implementation notwithstanding these elections have served as an impetus to pioneer elections for other positions of the Party and state apparatuses. All of these reforms, to be dealt with in more detail below, have raised the eyebrows of Western China-watchers.

While it appears easy to explain the attention paid to grassroots political reforms in rural China, the extent of these changes and their impacts remain hard to gauge given the huge area and diverse nature of the Chinese countryside.[2] In fact, Jonathan Unger aptly called rural politics in China "kaleidoscopic" because of the wide variations existing between different localities.[3] Nevertheless, it is probably not too early to raise questions pertaining to the nature of these political transformations. Specifically, this article addresses the question which driving forces behind them can be identified. I will argue that political change at the grassroots-level in rural China has neither been a story of top-down reform, nor of bottom-up initiative, but rather a mixture of both and that during the process new actors which I will term bureaucratic entrepreneurs, policy advocates and policy entrepreneurs came to play significant roles. First, it will be necessary to sketch the economic transformations in rural China during the reform era to elaborate different reform patterns. We will then turn to the political reforms taking place in this new context and attempt to identify which pattern best serves to explain these. In doing so, I will focus on political reforms defined as a restructuring of formal political institutions. Accompanying changes in political attitudes and the political culture of rural China will be addressed only where they are perceived as either driving forces or results of these institutional reforms.[4]

REFORMING CHINA'S RURAL ECONOMIC INSTITUTIONS

Major transformations of the Chinese rural economy have taken place during the 1980s and 1990s.[5] Indeed, the starting point of all reforms under Deng Xiaoping was de-collectivization of agriculture at the end of the 1970s and in the early 1980s which greatly boosted agricultural productivity during the first half of the 1980s. Yet, there have been greatly varying explanations of how these systemic changes came about. While some observers focused on intra-elite dynamics to explain this reform,[6] others depicted de-collectivization as a momentous reform from below in which peasants forced into similar circumstances by a seemingly overwhelming state acted in unison to replace the oppressive structures of collective farming with a family-farming system. In other words, in this

[2] For an assessment and comparison of village elections across China's provinces see: Robert A. Pastor and Tan Qingshan, "The Meaning of Village Elections," *China Quarterly* 162 (2001): 490-512.

[3] See Jonathan Unger, *The Transformation of Rural China* (Armonk: M. E. Sharpe, 2002), 197.

[4] On possible and actual impacts of VC-elections on political attitudes see: Li Lianjiang, "Elections and Popular Resistance in Rural China," *China Information* 16, no.1 (2002): 89-107.

[5] Since these are generally well documented in the literature, I will not unnecessarily repeat them here. See for example David Zweig, *Freeing China's Framers: Rural Restructuring in the Reform Era* (Armonk: M. E. Sharpe, 1997); Jonathan Unger, *The Transformation of Rural China* (Armonk: M. E. Sharpe, 2002).

[6] See Joseph Fewsmith, *Dilemmas of Reform in China: Political Conflict and Debate* (Armonk: M. E. Sharpe, 1994), chapter 1.

perspective the driving force of the adoption of this so-called household responsibility system (HRS) in agriculture has been the peasantry.[7] While the elite-focused approach is linked with a "top-down pattern" of reform in which reform progresses only as far as the leadership allows, the second explanation will be called a "bottom-up pattern." In the case of the HRS both have their virtues, but their explanatory power is obviously limited, especially regarding the regional variations in the adoption of a certain policy.

Therefore, other authors refined the argument to what can be termed an interactive pattern of reform:[8] Preceding initiative from below, a relaxation in economic policy emanated from higher political levels.[9] This created an opportunity for experimentation which some peasants and local cadres seized upon. After initial success of less radical forms of the HRS provincial-level reformers acted as patrons of these experiments and legitimized them post facto. Again, this encouraged initiative from below resulting in more small-scale, low-risk infringements of existing rules, called fence-breaking.[10] While this cumulative pressure from below led to step-by-step reforms and clearly went beyond initial expectations of Deng Xiaoping and other "reformers," earlier attempts in a very similar vein did not succeed because of the very different political macro-climate.[11] Only the power struggle at the top between Deng Xiaoping and Hua Guofeng opened the necessary window of opportunity for these local initiatives to be sustainable. Elite policy champions in the provinces, such as Wan Li in Anhui and Zhao Ziyang in Sichuan, used the early success of this reform initiative to bolster the reformist position. Significantly, the central-level reformers at one point chose to adopt the HRS as a nation-wide policy, even implementing it against resistance in some localities.[12] Therefore, only the interactive pattern of reform seems an adequate explanation for de-collectivization in China. I will argue below that this explanatory pattern also goes a long way in analyzing rural political reforms in the 1980s, but that it has its limitations, too.

POLITICAL REFORMS

The change from collective to family-farming under the HRS created a new political situation in the villages. Functions of rural basic-level cadres as well as their relationships to the populace were radically altered. Peasants had considerably more decision-making power in production and control over their harvest under the new HRS. Tensions between cadres and villagers centered on the extraction of grain and taxes and coercive state policies like birth-planning, in some places rising to a crisis of governance. Popular protests in rural areas

[7] See Daniel Kelliher, Peasant Power in China. The Era of Reform, 1979-1989 (New Haven: Yale University Press, 1992), 40-69; Kate X. Zhou, *How the Farmers Changed China: Power of the People* (Boulder: Westview Press, 1996), 46-75; Thomas Heberer, "The Power of the Fait Accompli: The Peasantry as the Motive Force of Change in the People's Republic of China," *Occassional Papers* 3 (University of Trier, Center for East-Asia and Pacific Studies).

[8] See Dali L.Yang, *Calamity and Reform in China. State, Rural Society, and Institutional Change Since the Great Leap Famine* (Stanford: Stanford University Press, 1996), 144-179; Zweig, China's Framers, 12-5.

[9] While most observers mention the documents of the famous third plenum of the eleventh CCP Central Committee in December 1978 as the starting point, Xu Yong points to the so-called Six Agricultural Articles of Anhui Province from November 1977 as the first opening-up document. Xu Yong, *Bao chan dao hu shenfu lu* [*A Thorough Record of Contracting Output to the Household*] (Zhuhai: Zhuhai chubanshe, 1998), 225.

[10] Thomas Heberer, Unternehmer als Strategische Gruppen: Zur Sozialen und Politischen Funktion von Unternehmern in China und Vietnam (Hamburg: Institute of Asian Affairs, 2001), 57-9.

[11] See Xu (1998) for a detailed analysis of these attempts starting as early as 1956.

[12] See Jonathan Unger, *The Transformation of Rural China* (Armonk: M. E. Sharpe, 2002), 95-109.

erupted more regularly and more violently during the two decades of the reform-era than before. Without direct leverage on villagers cadres now sometimes used excessively harsh methods to extract taxes and fees from the populace or to impose birth quotas or in birth-planning campaigns actually abortion quotas. Without a functioning judicial system to rely on to redress their grievances villagers reacted with open violence or stealthily retaliated against local cadres.[13] On the other hand, the general relaxation of political climate and ideological control throughout the system led villagers and cadres alike to concentrate on seizing the newly available economic opportunities. Many basic-level cadres quit their posts or neglected their duties, thus incapacitating village administrations.[14] Others used their remaining control of collective assets to profit from the boom of rural industries, combining political and economic clout.[15] Either way the power of the central state to control its basic-level cadres and through them the rural population was considerably weakened. Again, it was a combination of central political reforms and local initiatives which lead to institutional innovation. The creation of elected villagers' committees (VCs) to step into the political vacuum is commonly credited to "spontaneous" initiatives on the part of some villagers in Guangxi Autonomous Region.[16] However, it should be noted that the CCP Central Committee had in December 1978 issued a document which called for a democratization of the election procedures for village cadre positions.[17] And in 1979 Deng Xiaoping exclaimed: "Without democracy there can be no socialism, and no socialist modernization."[18] Although the socialist democracy Deng had in mind is a far cry from Western liberal concepts of democracy and his use of the term might have been part of a ploy in the intra-Party struggles of that time, this still constitutes an unambiguous signal that change was in the air and Deng proved to be serious about administrative reforms. Therefore, Xu Yong is right to conclude that "[i]f one says that reforms of the economic structure created the necessary economic conditions for villagers' self-administration, then the process of democratization of the state directly promoted its rise."[19] Even if it remains murky whether the villagers in Guangxi knew

---

[13] On popular protests see Elizabeth J. Perry, "Rural Collective Violence: The Fruits of Recent Reforms", in *The Political Economy of Reform in Post-Mao China*, ed. : Elizabeth J. Perry and Christine Wong (Cambridge: Harvard University Press, 1985), 175-92; Thomas P. Bernstein and Lü Xiaobo, "Taxation Without Representation: Peasants, the Central State and the Local States in Reform China," *China Quarterly* 163 (2000): 742-63. An excellent case-study of birth-planning implementation in a village is Zhang Weiguo, *Chinese Economic Reforms and Fertility Behaviour. A Study of a North China Village* (London: China Library, 2002), 168-98; and more general Thomas Scharping, *Birth Control in China 1949-2000. Population Policy and Demographic Development* (London: RoutledgeCurzon, 2003), 169-76.

[14] See John P. Burns, "Local Cadre Accommodation to the 'Responsibility System' in Rural China," *Pacific Affairs* 58, no. 4 (Winter 1985-1986): 612-4; Tyrene White, "Political Reform and Rural Government," in *Chinese Society on the Eve of Tiananmen. The Impact of Reform*, ed. Deborah Davis and Ezra F. Vogel (Cambridge: Harvard University Press, 1990), 48-52. However, rural cadres tend more to neglect those duties which are assigned to them with only 'soft targets,' and are more willing to fulfill 'hard targets,' see Kevin J. O'Brien and Li Lianjiang, "Selective Policy Implementation in Rural China," *Comparative Politics* 31, no. 2 (1999): 167-86.

[15] See in more detail Jean C. Oi, "Commercializing China's Rural Cadres," *Problems of Communism* (September-October 1986): 1-15.

[16] See for example Bai Gang, "Zhongguo cunmin zizhi fazhi jianshe pingyi" [Assessment of the Legal Construction of Chinese Villagers' Self-administration], Zhongguo Shehui Kexue 3 (1998): 88.

[17] See John P. Burns, Political Participation in Rural China (Berkley: University of California Press, 1988), 88; Sulamith H. Potter and Jack M. Potter, China's Peasants. The Anthropology of a Revolution (Cambridge: Cambridge University Press, 1992), 102-105.

[18] Cited in Xu 1997, p. 1; see also Wang 2001, pp. 6-7, for more on Deng's remarks on democracy during this era.

[19] Xu Yong, Zhongguo nongcun cunmin zizhi [Villagers' Self-administration in Rural China] (Wuhan: Zhonghua shifan daxue chubanshe, 1997), 27.

about new trends in central leaders thinking on basic-level administration, it is above doubt that these new trends had enabled grassroots initiatives to flourish. What is more, the central leadership decided to integrate the new institution of VCs into the formal administrative hierarchy when it abolished the people's communes. Communes were replaced by township governments and production brigades by administrative villages led by VCs enshrined in the 1982 constitution as basic-level self-administration organizations of the masses. This implied a certain degree of autonomy from township administration—the lowest level of formal state bureaucracy—although a definition of rights and duties of both were left to be defined by special laws.[20] Moreover, the constitution required that cadres serving on VCs are elected by the villagers. Therefore, one could argue that villagers' self-administration with elected VCs at its core had thus been institutionalized in an interactive pattern of reform very similar to the HRS. However, there are major differences between these two reforms. While the HRS was implemented nationwide without regard to local peculiarities within a matter of three years and has remained basically unchanged afterwards,[21] the system of villagers' self-administration remains only partially realized and proves still contentious even after two decades. The constitutional requirement to hold VC-elections was widely ignored even after promulgation of the Organic Law on Villagers' Committees in its trial version of 1987. Only after a final version of that special law which was already announced in the constitution of 1982 had been passed in 1998 did implementation become more forceful. Furthermore, during this long process of experimentation large revisions and profound additions have been made to the original shape of villagers' self-administration. We will address these in turn, when discussing driving forces for these political changes in the next sections.

Elite Policy Champions and Legislation

It is certainly true that without the support of some high-ranking Party leaders the system of villagers' self-administration would not have taken off. In fact, even the mentioning of elected VCs in the 1982 constitution is credited to the efforts of one single Party elder, Peng Zhen.[22] His backing also proved necessary to induce reluctant National People's Congress (NPC) delegates to pass the Organic Law on Villagers' Committees (Trial) in 1987 which defined more clearly the scope of self-administration and the functions of VCs. This law also required VCs to be elected directly by villagers although during the deliberations in the NPC many opponents had argued that this would make them less responsive to higher-level administration, thus aggravating, rather than ameliorating the rural governance crisis. In the end, with Peng's support the proponents' argument prevailed that elected VCs would be more able to carry out state-assigned but unpopular tasks because villagers would identify with

[20] See Xu, Zhongguo nongcun, 38-9. In fact, this process of administrative reform took three years and often involved a redrawing of administrative boundaries: During 1982-1985 54.342 communes were replaced by 91.138 townships and 719.438 brigades by 940.617 VCs; see Bai Gang and Zhao Taoxing, *Xuanju yu zhili: Zhongguo cunmin zizhi yanjiu* [*Elections and Governance: Studies on Chinese Villagers's Self-administration*] (Beijing: Zhongguo shehui kexue chubanshe, 2001), 44.

[21] This is of course not to say that China's land system is free from the need of reform; but, as Peter Ho argues, for the moment it serves both state and society well to delay reform. Peter Ho, "Who Owns China's Land? Property Rights and Deliberate Institutional Ambiguity," *China Quarterly* 166 (2001): 394-421

[22] See Kevin J. O'Brien and Li Lianjiang, "Accommodating 'Democracy' in a One-Party State: Introducing Village Elections in China," *China Quarterly* 162 (2001): 467-70. These authors link Peng Zhen's commitment to socialist democracy with earlier experiments in grassroots governance during the 1930s and 1950s.

them. Yet, again in the wake of the Tiananmen crackdown of 1989, it took Peng's efforts and the assistance of another Party elder, Bo Yibo, to rescue the Organic Law from being scrapped altogether.[23] These Party leaders succeeded in first passing the Organic Law and then saving it through the political retrenchment of 1989 to1990, but their victory was only partial and narrow. The law was merely passed for "trial implementation" and it took another ten years for a revised Organic Law to be promulgated by the NPC.[24] Thus, backing by parts of the highest echelon of Party leaders acting as policy champions proved a necessary condition for political institutional reforms, but by no means a sufficient one. The PRC's political system is as much characterized by authoritarianism as by fragmentation,[25] so that even had the law been less ambiguous it would have met with considerable opposition in its implementation. That the Organic Law left crucial issues ill- or undefined made matters worse. Most notably, the relationship of the township government to the VC was defined as one of "guidance"—not of "leadership"—which expresses respect for a certain autonomy of the VC vis-à-vis the lowest level of formal state administration. However, it remained unspecified how the VC would realize the prescribed cooperation with and assistance to the township government in carrying out state-set administrative tasks. Ever since de-collectivization this has been the most contentious point in rural governance reform.[26] Moreover, the village party branch, the highest organ in each village, was not even mentioned in the law. Only in party documents and the CCP statute the leadership of the party branch over the elected VC was clearly stated.[27] Of course, not even the most vocal proponents of villagers' self-government like Peng Zhen or Bo Yibo wanted the VCs to become independent of party leadership which to date remains the hallmark of the PRC's political system. But a clearer delineation of functions and authority would certainly have contributed to a successful development of village governance. As things stood, implementation of the Organic Law and direct VC-elections was sure to be obstructed by those who had most to lose from this reform: township administrations and village party branches. And the definition of the Organic Law as being only for trial implementation provided these opponents with a pretext to adopt a wait-and-see attitude. Obviously, something else had to happen to drive implementation forward.

---

[23] See Kevin J. O'Brien and Li Lianjiang, "Selective Policy Implementation in Rural China," *Comparative Politics* 31, no. 2 (1999): 131-4.

[24] On the Organic Law and its revision in 1998 see Björn Alpermann, *Der Staat im Dorf: Dörfliche Selbstverwaltung in China* [*The State in the Village: Village Self-administration in China*] (Hamburg: Institute of Asian Affairs, 2001), 27-43.

[25] On the concept of fragmented authoritarianism see Kenneth G. Lieberthal, "Introduction: The 'Fragmented Authoritarianism' Model and Its Limitations," in *Bureaucracy, Politics, and Decision Making in Post-Mao China*, ed. Kenneth G. Lieberthal and David M. Lampton (Berkley: University of California Press, 1992), 1-30.

[26] For a case-study on township-village relations see Björn Alpermann, "The Post-Election Administration of Chinese Villages," *China Journal* 46 (2001), 45-67. For a more general discussion see Jin Taijun and Shi Congmei, *Xiang cun guanxi yu cunmin zizhi* [*Township-Village Relations and Villagers' Self-administration*] (Guangzhou: Guandong renmin chubanshe, 2001), 195-247.

[27] See Xu Yong, *Zhongguo nongcun cunmin zizhi* [*Villagers' Self-administration in Rural China*] (Wuhan: Zhonghua shifan daxue chubanshe, 1997), 38. The fact that this leadership relation which includes the right to issue binding orders has never been in serious dispute has often been overlooked by Western observers.

Innovations by the Masses

Ever since the successful adoption of the HRS "innovations by the masses" have played a special role in rural reforms. These have the special credentials of being conform to the mass-line approach which has been a central tenet of Mao Zedong's thought about party work since the 1940s.[28] The mass-line is best described in Mao's own words:

> In all practical work of our Party, all correct leadership is necessarily 'from the masses to the masses'. This means: take the ideas of the masses (scattered and unsystematic ideas) and concentrate them (through study turn them into concentrated and systematic ideas), then go to the masses and propagate and explain these ideas until the masses embrace them as their own, hold fast to them and translate them into action, and test the correctness of these ideas in such action... Such is the Marxist theory of knowledge.[29]

There are obvious parallels between this spiraling process and what I termed an interactive pattern of reform. It is somewhat ironic, however, that this mass-line approach was in actual practice seriously disregarded during the Mao-era, and yet was revived in this new form as a major reform pattern under Deng in the 1980s. In rural governance reform, we regularly find the claim that some new mechanism is an invention of the masses even if involvement of local cadres is more than just likely. A case in point is the institution of villagers' representative assemblies (VRAs). These organs are composed of 30-50 members which are either elected in villagers' small-groups or proposed by groups of households. Because of their size they are more easily convened than an assembly of all villagers to deliberate and decide on important issues of the rural community. Apart from this participatory function they are also supposed to serve as a check on elected village cadres who often take part in VRA sessions.[30] Initially, assemblies of this kind seem to have been convened on an ad hoc-basis in villages in different parts of China during the 1980s to solve specific problems in village management. These local initiatives sometimes predated the promulgation of the Organic Law, but the institution spread more widely only with this law's implementation starting in 1988.[31] In other words, this institutional innovation would not have taken firm hold in the basic-level political system, but for the intervention of another driving force of political change, namely bureaucratic entrepreneurs—dealt with in more detail below—who helped to institute VRAs during this implementation drive. Another example is the case of village compacts and village charters. The first are rather simple codes of conduct, while the latter which are sometimes called 'small constitutions" regulate political

---

[28] See Kenneth G. Lieberthal, *Governing China. From Revolution Through Reform* (New York: W. W. Norton, 1995), 64-5.

[29] Cited in Tony Saich, *Governance and Politics of China* (Houndmills: Palgrave, 2001), 41.

[30] On limitations of VRAs' decision-making power see Jean C. Oi and Scott Rozelle, "Elections and Power: The Locus of Decision-Making in Chinese Villages," *China Quarterly* 162 (2001): 516-22. For a case-study of an unusually active VRA see Susan V. Lawrence, "Democracy, Chinese Style," *Australian Journal of Chinese Affairs* 32 (1994): 61-68.

[31] See Wang Zhenyao, Tang Jinsu et al, *Zhongguo nongcun cunmin daibiao huiyi zhidu* [*The Research Report on the Villagers Representative Assemblies in China*] (Beijing: Zhongguo shehui keyue chubanshe, 1994). 7-9; Zhu Hong and Yan Hao, "Yi ge you nongmin chuangzao de jiceng zhengzhi minzhu zhidu. Nanlou cun cunmin daibiao huiyi zhidu de diaocha" [A Democratic System at the Political Grassroots Created by Peasants. A Study of the Villagers' RepresentativeAssembly in Nanlou Village] *Zhongguo Minzheng* 4 (1989): 6; and Zhang Zhenxian, "Zhongguo nongmin de xin chuangju" [The New Pioneering Work of China's Peasants] *Zhongguo Nongcun* 5 (1997): 34.

live in the village.[32] The adoption of village compacts through an assembly of all villagers as an instrument to restructure community live and to strengthen rural governance was pushed in a national campaign starting in 1982.[33] As Ann Anagnost has shown, these village compacts have a history dating back to the Neo-Confucian revival of the eleventh century, yet "these historical antecedents are never mentioned. On the contrary, the compacts are consistently portrayed as an organizational *innovation* of 'the masses'."[34] Village charters which clearly share these historical antecedents are supposedly an invention of the masses of Zhangqiu County, Shandong Province during the implementation of the Organic Law.[35] From there their adoption spread nationwide during the MCA-led movement to create demonstration-sites for villagers' self-administration after 1990.[36] But very often the wide-spread adoption of village compacts and charters could only be attained by sacrificing the original procedure of the document being drafted by the villagers themselves. Instead various administrative levels simply took the initiative to issue these documents to the villagers.[37] An example is the county-level city of Anqiu, Shandong Province, where cadres of the Party's organization department at that level seemingly promoted the distribution of these documents starting in 1989.[38] The motives of cadres seizing such initiatives will be explored in the next section.

A last example of a local innovation—this time going back to a public protest of ordinary villagers well-documented by an independent researcher—is the two-ballot system for the election of the village Party secretary.[39] Due to the leadership role of the CCP throughout the political system which is enshrined in the PRC's constitution the village Party branch, headed by the Party secretary, usually dominates local decision-making although there might be exceptions if the VC controls more income-generating activities.[40] According to the CCP's Provisional Regulations on Election Work for Basic-Level Organs all Party members are eligible to elect the relevant committee of their own units. However, candidates have to be examined and approved by the party organ on the next higher level. And after election the

---

[32] See Kevin J. O'Brien, "Implementing Political Reform in China's Villages," *Australian Journal of Chinese Affairs* 32 (1994): 43-4.

[33] See Ann Anagnost, "Socialist Ethics and the Legal System," in *Popular Protest and Political Culture in Modern China. Learning from 1989*, ed. Jeffrey N. Wasserstrom and Elizabeth J. Perry (Boulder: Westview, 1992), 182.

[34] Anagnost, "Socialist Ethics," 188-9. (emphasis in the original).

[35] See Wang Wen, *Xiangzhen zhengquan jianshe* [*Construction of Rural Political Power at the Township-level*] (Guangzhou: Zhongshan daxue chubanshe, 1993), 139.

[36] See "Implementing Political Reform," 43; and Wang, Xiangzhen, 142-6.

[37] See Bai Gang, "Zhongguo cunmin zizhi fazhi jianshe pingyi" [Assessment of the Legal Construction of Chinese Villagers' Self-administration], *Zhongguo Shehui Kexue* 3 (1998): 88-104.

[38] See Zhonggong Shandong sheng Anqiu shiwei, Shandong sheng Anqiu shi renmin zhengfu (1996): "Hu wei jidian. Yifa zizhi. Cujin nongcun liang ge wenming jiankang fazhan" [The Household as the Basis-point. Govern according to the Law. Foster the Healthy Development of the Two Civilizations in the Villages], in Bai Yihua and Wang Zhenyao, eds., *Quanguo cunmin zizhi shifan gongzuo jingyan jiaoliu ji cheng xiang jiceng xianjin jiti he xianjin geti biaozhang huiyi wenjian huibian* [*Documents of the National Conference to Exchange Experiences in the Work on Models for Villagers' Self-administration and to Honor Urban and Rural Progressive Collectives and Individuals*] (Beijing: Zhongguo shehui chubanshe, 1996), 96-102. Similar observations were made by the author during fieldwork conducted in two counties of southern Hebei Province in 1997.

[39] See Li Lianjiang, "The Two-Ballot System in Shanxi Province: Subjecting Village Party Secretaries to a Popular Vote," *China Journal* 42 (1999): 103-118.

[40] See Oi and Rozelle, "Elections and Power," 530-1. On reconfigurations of the village authority structure under reforms see Guo Zhenglin, "Guangdong nongcun quanli jiegou de minzhu zhuanxing" [Democratic Reconfigurations of the Authority Structure in Rural Guangdong] (paper presented at the International Symposium on Grassroots Governance in Contemporary China, 30 August – 1 September 2002, Shizuoka, Japan).

same organ again has to approve the elected secretary and vice-secretary.[41] However, villagers of Hequ County, Shanxi Province, protesting in 1991 against their village party secretary's alleged wrongdoings forced a party work team dispatched to solve the crisis to apply a new election procedure. The villagers' demand for participation in the selection of the party secretary was accommodated by a two-step process in which an all-village assembly could nominate two candidates for the position. Then all village party members could cast a second ballot to decide which of the two would serve as secretary. This innovative election method worked so well that it was soon instituted in the whole county.[42]

These cases demonstrate that societal pressures for institutional reforms exist in many parts of the Chinese countryside. However, there is nothing to suggest that a spontaneous, unorganized, leaderless, nonideological, apolitical movement of the rural populace is about to introduce sweeping changes in grassroots governance structures. Advancing her version of the bottom-up pattern of policy-making Kate Xiao Zhou's claimed that such a movement was responsible for most rural reforms in the 1980s and early 1990s.[43] This claim has proved dubious as shown above and would surely be all the more so had it been made for the rural political reforms treated here. Moreover, even in combination with support by some of the highest party leaders acting as policy champions these societal pressures proved not enough for any sweeping changes as the actually very arduous implementation of political reforms at the rural basic-level during the last decade testifies. What is still lacking in this picture to explain even the limited successes that these reforms have achieved are the driving forces of reform in the middle between the apex and the bottom of the political system.[44]

BUREAUCRATIC ENTREPRENEURS

Building on the work of Nancy Roberts, Kaye Bragg introduced the concept of public entrepreneurship into the study of policy-making in the PRC. An entrepreneur is conceptualized as someone engaged in each of the three phases of creation, design and implementation of a policy. Furthermore, Bragg differentiates four subtypes and identifies bureaucratic entrepreneurs as those holding formal positions in government below the level of leadership of a nationwide bureaucracy.[45] Of course Bragg is not the first to deal with the roles of bureaucrats in the Chinese political process.[46] Yet, her concept proves useful to

---

[41] See Zhongyang jinrong gongwei zuzhibu, *Dang de zuzhi gongzuo shiyong shouce* [*A Practical Handbook for the Organizational Work of the Party*] (Beijing: Zhonggong zhongyang dangxiao chubanshe, 1999), 228. These regulations were promulgated on the June 27, 1990, and remained in force throughout that decade.

[42] See Li, "The Two-Ballot System," 103-5.

[43] See Zhou, Farmers.

[44] A mutual empowerment of the political center and the peasantry through VC-elections at the cost of bureaucrats in the middle is the central thesis of Wang (1997). This huge middle ground is, however, omitted in his analysis. Wang Xu, "Mutual Empowerment of State and Peasantry: Grassroots Democracy in Rural China," *World Development* 25, no. 9 (1997): 1431-42

[45] See Kaye C. Bragg, "'Crossing the River by Groping for Stones': Factors Reshaping the Policy Innovation Process for Chinese Water Policies" (paper presented at the 2nd International Convention of Asia Scholars, Berlin, Germany, August 9-12, 2001), 5-6. The other three subtypes are also identified according to their positions as political entrepreneurs (elected leadership positions in government), executive entrepreneurs (not elected leadership positions) and policy entrepreneurs (without formal positions; these are dealt with in the next section). See also the discussion of entrepreneurship and political innovation in Heberer, Unternehmer, 92-5.

[46] See for example the seminal work by Kenneth G. Lieberthal and Michel Oksenberg, *Policy Making in China. Leaders, Structures, and Processes* (Princeton: Princeton University Press, 1988).

understand the crucial role played by mid-level bureaucrats in current political reforms at China's rural grassroots because it systematically differentiates between the three above mentioned phases. Therefore, we can analyze more clearly the roles which bureaucrats play. Shi Tianjian has argued that mid-level officials of the Ministry of Civil Affairs (MCA) were essential in this process since this ministry was designated to implement the Organic Law after 1988. They applied an incremental approach first spreading the institutionalization of VC elections and thereby compromising on their quality. Only in a second step after 1993 these MCA officials began to raise election quality by reforming the nomination procedures and fighting manipulation.[47] However, this focus on policy-*implementation* obscured the fact that major *innovations* within the system of rural governance took place along with this process. As we have seen, neither VC- elections themselves nor some elements described in the above section were innovations of MCA officials. Nevertheless, an entrepreneur is not necessarily characterized by his ability for (technical) innovations, but also by his alertness to opportunities which he creatively exploits.[48] Understood in this way MCA officials acted entrepreneurial on a number of occasions greatly contributing to political reforms. VRAs again prove a good case in point. Seizing the opportunity provided by this locally initiated institution MCA officials promoted their large scale adoption since September 1990. After receiving the support of Song Ping, then member of the CCP's Politburo Standing Committee, MCA issued a circular on the construction of demonstration-sites for villagers' self-administration which also required the institutionalization of VRAs. Furthermore, through consulting provincial people's congresses in drafting implementation procedures for the Organic Law MCA succeeded in introducing relevant clauses in the majority of cases.[49] According to MCA about half of all Chinese villages had implemented this new organ by 1994.[50] The establishment of demonstration-sites throughout China itself served two of MCA's purposes. On the one hand, it created a favorable environment for further innovations as these are designated areas which are supposed to continuously improve the quality of VC-elections. Thus, it is their very purpose to experiment with new institutions in rural governance. On the other hand, MCA could cash in on local initiatives preceding the designation of a particular area as demonstration-site. This strategy could be called picking winners as the MCA would declare a particular local development a model and propagate it. An important example is the open nomination procedure called *haixuan*. Throughout the 1990s many localities still conducted non-competitive elections, that is an election with an equal number of candidates and positions to be elected. Other localities offered limited choice in conducting semi-competitive elections (number of candidates = number of positions +1 or +2). With the revision of the Organic Law in November 1998 this semi-competitive method has become the legally required standard.[51] Either way the nomination procedure and the process of reducing nominations to final candidates are of ultimate importance if any choice

---

[47] See Shi Tianjian, "Village Committee Elections in China. Institutionalist Tactics for Democracy," *World Politics* 51 (April 1999): 385-412.

[48] See Heberer, Unternehmer, 94.

[49] Out of sixteen provinces adopting implementation regulations after September 1990 only six had no provisions on VRAs or a similar organ. Fujian Province in 1993 revised its implementation regulations bringing the total of provinces adopting this system into local law to sixteen at the end of 1994; see Wang Zhenyao, Tang Jinsu et al., *Zhongguo nongcun cunmin daibiao huiyi zhidu* [*The Research Report on the Villagers Representative Assemblies in China*] (Beijing: Zhongguo shehui keyue chubanshe, 1994), 23-4.

[50] See Wang, Zhongguo nongcun, 35.

[51] On variations in provincial legislation see Alpermann, "Provincial Legislation," 9-11.

at all shall be provided. Most localities allowed nominations by groups of voters and certain village-level organs, including the party committee.[52] In a second step the number of nominations used to be whittled down to the desired number of final candidates by a process of consultation in which the party branch had considerable power to influence the choice of voters. In their effort to raise the quality of VC-elections MCA officials were looking for ways to reduce this influence.[53] With Lishu County, Jilin Province, they found a suitable opportunity to seize upon.[54] As early as 1986 there had been a case of open nomination by village voters which was reported to the central leadership and was allegedly well received by Peng Zhen. Similar to the development of the two-ballot system the starting point had been an effort to resolve the political problems of one particular village. After further explorations in VC-elections of 1988/89 and 1991/92 the Lishu government issued new election regulations in 1993 and pushed for the county-wide adoption of the *haixuan*-method. In this process, every voter first casts a ballot with nominations. Those nominees who receive most votes are eligible to run in the final election. In this way, a primary after nomination becomes unnecessary although some localities still prefer holding a primary to a decision based on nominations. Either way the power of village party secretaries or township governments to manipulate voters' choice is severely circumscribed by this process. Therefore, bureaucratic entrepreneurs at MCA decided to seize this opportunity and popularize the Lishu experience as a model to emulate.[55] As a fruit of this effort the revised version of the Organic Law, passed by the NPC in November 1998, clearly requires direct nominations by the voters thus abolishing all previously common forms of consultations and negotiations in that process.[56] However, it would be a simplification to credit only a handful of officials in the central-level MCA with this innovation. Obviously, the initial impulse was a local solution to a particular village's problems in governance. And even before the inception of the demonstration-site movement through MCA the Party committee and government of Lishu promoted the use of primaries and semi-competitive elections throughout the county in 1989.[57] With these requirements Lishu established itself as a frontrunner in rural governance reforms. This

---

[52] See Jørgen Elklit, "The Chinese Village Committee Electoral System" *China Information* 11 (1997): 7-9. Even publications by MCA-officials differ in their assessment which nomination method is the most common: Wang (1998) calls nominations by Party committees rare, whereas Liu (1998) lists these and nomination by the preceding VC as the most common methods. See Kennedy (2002) for an assessment of the effects of these different nomination methods. Wang Zhenyao, "Village Committees. The Basis for China's Democracy," in *Cooperative and Collective in China's Rural Development. Between State and Private Interest*, ed. Eduard B. Vermeer, Frank N. Pieke and Woei Lien Chong (Armonk: M. E. Sharpe, 1998), 250. Liu Xitang, "Cunmin zizhi yu woguo nongcun minzhu de dutexing" [Villager's Autonomy and the Distinctiveness of Democracy in China] *Zhongguo Nongcun Jingji* 12 (1998): 59. John James Kennedy, "The Face of 'Grassroots Democracy' in Rural China: Real Versus Cosmetic Elections" *Asian Survey* 42, no. 3 (2002): 456-482.

[53] See Robert A. Pastor and Tan Qingshan, "The Meaning of Village Elections" *China Quarterly* 162 (2001): 495-6.

[54] The following account of Lishu County's experiments is based on Bai Gang and Zhao Taoxing, Xuanju yu zhili: *Zhongguo cunmin zizhi yanjiu* [*Elections and Governance: Studies on Chinese Villagers's Self-administration*] (Beijing: Zhongguo shehui kexue chubanshe, 2001), 156-62.

[55] See Shi Tianjian, "Village Committee Elections in China. Institutionalist Tactics for Democracy," *World Politics* 51 (April 1999): 406.

[56] See Quanguo renda changweihui fazhi gongzuo weiyuanhui guojiafa xingfa shi, *Cunmin weiyuanhui zuzhifa xuexi duben* [*Study Book on the Organic Law on Villagers' Committees*] (Beijing: Zhongguo minzhu fazhi chubanshe, 1998), 35-6.

[57] See Yu Weiliang,"'Haixuan' guxiang de xuanju licheng. Jilin sheng Lishu xian cunweihui si ci xuanju de kaocha" [The Election History of the Native Place of 'haixuan.' An Analysis of Four Rounds of Elections in Lishu County, Jilin Province], in *Zhongguo cunmin zizhi qianyan* [*The Forefront of China's Villagers' Self-administration*], ed. Wang Zhenyao, Bai Gang and Wang Zhongtian (Beijing: Zhongguo shehui kexue chubanshe, 2000), 323-27.

position was formalized when several townships within Lishu County were designated as demonstration-sites during the VC-elections of 1991. In fact, prior to 1994 Lishu seems to have been the only county-level demonstration-site in the whole of Jilin Province.[58] So we can assume that it received considerable attention from regional-level Civil Affairs officials. Although it now seems impossible to accurately disentangle the different inputs that enlightened county leaders, Civil Affairs officials at the provincial- or district-level and MCA officials from Beijing have provided to Lishu's development it is obvious that all of these three groups of actors have acted as bureaucratic entrepreneurs and made considerable impact.[59] A more important question to answer is which motives these actors pursued in driving political reform forward. Shi Tianjian argued that a new generation of bureaucrats was responsible for the implementation of the Organic Law with personalities like Wang Zhenyao seriously committed to reforming the political process at the grassroots.[60] However, these bureaucrats needed to apply politically correct arguments to avoid offering an open flank for criticism.[61] This instrumental argumentation makes it hard to assess their genuine commitment to reform. Moreover, another equally compelling motive might be careerism. As MCA is the bureaucracy charged with implementing the Organic Law its officials could rightly assume successes in grassroots political reform to foster their individual careers as well as the prestige of the whole organization.[62] This careerist motive might be also be at work with bureaucratic entrepreneurs engaged in political reforms with positions in local and regional government and Party leadership positions. This point was made by Li Lianjiang after studying the few known cases of another attempted reform: the introduction of direct elections for the position of township head.[63]

According to the constitution and the Organic Law of Local People's Congresses the head of a township government is elected by the local people's congress (LPC). However, as this position falls within the purview of the Party's *nomenklatura* system the delegates are usually presented only with a single candidate pre-selected by the county party committee.[64] Nevertheless, this domination of CCP organs has recently been more vocally criticized within

---

[58] See Jilin sheng minzhengting, "Bawo jiyu. Jiji tansuo. Renzhen zuohao cunweihui xuanju gongzuo" [Seize the Opportunity. Explore Enthusiastically. Conscientiously Carry Out the Task of Villagers' Committee Elections], in Quanguo *cunmin zizhi shifan gongzuo jingyan jiaoliu ji cheng xiang jiceng xianjin jiti he xianjin geti biaozhang huiyi wenjian huibian* [*Documents of the National Conference to Exchange Experiences in the Work on Models for Villagers' Self-administration and to Honor Urban and Rural Progressive Collectives and Individuals*], ed. Bai Yihua and Wang Zhenyao (Beijing: Zhongguo shehui chubanshe, 1996), 304-5.

[59] In April 1988 a township in Lishu County was chosen by these regional Civil Affairs offices as experimental-site for the elections of 1988/89. The first visit by a MCA official, Bai Yihua, is recorded in March 1989. See the meticulous chronicle of events in Yu, "'Haixuan' guxiang de xuanju licheng," 365-6.

[60] See Shi, "Village Committee Elections," 390-2.

[61] See Shi, "Village Committee Elections," 397-8. The debate over villagers' self-administration is analyzed in more detail in Daniel Kelliher, "The Chinese Debate over Village Self-Government," *China Journal* 37 (1997): 63-86. See also Björn Alpermann, *Der Staat im Dorf: Dörfliche Selbstverwaltung in China* [*The State in the Village: Village Self-administration in China*] (Hamburg: Institute of Asian Affairs, 2001), 43-51.

[62] On this last point see Kelliher, "The Chinese Debate," 76.

[63] See Li Lianjiang, "The Politics of Introducing Direct Township Elections in China," *China Quarterly* 171 (2002): 722. A similar argument was made by Oi and Rozelle (2001): Power-holders in villages with a financial surplus might be attracted to hold contested elections because this would not threaten their position (they could buy out voters with favors) and would still polish their village's image as a progressive political unit. Jean C. Oi and Scott Rozelle, "Elections and Power: The Locus of Decision-Making in Chinese Villages," *China Quarterly* 162 (2001): 532-5.

[64] The elections of LPC delegates itself is carefully orchestrated by the CCP. For a detailed account of electorates and selectorates at the township level see Melanie Manion, "Chinese Democratization in Perspective: Electorates and Selectorates at the Township Level," *China Quarterly* 163 (2000): 764-82.

China.[65] And what is more, some localities experimented with more direct involvement of residents. The first of these experiments was conducted in Nancheng Township, Sichuan Province, at the end of 1998 and has been described as "essentially a carefully conducted political show"[66] since in the two-stage process of candidate selection voters' choice was severely circumscribed. Another author praised the historical significance of the fact that direct voting for the whole township leadership was possible, but criticized procedural flaws like the highly restrictive qualifications to stand as candidate and the adoption of mechanisms (like *haixuan*) developed for VC-elections but unsuitable for a wider electorate.[67] The controlled nature of the process is explained by the fact that the provincial CCP organization department took the initiative to arrange this election. Yet, the motivation of these cadres to do so remains obscure. In fact, the whole election was kept secret for more than two years.[68] Therefore, the first township election to grab the headlines in China and abroad was the now well-known election in Buyun, Sichuan Province, conducted only shortly after Nancheng's.[69] Here, the motivations of bureaucratic entrepreneurs, the leaders of Shizhong City, seem clearer. In the face of economic difficulties they attempted to regain legitimacy with the populace and to present themselves as successful in political reforms towards their superiors. However, these cadres legitimized their experiment with the general political trend after the 15th Party Congress of 1997 and instigated a demand for reform from below to share the political risks involved between different administrative levels.[70] Though not without flaws itself the Buyun election process surpassed the Nancheng experiment in being freer, fairer and more competitive in almost all aspects.[71] The central leadership reacted with a harsh condemnation of this election process and tried—but failed—to institute a news blackout. Although this condemnation itself was the target of a number of criticisms so far no other local experiment went that far again.[72] Those applied for example an open nomination process or a vote of confidence to align candidate selection and voters' preferences, leaving the final ballot to LPC delegates.[73]

Although not much is known about the motivations involved it is interesting to note that several of these testing grounds of electoral reform had been demonstration-sites for villagers' self-administration before.[74] Therefore, it seems plausible to assume that the officials

---

[65] See for example Jin Taijun and Shi Congmei, *Xiang cun guanxi yu cunmin zizhi* [*Township-Village Relations and Villagers' Self-administration*] (Guangzhou: Guandong renmin chubanshe, 2002), 158-60. See also Zhang Qingcai and Huang Qiang, "Kuoda jiceng minzhu zhi wo jian" [Our Views on the Expansion of Grassroots Democracy], in *Jiceng minzhu yu shehui fazhan* [*Grassroots Democracy and Social Development*], ed. Zhang Zhirong and Yang Haijiao (Beijing: Shijie zhishi chubanshe, 2001), 38.

[66] Li, "Politics," 710.

[67] See Li Fan et al., Chuangxin yu fazhan. *Xiangzhenzhang xuanju zhidu gaige* [*Innovation and Development. The Reform of the Township Head Electoral System*] (Beijing: Dongfang chubanshe, 2002), 386-8. Apart from the head of the township government, the vice heads were also elected.

[68] Li, "Politics," 709-10.

[69] For a detailed account see Li, Chuangxin yu fazhan, 115-52.

[70] See Li, "Politics," 710-13.

[71] Li, "Politics," 714-5.

[72] On this debate see Li, "Politics," 716-9. For a sample of arguments in defence of the election see Li, Chuangxin yu fazhan,182-4.

[73] On the experiments of Zhuoli Township, Shanxi Province, and Shenzhen's Dapeng Town, Guangdong Province, see Li, Chuangxin yu fazhan, 71-96, and on the experiment of Xincai County, Henan Province see Li, "Politics," 720.

[74] This is true of Meishan Prefecture, in which Nancheng is situated. (Li, "Politics,"709) This is also the case in Linyi and Hequ, where the two-ballot system for village Party secretaries was first developed. See Shi Weimin, *Gongxuan yu zhixuan. Xiangzhen renda xuanju zhidu yanjiu* [*Open Selection and Direct Election.*

involved had come to see political innovations as a way to improve career prospects as Li Lianjiang has suggested.[75] In any case, this is a more plausible explanation than the one offered by these cadres themselves that they were enthused about political reform by Jiang Zemin's praise for grassroots democracy during his address to the 15th CCP Congress. Seen in context, this eight line paragraph is hardly arousing, but rather the usual musing about "deepening reform" prevailing throughout this document of more than fifty pages.[76] If these cadres were encouraged by mixed signals from higher levels they seemingly were acutely aware of the risks involved, too.[77] Otherwise it would not be understandable why they attempted to keep the electoral experiments secret. An election would only be deemed successful if the chaos which opponents of too much democracy fear does not break out. Therefore, the hope of those local reformers probably was to let some time pass before claiming a successful political innovation.[78] However, the time obviously was not yet ripe for the adoption even of some experimental-sites in township electoral reform since these local bureaucratic entrepreneurs could obviously not find a policy champion in the highest level leadership.

POLICY ADVOCATES AND POLICY ENTREPRENEURS

A lively Chinese research community interested in rural political reforms has developed in the 1990s. Here, opponents of VC-elections are in the minority and we find many policy advocates who engage in both creation and design of policies.[79] This is largely done through case-studies—sometimes conducted with investigative methods—that point to local innovations, publicize them and add to their design in the form of policy proposals. Among the huge number of publications on the reforms discussed in this paper some of the most outstanding works emanated from Huazhong Normal University's Rural Problems Research Center where Xu Yong and Zhang Yan'an act as general editors of a book series on village governance. Another important research unit is the Center for Public Policy Research at the Chinese Academy of Social Sciences, headed by Bai Gang. Although the actual impact of scholarly work on the policy process is notoriously hard to assess, there can be no doubt that these think-tanks and other academics have played a role in the elaboration of villagers' self-administration legislation. And should a Party leader decide to act as policy champion for the

---

Research on the Electoral System of Township Peoples Congresses] (Beijing: Zhongguo shehui kexue chubanshe, 2000), 351, 360.

[75] See Li, "Politics," 722-3.

[76] See Jiang Zemin, "Gaoju Deng Xiaoping sixiang de weida qizhi, ba jianshe you Zhongguo tese shehui zhuyi shiye quanmian tuixiang ershiyi shiji" [Hold High the Great Banner of Deng Xiaoping Theory for an All-round Advancement of the Cause of Building Socialism with Chinese Characteristics], in: *Zhongguo gongchandang di shiwu ci quanguo daibiao dahui wenjian huibian* [*Documents of the 15th National Congress of the Chinese Communist Party*] (Beijing: Renmin chubanshe, 1997), 33.

[77] In the case of the Nancheng election the CCP organization department of Sichuan Province was the source of encouragement (Li, "Politics," 709). White (1998) even cites a CCP Central Committee document of June 1998 which "announced the Party's intention to 'make active efforts' to extend elections to the township level." Unfortunately, this quote is not set into its context, so its nature remains hard to judge. White Tyrene, "Village Elections: Democracy from the Bottom Up?," *Current History* (September 1998): 267.

[78] See Anne Thurston, "Democracy and Grassroots Change in China," in *Political, Economic, and Social Change in China: Prospects for Instability*, ed. Denise Groves (Berlin: Stiftung Wissenschaft und Politik, 2001), 52.

[79] See also the analysis of that debate in Liu Yawei, "Consequences of Villager Committee Elections in China. Better Governance or More Consolidation of State Power," *China Perspectives* 31 (2000): 21-4.

introduction of direct elections at the township-level he will probably turn to those academics who have previously released works on the topic to get their support in designing a policy. Another group of policy advocates in China has a uniquely strong presence in the field of rural governance reforms. Since the MCA has been quick to realize the potential of foreign academics and non-governmental organizations (NGOs) to strengthen its case for villagers' self-administration, those actors have been involved in the scene throughout the 1990s.[80] They have not only conducted election observations and brought international publicity to the program of village elections, but they also have made real impact on discussions and even the actual design of election laws.[81] Foreign academics and NGOs involved in discussions about future reforms will probably continue to exert an influence on policy-making, but they will have to be careful not to be seen as lecturing Chinese about democracy as doing so would not be politically acceptable to the party-state. One way to get around this is pursued by the Ford Foundation in collaboration with the Carter Center. In 2002 these institutions started to jointly publish a book series entitled Contemporary China's Rural Governance and Election Observation. Thus, they provide a forum for critical publications on rural governance by Chinese academics and practitioners of rural governance and act as policy advocates in an indirect way. It is the author's impression that the Chinese and international researchers as well as foreign NGOs and the MCA are connected in a strong network that as a community is driving for more reforms. There are now even signs that a new type of actor is about to emerge in China, namely the policy entrepreneur, that is "an individual working outside the formal government system to introduce and implement innovations."[82] In the 1980s Chinese intellectuals with a mind for political reform usually tried to work from within the system. Even the few cases left outside generally tried to be integrated into it.[83] Now at least some individuals are beginning to act as policy entrepreneurs. They are actively engaged in instigating local election experiments, contribute to policy design through commenting on political development in his own research publications and try to implement reformist policies on the ground in acting as consultants to local governments. The direction of their work is clear. According to one of this group "VC-elections have outlived their historical mission. Now it is time to move on to direct elections of the township head."[84] As shown above, some local officials are beginning to feel the same and there are definitely more local experiments underway than we know about since by intent these are kept secret at first.[85]

[80] On this see Kelliher, "Debate," 75-7.

[81] See Shi, "Village Committee Elections," 408-10. See also Becky Shelley, "Political Globalization and the Politics of Organisations: The Case of Village Democracy in China," *Australian Journal of Political Science* 35, no. 2 (2000): 130-1. Shelley also provides a fuller account of NGO activities in this policy area.

[82] C. Kaye Bragg, "Crossing the River by Groping for Stones: Factors Reshaping the Policy Innovation Process for Chinese Water Policies" (paper Presented at the 2nd International Convention of Asia Scholars, Berlin, Germany, 9-12 August 2001), 6.

[83] For a case study on Chen Ziming and Wang Juntao see George Black and Robin Munro, *Black Hands of Beijing. Lives of Defiance in China's Democracy Movement* (New York: John Wiley & Sons, 1993).

[84] Personal communication with the author, March 2001.

[85] See International Republican Institute, *Elections at the Grassroots. An Assessment of Local Elections in Guangxi, Hebei, Henan, Shanxi, and Yunnan Provinces, People's Republic of China* (Washington: International Republican Institute, 2000), 24-5. See also Thurston, "Democracy," 52.

CONCLUSIONS

This discussion of grassroots political reform in rural China has identified a number of actors playing significant roles in the initiation, design and implementation of new political institutions and governance mechanisms. Since the actual extent to which these changes to the basic-level political system have already taken hold in the Chinese countryside is impossible to gauge, we are at a loss to accurately assess the magnitude of the impacts these different reforms have had on rural political live in different regions. This article instead focused on the patterns according to which reforms were initiated, elaborated and adopted. The major finding is that no actor or single group of actors is in a position to successfully promote political reform on his or its own. In the context of a political system characterized by fragmented authoritarianism not even the highest leaders can see their policy initiatives implemented smoothly without building a coalition of supporters. Similarly, the actors trying to behave like entrepreneurs, that is innovating, designing and implementing a policy, need to rally policy advocates and policy champions around them to get their initiatives adopted. In other words, the different functions of the entrepreneurial process tend to become divided among several actors and public entrepreneurship is facilitated by a tentative coalition of actors functioning as nodes of a network.[86] The political reforms under scrutiny are best explained as products of this whole network rather than as emanating from either the apex or the bottom of the political system. The bottom-up pattern of reform tends to neglect that the peasantry needed a window of opportunity provided by a divided political elite to see its moves consolidated. Conversely, the top-down pattern is prone to ignore that leaders were consistently driven forward to more and more far-reaching reforms by initiatives from below. And both cannot account for the entrepreneurial role played by bureaucrats who engaged in far more than just policy implementation in being inventive themselves, creating environments conducive for inventions or appropriating innovations by others. In sum, the explanation for rural political reforms offered here points to another pattern of policy-making which could tentatively be called a nodal pattern since each of the nodes within the described network has a significant and necessary role to play to realize grassroots political reforms. Certainly, more research in this vein will be needed before such a reform pattern can be more confidently claimed in existence. For this research, this study can offer but a starting point.

However, a conclusion which can be drawn regarding the study of policy-making in China is that we sometimes might not be able to identify the single most important actor behind a particular policy, but instead need to look for the *processes* leading to change if we want to more fully account for the driving forces of political development. This finding parallels the conclusion some time ago drawn by Lieberthal and Oksenberg that the PRC's policy process is "*disjointed*, with key decisions made in a number of different and only loosely coordinated agencies and inter-agency decisional bodies."[87] But it extends this view by also taking societal actors into account which function as initiators, advocates or entrepreneurs of policies. Regarding further political reforms in the Chinese countryside the prospect for the moment is somewhat dim. Despite the usual pledge to extend grassroots democracy Jiang Zemin made in his address to the 16th National Congress of the CCP, the

[86] This is consistent with the findings presented by Bragg, "Crossing the River," 18-9.

[87] Kenneth G. Lieberthal and Michel Oksenberg, *Policy Making in China. Leaders, Structures, and Processes* (Princeton: Princeton University Press, 1988), 24.

Central Committee's Document No. 12 from July 2001 which declared direct elections for the position of township head unconstitutional and illegal remains in force.[88] However, as we have seen there is accumulating evidence of stirrings for further political reforms in the countryside. Therefore, if one or some of the leaders rising in the aftermath of Hu Jintao's succession to Jiang chose to act as a policy champion for such a reform he would find other actors to support his move. Nevertheless, given that the township-level belongs to the formal state bureaucracy and not the self-administration level this would be a bold move indeed since leading-cadre positions within the state administration fall within the purview of the Party's *nomenklatura* system. Furthermore, with the adoption of direct elections to executive positions at the township-level the conflict of elected officials and Party secretaries only accountable to higher levels which is currently widely perceptible at the village level would probably be moved one step up the administrative ladder. And finally, elections are but one side of the policy-cycle which also includes decision-making and policy implementation.[89] Therefore, even where elections are successfully instituted it is still too early to speak of full-fledged democracy and this would be true of the township-level, too.

[88] This document is cited in Li, "Politics," 704. For the English version of Jiang Zemin's speech refer to <www.16congress.org.cn/english/featires/49007.htm> (7 February 2003).

[89] See Björn Alpermann, "The Post-Election Administration of Chinese Villages," *China Journal* 46, (2001): 45-67.

In: China: Economic, Political and Social Issues
Editors: J. M. Phillips and L. J. Moore
ISBN: 978-60456-727-4

Chapter 9

CHINA'S RELATIONS WITH CENTRAL ASIAN STATES AND PROBLEMS WITH TERRORISM*

Dewardric L. McNeal

This chapter provides an overview of the Muslim separatist movement in China's northwestern Xinjiang Uighur Autonomous Region, China's attempts to stifle activities, which it considers terrorism, and implications for U.S. policy. Some analysts suggest that the U.S.-led campaign against terrorism may make it difficult to pressure the Chinese government on human rights and religious freedoms, particularly as they relate to Uighur Muslims in Xinjiang.

China also has reportedly stepped up its suppression of Uighur Muslims following the attacks in the United States on September 11, 2001. A policy question for the United States is how to balance the anti-terrorist campaign with traditional concerns over human rights in China's western region, and how to react should Beijing use the threat of terrorism to abrogate rights of autonomy in Xinjiang as provided for in China's constitution.

BACKGROUND AND OVERVIEW

Over one hundred years after Qing Dynasty troops gained control over East Turkestan,[1] currently known as Xinjiang Uighur Autonomous Region, some ethnic Uighurs in Xinjiang continue to aspire to reestablish sovereignty over their homeland. Uighurs did briefly establish the Republic of East Turkestan during the Chinese civil war (1945-1949), but self-rule came to an abrupt end when Communist troops entered Xinjiang in 1949. The Chinese government immediately began to consolidate its control over Xinjiang by sending retired ethnic Han Chinese soldiers into Xinjiang to form new units called "Production and Construction" Corps (Bingtuan).[2] The Chinese government has continued to resettle the

---

* Excerpted from CRS Report RL31213 dated 10-07-02.

[1] Qing Dynasty troops after encountering strong resistance to Uighur fighters established its rule in 1884 and renamed East Turkestan, Xinjiang, which means “new frontier” or “new territory”.

[2] See Human Rights Watch Report, *Xinjiang, China's Restive Northwest, 1998.*

Xinjiang area with ethnic Han Chinese migrants and with other ethnic minority groups. This has exacerbated tensions with the Uighurs, who have witnessed the Han population in Xinjiang, once a mere 6 to 7 percent, balloon to approximately 40 to 45 percent of Xinjiang's total population.[3]

Fearing continued cultural marginalization and religious persecution, Uighurs have become increasingly virulent in their protests against Chinese rule in Xinjiang. As a result of these protests and increased violence, in April 1996 the PRC government launched a series of new crackdowns and a controversial "Strike Hard" (Yan Da) campaign to reestablish order in Xinjiang. This has resulted in a number of Uighur leaders being killed, jailed, or driven into exile.[4]

The collapse of the Soviet Union in 1991 and the establishment of independent states by the former Soviet Central Asian republics, encouraged some Uighurs in their aspirations to reestablish an independent homeland. According to some analysts familiar with the region, many Uighurs in Xinjiang felt that having their own state "cuts to the core of their ethnic identity and ultimate survival as a culture."[5] Furthermore, other minorities in Xinjiang, the Kazakhs, Kyrgyz, Tajiks, Uzbeks, and Mongols, all can look to sovereign states that border China, as pillars of "cultural and ethnic pride."[6] However, with no real chance to see their own dream of an independent homeland become a reality because of the PRC government's strong determination to retain control of Xinjiang at all cost, a number of underground separatist groups began to spring up throughout Xinjiang and the Uighur diaspora.[7]

The PRC's Xinjiang fears were compounded by a number of significant events going on in Russia, Afghanistan, and Central Asia beginning in 1996. The Russians were prosecuting a second war in the break-away republic of Chechnya. Tajikistan was still suffering from the effects of its civil war. And the Uzbek government, led by President Islam Karimov, was dealing with an increasing threat from Islamic fundamentalists looking to establish a radical Islamic state in Uzbekistan. China feared that all of these events, which involved "Islamic fundamentalist" elements, would spread to Xinjiang and radicalize the Uighur groups in Xinjiang. However, the one event that would prove the most problematic to China and the entire Central Asian region was the fall of Kabul, Afghanistan to the Taliban Militia in September 1996.[8]

The Taliban movement has been accused by leaders in Beijing and secular leaders throughout Central Asia of spreading its radical views of Islam into many parts of Central and South Asia, leading in some cases to a rise of "Islamic fundamentalist" groups and activity, including bombing, assassinations, and other acts of terror and subversion. In particular, China and the Central Asian states over the years have charged that the Taliban and their

---

[3] See People's Republic of China, Year 2000 Census.

[4] See Uyghuramerican.org media reports, " Central Asia: Uighurs Say States Yield To Chinese," by Jean-Christopher Peuch, [http://www.uyghuraiiierican.org/mediareports/2001/CenasiayieldtoCHin.htrnl].

[5] See Asia Week Inside Story China: Beijing vs. Islam, by Michael Winchester, [http://www.asiaweek.com/asiaweek/97/1024/l~s l.html].

[6] Ibid.

[7] The Scotsman, Uighurs warn of return to terror, by Damien McElroy, May 31, 2000

[8] See transcripts from BBC News Report: ffl ho *Are the Taleban, December 20, 2000.*

close associate, Osama bin Laden, have been funding, arming, and training a number of Uighurs, Kyrgyz, Kazakhs, and Uzbeks in camps located inside Afghanistan.[9]

In 1996, China, Russia, Tajikistan, Kazakhstan, and Kyrgyzstan formed a group known as the "Shanghai-Five" to serve as a bulwark against the spread of Islamic fundamentalist subversion. It was initially designed to be an informal grouping to discuss ways to resolve old border disputes and fortify common borders against terrorist and separatist activity. However, the group's members soon decided they needed to cooperate more thoroughly to deal with what they called the "three evil forces"-terrorism, separatism, and extremism.[10] In the summer of 2001, the Shanghai-Five adn-fitted Uzbekistan into the organization and established a permanent regional group called the Shanghai Cooperation Organization (SCO). The new organization approved two joint communiques that stressed its intentions to cooperate on combating terrorism and to establish an anti-terrorist center in Bishkek, Kyrgyzstan.

However, the terrorist attacks against the United States on September 11, 2001 appear to have caused an unintended halt to a number of the SCO plans, at least for the near term. Shortly after the September attacks, the United States made counter terrorism its number one priority. Some China and Central Asian analysts indicate that now that the United States is taking on global terrorism, particularly in the Central Asian region, the Shanghai Cooperation Organization is beginning to feel a bit "overshadowed" and marginalized.[11] Surprisingly to some, Russia, Tajikistan, Uzbekistan, Kazakhstan, and Kyrgyzstan are all providing robust support for the U.S.-led counter-terrorism effort. Analysts say that with the United States now "monopolizing" the agenda on anti-terrorism in the region, the Chinese are starting to s fear that a major component of their Central Asian geopolitical strategy is being gradually neutralized.[12]

U.S. Policy Implications

The attacks on September 11, 2001 and the U.S.-led retaliation in Afghanistan has wide-ranging, policy implications for U.S. China policy in the short term, and may cause a number of policy shifts and challenges in the long term, One of the most difficult challenges is how the United States will balance its need to create a broadbased multi-state coalition to fight against terrorism with traditional American obligations to protect and defend religious freedoms and human rights. According to a number of analysts, China, Russia, and the Central Asian states, in exchange for lending support and cooperation to the U.S. in the fight against global terrorism, may want "support for their campaigns against groups they view as terrorists," and a reduction in the level of criticism over what the United States views as human rights abuses.[13] This may anger religious and human rights activists, who may view it as capitulation of American values and principles. Although it may be important to review

---

[9] BBC Monitoring Central Asia, "Central Asians, Uighurs training in Pakistan, Afghanistan for "subversive" Acts," July 11, 2000.

[10] See Institute for Peace and Conflict Studies article No. 521, Shanghai Five: Emerging Foreign Policy Dimensions, by P.A. Mathew, July 15, 2001.

[11] *Wall Street Journal*, "Chinese Goals Take A Backseat As U.S. Rises To The Fore In Asia," by Andrew Higgins and Charles Hutzler, October 19, 2001.

[12] Ibid.

[13] *South China Morning Post*, "Beijing Moscow support Afghan coalition government." October 11, 2001.

and reformulate those policies to make it easier to fulfill the requirements and goals of a multi-state coalition, some policy makers argue that an equally important consideration for U.S. policyrnakers pursuing the campaign against terrorism is ensuring that the terrorism campaign does not give a blank check to authoritarian regimes pursuing their own domestic agendas of civil, political, and religious repression. There is also the question of whether the U.S.-led campaign against international terrorism should apply to groups seeking religious and political rights in authoritarian countries. On the one hand, it may appear that some Uighurs' ties with extremist groups could justify a crackdown by Beijing similar to that occurring in other countries. On the other hand, the political unrest by some Uighurs could be a logical response to suppression of their constitutional rights and the settlement of traditional Uighur lands by ethnic Chinese. The policy dilemma for the United States therefore is the degree to which it may decline to react to possible human rights violations against Uighurs in Xinjiang in return for Chinese cooperation in the campaign against terrorism.

In the months leading up to the events of September 11, 2001, the United States and China seemed headed toward becoming "strategic competitors" or even adversaries. Before September 11, 2001, Sino-U.S. relations were plagued by a number of controversial issues such as national missile defense, U.S. weapons sales to Taiwan, the EP-3 spy plane collision, Chinese missile exports to Pakistan and elsewhere, and continued criticisms over China's violations of human rights and religious freedoms. But the tragedy of September 11, 2001, seemed to have pushed Sino-US relations in a different direction. The Chinese began to stress a common interest in combating terrorism, and U. S. policy makers began building a broad-based multinational coalition against terrorism that would include the PRC. Some see the anti-terrorism campaign as a new potential framework for a more constructive and cooperative relationship.

Despite this new cooperative environment and concessions that some in the foreign policy establishment consider as necessary to form the multi-state coalition against terrorism, the Bush Administration has also shown a willingness to stress the values and principles of human rights and religious freedoms, particularly with regard to China. Although the United States has lifted some sanctions against nations that are cooperating in the war on terrorism (e.g., Pakistan), neither the Bush Administration nor Congress, which has oversight authority on the waiving of sanctions placed on the PRC, has shown an inclination toward extending a waiver of any existing sanctions placed an the PRC.[14]

China reportedly expects the United States to moderate criticisms over the PRC's handling of Uighur separatism in Xinjiang. However, at the APEC Summit in Shanghai, in October 2001, President Bush made a statement that was interpreted as a strong reminder that the U.S. does not approve of China's policies toward ethnic minorities and does not intend to forgo its responsibilities to support human rights and religious freedoms. Bush stated that the Chinese should not attempt to use the war on terrorism as an "excuse to persecute

---

14 There are a number of existing sanctions contained in Section 902 of P.L. 10 1-246, put in place after the Tiananmen crack-down, which ban the sale and export of a number of items to China, such as criminal detection and crowd control instruments, munitions including helicopters and helicopter parts, and satellites for launch by Chinese launch vehicles. Shortly after the September 11 attacks, several media reports hinted that in exchange for Chinese support and cooperation in the war on terrorism, some of these sanctions would be eased or dropped.

minorities."[15] China nevertheless, insists that there are a number of Uighur groups that are actively involved in cross border "terrorism" and that it has the right to combat what it views as "terrorism" within and around its borders.

Also China and the SCO are being overshadowed by the U.S. presence and leadership in Central Asia at the moment, but Beijing may attempt to reassert its influence as a power broker in the region when the fighting in Afghanistan has died down by revitalizing the SCO mechanism. However, the terrorist attacks on September 11, 2001 and the U.S.-led retaliation has caused a range of geopolitical realignments among nations in Central Asia, most notably among the member states of the Shanghai Cooperation Organization. After the attacks on the United States, a number of SCO members immediately pledged fall support and cooperation to the United States. This apparent geopolitical realignment, combined with the possibility of long-term U.S. troop deployment in Central Asia, may raise concerns among the military and political elites in Beijing that the United States is engaged in a strategy of long term "containment" or "encirclement" of China on both its eastern and western borders. Analysts caution that the PRC has not lost its resolve to extend its sphere of influence into Central Asia nor has it abandoned its geopolitical strategy of using the SCO as its primary vehicle to achieve this goal, This could mean an increase in the possibilities for competition between China and the United States over influence in Central Asia.

History and Composition of Uighur Movement

By the 14th century, ethnic Uighurs, a Turkic speaking people from Central Asia were fully converted followers of Islam. They lived in ancient cities of great wealth and learning like Tashkent, in modern day Uzbekistan, and Kashgar in modem day Xinjiang, Western China. However, between the mid-1700's and the mid-1800's China conquered most of the Uighur homeland. The ethnic Manchu of Northern China[16]and Czarist Russian empires annexed the entire region of Central Asia by the late 1 800's. Turkic-speaking peoples from West and East Turkestan were eventually brought under the sovereignty of these two empires. Although the Uighurs reestablished East Turkestan just after World War II, Chinese Communist forces reincorporated East Turkestan into China at the end of the Chinese civil war, and East Turkestan became known as the Xinjiang Uighur Autonomous Region. The name was supposed to reflect the large degree of autonomy granted by the PRC to Uighurs in the constitution. However, some Uighurs allege that the name is only symbolic and that little autonomy and rights are enjoyed by Uighurs presently.

In 1991, Central Asian Muslims such as the Kazakhs, Uzbeks, Tajiks, Turkmen, and Krgyz-ethnic groups of the former Soviet republics-finally won their independence and set up sovereign states. For the first time in several hundred years they governed their own independent homelands. Although the Uighurs did not gain independence like their Central Asian cousins, some saw the sovereignty gains of the newly independent states of Central Asia as a source of inspiration for their own struggle and as a safety zone from which to

---

15 *The Washington Post*, "China Vows To Help in Terror Fight," by Mike Alien and Philip P. Pan, October 19, 2001.

16 The Manchu ethnic group launched the Qing Dynasty (1644-1911) after overthrowing the ethnic Han Chinese of the Ming Dynasty. It was the Manchus that first incorporated Uighur areas in Central Asia and later brutally repressed a rebellion in the late 1800's.

organize an independence movement. Analysts note that the Xinjiang Uighur Autonomous Region shares a relatively porous border with Kazakhstan, Tajikistan, Kyrgyzstan, Pakistan, and Afghanistan,[17] and according to a number of reports these states have increasingly become a source of ideology, information gathering, arms procurement, and training for some Uighur groups in their struggle against PRC rule.[18]

Although the Uighur opposition to Chinese rule has existed in many forms throughout history, it has become more violent in recent years. Although some Uighurs have been trying to attain independence for a number of years, they have remained largely out of the view of mainstream media and have gained relatively little support from the international community. Some analysts argue that this is because the Uighur community lacks a single charismatic leader like Tibet's Dalai Lama, and because the Uighur resistance groups are largely fractured and disorganized, and lack the ability to gain the full attention of key states such as Britain and the United States.[19] Other analysts and human rights activists argue that the reason that the Uighur resistance movement has trouble gaining robust support and international attention is because it lacks a well funded lobby effort such as that of Tibet and Taiwan for advocating its cause in the West. These analysts point out that Uighurs are generally extremely poor and geographically isolated in a corner of the world that is largely forgotten and overwhelmingly populated by Muslims.[20] Analysts also argue that Beijing has kept international attention away from the Uighur resistance movement by severely restricting access to Xinjiang Uighur Autonomous Region.[21] According to these analysts, the PRC did not want to cast any light on the "brutal tactics" that police have used to stamp out the resistance to Chinese rule.[22]

However, the events of September 11, 2001 have turned the attention of many analysts and journalists to the Uighur struggle, In particular, there appears to be interest in a number of reports about alleged links between some Uighur groups and the radical Islamic elements in Central Asia. Specifically, analysts have focused on the allegations that linkages exist between Osama bin Laden's Al Qaeda network and some Uighur groups throughout Central Asia. In a November 2001 briefing, PRC Foreign Ministry spokesman Zhu Bangzao listed more than 10 separate organizations based in Central Asia, Afghanistan, and Xinjiang that he accused of "conducting terrorist violence" in Xinjiang and other parts of China.[23]

---

17 Xinjiang Autonomous Region shares a 5,000km border with the five states mentioned above, roughly 1,500km of the border has Turkic-speaking peoples on both sides.

18 Center for Computational Science at the University of Kentucky, "Uighurs' Independence is Important to the Survival of Their People," by Gwynne Dyer, [http://www.ccs.uky.edu/-rakhim/doe_files/gwyne_dyer.html].

19 Dialog.com, "International Data Reference on Terrorist, Guerilla and Insurgent Groups Asia, Indo China and the Pacific Rim," May 1999, [http://www.dialog.com/info/home/australia/fastways/terrorism_in_china.html].

20 *Christian Science Monitor,* "Roots of a Race Riot," by Robert Marquand, July 18, 2001.

21 *The Wall Street Journal*, "China Provides Extensive Briefing On Separatists in Xinjiang," by Charles Hutzler, November 15, 2001.

22 Ibid.

23 Ibid.

Armed Uighur Groups Alleged to Be Active in Xinjiang

A number of armed Uighur groups are believed to be active in the opposition to what they view as Chinese "occupation" of East Turkestan. Some of these groups advocate total separation from China and have resorted to violence against the PRC over the last several years. In late 1990, the level of violence in Xinjiang began to increase when a small uprising erupted in Baren, a town near Kashgar.[24] The PRC government cracked down swiftly and harshly, and local security forces were given wide-ranging power to root out any element that "harms national unity" and "the solidarity of ethnic groups or social stability.[25] The Baren uprising, reportedly led by Abdul Kasim, laid the foundation for an underground-armed struggle against the Chinese in Xinjiang. In 1995, PRC security forces reportedly found a stowaway clutch of some 4,000 sticks of dynamite, 600 guns with ammunition, and 3,000ka of explosives.[26] In April 1996 Chinese security forces arrested more than 1,700 suspected "terrorists." One month later a high ranking official of the Xinjiang Peoples Political Consultative Conference[27] was assassinated, and a number of bombings occurred along Chinese railroad lines,[28]Uighur armed resistance groups allegedly detonated three time bombs on buses in Uighur on the day of Deng Xiaoping's funeral. By late 1998, China became concerned that the violence in Xinjiang was spiraling out of control. Beijing began to pressure the Central Asian states to assist with efforts to identify groups and leaders throughout the Diaspora. Beijing also insisted that any Xinjiang Uighur found outside Xinjiang be extradited to the PRC, and that all outside sources of assistance and shelter for the Xinjiang-based Uighur movement be cut off.

The PRC has accused a number of Xinjiang based Uighur groups of committing "terrorist" acts in Xinjiang and other parts of China and Central Asia, In light of the global anti-terror campaign, some western journalists have begun to focus more attention on these groups. They include:

United Revolutionary Front of Eastern Turkistan- led by 77-year-old Yusupbek Mukhlisi, also known as Modan Mukhlisi. This group claims to have more than thirty armed units working in and around Xinjiang, including expert bomb makers. Mukhlisi fled China in 1960, and for more than thirty years he advocated peaceful resistance to what he calls "Chinese rule" over East Turkestan.[29] However, this relatively moderate policy was disavowed in March 1997 when the United National Revolutionary Front of East Turkestan and two other Kazakhstan-based Uighur groups issued a joint declaration stating that they

---

[24] See Laogai Research Foundation Special Report, "The World Bank and Chinese Military. Ignorance-Incompetence- or Cover Up?," April 4, 1996.

[25] Dialog.com, "International Data Reference on Terrorist, Guerilla and Insurgent Groups Asia, Indo China and Pacific Rim," May 1999 [www.dialog.com/info/home/australia/fastways/terrorism_in_china.html].

[26] Ibid.

[27] The Political Consultative Conference an entity controlled by the Communist Party that is made up of minority or non-Communist political parties. It has no real power and serves no real political purpose such as being an opposition party to the Chinese Communist Party. There are National Peoples Consultative Conference and several Provincial Political Consultative Conferences in China.

[28] Dialog.com. "International Data Reference on Terrorist, Guerilla and Insurgent Groups Asia, Indo China and Pacific Rim, May 1999, [www.dialog.com/info/home/australia/fastways/terrorism_in_china.html].

[29] Radio Free Europe and Radio Liberty Online, "Kazakhstan: Exiled Uighurs Step Up Fight Against Beijing," by Jeremy Bransten, 14 October 1997, [http:www.rferl.org/nca/features/1997/10/F.RU.971014135113.html].

were "taking up arms against Chinese oppression."[30] In a recent article published in the *Japan Times*, Mukhlisi boasts of having a "well developed" movement in Xinjiang and says that he has "twenty-two million Uighurs" ready to conduct armed struggle against the Chinese. He claims to have "ties to several groups" across the border in Kazakhstan.[31]

Organization for the Liberation of Uighurstan- led by Ashir Vakhidi. This group is said to be internally divided over many personal and political issues. Reportedly these divisions include disagreement over whether to use East Turkestan or Uighurstan as the name of an Uighur sovereign state.[32] However, the group is committed to armed struggle against Chinese "occupation" of the "Uighur homeland."

Wolves of Lop Nor- this group has not publicly listed its leader, but it is reported to have claimed responsibility for a number of bombings on trains and for several assassinations in Xinjiang. According to reports, this group released a statement to Taiwan radio stating that all of its attacks are in response to "suppression of pro-independence activism" of Uighurs in Xinjiang by Chinese government forces. Additionally, following a Beijing bombing, this group revealed that the attack had been planned by Uighur exiles in Kazakhstan and that more events would be planned. Although there have been no incidents or threats against Chinese nuclear facilities, some China watchers point out that the city of Lop Nor in Xinjiang Uighur Autonomous Region, home of the "Wolves," is also the site of one of China's largest nuclear test sites.[33]

Xinjiang Liberation Organization and Uighur Liberation Organization (ULO)- reportedly active in Uzbekistan and Kyrgyzstan. According to some reports, they are responsible for the assassinations of Uighurs who they viewed as "collaborators" with the PRC and Central Asian governments.[34] There are also reports that Uighurs from this group are dispersed throughout the region;[35] and that the countries of Tajikistan, China, Uzbekistan, Afghanistan, and the Russian republic of Chechnya are home to ULO members.[36]

Home of East Turkistan Youth- (branded as Xinjiang's Hamas) is a radical group thought to be committed to armed struggle against the Chinese in Xinjiang. This group reportedly has over 2,000 members and allegedly has undergone explosives training in camps inside Afghanistan.[37]

Free Turkistan Movement- led by Uighur and reported "Islamic fundamentalist" Abdul Kasim, this group led an uprising in April 1990 in the Xinjiang town of Baren. Although figures vary, PRC officials report 22 people were killed in the incident. The Baren incident touched off harsh crackdowns on religious activity throughout Xinjiang. Additionally,

---

[30] Ibid.

[31] *The Japan Times Online*, "Fighting for independence in the shadow of a Goliath," by Russell Working, November 6, 2001, [http://www.japantimes.co.jp/cgi-bin/getarticle.pl5? eo200lllO6al.html].

[32] Dialogue.com, "International Data Reference on Terrorist, Guerilla and Insurgent Groups Asia, Indo China and the Pacific Rim, May 1999.

[33] Ibid.

[34] See stratfor.com, "Chinese Cleanup Targets Uighurs," May 16, 2001, [http://www.stratfor.com/asia/commentary/0105162140.html].

[35] These reports from Strategic Forcasting Service, an analylitical new service, are attributed to Aziz Soltobaev, on the staff of the American University of Kyrgyzstan.

[36] See Stratfor.com, "Chinese Cleanup Targets Uighurs," May 16, 2001 [http://www.stratfor.com/asia/ commentary0105162140.html].

[37] Federation of American Scientist: Intelligence Resource Program," Uighur Militants: Committee for Eastern Turkistan."

Chinese officials claim that the weapons used in the Baren incident came from Afghan Mujahadeen.[38]

Other Extremist Groups and the Uighur Opposition

Xinjiang Uighur Autonomous Region is home to an estimated 10 million Uighurs, According to some reports there are an additional 500,000 Uighurs in "Western Turkestan," which includes Uzbekistan, Kazakhstan, Tajikistan and Turkmenistan, and another estimated 150,000 Uighurs in Pakistan, Saudi Arabia, Afghanistan, Western Europe, Turkey, and the United States.[39] According to the figures and information listed above, the Uighur Diaspora is surprisingly large and spread throughout several countries. Chinese government officials and a number of Western sources suggest that some of the groups in the Uighur Diaspora are linked to extremist elements in the countries in which they reside. PRC officials allege that these include links to Osama bin Laden's terrorist network. On June 9, 2000, a Bishkek journalist named Aleksandr Knyazev, stated what the Chinese government has believed for several years, that "it is widely known" that "Uighurs are fighting on the Taliban side" in the war in Afghanistan.[40] Knyazev named several well-known groups, such as the Hizb-ut-Tahrir Party and the Islamic Movement of Uzbekistan as having trained and recruited Uighurs. He also stated that he had the opportunity to meet and interview a Uighur captured by the Anti-Taliban forces in Northern Afghanistan; the captured Uighur came from the small town of Aksu in Xinjiang. According to comments made by the Uighur captive, he had received his training in a camp near the Pakistani town of Peshwar.[41]

In another report, the Russian special envoy to Pakistan in September 2000, pointed out that he had identified five camps in Pakistan used to train terrorists, and that there is proof of Chechens, Uzbeks, Tajiks, and Uighurs from China being trained in those camps.[42] According to other reports, some Uighur resistance groups have ties to other groups listed below. This listing, however, does not imply that the groups have significant, or even recognizable, influence on Uighurs living in China.

Tableeghi Jamaat- a Pakistani Islamic missionary organization that China believes has supplied Uighurs with arms and recruited Uighurs to train and fight in Afghanistan. In 1998, Krygyz authorities broke up a faction of this group led by a Chinese-born Uighur called 'Kasarli,' showing that China and the Central Asian states were beginning to cooperate on cracking down on the violent groups in Central Asia and Xinjiang.[43] This group has also caused some difficulty in the Chinese-Pakistani relationship over the last couple of years. According to reports that appeared in the ITAR-TASS Russian news agency and Reuters news service in February of 1997, the Chinese government accused this group, and indirectly

[38] *The Pioneer*, "China Tries to quell the Xinjiang uprising", by Aditya Bhagat, February 27, 1997.

[39] See Federation of American Scientist: Intelligence Resource Program, "Uighur militants: Committee for Eastern Turkistan."

[40] BBC Monitoring Central Asia, "Central Asians, Uighurs training in Pakistan, Afghanistan for "subversive" acts," July 11, 2000.

[41] Ibid.

[42] BBC Monitoring South Asia, "Putin envoy says Afghan Taliban training Uighurs, Chechens, Central Asians," September 27, 2000.

[43] Dialogue.com, "International Data Reference on Terrorist, Guerilla and Insurgent Groups Asia, Indo China and the Pacific Rim," May 1999.

the Pakistani government, of distributing religious materials in Xinjiang and with being "actively involved" in violence and unrest in Xinjiang.

Hizb-ut-Tahrir (Islamic Revival)- has a number of cells throughout Central Asia. According to some reports, the goal of this group is to create a "Caliphate" or independent state within the territory that includes parts of China's Xinjiang, Uzbekistan, Tajikistan, and Kyrgyzstan.[44]

Committee for Eastern Turkistan- based in Alma-Ata, Kazakhstan, this group was originally formed by Uighur Guerillas who fought against the Peoples Liberation Army from 1944-1949.[45]

Jamaat-i-Islami- is Pakistan's largest Islamic political party, and is led by Qazi Hussain Ahmad. Several reports indicate that a number of Uighurs, some say hundreds, have been recruited by Jamaat-i-Islami and trained by the Afghan Mujahadeen.[46]

Islamic Movement of Uzbekistan (IMU)- military wing is led by Juma Namangani, who has been recently identified as a top Lieutenant to bin Laden and is accused by many Central Asian states and China of actively recruiting and training a number of Uighurs in the IMU's paramilitary centers in the city of Mazar-e-Sharif, Northern Afghanistan. In addition to being linked to the Taliban and Al Qaeda, the IMU has also been linked to Hizb-ut-Tahrir. The IMU was one of three groups, in addition to the Taliban and Al Qaeda, named in U.S. President George Bush's address before a joint session of Congress on September 20, 2001. Although not independently confirmed, Namangani was reportedly killed in late November 2001, during a battle with the anti-Taliban forces to retain control over Mazar-e-Sharif.

Osama bin Laden's Al Qaeda Organization- reports suggest that some 6,000 to 7,000 foreign fighters and guerillas are in Afghanistan. These mercenaries reportedly include some who are Pakistani, Kyrgyz, Arab, Uzbek, Tajik, Chechen, and also reportedly includes Uighurs from Xinjiang and other parts of the Uighur Diaspora. Allegedly, most of these foreign mercenaries were funded and trained by Osama bin Laden's Al Qaeda organization in Afghanistan.

Non-Violent Uighur Groups and Associations

A number of Uighur groups and individuals advocate only a modicum of autonomy from the PRC. They also claim to want the PRC to only honor its promises of autonomy for minorities as presented in the Chinese Constitution. Some other Uighur groups within Xinjiang and abroad seek independence from the PRC, but seek it through non-violent political activities. For example, there are "Uighur opposition-in-exile" groups in countries such as the United States, Germany, and Turkey. They belong to groups such as the Uyghur American Association and the East Turkestan National Congress, which is a federation of a number of Uighur associations. Some of these non-violent groups, such as the Regional Uighur Organization, also are based in Central Asia.[47] In addition to these groups and

[44] See Uyghuramerican.org, "Central Asia: Uighurs Say States Yield To Chinese," by Jean Cbristophe Peuch, March 29, 2001.

[45] See Federation of American Scientists: Intelligence Resource Program, "Uighur militants Committee for East Turkistan."

[46] *The Pioneer*, "China tries to quell the Xinjiang uprising," by Aditya Bhagat, February 27, 1997.

[47] See Human Rights Watch Backgrounder, China: Human Rights Concerns in Xinjiang, October 11, 2001.

associations, Uighur news groups and media sources are dedicated to reporting on the situation of Uighurs in Xinjiang. For example, the East Turkestan Information Bulletin, published by the East Turkestan Union in Europe (ETUE), a Munich based organization, says that its mission is to "disseminate objective current information on the people, culture and civilization of Eastern Turkestan and to provide a forum for discussion on a wide range of topics and complex issues."[48] According to some analysts, most of these groups and associations have "consistently advocated peaceful means" to gain their independence from the PRC.

Human Rights Issues in Xinjiang

Although for a number of years the PRC government has claimed that some Uighur groups are linked to terrorist groups in Central Asia, until recently the allegations were viewed by many in the West as mere "propaganda" or as an excuse to persecute political dissidents in Xinjiang. According to some analysts and rights activists, one reason that Chinese allegations against Uighurs are so highly disregarded by many in the West is that Beijing is prone to group all Uighurs into the "terrorist" category. Since September 11, however, there has been an increase in the number of reports by outside sources about Uighur violence in Xinjiang, and some of the reports make claims similar to those that have been made by the PRC over the past five years.

However, since the terrorist attacks on the United States, a number of international Uighur groups and activists have been concerned that as the U.S. prosecutes the war on terrorism, the Uighur cause will be viewed in a new unfavorable light by the international community. Uighur activists fear that Chinese complaints about terrorism are becoming more accepted in the west. In a recent interview with the *Washington Post*, imprisoned Uighur businesswoman Rebiya Kadeer's son expressed his concerns that the U.S. will "weaken" its support for human rights among China's minority populations, "especially the Turkic speaking, Uighur Muslims" of Xinjiang.[49]

According to Turdi Ghoja of the Uyghur American Association, the PRC is taking "advantage of the global war on terrorism" to indulge in "killing, torturing, and imprisoning" Uighurs in Xinjiang "without causing too much criticism from the international community."[50] Recently, U.N. High Commissioner for Human Rights Mary Robinson in a meeting with PRC leaders, stressed that the war on terrorism "must not infringe on the human rights of China's Muslims." Robinson told PRC officials that since the September I I attacks, her office has seen a rise in allegations of "summary executions, imprisonment, and torture" of Uighurs, which is considered a serious violation of the principles embodied in the United Nations Covenant on Civil and Political Rights and the Universal Declaration of Human Rights. China is a signatory of both documents.[51]

---

48 See East Turkestan Information Bulletin, [http://www.caccp.org/et/etib3_5.html].

49 *Washington Post*, "Uighur Activist Back U. S. but Worry Their Cause Will Suffer," by John Pomfret, October 13, 2001.

50 See *National Review Online's* Guest Comment, "Meanwhile, In China: On Persecution of Muslims, Christians, and the Falun Gong," by Ann Noonan (Laogai Research Foundation), November 9, 2001.

51 *Los Angeles Times*, "U.N. Voices Concern Over Rise in Alleged Abuse of Chinese Muslims," by Anthony Kuhn, November 10, 200 1.

Additionally, China has drawn criticism from a number of Uighurs and human right advocates because it "consistently fails" to live up to its own constitutional provisions governing autonomous regions.[52] For example, Amnesty International cites several instances of Uighurs being detained "merely for being relatives or friends of political prisoners or fugitives," or they say Uighurs could be detained and held without charge for a number of months, just for rousing suspicions that they are involved in acts deemed harmful to the national security of the state.[53] Chinese Vice Premier Qian Qichen denies these allegations and insists that "China strictly distinguishes the separatists from the rest of the 10 million Chinese Muslims in the Xinjiang region."[54]

SHANGHAI COOPERATION ORGANIZATION

On June 15, 2001, in Shanghai, the heads of states of China, Russia, Kazakhstan, Kyrgyzstan (Kirghizia), Tajikistan, and Uzbekistan, formerly known as the "Shanghai Five" and later the "Shanghai Forum," released a joint-press communique describing what they called their intention to "raise the Shanghai Five to a higher level" and "build a regional organization of multilateral cooperation covering various fields,"[55] This joint communique announced that the new regional organization would be called the Shanghai Cooperation Organization (SCO). The establishment of the SCO, largely spearheaded by the Chinese, is seen by many observers as part of a security strategy to prevent Kazakh or Uyghur separatists from using Central Asian states as a safety zone to plot separatist activities in Xinjiang. It is also seen by some analysts as an organization that the Chinese have used to spread their sphere of influence, both economic and geopolitical, throughout Central Asia.

SCO and the Aftermath of September 11

In the days and weeks after the terrorist attacks on the U.S. in September 2001, China has reportedly become increasingly concerned that its strategy for expanding its presence and influence in the Central Asian region through the SCO mechanism is in jeopardy.[56] They point out that the U.S. efforts to build and lead an international coalition against terrorism, particularly in Central Asia, have been swift and effective. The U.S. appears to have completely seized the initiative from the newly formed SCO regional grouping, and has provided SCO members with an unanticipated alternative for addressing the issue of regional terrorism.[57] Indeed, the willingness and level at which a number of SCO member states have offered their support and cooperation to the United States is disturbing to a number of

---

52 See Chinese Constitution Section VT Sections 112-122 The Origins of Self Government of National and Autonomous Areas and Chapter Two: The Fundamental Rights and Duties of Citizens, with particular emphasis being placed on Articles 35, 36, and 37.

53 See AmnestylntemationalOn-line, "Peoples Republic of China Uighurs arbitrarily detained and tortured," February 4,1999, [http://www.web.amnesty.org/ai.nsf/priiit/ASA170051999?OpenDocument].

54 Ibid.

55 *BBC Monitoring Asia Pacific,* "China: Press communique of Shanghai summit," June 16, 2001.

56 *Wall Street Journal*, "China Worries That Rising U.S. Influence In Central Asia Could Harm Its Interests," by Charles Hutzler, September 24, 200 1.

57 Ibid

Beijing's elites. Several western diplomats and Asia specialists note that many in Beijing are deeply concerned that Washington could so quickly project its power into Central Asia and even develop close working relations with China's closest ally in the region, Pakistan.[58]

The New 'Great Game'

The PRC's reported plans to expand its influence throughout Central Asia may be put on hold because of rapidly unfolding events in the region. However, prior to September 2001, it appeared that China was well on its way to establishing a powerful presence in Central Asia. According to some western analysts, by the Spring of 2000, China and Russia both seemed poised to take advantage of what was viewed by the Central Asian states as U.S. indifference toward the region. As an example of the latter, analysts point to former Secretary of State Madeleine Albright's "whirl-wind" tour of the region in 2000. In an unsuccessful attempt to address the pleas from the governments of Uzbekistan, Kazakhstan, and Kyrgyzstan for security assistance, the U.S. offered a mere $16 million dollars of combined assistance for all three states.[59] They reportedly considered Washington's $16 million dollar offer a "declaration of disinterest" in the region and its security concerns.[60] Analysts argue that this sent an immediate signal to China that the time was ripe to capitalize on Washington's perceived "ambivalence" toward the region.

Although the United States had delivered around $1.5 billion in aid to the region between 1992 and 1998, this assistance was accompanied by pressure on the Central Asian states to establish pluralistic and democratic societies. On the other hand, the Central Asian states were more concerned about security and consolidation of their secular governments in the wake of increased "Islamic fundamentalism" than they were with democracy and pluralism in their societies.[61] China, which was much less concerned about democracy and pluralism, saw an opportunity. For example, China provided military and technical aid to Uzbekistan, Kazakhstan, and Kyrgyzstan. China also increased trade and economic ties with most of its western neighbors, hoping to ensure access to valuable Central Asian oil and natural gas resources.[62] Additionally, Beijing was using the SCO to develop closer ties to Moscow than it had enjoyed at any other time since the Sino-Soviet split in the late 1960's. Most of these relationships were further enhanced by the signing of the Declaration of the Establishment of the Shanghai Cooperation Organization, the Shanghai Covenant on the Suppression of Terrorism, Separatism, and Extremism, and the Sino-Russian Friendship Pact, signed this past summer in Moscow.[63] An important component of this process was the development of a potential Sino-Russian counter-weight to closer ties between Russia and the United States. This potentially significant gain for China was undermined by the geopolitical and policy shifts following the September 11 attacks. At the same time, many in China believe that heightened U. S. awareness of possible threats posed by Islamic fundamentalist groups could serve Chinese interests.[64]

---

[58] *The Christian Science Monitor*, "China's new balancing act~" by Robert Marquard, November 8, 2001.

[59] Ibid.

[60] *The Wall Street Journal Europe*, "Shanghai Five: The 'Great Game' Returns," August 23, 2001.

[61] Ibid.

[62] See Central Asian Caucus: Analyst, "Did Putin Shanghai Bush?," by Robert M. Cutler, July 4, 2001.

[63] *The Christian Science Monitor*, "China's new balancing act" by Robert Marquand, November 8, 2001.

[64] On December 6, 200 1, while meeting with terrorism officials in Beijing, Francis X. Taylor, the U.S. State Department's top counter terrorism official, noted that some Chinese Muslims had fought for Al-Qaeda in

However, since September 11, the eagerness of some member states to assist the United States bilaterally in the war on terrorism raises a number of questions about the future of the SCO and China's plans for spreading its influence and presence in the region. For example, Uzbekistan, Kazakhstan, and Kyrgyzstan, all key members of the SCO and recipients of Chinese security and technical assistance, have offered their broad support to the U.S. efforts to fight global terrorism, and each state appears to have pushed its own domestic interests and agenda over those of the SCO.[65]

Bilateral versus Multilateral Cooperation

The absence of the SCO as a regional player in the war against terrorism has surprised a number of China watchers, who believed that the Shanghai Cooperation Organization had, on paper at least, a number of options that it could have offered the United States to assist in the war on terrorism. Some analysts argue that the SCO had been involved in the fight against "terrorism" and what it calls the "three-evils forces" in the Central Asian region since 1996 and could have used this collective experience and its new antiterrorist center in Bishkek, Kyrgyzstan to offer multilateral regional support to the war on terrorism. Instead, it appears as though the multilateral SCO option has been put on hold as each state is offering bilateral support to Washington and possibly looking to gain military and security aid along with other support.

Afghanistan. However, Taylor stressed that Washington did not -support the PRC's insistence that Muslim separatists in China's northwest are a part of a global fundamentalist terror threat.

65 *The Wall Street Journal Europe*, "Shanghai Five; 'Great Game' Returns, by Ilan Berman, August 23, 2001.

In: China: Economic, Political and Social Issues
Editors: J. M. Phillips and L. J. Moore

ISBN: 978-60456-727-4

Chapter 10

INNOVATION TO THE DEVELOPMENT OF CHINA TECHNOLOGY MARKET: STRATEGIC ISSUE ON TECHNOLOGY TRANSFER OF CHINA

Yanmin Ma

1. TECHNOLOGY MARKET – THE BASIC SYSTEM OF TECHNOLOGY TRANSFER

1.1. Background of the Development of China Technology Market

The Technology market was built upon under the circumstance of the large-scale reform on the system of economy as well as science and technology. The core of the reform was to improve the integration among Science and Technology with economic and social development, accelerate the application and dissemination of the S&T achievements as well as give full play to S&T as the primary productive force.

In accordance with reforming on the whole system of science and technology, China also reformed the technology transfer system. The orientation was to discard the drawbacks of the former application and dissemination system on S&T system, to establish a market-guided technology transfer system and enhance the motivation and energy of technology development and transfer.

1.2. Two Breakthroughs of the reform on China Technology Transfer System

Breakthrough 1: Reforming the System of Research Institutes

Reform the system of financing, push development-oriented R&D institutes changing to enterprises and being engaged in market-guiding R&D activity afterwards.

Breakthrough 2: Opening up Technology Market

Bring about the commercialization of S&T achievements, carry technology contract regulations into effect and build the system and mechanism which are beneficial to commercialization and industrialization of S&T achievements

1.3. Framework of China Technology Market

Having been built up and developed for 20 years, China technology market has formed a comparative integrated system and structure, which includes the policy, regulation and Law system, the management and supervision system and the services and exchange system.

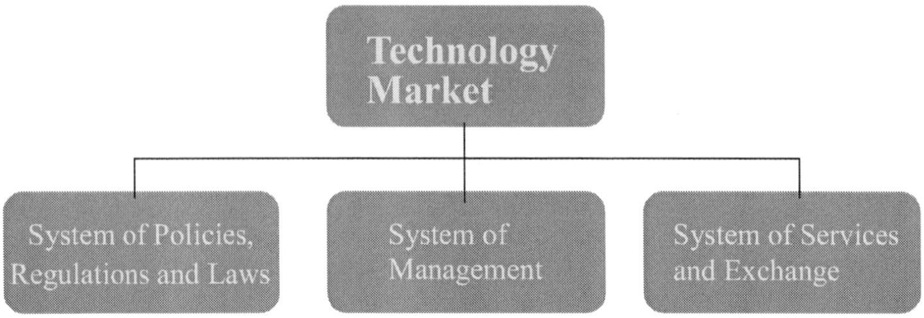

1.3.1. Legal Framework

The main laws that technology market rests on are the followings:

Law on the Advancement of Science and Technology, Law on the Application and Dissemination of the S&T, The Patent Law of PRC, The Contract Law of PRC, and these constitute the regulation and Law system of technology market with the regional regulations.

1.3.2. System of Policy Supporting

The system of policy supporting includes the preferential taxation policy, encouraging policy and so on. This summary just highlights a few of the richness, and is mostly relating to the foreign and foreign invested enterprises, those who are engaged in technology transfer in China:

- For enterprises and individuals including foreign invested R&D centers, foreign enterprises and individuals, the income gained by technology transfer, technology development and relevant technology consulting and technology service, is being exempted from business taxation.
- For foreign invested enterprises or foreign enterprises that subsidize the R&D activity of non-relating R&D institutes and colleges, the income gained by intangible property transfer is being deduced from the overall income when calculating income taxation.
- For using advanced technologies listed on 'National High and New-tech Catalogue', the software fees paid overseas by enterprises in line with contracts is duty-free and exempted from import added-value taxation.

– For enterprises purchasing advanced technologies listed on 'National Hi and New-tech Catalogue', the software fees paid overseas in line with contracts is duty-free and exempted from import added-value taxation.

1.3.3. Management and Supervision System

There is a three-level management and supervision system of Technology Market. The Ministry of Science and Technology is the state-level administration of technology market, and Sinotechmart is the executive institute being charge of the daily work. Additionally, there are totally 1532 administrations at provincial-level (mostly in Science and technology Bureau) and those at city or county levels. Furthermore, there are 1280 registration institutions of technology contract all over the country.

1.3.4. Exchange and Service System

Exchange and service system of technology market was constituted by two parts: One includes 355 technology exchange markets all over China, and among them there are 287 Comprehensive ones, 34 agricultural ones and 14 others. The other part includes 35287 technology trade institutions and 0.85 million personnel all over the country.

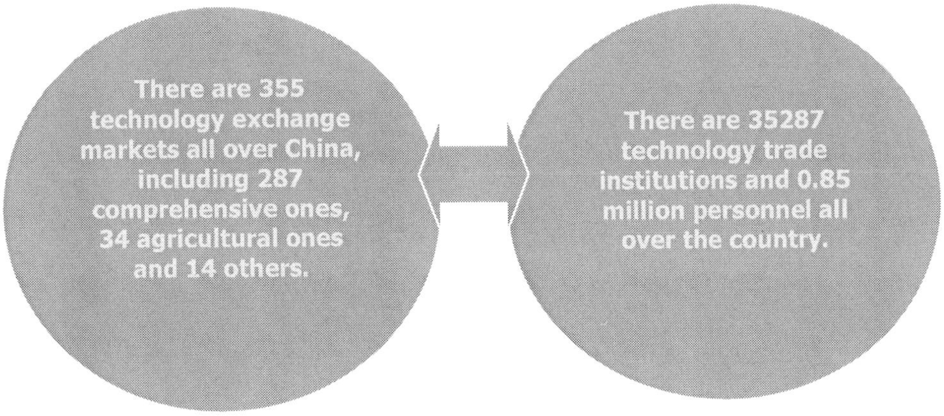

1.4. Accomplishment Achieved by the Development of China Technology Market

The construction and development of technology market especially introducing competitive mechanism into scientific research made large amount of S&T achievements flowing to industry. Since 1990, the average annual increasing rate of the total exchange amount of technology contracts is over 15%. In 2005, the contract number was 264929, and the total exchange amount reached 1551 billion Yuan, increasing 16.24% of that in 2004.

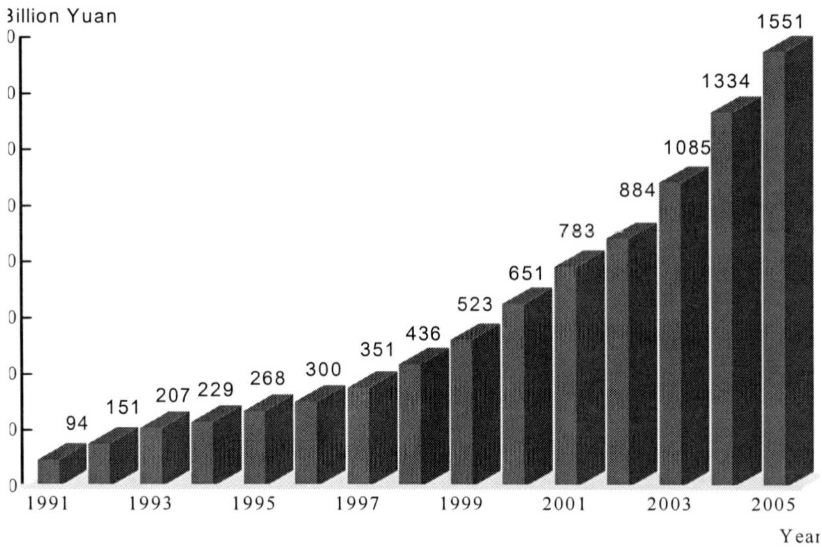

2. Supporting Innovation Is the Main Task of Building Up China Technology Market

The Fourth National Conference on S&T was held on January 1st, 2006. In accordance with the chance and challenge brought by the worldwide new revolution of science and technology, as well as the overall situation of China modernization construction, China government calls up to enhance the country's Innovation capability and building up an Innovation-oriented country.

2.1. Challenges for Technology Market Rising from the Strategy of Innovation

2.1.1. Raising Innovation Capability of Enterprise and Enhancing Core Competitiveness Are the Strategic Motif of China's Science and Technology Development

- As a huge developing country, the S&T advancement must base on the motif of innovation.

- Enhancing innovation capability is the key to readjust industrial structures and shift growth modes.
- Enhancing innovation capability is the urgent requirement for China enterprises to cope with international competition.

2.1.2. Applying the Innovation Strategy Calls for Mature Technology Market Environment and System

Innovation is the activity that the innovators push forward the technology innovation independently, complete the commercialization of technology and achieve huge commercial benefits. Applying the strategy of innovation persistently will be beneficial to keep competitive superiority, but more input will be needed and of course, the innovator will take more risks.

Growth of the innovation-oriented enterprises needs a course of development, and during this course a sound market environment and system is necessary for promoting the innovation of enterprises. These include:

- Uniform, open, competitive and orderly market environment
- Sound system of law and regulation on intellectual property protection and technology exchange.
- Perfect mechanism of technology transfer and intermediary service system for innovation and diffusion.
- Effective mechanism of venture investment and financing.
- High-quality work force of technology innovation and technology agencies.
- Culture of encouraging innovation and tolerance of failure.

2.2. Main Problems of China Technology Market

In light of above situation, there are some problems of China Technology Market. A few of noticeable ones are listed below:

- Deficiency of effective supplement of technological commodity;
- Imperfection of laws and regulations regarding technology market;
- Lag of infrastructure construction and means of exchange;
- Lack of high-quality technological marketing personnel, meanwhile the capability of S&T intermediary and their service level are to be improved urgently;
- Lack of organic linkage among technology market with capital and labor market.

2.3. Analysis of Innovation Environment For Private S&T Enterprises

Southeast University has completed an environmental analysis report on establishment and growth mode of private S&T enterprises. Based on the analysis, the clues of the orientation of the technology market have been found.

Technology Environment

The report indicates that in current technology environment, 21.7% enterprises express that innovation is lack of effective technology supplements, 19.9% express that innovation is lack of the service system of technology application and dissemination, and 26% regard that effective encouraging policy is absent.

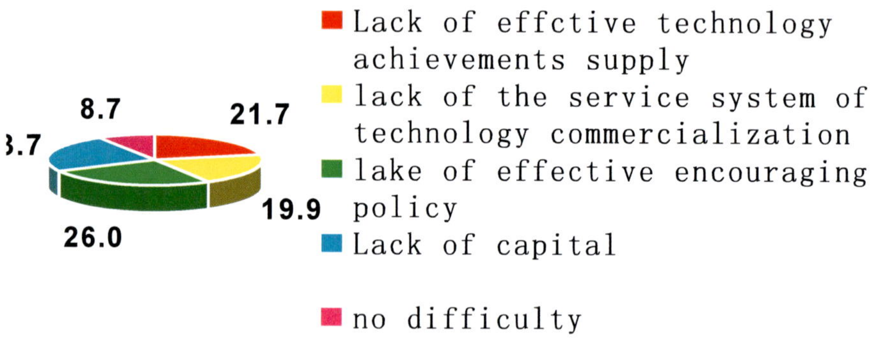

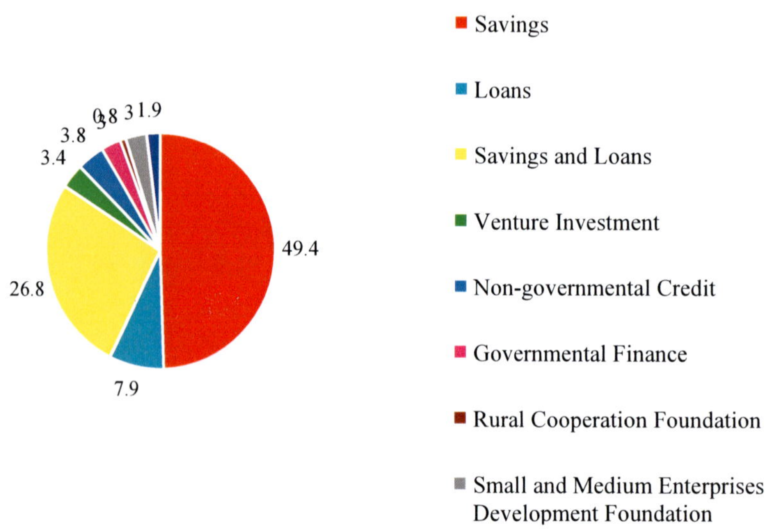

Capital Environment

According to the analysis on capital environment, 49.4% enterprises use their own savings to carry on Innovation, 7.9% rely on the bank credit, 26.8% rely on both, and 3.4% can obtain venture investments.

Personnel Environment

According to the analysis on personnel environment, 32.7% enterprises express lacking of high quality technology personnel, 20.5% express lacking of high quality management personnel while 17% express lacking of skilled workers.

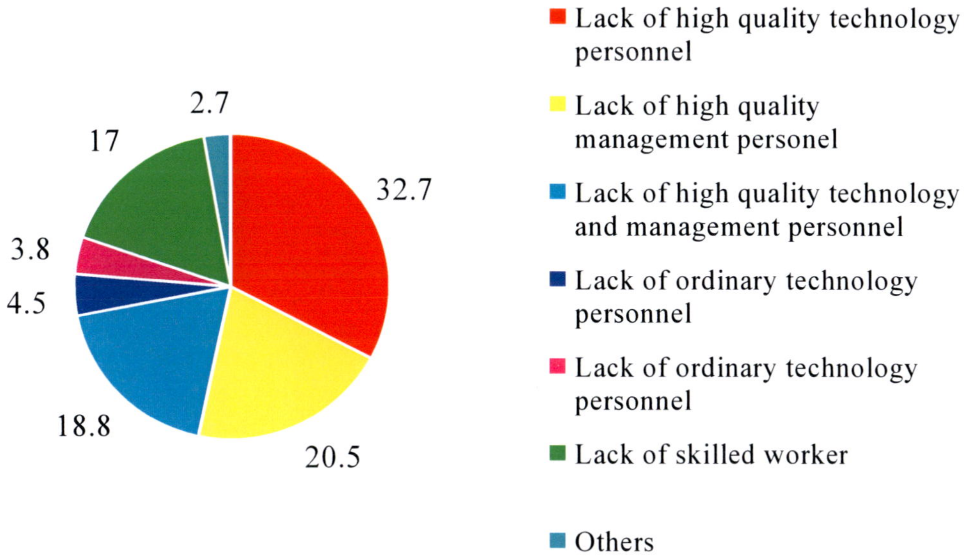

Social Culture and Policy Environment

According to the analysis on Social Culture and Policy Environment, 50% enterprises think it is good, 36% think it is ordinary, and only a few enterprises express it is excellent or not good. That indicates that these are still some problem with the social culture and policy environment of innovation.

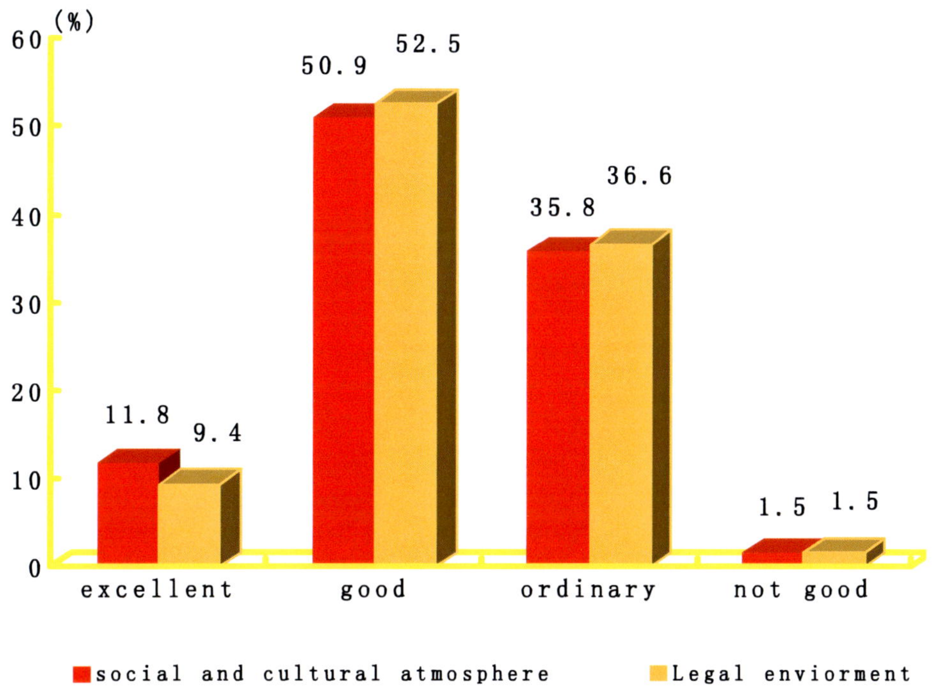

Intellectual Property Protection Environment

According to the analysis on intellectual property protection environment, 45.3% enterprises think it is good, 43% think it is ordinary, and only a few enterprises regard it is excellent or not good. This indicates that the intellectual property protection environment has been improved, but there is still a long way to run.

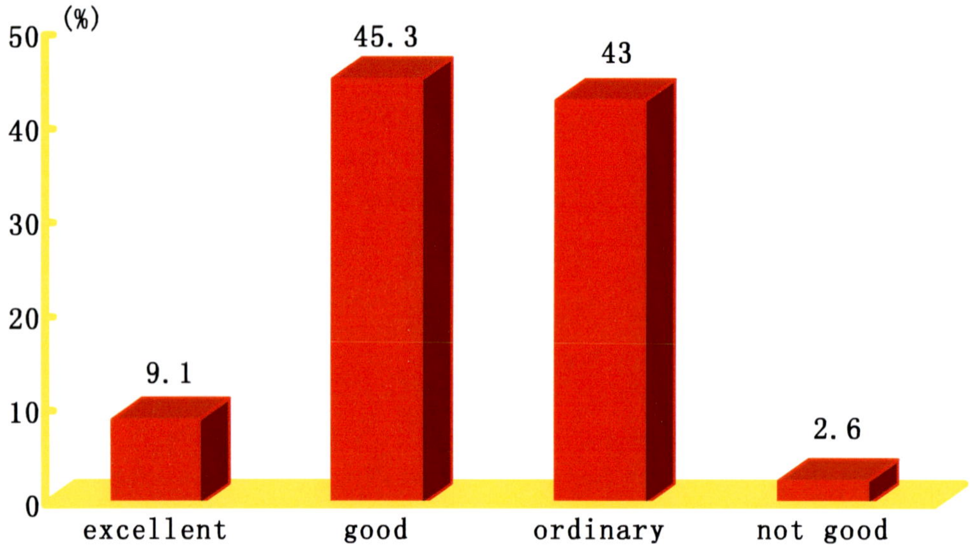

3. Accelerate and Improve the Development of Technology Market

According to the above analysis, China technology market will consider to take the following measures to encourage innovation of enterprises:

3.1. Speed up policy system construction of technology market; tighten technology market supervision and management; strengthen protection of intellectual property rights;

Further strengthen the study on policies aimed at stimulating S&T innovation and achievements transformation, encourage close integration of industry, academy and research, reveal the role of technology on profit allocation and create a favorable innovation environment.

3.2. Speed up public platform construction for technology exchange, set up information release and sharing regulations regarding technology exchange and provide equal competitive opportunity for the participants of the market

3.3. Raise the service capability of technology intermediary institutions, support and foster regional leagues of technology transfer, constitute reputation evaluation system S&T intermediary institutions and credit evaluation system of technology market, enhance service level for innovation.

3.4. Accelerate the linkage of technology market with capital, labor and property market, promote financing of technology property and the acquisition of enterprises, explore suitable mode of S&T investment and financing mechanism and methods of technology property exchange.

3.5. Strengthen the construction of work force of technology market, set up personnel evaluation system and qualification certificate system, set up professional course on technology transfer, improve the quality of the personnel who are engaged in administration and commercial activity of technology market.

3.6. Actively participate in international technology transfer and trade, tighten the linkage and cooperation with leading technology transfer institutions of the world, build up the system of technology trade, technology commodity admittance and intellectual property protection system in accordance with the international convention, create favorable circumstance for Chinese enterprises to participate in international competition.

INDEX

A

B

C

D

E

F

G

H

I

J

K

L

M

N

Q

R

T

U

V

W

X

Y

Z